A HISTORY
of the AMISH
THIRD EDITION

STEVEN M. NOLT

Good Books

New York, New York

Photography Credits
Covers: front and back, Jerry Irwin.

Jerry Irwin/Good Books, 2, 240, 244, 349; Jan Gleysteen, 5, 10, 15, 22, 25, 27, 29, 33, 36, 53, 59, 100, 109, 110; Mirror of the Martyrs (copyright 2003, Good Books, New York , NY), 11; The People's Place, 32, 73; Pearl L. Sensenig/Mennonite Disaster Service, 38; Mennonite Historical Library, Goshen, IN, 51 (both), 55, 74, 102, 107, 152, 282; John A. Parmer, 76; Doyle Yoder, 79, 106, 300, 325; J. Lemar Mast, 121; Mennonite Church USA Archives, Goshen, IN, 131 (Edward J. Yoder Collection), 170, 171 (John E. Sharp Collection), 202 (Historical Committee Collection), 224 (both, Michael Richard Collection), 241 (S.D. Guengerich Collection), 302 (Mennonite World Conference Collection); John Stahly, 133; Thomas J. Meyers, 144; Steven M. Nolt, 147; Heritage Historical Library, 155; Steven R. Estes, 185, 271; Louetta M. Miller, 188; Illinois State Historical Library, 191; Harold Thut, 199; James R. Burkett, 210; Della Bender Miller, 213; Nelson P. Springer, 222; Pennsylvania Mennonite Heritage, 225 (both), 228; Friends of Chrisholm, Trenton, OH, 231; Horst Gerlach, 232; The Amish in America: Settlements that Failed, 1840-1960 (Pathway Publishers, Aylmer, ON), 235; Ivan H. and Alice Martin Stoltzfus, 251; Lancaster (PA) Mennonite Historical Society, 264; Mennonite Library and Archives, North Newton, KS, 273; Kenneth Pellman, 279; Melvin S. and Mary Ellen Stoltzfoos Stoltzfus, 284; Richard Reinhold, 296; Ed Sachs, 305; BERRY'S WORLD reprinted by permission of NEA, Inc., 311; Wide World Photos, 312, 318; Globe and Mail (Toronto), 319; Christian Aid Ministries, 336.

Good Books books may be purchased in bulk at special discounts for sales promotion, corporate gifts, fund-raising, or educational purposes. Special editions can also be created to specifications. For details, contact the Special Sales Department, Good Books, 307 West 36th Street, 11th Floor, New York, NY 10018 or info@skyhorsepublishing.com.

Good Books is an imprint of Skyhorse Publishing, Inc.®, a Delaware corporation.

Visit our website at www.goodbooks.com.

10 9 8 7 6 5 4 3

Library of Congress Cataloging-in-Publication Data is available on file.

Cover design by Cliff Snyder
Cover photos: front and back, Jerry Irwin

Print ISBN: 978-1-68099-065-2

Printed in the United States of America

In memory of
Abner F. Beiler (1917-2002)
who encouraged me to write the first edition of this book.

Contents

Acknowledgments

The themes of community and mutual aid are important in Amish history, and they have been critical to the process of writing and revising this book, as well. I received generous assistance and advice from numerous people. Special recognition goes to staff members of the Mennonite Historical Library of Goshen (Ind.) College, Archives of Mennonite Church USA, Goshen, Indiana; the Young Center for Anabaptist and Pietist Studies at Elizabethtown (Pa.) College; and the Heritage Historical Library, Aylmer, Ontario. Several Amish people in Indiana, Ohio, Ontario, and Pennsylvania read portions of the manuscript and offered suggestions and corrections. Individuals who supplied helpful information and critiques include Donald B. Kraybill, Thomas J. Meyers, Joe Springer, and Karen M. Johnson-Weiner. Steve Scott (1948-2011) deserves special mention for his insights, assistance, information, and friendship. I marvel at the confidence that Merle and Phyllis Good showed for a novice author's first book so many years ago, and I appreciate their interest in keeping the book updated and current.

For some reason it is customary to thank family members last, even though their contributions are most important. To Rachel—who has lived with Amish historical work for more than two decades now—and Lydia, and Esther, thanks for all your love.

Steven M. Nolt
Summer, 2015

—1—

A Reformation Heritage

"We have been united to stand fast in the Lord."
—Anabaptist leaders, 1527

A peculiar people in a land of grand expectations

For many Americans, the early 1960s seemed an era of buoyant optimism and impressive progress. Poverty rates were falling, life expectancy increasing, and modern medicine promised to end a host of dread diseases. A decade and a half of economic growth had boosted national and personal incomes to new heights and with it remarkable new consumer goods, from air conditioning to transistor radios. Weather satellites, jet airplanes, and other technological wonders gave people confidence that President John Kennedy was right when he vowed that humans would walk on the moon before the decade ended. Undergirding national prosperity was an expanding system of education and technical know-how, and the security that came from residing within the boundaries of a superpower whose global influence and military muscle supported an "American way of life." Cold war tensions could put people on edge, but in the years before a deepening war in Vietnam, the assassination of Martin Luther King, or the cynicism of Watergate, the spirit of the times was one of grand expectation.[1]

Amish families going home from church, Conewango Valley, New York. While the Old Order Amish are hardly isolated from modern society, they remain decidedly out-of-step with twenty-first century North American culture.

Near the crossroads community of Winesburg, in eastern Holmes County, Ohio, thirty-one-year-old Elizabeth Miller was not so sure. That year, Miller, an Old Order Amish farm wife and mother, penned several essays on church history and contemporary life. Apparently well-read and familiar with current events, Miller was nonplussed by many of the developments that others took to be progress. She had heard the puzzled questions often enough: "Don't [you] care for the use of electricity and the pleasure of owning an automobile?"

"Surely Christ would not have led a homeless poor life as he did" if it wasn't "necessary for a follower of Christ to live a humble life" as well, Miller reasoned, but in a society celebrating abundance it was difficult to explain why her family did not seek "anything more than what is needed to live."[2] Yet modernity bore more than curious questions. It had a coercive edge. Miller felt mounting pressure on Amish parents to send their youth to consolidated high schools that featured "basketball games, dances, [and] shows" and that assumed one can "learn to plow straight by reading how to do it," rather than getting one's hands dirty through experience. In response to state demands, faithful Amish "mothers and fathers sorrowfully have been apprehended and served prison terms" rather than subject "their beloved children" to such higher schooling.[3]

In some ways, Miller's reflections on life in the 1960s expressed noticeably American themes. She condemned "godless communism," for example, and gave money to the Red Cross and to fund a cure for polio. But her brand of patriotism differed from those who "believe in fighting for their country . . . with guns and bombs." She knew that the pacifist Amish "are looked upon with scorn because they refuse to take up arms." She had attended the court hearings of Amish men sent to prison by military draft boards. Rather than seeing better days ahead, Miller wondered aloud whether her people could persevere in an environment where those "in high places who administer the laws" considered the Amish "ignorant, illiterate, and unlettered."[4]

A half century later, Miller's community of faith has not only persisted in the midst of hypermodern society, but is a growing, vibrant group. As a "plain and peculiar people," in Miller's self-description, the Amish attract the attention of tourists and mass marketers who see the Amish as everything from examples of nostalgic conservatism to icons of postmodern environmentalism. For their part, the Amish insist they are not exactly any of these things. They are not timeless figures frozen in the past, nor the poster-children of political activists. Taken on their own terms, the Old Order Amish are a community that takes seriously the task of personal discipleship and collective witness to a particular Christian way of life that values humility, simplicity, and obedience. From their 1693 beginnings in Switzerland and the south Rhine Valley, to their immigration to North America and settlement in thirty U.S. states and the province of Ontario, the Amish have charted a distinctive history. At times, like Elizabeth Miller's musing on current events, that story has been recognizably North American, yet it has also been markedly different from the dominant narrative of individual achievement and scientific progress that has shaped modern life.

One of the striking features of Elizabeth Miller's writing was the ease with which she invoked the past. Her reflections on the present instinctively and repeatedly turned to stories from Amish history and accounts from old church martyr books. That Miller situated her people's contemporary life in a long tradition of dissenting and suffering forebears is no surprise. The Amish are one of several spiritual heirs of the Protestant Reformation's Anabaptist movement, and the source of Miller's faith had roots deep in sixteenth-century Europe.[5]

Turbulent times

In the early 1500s, an array of political and economic woes troubled Western Europe. For more than fifty years, a population explosion had seemed to outstrip the continent's ability to feed itself. The Spanish conquistadors, who brought news of exotic "new worlds" across the sea, also brought shiploads of silver, plundered from the Americas. This destabilized European economies, producing inflation of prices and rents that drove land-owning peasants into poverty. In towns and cities, a growing class of wealthy merchants and craftspeople challenged the authority of hereditary nobles, while university scholars and disgruntled students voiced sharp criticism of public corruption.

The growing power of the Ottoman Turks to the east threatened Western Europeans' sense of security. Kings

The Grossmünster (Great Church) in Zurich, Switzerland, where Reformer Huldrych Zwingli presided. The Anabaptist movement in Zurich began in 1525.

struggled not only to wrest power and authority from local nobles, but also from rival monarchs. Anxiety only grew as the printing press seemed to shrink the European world. No longer were events in Paris and Vienna so distant. The printed page relayed messages of trouble, defeat, and social unrest from city to city in a matter of days. Free from direct state control, the new press circulated ideas and arguments in a way that often increased unease and discontent.

Amid all the turbulence, however, the church had still stitched the social fabric together. For more than a thousand years, Western Europe had been united in "One Holy Catholic and Apostolic Church." During the fourth century, with the support of the Roman emperors, Christianity had evolved from a persecuted movement to the only sanctioned religion in the Roman Empire. Under a now presumably Christian empire, bishops and priests received special privileges, and eventually the bishop of Rome was accorded particular prestige. The church and the imperial state were linked in building a common, unified, and Christian civilization. Dissent against the One Church also became a crime against state and society.

In time, the western half of the Roman Empire crumbled, but the church remained to pick up the pieces. Throughout the Middle Ages, the pope, as bishop of Rome, led Christians in building a holy civilization in Western Europe. The church offered God's salvation to all who sought divine grace through participation in the sacraments (especially the Holy Communion), which the church regulated carefully. But the church did more than oversee the way to heaven. The church mediated national conflicts, crowned rulers, patronized the fine arts, sponsored higher education, and encouraged trade and exploration.

The church had led Western Europe for a millennium, but now, in the early sixteenth century, as society was splintering, the church itself was breaking up—and that fact unsettled many people as much as any political or economic bad news.

To be sure, some medieval popes had been pawns of French kings and German emperors, and church councils had frequently called for churchly reform of one kind or another. But after 1517, the trouble in the church was different. The Roman Catholic Church was actually losing its moral and political authority in some parts of Europe. That year, the Wittenburg monk and lecturer Martin Luther had proposed a whole set of changes, not only of church structure—as many reformers had done before—but also of the interpretation of key church doctrines.[6]

Luther and the Protestant Reformation

Luther proposed revolutionary challenges to some of Rome's basic teachings. Luther insisted that "salvation by grace through faith alone" meant that God's saving grace comes directly to each Christian on the basis of his or her individual faith, and that it is not mediated through the church's sacraments. Such thinking undercut the church's importance and authority. By the time he officially broke with Rome in 1521, Luther was also championing church decision-making based solely on appeals to the Bible instead of tradition or canon law, and the use of the German language instead of Latin to make worship more understandable to lay people.

Printers promoted Luther's ideas throughout German-speaking Europe and beyond. A number of German princes also supported him, both for political and theological reasons. Church leaders in other places began introducing some of Luther's teachings into their own parishes. An important fellow-reformer was Huldrych Zwingli, priest at the Great Church in the Swiss city of Zurich. Like Luther, Zwingli preached salvation by grace through faith alone, rejected the doctrine of purgatory, and advocated the marriage of clergy. Zwingli also taught the symbolic, rather than physical, presence of Jesus' body and blood in the bread and wine of communion.

As early as 1518, Zwingli's teaching attracted reform-minded young men and women in the Zurich area. By 1522 small groups of these students and craftspeople began meeting in private homes for Bible study.[7] They were excited by the ideas of the Reformation, but were also troubled because they feared Zwingli's reforms were losing momentum and might even be reversed by the Zurich city council. Zwingli, like Luther, often relied on the government to implement religious change. Luther and Zwingli seemingly could not imagine a society without a strong leader. When they removed the pope from their social scheme, they replaced Rome's power and authority with that of a local prince or magistrate.

Radicals in Zurich

This state-church strategy troubled the young people around Zwingli. They feared the Zurich city council was now controlling the church. When Zwingli's reforms strengthened the council's power (such as his rejection of Rome's authority over Zurich), the city fathers readily agreed. But when the changes involved the council's own sacrifice (such as relaxing the unjust tithes that the city extorted from the surrounding rural villages), the council balked.

Moreover, because the church routinely baptized all infants, it automatically included all citizens among its members. In practical terms this meant that the church had to adjust its moral expectations downward, seeking a lowest common denominator to support its inclusive character. Virtually everyone was a member of the church, regardless of their commitment or interest. The church could not expect the rigorous ethics of Christ's Sermon on the Mount from those who were nominally Christian simply because they were citizens. Instead it settled for expedient personal and social ethics, and Jesus' teachings often were disregarded in the face of political realities. In Catholic lands monks and nuns still aspired to biblical "counsels of perfection," but reformers such as Luther and Zwingli had done away with those religious orders.

The course of reform in Zurich bothered the young dissenters. If the Word of God was to form the church, they contended, no human government should stand in the way. In 1524, when Zwingli concluded that aspects of the Catholic mass should be discarded, the city council stalled. Zwingli conceded to the council, irking the radicals.

Gradually the dissenters realized that the recovery of the church as they understood it from the New Testament could occur only on radically different grounds from those being used both by Rome and by the reformers. These radicals, it turned out, were working with a different concept of the church. For them the church was a community of Christians voluntarily committed to imitating Christ and to supporting one another. Baptism—the sign of church membership and commitment—was only for those old enough to choose the path of discipleship. Moreover, the state should have no part in controlling or directing the activities and doctrines of the church.

Salvation came by grace through faith, these radicals believed, but it was more than a future ticket to heaven. It transformed one's present life with God and with other people. Since Christ taught peaceful nonresistance to worldly enemies, radical Christian obedience rejected participation in either the military or the judicial arms of the state. The New Testament church demonstrated sharing of personal goods and practicing mutual aid among Christians, and the dissenters took those examples seriously as well.

Anabaptism is born

Before long, the ideas of the "free church" radicals clashed with the Zurich council, which demanded a unified church and state on its own terms. Some dissenters refused to have their infant children baptized because the children were not yet old enough to understand the implications of Christian discipleship. The city demanded that the radicals stop meeting, have their children baptized, and expel the non-Zurichers from among them. Snubbing the council, the dissenters met on January 21, 1525 and baptized one another, signaling their own conscious decision to follow Christ and form a church apart from the state. Since they all had been baptized as infants many years earlier,

Anabaptists met secretly for worship in this Swiss cave near Wappenswil.

these new adult baptisms were literally second baptisms (in Latin, *anabaptismus*). For their part, the Anabaptists, as they were now called, claimed that their infant baptisms had been meaningless.

Such disobedience was intolerable in Zurich. Both Zwingli and the council sensed that Anabaptist ideas challenged the unity of the church and the state and was politically and socially subversive. In rejecting infant baptism, the Anabaptists separated the political tie between church membership and citizenship. By challenging the unity of the church, the Anabaptists shredded the social fabric. In rejecting the state's authority in matters of religion, the Anabaptists threatened anarchy, and, by refusing military service, the Anabaptists made the city vulnerable to foreign attack.

Anabaptists were imprisoned and exiled, fined and threatened. Meanwhile, their ideas, already present in the rural countryside around Zurich, spawned a number of rural fellowships beyond the city walls. Even the threat of the death penalty failed to halt the movement. Within several years, Anabaptist groups emerged elsewhere in Switzerland and in southern Germany, the Austrian Tyrol, and Moravia. Itinerant preachers, dissident booksellers, and traveling merchants spread the message, calling people to receive God's grace and form a faithful church free of state interference and practicing Jesus' teaching in their ordinary lives.[8]

The predicament of persecution

Anabaptists faced fierce opposition from both Catholic and Protestant authorities. Some Anabaptists were impris-

During the sixteenth century, several thousand Anabaptists were executed, including Maria and Ursula van Beckum in 1544. Etching by Jan Luyken.

oned and tortured, others were burned or beheaded, and still others were sold as galley slaves forced to row themselves to death on the Mediterranean. Swiss city-states employed "Anabaptist hunters" who tracked down suspected citizens and were paid by the head. When Anabaptist groups sprang up in northern Germany and the Netherlands, authorities there also reacted harshly. As many as 2,500 Anabaptists were killed in the decades after 1525, accounting for 40 to 50 percent of all Western European Christians who were martyred for their faith during the sixteenth century.[9]

As a result, Anabaptist meetings might take place at night, in the woods, or only in small groups. Leaders traveled secretly and had to hide precious and illegal tracts and devotional materials. Members lived in fear and some recanted their beliefs, returned to the state churches, and even betrayed one-time associates. This period of nearly a century of persecution shaped the Anabaptist movement in important ways.[10] The re-baptizers developed a deep distrust of larger society and a fairly negative view of government, which they encountered most often in the form of judicial brutality. Generations later and half a world away in North America, Anabaptist descendants still recounted the stories of those who suffered.

In addition to fostering a tendency to separation, the fierce opposition encouraged values of simplicity and piety that the Anabaptists already saw in the Bible. The line dividing the suffering church and the cruel world became all too clear. The world was arrogant, wealthy, proud, and violent. The Anabaptists saw themselves as meek, simple, humble, and nonresistant. While some of these characteristics may have been typical of rural Swiss and south German people generally, the experience of persecution accentuated them among the Anabaptists.

With its rather flexible nature, Anabaptist church life also came to reflect these desperate times. Congregations were fairly autonomous, each with its own resident ministry who preached and provided pastoral care, as well as looked after the material needs of members by collecting and distributing money for the poor. Swiss Anabaptists allowed lay members to lead worship and teach if no ordained leader was available, although performing the rites of baptism, communion, and marriage was reserved for senior ministers called *elders* (later, in North America, they came to be called *bishops*). In many respects, the most important roles for Anabaptist leaders—elders or junior ministers—were modeling daily Christian discipleship and guiding ethical discipline.

Anabaptist agreement

If the rather decentralized nature of the Anabaptist movement was something of a survival strategy, it also posed problems. Within two years of Anabaptism's beginnings, some leaders sensed a need to outline what held their diverse collection of scattered churches together. Gathering in the village of Schleitheim on the Swiss-German border, Anabaptists who called themselves simply "Brethren" or "Swiss Brethren" drafted a document that began with their definition of church. "We have been united to stand fast in the Lord," they announced, "as obedient children of God, sons and daughters, who have been and shall be separated from the world in all that we do and leave undone, and . . . completely at peace."[11]

The statement went on to outline seven foundational elements of church life and Christian conduct, beginning with adult baptism and church discipline. Swiss Brethren were considering church discipline in a context in which they themselves were being subjected to discipline in the form of imprisonment and torture for abandoning the official church. In contrast, Anabaptists gathered at Schleitheim insisted that discipline was to be nonviolent. The church would excommunicate and bar from fellowship those who fell into unrepentant sin, but they renounced the use of force to coerce right behavior.

While milder than that meted out by state executioners, church discipline was nevertheless a key issue for the Swiss Brethren and would remain so for their spiritual descendants. Since they affirmed both the voluntary nature of the church and the high ethical standards of personal discipleship, Swiss Brethren also had to grapple with what to do when people stopped following the way of Jesus. They believed that a committed community required the discernment of definite boundaries. But if the New Testament seemed clear that Christians should avoid "the world," it was less clear what such avoidance involved. For the time being, the Swiss Brethren seemed to suggest that barring the unrepentant from the communion table safeguarded the integrity of the church.

Trouble in the north

Anabaptists in northern Europe soon had to wrestle with church discipline in a situation that was less theoretical. Anabaptism had arrived in northern Germany in 1530 and spread immediately in the Netherlands, where the movement grew rapidly. This northern strain of Anabaptism developed some different emphases than those found in Switzerland and the south Rhine Valley. Notably, in the north there was great enthusiasm for the imminent second coming of Christ, with bold predictions of dramatic events preceding that Divine Return. Some Anabaptists were uncomfortable with the fanaticism associated with these predictions and preferred a "quiet and peaceable life" of obedience to Jesus' teachings.

Anabaptist leader Menno Simons.

Others, however, set out to usher in the Messianic Age. Ironically, these Anabaptists took up the sword in order to create an Anabaptist church-state. Capturing the city of Münster in 1534, they turned the tables on the state churches and began to persecute anyone who refused to be baptized as an adult!

Within a year, an army jointly raised by Catholics and Protestants crushed the Münster uprising. But the aftershocks of the struggle shook the nonviolent northern Anabaptist community, which had rejected the actions at Münster from the start. Angry authorities connected the events of Münster with all Anabaptist groups, even those that denounced violence. Following Münster, persecution of Anabaptists became severe in the Netherlands and northern Germany, since officials believed they had clear evidence that Anabaptism could spark militant revolution.

With its members scattered and scared, peaceful Dutch Anabaptists struggled to reconstitute their movement. Into this scene came a former Dutch Catholic priest named Menno Simons.[12] Menno had privately been an Anabaptist sympathizer for some time, but in 1536 he publicly joined the peaceful wing of the Anabaptist movement. For the next quarter century, Menno and others worked to nurture nonviolent Anabaptist churches across northern Europe. So influential was Menno's role that by 1545 some officials were linking Anabaptism with his name and the label *Mennonites*.

Menno needed to distance his fellow believers from the mayhem of Münster. No longer was it possible simply to refuse spiritual fellowship with the fanatical Anabaptists of the Münster stripe; peaceful Anabaptists could not risk associating with them. Unrepentant Anabaptists who espoused violence had to be avoided in social and personal relationships, Menno and others taught.[13]

Other questions challenged Dutch Anabaptism, as well. Some European theologians and church reformers had begun to promote the notion that the church was merely "spiritual" and other-worldly, which opened for question the significance of Christian relationships and the importance of ethics in this life. In corrective reaction to such teaching, Menno and the Mennonite Anabaptists placed even more emphasis on purging sin from the ranks of the church and on the separation of believers from the apostate. Christians needed to avoid, or "shun," the unrepentant.[14]

In the course of a few years, some northern Anabaptists became increasingly extreme in their practice of shunning excommunicated members (the practice was known as *Meidung* in German). Some would have nothing at all to do with ex-church members. Others called for suspending the marriage relationship if a spouse was excommunicated. Menno tried to play a mediating role between those who called for stricter and milder application of excommunication, but in the end Menno often sided with those who demanded social avoidance.[15]

Disagreement over shunning repeatedly stifled church unity among the Anabaptists. In 1554, when the Dutch and northern European Mennonites finally formulated a specific statement on avoidance and excommunication, the Swiss and south German Mennonites* rejected it as too harsh. Three years later, a well-attended conference of Swiss and southern leaders sent a delegation north to visit Menno and to suggest that the Dutch practice of shunning had gone too far.

Eventually Swiss and south German Mennonites agreed to recognize the value of social avoidance, at least to some degree. Perhaps they made this concession to their Dutch brothers and sisters for the sake of unity. Or perhaps some Swiss and south Germans actually were persuaded that the New Testament called on Christians to limit social contacts with the wayward as a means of urging them to repent. Either way, in 1568 and again in 1591, south German Mennonites adopted confessions of faith that called for socially avoiding those who had left the church and remained unremorseful.[16] To what extent the south Germans actually practiced what

---

* Swiss and south German Anabaptists did not use the term *Mennonite* to describe themselves. Typically they went by the name *Swiss Brethren.* In the interest of simplifying terminology, however, this chapter and those that follow will use the term Mennonite to identify these Swiss and south German Anabaptists.

they preached is unclear. Meanwhile, in the north, decades of harshly administered church discipline were starting to tear Dutch Mennonites apart.

Decisions at Dordrecht

In 1632 the debate over shunning in the north seemed to be largely resolved. In an historic meeting in the Dutch city of Dordrecht, Dutch and northern Mennonite leaders drew up a church unity agreement known as the Dordrecht Confession.[17] The confession became a long-lasting and highly influential Mennonite document. It outlined an understanding of Christian faith that stretched from creation to Christ's second coming. The next-to-last of its 18 articles dealt with the avoidance of those who were brazenly unrepentant and called for ending business and most ordinary social interaction with those who broke their baptismal vows. The faithful could not conscientiously support the life and lifestyle of those who rejected the way of discipleship, the document argued.

But Dordrecht also called for Christian moderation in the use of avoidance. The church was still to feed, clothe, and otherwise assist excommunicated members when they were in need, "according to the love and teaching of Christ and the apostles." The church must not view those it shunned as "enemies," but rather should ask erring ones to amend their lives and "be reconciled to God" and the church.

The Dordrecht Confession tried to strike a balance by teaching a moderate form of shunning. Accepted by many congregations in the north, the document circulated among the Mennonites in south Germany and Switzerland as well, as did many of Menno's writings that advocated social avoidance. Swiss Anabaptists had generally rejected shunning, but even they offered the Dordrecht Confession, with its teaching on avoidance, when the government in Bern demanded an

Martyrs Mirror:
Anabaptist History among the Amish

In the late sixteenth century, the Dutch government adopted a tolerant stance toward Anabaptism. Socially accepted, Mennonites moved into many avenues of mainstream culture and prospered economically. By the mid-1600s, they enjoyed a "golden age" and joined the ranks of influential merchants, physicians, artists, and artisans.

Dutch Mennonite minister Thieleman Jansz. van Braght feared his people were acculturating too much. As they became more socially secure in this life, would they forget Jesus' teaching of simplicity, humility, and the suffering church? Braght believed that one way to call the church to faithful discipleship was to remind it of its martyr past. He began collecting stories of Anabaptist martyrs from court records and drew on earlier Mennonite martyr collections. In 1660, he published these stories in a 1,478-page tome entitled *The Bloody Theater, or Martyrs Mirror*.

The book included explanation of Mennonite beliefs (including shunning), as well as hundreds of gripping martyr tales. About 100 of the stories were made more graphic in the book's second edition of 1685 when Dutch Mennonite artist Jan Luyken provided 104 copper engraved illustrations.

Mennonite readers believed the book implicitly taught nonresistance to violence since the stories valorized those who chose suffering over fighting back or taking revenge when faced with persecution. In 1748, confronted with the threat of colonial warfare, Pennsylvania Mennonites had the book translated into German as a resource for teaching their youth.

In 1780, Amish elder Hans Nafziger of Essingen, Germany made arrangements to reprint the Pennsylvania edition in Europe for his German-speaking Amish congregations in the Palatinate and Alsace. Nafziger worked on the project with Peter Weber, a neighboring Mennonite minister. In war-torn Europe, these stories would do their people good, they believed. Meanwhile, the Amish in North America were also reading the German *Martyrs Mirror*, and several decades later, in 1849, Amishman Shem Zook of Mifflin County, Pennsylvania, issued a new German edition of the book. Amish-owned Pathway Publishers still keeps a German edition of the martyr book in print.

Today, the *Martyrs Mirror* is found in most Amish homes, and references to it are common in Amish circles. The book has supported the idea that the world is not to be fully trusted. The themes of separation, suffering, and faithfulness ring from its pages. No doubt the piety and experiences of martyrs in the sixteenth-century shape Amish life and thought in the twenty-first.

See Thieleman J. van Braght, *The Bloody Theater; or Martyrs Mirror of the Defenseless Christians* (Scottdale, Pa.: Herald Press, 1998). See also John S. Oyer and Robert S. Kreider, *Mirror of the Martyrs*, sec. ed. (Intercourse, Pa.: Good Books, 2003).

outline of their doctrine.[18] And in 1660, Alsatian Mennonite ministers and deacons representing churches comprised of recent immigrants from Switzerland adopted Dordrecht as their statement of faith (although at least one of those leaders did not approve of the confession's article on shunning).[19] After more than a century of Anabaptist debate, controversy over social avoidance seemed to die down after 1660. Had Mennonites achieved "unity in the Lord" when it came to the practice of church discipline, or was the issue still unresolved?

Survival strategies

While the south German and Swiss Mennonites were trying to resolve their disagreements over discipline, they also confronted continued opposition from government and the state church. After 1614, Swiss authorities avoided creating religious martyrs. Instead of public executions, civic leaders used imprisonment, fines, and exile to discourage Anabaptist growth. Beginning in 1635, Swiss city councils, especially the one that governed the area around Bern, tried systematically to rid their lands of Swiss Brethren.

In 1648, Europe hailed the end of the terribly destructive Thirty Years War. Fought over political ambitions and alliances that were often complicated by Protestant and Catholic rivalries, the war had taken the lives of more than half the inhabitants of some areas. The enormity of death and devastation was staggering. Farmland that had lain untilled was reverting to forest, threatening survivors with famine.

Within the dire conditions left by the war, princes hurried to find settlers willing to cultivate their war-ravaged acres. The situation was so desperate in some places that landowners considered taking on outcast Anabaptists as tenants. By at least 1653, persecuted Swiss Brethren began to move down the Rhine River into the ravaged lands on its west bank known as the Palatinate. Eleven years later, one of the Palatinate's dukes issued a special offer of toleration to the Swiss Brethren (he called them "Mennists," correctly associating them with their fellow Mennonites in the North). The Mennonites would receive religious freedom for themselves, the duke promised, but they could not proselytize, meet in large groups, or construct church buildings. Despite these restrictions and heavier taxes, some Mennonites saw

A prison cell at Trachselwald Castle, Switzerland, in which Anabaptists were imprisoned.

the offer as better than the harassment and continued threat of deportation they faced in Switzerland.[20]

Simultaneously, several French nobles invited Swiss Brethren to move into lands just north of Switzerland on the west bank of the Rhine. Known as Alsace, the region was home to German-speaking Alsatians, but was governed by religiously tolerant French aristocrats. Small numbers of Anabaptists had lived in both the Palatinate and Alsace for several generations, but the large migrations after 1670 changed Mennonite church life there.[21] The new immigrants came in large numbers and maintained their social and churchly ties to Switzerland. Mennonite congregations in Switzerland, the Palatinate, and Alsace were now more closely connected than before.

Anabaptist survival into the mid-1600s had not been easy, and opposition had surfaced from many quarters. Still, these often marginalized members of society had tried to live as committed disciples of Christ. At times, this vision itself had been a stumbling block, as Anabaptists disagreed on how the church should relate to those who rejected discipleship. The tension of being *in* the world, but not *of* it, had sometimes been too great and had produced division. Still, most Anabaptists had not given up living in that tension, choosing rather, they said, "to persevere along the path we have entered upon, unto the glory of God and of Christ His Son."[22]

Ausbund:
Anabaptist Hymnal of the Amish

In 1535, a group of Anabaptists traveling from Moravia to southwestern Germany were captured on the Bavarian border. Placed in a Passau castle prison, some spent nearly five years there before being released, and others died in the dungeon. During the imprisonment, to occupy themselves and encourage one another, the prisoners wrote 53 hymns. The lyrics spoke of sorrow, loneliness, and the imminence of death, but the hymns were also hopeful, since their authors believed that suffering was to be expected in this life and that a heavenly reward awaited them.

By at least 1564 the hymns were printed in book form. The book proved popular among Anabaptists, and soon other favorite songs, including lengthy martyr ballads with dozens of stanzas, joined the Passau collection. Nineteen years after its first known edition, the prison hymnbook was reissued with 130 songs. This printing was the first to receive the *Ausbund* title.

The hymns stress Anabaptist themes such as believer's baptism, nonviolence, and the suffering of Christ's followers. Many of the tunes associated with the hymn texts were popular secular ones now matched to religious lyrics. The *Ausbund* was the Anabaptists' most common worship book other than the Bible. German-speaking European Mennonites and Amish continued to use the *Ausbund* some 300 years after its first words were sung in the Passau prison.

In North America, Mennonites used the book regularly until about 1800. The Amish continued to sing from the book, and today nearly all Old Order Amish congregations use it or variations of it. Today's *Ausbund* contains 140 hymns, a brief doctrinal statement, and a short selection of Swiss Anabaptist martyr biographies. No printed music is included in the volume; all tunes have been passed on orally over time. While some of the tunes have been forgotten and many greatly embellished, the Amish have preserved an important piece of Reformation-era hymnody. Contemporary Amish church life has been enriched by singing from the *Ausbund*. The stories of martyrdom and persecution strengthen the Amish sense of humility and dependence on God and remind them of their heritage.

See *Ausbund: das ist, Etliche schöne Christliche Lieder* (Lancaster, Pa.: Verlag von den Amischen Gemeinden in Lancaster County, Pa., 1997). For more information, see the Amish-authored volume Benuel S. Blank, *The Amazing Story of the Ausbund* (Narvon, Pa.: the author, 2001). English translation of *Ausbund* hymn texts have been published as *Songs of the Ausbund: History and Translations of Ausbund Hymns* (Millersburg, Ohio: Ohio Amish Library, vol. 1, 1998; vol. 2, 2011).

The castle at Passau on the Danube River. Anabaptists imprisoned here wrote hymns that became the nucleus of the Ausbund *hymnal.*

—2—

Amish Beginnings, 1693-1712

"There you have it."

—Peter Zimmerman announcing
the beginning of the Amish church

A time of paradox

The late 1600s were paradoxical times for Swiss Mennonites. On the one hand, these were years of insecurity and persecution, reminiscent of the early days of Anabaptism. At the same time, Mennonites were garnering respect and even admiration from some of their neighbors.[1] This curious mix of confrontation and appreciation created a context for heated Mennonite debate about their church and its relationship to wider society—debate that eventually produced division.

Hostility from civil authorities, especially in the Canton of Bern, had been a persistent reality throughout the 1600s. Waves of harassment, peaking in 1670 and the early 1690s, included rounds of official mandates decreeing various fines and the loss of civic privileges, as well as threats of banishment or imprisonment. These attempts to expel Anabaptism from Swiss soil prompted the emigration of some Swiss Mennonites to Alsace and the Palatinate during these years.

The Emme River Valley in Switzerland, home of many Swiss Brethren (Mennonites), including Hans Reist.

Those who remained in the Swiss heartland often survived through a combination of strategies that could include occasional attendance at state churches or public denials of Anabaptist affiliation.[2] In other cases, making it through trying times was easier with the support of sympathetic, non-Anabaptist neighbors. And as the century wore on, there were a growing number of such neighbors. Common people, tired of civic corruption and formal religiosity, saw the separatist Anabaptists as model Christians. An official investigation in 1692 unearthed opinions such as that of a women who, when asked if she were a Mennonite, replied, "No, to tell the truth I am not worthy to be an Anabaptist . . . they are such a holy people." The depth of this popularity, in fact, was embarrassing to magistrates and resulted in targeted efforts to pressure village leaders and state church members to comply with anti-Anabaptist mandates. Early in 1693, a Swiss Reformed pastor named Georg Thormann authored a book against the Anabaptists, driven to do so by the fact that too many common people saw Mennonites "as saints, as the salt of the earth, as the true and chosen people and the proper core of all Christians."[3]

The combination of renewed legal harassment and newfound public favor meant that the issue of the church's relationship to the wider world was complicated. During times of persecution, friendly neighbors interceded on behalf of Mennonite acquaintances or even hid them. But this environment placed Mennonites in a peculiar position. Having long seen themselves as a people separate from and in opposition to "the world," what did it mean that at least some in that world now seemed to like them?

Mennonites were unsure how to regard their sympathetic friends. The designations they gave their admirers— Half-Anabaptists (*Halbtäufer*) or True-Hearted (*treuherzige*) people—suggested some of the Mennonite ambivalence. Yet, facing discrimination and social stigma, many Mennonites turned to the True-Hearted for help, especially in Switzerland where official opposition was harshest and families had built up generations of neighborly connections with the True-Hearted. Ties to the True-Hearted were less important in Alsace and the Palatinate.

In an era when all churches—Catholic, Lutheran, and Reformed—branded most of those outside of their own groups as heretical, the Mennonites were not alone in viewing ecumenical relations as problematic. For the Anabaptists, however, the difficulty was all the more perplexing because they advocated voluntary baptism and separation from worldly society as a mark of true Christian discipleship. Were the True-Hearted saved? They exhibited Christ-like ethics, such as "giving a cup of cold water" to their persecuted neighbors, yet they would not give up their socially secure state church

*The Alsatian village of Markirch (today Sainte-Marie-aux-Mines).
Jakob Ammann lived in this area from about 1695 to 1712.*

memberships and continued through their tithes to support
the very apparatus that persecuted Mennonites.

An old Anabaptist perspective on the issue was that
Mennonites simply could not know whether the True-Hearted
were saved; only God knew. Mennonites should pray for them
and be grateful for their friendship. Another traditional line
of reasoning drew on a strict Anabaptist distinction between
the church and the world. For those who held this worldview, there was little middle ground: Mennonites should not
pretend that the True-Hearted were truly obedient to God's

will, nor rely too much on them in times of trouble. God alone would see the persecuted through.

Mennonites who held to this more dualistic view also made much of the Anabaptist practice of shunning those who recanted their professions of faith and joined (or rejoined) the state church. Drawing on streams of earlier Mennonite thought, those who advocated this perspective had biblical and historic Anabaptist support for their call for separation and social avoidance. Since salvation and church membership had day-to-day social implications, it followed that reneging on one's baptismal vows carried consequences that were equally concrete and relational.

A bold reformer

Swiss Anabaptism not only attracted secret sympathizers in the 1600s. It also gained a steady stream of converts—people who were not merely True-Hearted but who made the socially costly choice to join the dissident movement through adult baptism. Since the early 1670s, Anabaptist preachers, such as Ulrich Müller, had won converts, particularly in the Bernese Oberland that lay in the southern part of the Canton of Bern. These zealous new members may have had less patience with the partial commitment of the True-Hearted.[4]

This yeasty mix of persecution and esteem, secret admirers and dedicated converts, generated calls in Mennonite circles for clarifying theology and reforming church life. Perhaps the most prominent of these voices was that of Jakob Ammann, a man who had himself converted to Anabaptism around 1680 and sometime thereafter become an elder (a minister ordained with authority to baptize and preside at the Lord's Supper). Ammann and his family had left Switzerland in the early 1690s and moved north, settling in Alsace, eventually near the village of Sainte-Marie-aux-Mines. The Ammann household was not alone. During the late 1600s, more than a thousand

Swiss Anabaptists had taken flight to more tolerant territories in Alsace and the Palatinate seeking a respite from religious harassment.

Relocation also offered Mennonites an opportunity to reboot their church life, and it was in that context that Ammann began calling for spiritual renewal, along with a recommitment to separation from corrupting influences of the world. Alsace had long been home to a small number of Anabaptists. The new Swiss refugees swelled these ranks, but the newcomers, who had been among the fervent converts to Anabaptism, were chagrined by how an atmosphere of toleration had eroded the Alsatian's sense of separation from worldly society. The greatest tension, however, emerged between the Swiss refugees in Alsace and the Palatinate and fellow Mennonites they had left behind in Switzerland, and it centered on Ammann's agenda for spiritual renewal.

Ammann's program of reform began with a proposal for more frequent communion services.[5] Swiss Mennonites had observed communion once a year because the first Lord's Supper, instituted by Jesus, had been a part of an annual Jewish Passover meal. Ammann urged Anabaptist congregations to commune twice a year. Since Mennonites stressed preparing for the Lord's Supper by closely examining their lives and relationships with God and other people, more frequent communion would encourage greater attention to Christian living.

Also, since Anabaptists excluded the unrepentant from the communion table, a more frequent observance of the rite would also prompt churches to address more often situations of wrongdoing and offense. Since Ammann represented those who believed that Mennonites were becoming spiritually lax, he welcomed more attention to church discipline.

Ammann's churches instituted more frequent communion, but when people in other congregations asked for the same change, their ministers, notably a Swiss elder named

The confrontation between Jakob Ammann and Hans Reist as carved by Aaron Zook, a member of the Beachey Amish church.

Hans Reist, balked at introducing new practices. Perhaps threatened by Ammann's strong personality or his popular appeal, Reist and other elders rejected the idea. Ammann and those who agreed with him could do as they wished, but Reist and his associates made it clear that they considered the innovation unnecessary.

To avoid or not to avoid

Ammann seems to have believed that Reist represented a weakening of Mennonite resolve, a weakening that Ammann abhorred. Reist suggested that the True-Hearted were saved without needing publicly and personally to confess God's grace through baptism. Nor did Reist ritually avoid those who left the church by refusing to eat with them. He thought

The Niklaus Moser farm at Fridersmatt, in the Emme River Valley, was the site of numerous secret Swiss Anabaptist meetings. In 1693 it also served as a meeting place for one of the debates between Jakob Ammann and his supporters and those who sided with Hans Reist.

it was enough merely to exclude them from the once-a-year communion service. So when some Mennonites in Reist's region continued to clamor for more frequent communion, and Reist called fellow ministers Niklaus Moser and Peter Giger for counsel, Ammann decided to open the debate further. Ammann asked Moser and Giger to find out what Reist really believed about shunning.

Reist answered with the words of Jesus, replying that, "What goes into the mouth does not defile the person but what comes out of the mouth, that defiles a man" (Matthew 15:11).[6] Reist had no interest in practicing literal shunning of errant members in an attempt to win them back to the church.

Jakob Ammann

In recent years, historians have learned more about Jakob Ammann. The son of Michael and Anna (Rupp) Ammann, Jakob was born in 1644 near Erlenbach in the Swiss Canton of Bern. He was married to Verena Stüdler. As late as 1671, Jakob was a member in good standing of the Reformed Church, but by 1680, Swiss officials reported his conversion to Anabaptism. Records reveal suspicion that his father had also become an Anabaptist.

Prior to his public dispute with Hans Reist, Ammann probably lived near Steffisburg in the Bernese Oberland and likely moved to Alsace in the very early 1690s, first near the town of Heidolsheim and later to the village of Sainte-Marie-aux-Mines in the Lièpvre valley. Non-Anabaptist observers in Sainte-Marie-aux-Mines recognized his leadership and influence. In 1696, a magistrate called Ammann the "leader of the new Anabaptist sect" and noted that he was "commonly called 'the Patriarch.'" Ammann successfully negotiated his people's exemptions from militia duty and from serving as municipal tax collectors (a task that involved carrying threatening weapons). In 1701, he won approval for an Amish family to raise several orphans in a case where the village clerk had wanted to assign the children to foster parents in the state church.

In 1712, the French King Louis XIV forced local authorities to expel Anabaptists from Alsace "with no exceptions," and Ammann's whereabouts thereafter are unknown. In 1730, Ammann's daughter asked to resettle in the Canton of Bern. She told authorities that her father had been an Anabaptist minister, but that he was no longer living and had died outside the canton. As part of her repatriation she was ordered to join the Reformed Church, but she probably never did.

Like his father, Jakob Ammann was a tailor by trade. French researcher Robert Baecher has written that it is "fitting that a tailor, one sensitive to the style of dress around him, would extend this concern to the strict and regulated attire that eventually became a hallmark of the Amish community."

Today, few Amish know much about Ammann. When asked about their church's origins, most typically stress the biblical or Reformation roots of their faith. "The birthplace of Jacob Aymen [sic] we have not yet ascertained," wrote two Pennsylvania Amishmen in 1830, "nor yet the exact place of his residence—having never considered him a man of note, we do not deem the place of his nativity a matter of consequence." Nevertheless, today nearly 300,000 people call themselves *Amish*.

For biographical material on Ammann, see Robert Baecher, "The 'Patriarche' of Sainte-Marie-aux-Mines," *Mennonite Quarterly Review* 74 (January 2000), 145-58; John Hüppi, "Identifying Jacob Ammann," *Mennonite Quarterly Review* 74 (April 2000), 329-39; and Mark Furner, "On the Trail of Jacob Ammann," *Mennonite Quarterly Review* 74 (April 2000), 326-28.

Ammann now sensed that church renewal was all the more urgent if even seasoned leaders such as Hans Reist were not committed to thoroughgoing separation from the world. In 1693, Ammann and three like-minded ministers traveled among Swiss Mennonite communities, explaining that shunning was a clear corollary to Anabaptist beliefs: if church membership had social implications, so did severing one's ties with the church through disobedience or persistent sin.

The party soon found that Reist's friend, Niklaus Moser, admitted that social avoidance was important, and he

The mill at Ohnenheim in Alsace. In 1660, Alsatian Mennonites met here and adopted the Dordrecht Confession as their statement of faith. Later, during the Ammann-Reist controversy, Palatinate Mennonites called a unity conference at the mill. That March 1964 gathering failed to bring peace, and the two groups remained divided.

rejected the notion that the True-Hearted were saved. In the next town, another of Reist's colleagues, minister Peter Giger, also seemed to confess the importance of shunning. Buoyed by these sympathetic encounters, Ammann's group traveled down into the Swiss Emme River Valley and summoned Hans Reist himself. The exchange between Reist and Ammann was heated. Reist rejected Ammann's call for shunning on the grounds that Jesus had eaten with sinners but had kept himself pure. Christians in the late seventeenth century could do the same, Reist claimed.

But, Ammann countercharged, Reist was not keeping the church pure. A woman who had lied, and then repeatedly lied about her lying, remained a member of Reist's congregation even though her untruth had been revealed. Reist had not practiced the sort of accountability he espoused. Here was proof for Ammann that Reist was drifting from the vigorous Christianity of the Anabaptist tradition.

Ministers in a neighboring town suggested that Ammann call a general meeting of Swiss Mennonite leaders and discuss the matter publicly. Niklaus Moser's barn served as the meeting place. Few elders and ministers showed up, and Hans Reist was noticeably absent. Sensing the rift between Ammann and Reist, Moser and Giger backed away from their earlier acceptance of shunning. Instead, they told Ammann that they would like to decide the issue only with the counsel of all of the ministers and a reconsideration of relevant Bible verses. After some discussion, those present decided to invite leaders and lay members to another gathering in two weeks.

The next 14 days were filled with personal meetings and private correspondence. Through emissaries, Ammann tried to contact Reist, who still refused to say that the True-Hearted were not saved. Reist also circulated a letter sharply critical of Ammann and warning ministers "not to give too much regard to the teachings and discipline of the younger [ministers]."[7] Ammann complained that Reist claimed to hold "more authority" than Ammann, even though both held the same church office. While the simmering dispute involved more than a simple personality clash, Reist's condescending attitude seemed to invite confrontation.

Today Amish and Mennonites participate together in several cooper-ative ventures. Here Old Order Amish men help rebuild a structure near Salisbury, Pennsylvania, soon after tornadoes destroyed it in June 1998. The Salisbury cleanup and reconstruction was coordinated by Mennonite Disaster Service, a volunteer relief response effort supported by both Mennonites and Amish.

Days of division

When the day for the general gathering arrived, Hans Reist and several other ministers sympathetic to him did not appear. In the tense moments that followed, Ammann assured everyone that he did not want to cause a schism, but he reminded them that matters could not be settled until Reist arrived. One of the women waiting for the discussion to start left to find Reist and tell him that the group was waiting.

But Reist had no intention of meeting with Ammann or debating the issues under consideration. He sent word back to those at the Moser barn that he and other ministers were involved in farm work and could not be bothered. Hearing this, Ammann "almost became enraged and immediately placed Hans Reist, along with six other ministers, under the ban as a heretic."[8] The startling course of events left onlookers "horrified," and several people begged Ammann to be patient and let his temper cool.[9] Instead, Ammann turned and questioned five other men as to their views on shunning. When their answers were conditional, Ammann expelled them as well. Stunned by the splintering of their church before their eyes, those gathered waited for someone to speak a word of peace—some word to undo all the harsh words that had just torn their church apart.

Instead, as if to validate what had transpired, Ammann's associate, Peter Zimmerman, said, "There you have it," and the meeting broke up in confusion, with neither side offering the customary handshake.[10]

In the hours following that encounter, a number of leaders tried to resolve the crisis. Two of the ministers whom Ammann had excommunicated offered to hold a discussion and try to work out the groups' differences. After some hesitation, Ammann and his supporters agreed to attend the forum, which included Peter Giger and people from his congregation. The sides consented to one guideline: "that when someone is speaking, the other should listen."[11]

Ammann addressed the group first. When Giger then began to present the views of the Reist group, Ammann walk out. Angry that Ammann would not offer the same hearing he had just received, Giger grabbed Ammann's shirtsleeve and said, "Let me also finish my speech." But Ammann "shook his arm loose" and left the room, dramatically bringing the meeting to a premature end.[12]

If before this encounter Swiss church leaders had underestimated Ammann's resolve or the seriousness with which he regarded reforming church life, they could do so no longer. Although division was not inevitable at this point, the confrontation suggested the emergence of two factions: a larger Mennonite community represented by Hans Reist and the reforming "Ammann-ish" faction led by Jakob Ammann.[13]

Schism spreads

The story of what had transpired in Switzerland during 1693 soon spread to the other south Rhine Mennonite communities and eventually to Dutch and north German Mennonites, as well. Thereafter, letters flew back and forth, with all parties advising, scolding, questioning, and challenging both the Reist/Mennonite and Amish parties. Some Palatinate ministers wrote to the Amish and counseled them to be reconciled with the Reist group and wrote, too, to Alsatian Anabaptists and warned them not to listen to Jakob Ammann.

Alsatian church leaders, however, claimed that Reist was the one to ignore. They were confused as to why Reist thought that social avoidance was a new teaching. Alsatian congregations contended that Swiss Mennonites had accepted the biblical teaching of shunning some thirty years earlier. Why had Reist not practiced it, they wondered? Most Swiss refugees in Alsace saw Ammann as a true reformer, struggling to restore classical Anabaptist doctrines that the Swiss had let slide. Earlier, Ammann had excommunicated several members of a Mennonite congregation near Sainte-Marie-aux-Mines who had tried to curry public favor by attending services of the state church. Ammann and other Alsatian leaders would allow no such compromise of faith for personal gain and social status.

Returning to Alsace, Ammann responded to the past months' events with a long letter. He reminded those who called him a troublemaker that he had followed the three-part practice of church discipline outlined by Jesus in Matthew 18. Ammann had privately confronted those who were erring and asked them to mend their ways. When they refused admonition, he visited them with several witnesses, and only as a last resort was he forced to excommunicate those who would not reform.

But Ammann also had words for those who as yet were not involved in the Reist-Ammann division. Ammann sent a "letter of warning" to the Mennonite churches in the south Rhine and Swiss regions in which he stipulated that men and women, ministers and lay members alike, declare by February 20, 1694 whether they supported Reist or him. Although Ammann said he was open to being shown with Scripture that he was in error, he served notice that the Amish would shun, "according to God's Word," those who did not stand with them by March 7.[14]

In response to events that seemed to be spinning out of control, Palatinate Mennonites called a conference of reconciliation at a mill in Alsace. The Palatinates proposed a compromise. They suggested that Reist had, in fact, been negligent in exercising church discipline and in teaching that the True-Hearted were saved, but the Palatinates rejected Ammann's teaching on shunning. Grudgingly, the Swiss Mennonites—including Reist himself—agreed to the compromise.

The Amish, however, would not accept the proposed solution. The social avoidance of those who left the church, even to the point of not eating common meals together, was one of Ammann's major reforms. He believed it was biblical and that it aligned with the historic understanding of many Anabaptists. The only Amish response to the meeting at the mill was Ammann's banning and shunning most of the Palatinate ministers, along with a large group of other people whom he had apparently not met.

Different contexts, different perspectives

The Swiss and south Rhine Valley Mennonites had remained a fairly cohesive, if dispersed, group for more than a century and a half. During several months spanning 1693-1694 their relationships were torn apart and mired in mutual resentment. Were the disagreements trite matters of no lasting concern? Did schism result from personality conflicts blown out of proportion?

Although personality differences seem to have contributed to the impasse, the issues were not insignificant and stemmed from old Anabaptist convictions about the nature of the church. From the perspective of both sides, the church was at risk.

For Ammann, the danger was compromise and the possibility that church might be reduced to a private experience. As he saw it, Anabaptist reformers of 150 years earlier had given their lives for a church that would be a visible alternative to corrupt society. But now Mennonites were willing to play the part of state church members in public, agreeing even to have their infants baptized in order to avoid exile.

In this setting, relations with the True-Hearted were especially problematic, Ammann charged, because the half-commitment of such folks mirrored the lack of full-fledged commitment on the part of many Anabaptists themselves. If Anabaptists really believed that salvation was given by grace through faith, then the True-Hearted, who had not personally and publicly recognized such grace and submitted to baptism, were not part of the church.

The same was true for what Ammann saw as a clear New Testament teaching of social avoidance: there was no middle ground.[15] In those regions where persecution was relatively light—Alsace and parts of the Palatinate—compromise seemed a greater threat and Ammann received most of his support. He championed strict interpretations and an activist approach that appealed to Mennonites desiring strong group identity in an atmosphere of relative tolerance.[16]

For Reist and the old Mennonite communities in the Emme River Valley and parts of the Palatinate, the threat they perceived was anything but lost identity. Their identity as outcasts and the targets of persecution was all too clear. For the Reist group, the threat to the church was a cold legalism. They already faced enough external threats. Shunning that would divide them from within was the last thing they needed. Nor were they keen to receive lectures on faithfulness from those who lived in the relative safety of Alsace.[17]

Additionally, Reist could claim—quite rightly—that Swiss Anabaptists had never practiced social avoidance, at least not in the form Ammann advocated, even if they had seemed to agree to it in principle when they made use of doctrinal works written by their northern European Mennonite cousins. Ammann's insistence on implementing shunning now only stirred up trouble. Social avoidance was simply not taught in the New Testament as Reist read it. And as for the True-Hearted, Reist thought that it was presumptuous for humans to declare whether or not a person was saved, baptism notwithstanding.

Yet despite their emphasis on flexibility, it was Reist's group that seemed to practice shunning when opportunities for reconciliation surfaced.

Amish ask for forgiveness and Mennonites refuse

Several years after the Mennonite and Amish schism, a number of Amish leaders felt they had acted too quickly in excommunicating so many people. They wondered if their

Hans Reist

Hans Reist, also known as Hüsli Hans, was a Swiss Brethren elder in the Emme River Valley east of Bern, Switzerland. Little is known about his life aside from bits of information preserved in letters chronicling his disagreements with Jakob Ammann. He was married to Barbara Ryser.

Reist had experienced religious harassment firsthand. In 1670, authorities expelled Hans and Barbara, penniless, from their village of Rotenbaum because the couple were Anabaptists. Bern's government confiscated the Reist house and sold most of their grain, animals, and furniture, including a loom, suggesting that Reist was a weaver. The state settled Reist's outstanding debts with the proceeds, and then kept about half the profits from the liquidation of the family's property.

Like many expelled Anabaptists, Reist broke exile in a few years and returned home. State records mention him again in 1686. In 1701, officials again arrested Reist, and he promised to attend state church services and take the holy sacraments. Reist may have had no more intention of keeping that pledge than he had had of remaining in exile thirty years earlier, or he may have been willing to engage in acts of public piety in exchange for some measure of toleration.

Reist was a leader who knew how to survive tough times and understood his own ability to compromise. Apparently he sympathized with the weaknesses or calculating choices of others and granted his church and the True-Hearted a generous degree of latitude.

A small collection of Reist's writings remain in the form of a sixteen-page booklet containing a prayer and a hymn. In line with Ammann's charge that Reist promised salvation for the True-Hearted, Reist's prayer petitions God "on behalf of all those peoples who do so much good unto us with food and drink and house and shelter, and who produce and show unto us great love and loyalty. Lord God, be their rich reward here and in the life eternal."

Reist's prayer suggests the pain he experienced in the schism with Ammann. "Draw us together," the elder prayed, "in Thy great love, and let no dissention or scattering come among us anymore, but rather let us see, O Lord of Harvest, how great the harvest but how few Thy faithful workers are." Reist's hymn was a forty-six-stanza ballad recounting the biblical story of Abraham and Isaac.

For more information see Samuel Geiser's entry "Reist, Hans" in *The Mennonite Encyclopedia, vol. 4* (1959); Isaac Zürcher, "Hans Reist House and the 'Vale of Anabaptists,'" *Mennonite Quarterly Review* 66 (July 1992), 426-27; and Robert Friedmann, *Mennonite Piety Through the Centuries: Its Genius and Literature* (Goshen, Ind.: Mennonite Historical Society, 1949), 184-85. Mark Furner, "Lay Casuistry and the Survival of Later Anabaptists in Bern," *Mennonite Quarterly Review* 75 (October 2001), 455-56 (esp. n.105), 466. Reist's prayer appears in John D. Roth, ed., with Joe Springer, *Letters of the Amish Division: A Sourcebook* (Goshen, Ind.: Mennonite Historical Society, 1993), 147-52.

actions had been justified because they had not first discussed matters with their own congregations before expelling the Reist group. Several Amish leaders—including Ammann himself—then excommunicated *themselves*, symbolically demonstrating their repentance and desire to mend the broken Anabaptist fellowship. The response of the Mennonites was cool. Some of the Reist group reveled in the Amish admission that they had been too quick. Others wrote letters likening Jakob Ammann to symbolic biblical figures of evil and doom.

In 1699 and 1700, Mennonite leaders again rebuffed Amish attempts to seek peace. Amish minister Ulli Ammann, who was Jakob's younger brother, later wrote that the Amish had hoped to come to some agreement. "But this was all for naught. Our efforts could find no place among them," Uli Ammann lamented. "Instead, when they [the Mennonites] said something about the matter, they began with our faults and did not want to acknowledge that they themselves were guilty of making mistakes or had been a cause of our mistakes. So contention and division continued among the people."[18] In 1711, some sort of reconciliation talks apparently began between Alsatian Mennonites on the one hand, and Ulli Ammann and other Amish ministers on the other, but produced no concrete results.[19]

Instead, two distinct groups began coalescing among Anabaptists of Switzerland and the south Rhine Valley region. Markers that distinguished the Amish included the practice of shunning and the fact that Amish church members ritually washed one another's feet. They did this as part of their observance of communion, following the example of Jesus who had washed his disciples' feet during the Last Supper before his crucifixion (John 13). Swiss Mennonites thought that literal footwashing was an unnecessary ritual, even though it, like avoidance, was a part of the historic Dordrecht Confession.

Diverging paths

Throughout the turbulent years of Swiss and south Rhine Mennonite division, the War of Palatinate Succession ravaged parts of Alsace and the Palatinate. Meanwhile, the Bern government in Switzerland redoubled its efforts to drive Mennonites of any sort from its territory. Amid such hardship along the Rhine and persecution in the Alps, the small group of Anabaptists split.

Four days before Christmas 1697, a north German Mennonite patriarch, eighty-five-year-old minister and merchant Gerrit Roosen of Hamburg, wondered about the connections between the larger events of European politics and Mennonite church life. Roosen worried over the war's effects on his people, and about new political divisions created by France's influence in Alsace and over the city of Strasbourg. He was also deeply saddened by the Mennonite-Amish division, which was well-known among Mennonites in northern Europe. Although the Dutch and north German Mennonites of Roosen's region had once advocated shunning, they now practiced it less often. And Roosen flatty rejected Ammann's concern for plain clothing and appearance. In all of the Apostle Paul's letters, the old minister wrote, there was "not a single word in which he gave a law to any believers regarding what style of clothes they should have." Avoid undue luxury, of course, he added, but otherwise "I think it appropriate to follow the customs of the land and that of the people one is with and of one's surroundings."[20]

Roosen's ideas represented an emerging consensus among European Mennonites. In the north, an emphasis on inner piety over outward appearance meant that a simple lifestyle and social separation from the world were less important so long as a person's heart was right. In the south, Mennonites' very struggle to survive had nurtured ties with the True-Hearted and softened a sense of separation. Ammann's position represented a different approach. The church as a visible and social reality needed boundaries equally physical and social. Separation from the world was not merely a matter of inner feeling, nor even the result of being a persecuted minority group. Church renewal came by way of commitment and community.

Yet despite their renewed commitment to separation from the world, the Amish shared some things in common with other Western Europeans. After 1700, for example, the

Amish were taken with the prospect of immigration to "new worlds" in the Western Hemisphere. North America beckoned the Amish as persuasively as it called their worldly neighbors. The lure of the Atlantic shunned no one.

Distinctive Dress

Today, distinctive dress is among the most recognized marks of Amish life. Yet clothing was not a major issue in the debates between Jakob Ammann and Hans Reist. In 1693, Ammann did admonish those who want "to be conformed to the world with shaved beard . . . and haughty clothing" and said the church must discipline members who did not adopt a more humble appearance. Otherwise, plain clothing did not figure prominently in Ammann's writings. Did that mean Ammann did not care about clothing?

In fact, in the 1600s, dress was a matter of general civic concern, and clothing was highly regulated in Switzerland and some other parts of Western Europe. Governments issued "sumptuary laws" that detailed what kind of clothing people in each social class were allowed to wear. For example, rules for the Canton of Bern forbade pointy shoes, silk lace, ornamental ribbons and pearls, and the use of extra fabric to make billowing sleeves.

Like his father, Jakob Ammann was a tailor, so he would have been quite familiar with sumptuary codes and would even have been responsible for enforcing such rules before he converted to Anabaptism. Tailors could be held liable if they made clothing that did not conform to sumptuary law, and they were obliged to tell customers what kinds of attire they were legally permitted to wear. In short, restrictions on what people could wear were not uniquely Anabaptist concerns but widely shared social norms.

Although there is no evidence that early Amish dress differed radically from that of their neighbors, it seems the Amish were noticeably plain in a context where all peasants were limited in what they were allowed to wear. In 1702, an Alsatian Catholic priest wrote that among the Amish "the men . . . have a long beard and the men and women wear clothing made only of linen cloth, summer and winter." In contrast, the Mennonites who had not sided with Ammann had "shorter beards" or dressed "about like the Catholics."

Historian Mary Ann Bates has suggested that Amish commitment to plain dress may have demonstrated more than just Christian humility. It may also have been something of a political strategy. By scrupulously following laws that required peasants to avoid fancy dress, the Amish were obedient, model subjects rather than socially dangerous dissidents. Indeed, in 1693, when a Reformed Church pastor published a sharp critique of Anabaptists, he admitted that they obeyed government sumptuary codes more conscientiously than did most members of his state church.

Amish clothing patterns evolved in North America during the nineteenth and twentieth centuries, but the basic outlines of Amish commitment to plain dress were present in the late 1600s. The Amish accepted the widely held idea of their day that dress could and should be regulated. Where they differed from others of their era was in their belief that the church, not the state, should regulate clothing styles.

For more information, see Mary Ann Miller Bates, "Insubordinate Anabaptists in Virtuous Clothing? Amish Anabaptists as Model Subjects in the Context of Bernese Sumptuary and Morals Mandates," *Mennonite Quarterly Review* 82 (October 2008): 517-31; and John Martin Vincent, *Costume and Conduct in the Laws of Basel, Bern, and Zurich, 1370-1800* (Baltimore: The Johns Hopkins University Press, 1935). For an Amish discussion, see David Luthy, "Clothing and Conduct in Swiss Laws, 1450-1700," *Family Life* (July 1994): 23-26.

—3—

Migration and Persistence: The Amish in Europe, 1693-1801

> *"You are still one with us . . . in keeping to doctrine and congregational practice according to the old customs."*
> —European elder Hans Nafziger to a
> minister in North America, 1788

Searching for stability

The first century of Amish life was marked by the church's status as a marginal and maligned group, and by the emergence in many places of amiable relations with influential non-Amish neighbors and patrons. Both of these realities encouraged the group's geographic dispersion. In 1693, the Amish were a tiny party concentrated in Alsace, with smaller numbers in the Palatinate and Switzerland. Political pressure and social hostility in these areas, invitations to lease farms in other parts of Germany and in Eastern Europe, and the lure of North America, all prompted migration, so that by 1801, Amish communities were scattered from western Pennsylvania to Russian Volhynia.

Popular images of eighteenth-century Swiss Anabaptists.

Despite the church's dispersal during the 1700s, its members seem to have maintained a sense of connection and nurtured their religious ties. In the late 1700s, elder Hans Nafziger of Essingen, Germany visited Amish congregations in the Netherlands, ordained leaders in Alsace, and corresponded with minister Christian Schowalter in Lancaster County, Pennsylvania. Such activity, along with Nafziger's arranging to publish a German translation of the Dutch Anabaptist history book *Martyrs Mirror*, pointed to ways that past experiences and contemporary relationships shaped Amish identity.

The tension between social inclusion and exclusion was apparent even in the earliest years of the Amish church. After the 1693 division, many of the Swiss Anabaptists who sided with Ammann moved north to Alsace, settling in the Lièpvre valley near the town of Sainte-Marie-aux-Mines, which was then ruled by the religiously tolerant Lords of Ribeaupierre. While Anabaptists had been living in the Alsatian lowlands for some time, the influx of as many as sixty new families—including

Ammann's household—into the Sainte-Marie-aux-Mines area created a sizable new Amish community there.

Writing in 1702, a local Catholic priest noted that "in Sainte-Marie-aux-Mines [the] Anabaptists . . . are divided in three different sects and have no communication with each other as far as their religion is concerned." The largest was Ammann's notably plain group in which men "have a long beard and the men and women wear clothing made only of linen." A few Swiss refugees, perhaps those aligned with Hans Reist, "have shorter beards and everyone dresses in coarse cloth," while the third group—those Anabaptists who had been living in tolerant Alsatian villages for decades— "are about like the Catholics [in appearance]." None of the three groups had a "church building but meet in one of their homes (each one in his sect) which are often scattered in the mountains."[1]

Clearly the Amish were distinguishable even from other Anabaptists, especially those whose long-standing presence in tolerant Alsace had resulted in their adaptation to local customs and appearance. Yet even as outsiders, the Amish were able to find a welcome in Sainte-Marie-aux-Mines. Evidently, in fact, members of the local French Reformed (Huguenot) congregation had housed Amish refugees when they first arrived after 1694.

As the Amish established themselves in the area, they rented or even purchased some of the largest farms in the valley. Others took over area mills and lumber operations. Meanwhile, civil authorities appear to have sided with them when neighbors complained that the Amish should have to serve in certain civic roles. The Amish received a waiver in exchange for a fee.

This economic integration and even limited civic acceptance, however, existed in tension with the reality of being religious outsiders. During the early 1700s, Amish leaders were repeatedly involved in conflicts over conversion as individuals from state church backgrounds joined or sought to join the Anabaptists. Some disputes were quite public, such as Ammann's vocal arguments in the middle of the street with a Catholic priest upset over the possibility of proselytism. In the end, these religious tensions outweighed the ability of the Amish to find an economic and neighborly niche in the valley. In 1712, the French government overruled locally tolerant lords and ordered the expulsion of all Anabaptists from Alsace. Although the order never completely rooted out the Amish presence, it effectively dispersed the Sainte-Marie-aux-Mines Amish.

While the expulsion order pushed the Amish out, the possibility of settlement pulled them to nearby areas outside direct royal jurisdictions, such as Salm, Montbéliard, Hesse-Darmstadt, and the duchies of Lorraine and Zweibrücken. In some cases, refugees moved to territory open to

The Schaaken Estate, near Korbach in Waldeck. Vinzenz and Anna (Zimmerman) Schwarzentruber were leaseholders here beginning in 1759.

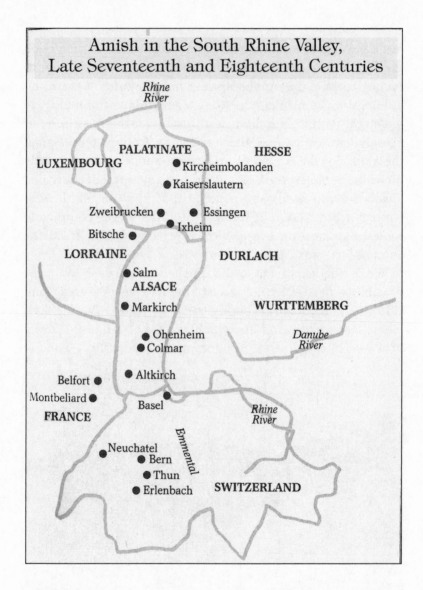

Amish in the South Rhine Valley, Late Seventeenth and Eighteenth Centuries

Anabaptists for the first time, while in others, they went to places where fellow church members had already been living. As early as 1704, for example, Amish families had been living in Montbéliard, but the expulsions from Sainte-Marie-aux-Mines swelled these numbers considerably. Eventually, most Amish were forced out of the very areas in which Anabaptism had sprouted. Only three small Amish congregations survived in Switzerland, all close to the Alsatian border.[2]

An Amish couple from Kampen, the Netherlands, late eighteenth or early nineteenth century.

A Voyage of Eighty-Three Days

An eighteenth-century Atlantic crossing involved uncertainty and danger as storms and disease resulted in delay and death. In 1737, many of the earliest Amish families to settle in North America arrived in Philadelphia on the *Charming Nancy*. A journal presumably kept by one of the ship's passengers recorded these voyage details:

"The 28th of June while in Rotterdam [the Netherlands] getting ready to start my Zernbli died and was buried in Rotterdam. The 29th we got under sail and enjoyed one and a half days of favorable wind. The 7th day of July, early in the morning, Hans Zimmerman's son-in-law died.

"We landed in England the 8th of July, remaining 9 days in port during which 5 children died. Went under sail the 17th of July. The 21st of July my own Lisbetli died. Several days before Michael's Georgli had died.

"On the 29th of July three children died. On the first of August my Hansli died and the Tuesday previous 5 children died. On the 3rd of August contrary winds beset the vessel and from the first to the 7th of the month three more children died.

"On the 8th of August, Shambien's Lizzie died and on the 9th Hans Zimmerman's Jacobli died. On the 19th Christian Burgli's Child died. Passed a ship on the 21st. A favorable wind sprang up. On the 28th Hans Gasi's wife died. Passed a ship 13th of September.

"Landed in Philadelphia on the 18th and my wife and I left the ship on the 19th. A child was born to us on the 20th—died—wife recovered. A voyage of 83 days."

Excerpted from S. Duane Kauffman, "Miscellaneous Amish Mennonite Documents," *Pennsylvania Mennonite Heritage* 2 (July 1979): 12. On the document's authorship, see the article's note 3.

In most places, Amish and other religious minorities did not own land outright, but leased estates from landed nobility who sought reliable tenants. The relationship between landlords and renters benefited both parties. Leaseholders received toleration, while owners found a pool of especially loyal tenants who were dependent upon them for protection.[3] Landed nobles typically rented estates for periods of six to nine years, handing over responsibility for the estate farm, granting freedom of worship on estate land, and allowing leaseholders use of the nearby forests for raising livestock. Leaseholders could supplement their income by taking up a trade in weaving or operating an estate's distillery. In Waldeck, some renters began making cheese.[4]

Often more than one household leased a single estate, and in the case of Amish renters, they sought to pass the lease to fellow church members. For example, in 1713 Christian Rupp leased an estate near Freiburg, which he renewed until his death in 1746, whereupon Michael Müller became the tenant. By that time, Müller had to pay nearly twice as much in annual rent and took a co-leaseholder. In 1772, the estate— still under the management of Müller and Zimmerman families—included ten horses and foals, thirty-two oxen, sixteen cows, twenty calves, twenty-six sheep, and twenty-three pigs. In 1800, the farm had a workforce of twenty-three who oversaw 231 acres of tillable land, 128 acres of meadow, 119 acres of pastureland, and up to five acres of garden. All of this had to feed thirty-five people and generate enough cash to cover the annual lease payment.[5]

Identifiable Amish communities developed as leaseholders clustered in particular areas. The French-speaking territory of Montbéliard, for example, developed into a thriving Amish community, especially after 1750 under the leadership of elder Hans Rich.[6] As the eighteenth century wore on, the needs of growing families and the interests of territorial landlords both resulted in the formation of more communities. About 1775, Prince Carl Christian of Nassau-Weilburg invited four families—Nafziger, Unzicker, Schanz, and Schwarztraub households—to take up estates near Frankfurt, which they did. And by 1780, Amish were invited to Austrian-controlled land in Baden-Durlach.[7]

Harassment and hospitality

The welcome some found on the estates of wealthy landowners was part of the paradox of Amish life in these years: havens of toleration made necessary by continued waves of harassment. Into the eighteenth century, Swiss authorities in the Canton of Bern posted commissions for citizens who turned in their Anabaptist neighbors to the state.[8] Certainly the Amish were not alone in suffering intolerance. In 1699, the government of Bern expelled the pastor of the city's largest state church because he had held unauthorized Bible study meetings.[9] In many places, both Catholics and Protestants—if they were minority members of their home territories—felt unwelcome. Nor were the Amish the only ones to benefit from the land-leasing agreements offered by nobles. Swiss Reformed households were also leaving Alpine valleys to become tenants on German and French farms to the north.

Yet if lease agreements afforded the Amish some relief from religious persecution, they also could produce new tensions. As Swiss outsiders, the Amish—along with other Swiss leaseholders—were "free" people, not bound by traditional local rules that regulated the economic lives of surrounding peasants. Moreover, peasant farmers typically were banned from allowing their cattle, sheep, or pigs to use the estate forests, which were open only to the leaseholders. Opposition to the Amish, then, might have stemmed from nonreligious resentments, or might have become entwined with religion, only as frustrated peasants enlisted the help of sympathetic

In 1782, Daniel Joder was leaseholder on the Vogelstocker Estate, near Speyer in the Upper Palatinate.

priests or pastors to protest the presence of Anabaptists. Such protests rarely resulted in nobles turning down leases, but they added to a context in which the Amish status as ethnic and religious outsiders remained, even though some nobles gave them a friendly welcome.

Despite such tensions and Amish commitments to separation from worldly society, there were notable examples of assistance and friendship across religious lines. If the Amish were separate, they were not necessarily withdrawn. Not only were landlords dependent upon them, but the Amish themselves at times relied on the goodwill of their non-Amish neighbors—even in cases where the issues clearly were matters of Amish concern.

In 1729, Hans Hochstättler, a leaseholder near Freiburg, appealed to a nearby Reformed Church pastor to perform the marriage of Hochstättler's daughter Barbara and an Alsatian Anabaptist named Hans von Gunten. Barbara's pregnancy out of wedlock had resulted in her excommunication from the Amish church and the refusal of Amish elders to perform the wedding.

The Reformed clergyman also refused at first, citing the fact that services of the state church were unavailable to religious dissenters. Yet apparently the pastor liked Hochstättler, and so he wrote to his own superior, asking permission to marry the couple as a gesture of goodwill. Clearly he did not approve of Amish religious customs, referring to Amish discipline as "their strange way of thinking," but he respected Hochstättler enough to put his own professional reputation on the line and to marry the couple "in a private ceremony and without pomp."[10]

Another somewhat surprising feature of Amish family life in this era was the number of mixed marriages between Amish and non-Amish partners. Because the Amish insisted that marriages could take place only if both partners were members of the Amish church, it seems these religiously-mixed marriage situations resulted when one spouse within a state church household converted to the Amish later in life and the other spouse remained a state church adherent.[11] These sorts of ties—in addition to the economic links of leaseholding—connected Amish and non-Amish families and communities in peculiar ways.

If all of this seems a bit remarkable in light of Jakob Ammann's insistence on separation and avoiding dependence on the True-Hearted, perhaps it can be understood in a larger context. Amman had keenly opposed religious compromise as a means of currying state favor. The Amish of the 1700s were still committed to those principles. If their daily conduct won them friends and some respect, that was another matter.

Even if the development of neighborly connections resulted in some goodwill, the Amish were still spiritual outsiders subject to social sanction. In 1744, for example, when Nicholas Stoltzfus, a Lutheran hired-hand on an Amish farm, asked to marry an Amish woman, state authorities permitted the nuptials only if the couple agreed to leave the area after the wedding.[12]

Such sanctions, though, were often rooted as much in tensions accompanying economic competition as they were in theological debate. In Baden-Durlach in the 1760s, for example, the Hochberg weaver's guild protested the presence of non-guild Amish weavers such as Christian Gautsche and succeeded in keeping Gautsche from hiring a journeyman. After 1780, when Anabaptists moved into Austrian-ruled areas of Baden, economic resentments surfaced even more frequently. Locals denounced the Amish as foreigners and complained that nobles who rented estates to outsiders were unconcerned with the economic plight of local folks. One notable case of conflict involved a Catholic would-be renter who railed against a Catholic nunnery for preferring to lease its acres to Anabaptist heretics on the grounds that they were skilled farmers, instead of to him.[13]

North to the Netherlands

Some migrations took Amish families further afield—to the Netherlands, North America, and Eastern Europe. The movement northward grew out of persecution and international diplomacy. In 1711, the Swiss Bernese government decided to rid its territory of Anabaptists by shipping them elsewhere. Already in 1699, Bern officials had asked the Dutch East India Company to take Swiss Anabaptists to islands in the Pacific Ocean.[14] When the shipping company did not respond, the Swiss drew up their own plans to export the Amish and Mennonites to North America.

An initial attempt to send Anabaptists out of the Alps failed. But in the summer of 1711, the Bern government was gearing up efforts to try again, when officials in the Netherlands intervened with the humanitarian promise of safe passage from Switzerland to Dutch territory. Once there, the refugees could decide where they wanted to go, the Dutch announced.[15]

But complications troubled this scheme as well. First, the Swiss could round up only enough Anabaptists to fill four of the five ships they had contracted. Then, to the chagrin of the Dutch ambassador, the Mennonites nearly refused to ride on the same boats with the Amish.[16] Apparently the division of 1693 was still sore. Finally, organizers persuaded the Mennonites to go along, though many jumped ship downriver and tried to make their way back to Switzerland. In August, the boats arrived in the Netherlands with an almost entirely Amish cargo. (The Mennonites who did stick it out to Dutch territory grumbled and complained and eventually headed south toward the Palatinate.)

Arriving in Holland, the Amish were invited to settle in Prussia (now northern Poland), but decided to remain in the Netherlands instead. They formed several congregations, and with the aid of Dutch Mennonites established themselves in farming. The culturally refined Dutch Anabaptists found the traditional dress and untrimmed beards of the Amish quaint, if not odd. The Amish use of a Swiss-German dialect also set them apart in the Netherlands. An old story handed down from that time reports that Amish worship seemed so peculiar to the Dutch that, at times, town constables needed to keep curious crowds away from Amish church meetings.[17]

To North America and Eastern Europe

While the Bern government continued trying forcibly to move Amish and Mennonites to North America, some Mennonites had been immigrating there voluntarily. Already a decade before the Mennonite-Amish division itself, a Mennonite couple named Jan and Mercken (Schmitz) Lensen had settled in Germantown, Pennsylvania, marking the start of the first continuous Mennonite community on the other side of the Atlantic. For the next eighty years or so, Mennonites—especially from the Palatinate and Switzerland—felt the pull of Penn's Woods. In the eighteenth century, Pennsylvania was the destination of virtually all Mennonites who left Europe, and it would become the Amish destination, as well.

In 1681, Englishman William Penn had received a royal land grant and set out to create the colony of Pennsylvania as a "holy experiment." Penn was a member of the Religious Society of Friends (Quakers), a group that was itself a persecuted minority in England and continental Europe. In Pennsylvania, Penn established a colony where religious toleration would be the order of the day.[18] He advertised especially in the Rhine Valley for immigrants to settle in his province, and Pennsylvania became one of North America's havens for marginalized religious minorities, including Quakers, Moravians, Schwenkfelders, Mennonites, Dunkers, and Amish, along with larger contingents of Lutheran, Reformed, and Presbyterian church immigrants.

Exactly when Amish families first left Europe for North America is unclear. Perhaps none sailed until 1736; information on any Amish who emigrated before that time is sketchy. In 1737, significant movement began when the *Charming Nancy* sailed for Pennsylvania with twenty-one Amish families aboard.[19] Once the Amish began to emigrate, they did so relatively quickly. Within about three decades, approximately 100 households made their way to Pennsylvania. Amish migration matched the broader pattern of German trans-Atlantic movement during these years, and most Amish came during the peak years of German arrival in Philadelphia.[20] Some ships carried sizable groups of Amish, while others bore only a family or two.

No matter the method, a European exodus was expensive. In 1710, generous Dutch Mennonites had established a Commission for Foreign Needs to help both their fellow Mennonites and the Amish with immigration costs. By 1742, though, one Mennonite pastor was complaining that the Dutch Commission was partial to the Amish. His own Mennonites were not getting as much financial assistance from the Dutch as some Amish received, he thought. Perhaps that was because the Amish needed less help than the Mennonites. The Dutch seemed more willing to offer aid to those families or groups who made an effort to help themselves. The Amish, suggested one Mennonite historian, "seem to have been better able to finance their own emigration" than were many Mennonites. Perhaps the "reason may well have been a more close-knit group structure."[21]

As some families sought the freedom promised by Pennsylvania, others set out for Eastern Europe on a similar search for places where they could live productive and unmolested lives. As with the dynamics of Atlantic migration, Amish movement to the east was a tiny part of a much larger people movement that took many German-speakers into lands ruled by Russian, Lithuanian, or Austrian nobles.

In 1781, the Austrian emperor invited German farmers to settle in Galicia (now southeastern Poland). Three years later, some 20 Amish families were among the 3,300 German households who responded to the invitation.[22] Others moved to the neighboring Wlodawa area of what was then southern Lithuania. The Amish hailed from the Palatinate, Alsace, and Montbéliard and were accompanied by a number of Mennonite households from the same regions. Although the Amish and Mennonites wintered together after arriving in Galicia, by 1785 they were meeting separately for worship, with the Amish group under the leadership of a Catholic-turned-Anabaptist convert, Joseph Mündlein.[23]

In 1796, a few of the Amish joined some Mennonites in moving farther east and joining a Hutterite community. Like the Amish and Mennonites, Hutterites traced their origins to the Anabaptist movement of the sixteenth-century Reformation, but Hutterites also had a distinctive communal lifestyle and rejected private property. Hutterite families lived on large rented estates where they held property in common, ate group meals, and performed community-assigned tasks and trades.[24]

Though stemming from common religious roots, Amish and Hutterites expressed their faith in different ways, and the mixed community lasted only about a year. Perhaps the Amish were not prepared for the sort of strenuous Hutterite work ethic. In any case, the Amish claimed the Hutterites were interested only in material profit and left in disgust. Two young Amish women remained behind and married Hutterite men.

By 1801, these wandering Amish families had settled on estates in Russian Volhynia (now northwestern Ukraine), where they joined other Amish who had moved to the area from nearby Galicia or directly from Western Europe. During the next decades, in fact, almost all the Galician Amish relocated to Volhynia. The Volhynians adhered to the same church discipline as fellow church members in Western Europe, and they sang from the *Ausbund* hymnal. Correspondence from elder Mündlein, who had moved from Galicia to Volhynia, and the comments of area observers, indicate that the Volhynia churches followed customary Amish communion and footwashing practices, upheld the discipline of shunning, and maintained Amish clothing customs such as untrimmed beards for men and hook-and-eye fasteners instead of buttons on coats.

Persistent peoplehood

The Volhynian Amish illustrate the evolving nature of Amish life a century after Jakob Ammann debated fellow Anabaptists in the Rhine and Swiss valleys. The church in Eastern Europe included households that had been Anabaptists for generations, as well as recent converts like Mündlein. Distinctly identifiable in appearance, the Amish also were

---

A Baptismal Service, 1781

An eighteenth-century church discipline provides a window onto the rhythms of Amish church life, including this description of baptism. According to the document, elders and ministers were to instruct applicants for baptism by recounting the grand biblical narrative, beginning with the account of creation. Next, the ministers told of the sin of Adam and Eve and their consequent expulsion from Paradise. They were then to preach "the gospel of grace . . . with repentance and improvement of life, unto faith in the Holy Gospel."

Following this instruction, applicants entered a period of study, during which the congregation was "admonished to diligently watch over" them "and support them by their good example." If the congregation agreed that the candidates were sincere in their confessions and repentance, the applicants could be baptized. Sermon texts were to include John 3, Acts 2, and Romans 6. The account continues:

"With these words the applicants are requested to come before the ministers and when they [the applicants] have fallen on their knees the story of Philip and the Ethiopian eunuch [Acts 8:26-40] is told them, how he was reading the prophet Isaiah but did not understand it and how then Philip preached the Gospel to him, so that he desired to be baptized, and Philip baptized him. Then the applicant for baptism is asked: Do you believe from your whole heart that Jesus Christ is the Son of God? Answer, yes. Do you also believe that God raised him from the dead, and are you willing to be obedient to God and the Church, whether to live or die? Answer, Yes.

". . . The bishop [elder] places his hands on the head and a fully ordained deacon pours water on his [the bishop's] hands, whereupon the bishop calls him [the baptismal candidate] by name and says: On this confession of faith which thou hast confessed, thou art baptized in the name of God the Father and of the Son and of the Holy Ghost. Then the bishop gives him [the new member] his hand and raises him up, pronounces peace and says: The Lord continue the good work which he hath begun in you and complete it unto a blessed end through Jesus Christ."

Excerpted from "An Amish Church Discipline of 1781," *Mennonite Quarterly Review* 4 (April 1930): 140-48.

integrated to some degree into local economies through their leasing agricultural estates from landed nobles. Separated across hundreds of miles from fellow believers to the west, they corresponded and shared common devotional practices.

The Volhynian churches subscribed to a sixteen point church discipline that elders and ministers from nineteen congregations had drawn up at a November 1779 meeting near the Palatinate village of Essingen. The Essingen agreement was one of several formulated by Amish leaders during those years, first at Steinseltz in April 1752, and then by representatives of a dozen churches at Essingen in 1759.[25] The congregational nature of the Amish church meant that churchly decisions were not handed down from higher authorities, so much as they emerged from the consensus of leaders who discerned common problems and agreed on collective responses. The decisions of these meetings, then, point to areas of contemporary discussion and debate.

The 1752 meeting clarified contested matters related to shunning and warned against pride in the form of fancy clothes and stylish grooming. Leaders also addressed conflicts stemming from leaseholding, counseling members to think of the welfare of the entire church and not just their immediate families. No one was to take on excessive debt, "thereby burdening the congregation or bringing hardship and shame to it," nor should competition among leaseholders undercut the ability of poorer households to obtain leases. Seven years later, the first Essingen conference revisited some of these issues, and also lamented that the practice of shunning "has been heeded poorly," and resolved "not to take God's discipline so lightly."

The 1779 Essingen discipline was more detailed and offers a window on the world of eighteenth-century Amish church life. Opening resolutions affirmed the confession of faith printed in the Anabaptist *Martyrs Mirror* and discussed the incarnation of Christ. Other statements outlined the ways Amish churches should relate to one another and urged ministers to make fraternal visits to other congregations as a means of maintaining accountability among a scattered people. There was no room for "pride or arrogance" among the ministry, "but in lowliness and humility" they were to use "caution" and "introduce nothing new or unusual, so that they not be led astray from simplicity in Christ." Economic decisions were to be made with the welfare of the whole church in mind and preference in employment given to fellow church members.

The Essingen conference also urged care for widows and orphans. Finally, a number of resolutions condemned smoking and snuff tobacco, shaving beards, and wearing silks, printed fabrics, or pointed high-heeled shoes "made according to worldly styles."

Migrating Amish copied and recopied the Essingen discipline, taking versions of it with them into Eastern Europe and on to North America. Its mix of congregational accountability, meaningful church discipline, and attention to a simple lifestyle made it a key document in Amish circles and pointed to common aspects of Amish identity. Much had changed in the social and religious scene since the Reformation, and even since Ammann's 1693 reform movement, but the elements of Essingen pointed to persistent and practical peoplehood.

It is likely that the 1759 and 1779 ministers' gatherings convened in Essingen because it was the home of the respected elder Hans Nafziger. Nafziger understood the challenges facing his church. On the one hand, he was aware of the welcome and toleration in some quarters for those Amish deemed economic assets. At one point he optimistically exuded that, "Our articles of faith . . . have become so clear and well known that the mighty of this world have taken a change of opinion," citing the openness of the Austrian emperor to Amish settlement in Galicia.[26]

Yet Nafziger also knew that the world did not fully accept him or his convictions. Around 1780 he had been arrested for baptizing two young women who had not been raised Amish, having been taken from an Amish widow and raised in a state orphanage. After coming of age, the two returned to live with their mother and soon asked to join her church. When word of their baptisms reached their former guardians, local officials moved to banish the sisters and punish Nafziger. Although the elder spent some time in prison, the potential punishments were never carried out, due in large part to the good reputation that Nafziger and his church had with the area's state church bishop and other imperial authorities.[27] Routinely reminded of their outsider status, Nafziger and other Amish also knew that states sometimes had an interest in curbing persecution.

Nor did the challenges facing eighteenth-century Amish all come from without. Conflict within the church troubled Nafziger and his fellow leaders, who engaged in remarkable amounts of travel as they mediated churchly disputes. Some of the sharpest occurred among Swiss Amish settlers in the Netherlands. German elders made no less than four extended pastoral visits there in the 1760s and 1770s.[28]

As senior leaders in other communities died, Nafziger and others undertook additional trips to provide pastoral oversight or to ordain successors. "[As to] how it is going otherwise in our congregations," he admitted at one point, "we must lament with Paul the Apostle that we have come short of the glory that we should have before the Lord. But the ban and avoidance is still kept fairly strictly, but the young ministers are yet in need of much teaching."[29]

Nafziger's correspondence with churches from Eastern Europe to North America suggest the sort of common concerns that united a people now spread far beyond the Alsatian villages and Swiss valleys where they had begun a century earlier. His 1788 and 1790 letters to minister Christian Schowalter, who had immigrated to Lancaster County, Pennsylvania, include news about crops and the weather, the Reformed church family who now leased the farm where Schowalter once lived, and events from the Russian-Turkish war and the French Revolution. Nafziger passed on news from the Volhynian Amish and kept the Amish in America up-to-date on recent European ordinations. Despite geographic separation, he hoped Schowalter was "still one with us in the articles of faith, baptism, the Lord's Supper, footwashing, ban and avoidance, solemnization of marriage, in keeping to doctrine and congregational practices according to the old customs."[30]

Nafziger's hope was not in vain. Across the Atlantic, the convictions the old elder held so dear had, in fact, persisted, even as that new environment was also shaping the tradition in distinctive ways.

— 4 —

Settlement and Struggle in a New World: The Amish in Eighteenth-Century Pennsylvania

> *"In this country is a very good living."*
> —Amish man Hans Lantz

Putting down roots

The Amish who arrived in North America were distinctive but not unique. During the decades before the American Revolution, some 80,000 German-speaking Europeans came through the port of Philadelphia, and the Amish were one small part of this larger movement of people. While some Germans who rode this immigrant wave had no religious affiliation, the vast majority were Lutheran or Reformed, with smaller numbers of Moravians, Catholics, and various Pietist and Anabaptist groups. English onlookers quickly labeled all these German newcomers "Pennsylvania Dutch."

These Pennsylvania Dutch (sometimes called Pennsylvania German) settlers soon developed a common dialect—also

During the eighteenth century, Amish immigrants to North America entered through the port of Philadelphia. This scene was carved by Aaron Zook.

Ruins of a Chester County, Pennsylvania, church and schoolhouse. The Amish and their neighbors jointly constructed and shared the use of the building in the early nineteenth century. Photo from 1935.

known as Pennsylvania Dutch—which, along with other customs and folkways, set them apart from their British-rooted neighbors. For example, Pennsylvania Germans were more likely than other immigrants to settle in communities composed of fellow ethnics, and their clothing styles, architecture, and patterns of food preparation were also distinct. The Pennsylvania German settlement was concentrated in southeastern Pennsylvania and spread into the Maryland and Virginia "backcountry." Rather than being attracted to land near county seats or market towns, Pennsylvania Germans of all religious stripes gravitated to townships where fellow church members lived. Immigrant Amish life was one piece of this larger Pennsylvania German pattern.[1]

It is difficult to know with certainty exactly who was the first Amish arrival in Pennsylvania, but it is clear that the first Amish settlement was in what became Berks County, Pennsylvania. In 1736, the Detweiler and Sieber families— perhaps the earliest of roughly 500 Amish immigrants during the 1700s—put down roots there. Hans Sieber and another early immigrant, Jacob Beiler, bought land in the Northkill Creek and Irish Creek areas of Berks County. At its height, this settlement may have had nearly 200 Amish residents. By 1750, it included families with such common twenty-first century Amish surnames as Fisher, Hershberger, Hertzler, Hochstetler, Kauffman, King, Lantz, Miller, Speicher, Troyer, Yoder, and Zug (Zook).[2]

Other Amish households took up land in Lancaster County, launching a small community sometimes called the Old Conestoga settlement. It persisted through most of the eighteenth century and then broke up as its families moved to other locations. Some Amish households may also have lived in northern Lancaster County's Cocalico region for a time, and later in the far eastern part of the county near the future village of Cains.

Although Lancaster County eventually became one of America's largest Amish population centers, during the colonial period most Amish lived outside of its boundaries. More families lived in places like Berks County's Cumru Township (along Maiden Creek) and on the Berks-Lancaster border along the Conestoga Creek. Others settled in the Tulpehocken Valley in a settlement that extended from Berks into what later would become Lebanon County. By 1767, Amish newcomers, along with households who had been in North America for some years, were heading west to Somerset County, Pennsylvania, where, in the eighteenth century, they formed three distinct clusters. And in 1791, Amish families were living in central Pennsylvania's newly organized Mifflin County.[3]

While the western backcountry attracted some Amish, others headed east. By 1768, a congregation had organized closer to Philadelphia, in Chester County's Great Valley. The Chester County group was unusually connected to non-Amish neighbors, joining with them in starting a cemetery, building a schoolhouse, and helping to execute wills. By the early 1800s, these Amish were, even more unusually, using their community school as a meetinghouse for Sunday morning church services.[4] In Europe, Swiss and south German

The home of immigrant Nicholas Stoltzfus (c. 1718-1774), built about 1770 along the Tulpehocken Creek in what was then Cumru Township, now Wyomissing Borough, Berks County, Pennsylvania. Son Christian Stoltzfus and his family lived here until 1804, when they moved to Lancaster County. This home is being restored by the Tri-County Heritage Society, Pequea Bruderschaft Library, and Stoltzfus descendants.

Amish and Mennonites had worshiped in homes or barns. Perhaps out of frugality or necessity, or perhaps to emphasize that people, and not buildings, were really the church, they had rejected specially-designated structures for worship.[5]

Lewis Riehl

Although some Europeans saw North America as a place of possibility and promise and immigrated voluntarily, many others did not cross the Atlantic so freely. Around 1750, when Ludwig Riehl was about eight years old, he was playing and exploring in a European harbor where ships were preparing to sail. Someone persuaded Ludwig to board a ship, and once the boy was on deck would not allow him to leave. Ludwig discovered too late the intent of the captain to carry him across the Atlantic and sell him in Philadelphia.

A Chester County, Pennsylvania, family paid the cost of his transit as a redemptioner and he was required to work for them until he turned twenty-one. According to Riehl family tradition, the farmer who owned Ludwig—who became known as Lewis—treated him badly, and as soon as his contract was completed, he left and found a welcome among the Chester County Amish living around Malvern.

Lewis later joined the Amish church and married Veronica Fisher. In the 1790s, Lewis and Veronica left the old Chester County settlement and were among those who formed the Mifflin County, Pennsylvania, Amish community.

See David Luthy, "New Names Among the Amish, Part 3," *Family Life* (November 1972): 22.

Although the Chester County Amish settlement was never large, it played an outsized role in Amish life because of its location along the route taken by new arrivals traveling west from Philadelphia. Into the nineteenth century, the Chester church offered hospitality and aid to fellow Amish immigrants moving inland.[6]

In the later 1700s, a few Amish also may have been among those Pennsylvania Germans who followed "the Great Wagon Road" from Pennsylvania south into Virginia and North Carolina. Evidence of settlers with typical Amish surnames in those states are suggestive but inconclusive. In neither place did ongoing Amish congregations form, so if some Amish did end up in the Shenandoah Valley or western North Carolina, they likely blended with Pennsylvania Dutch-speaking neighbors, perhaps intermarrying with them and joining one of the German-speaking churches in those regions.[7]

Due to their relatively well-organized and well-financed immigration to America, Amish families were often prepared to purchase land in North America. Some bought heavily and then resold to their children, to other Amish families, or to non-Amish neighbors. When describing the land holdings of early settler Christian Beiler, one twentieth-century Amish historian concluded, "All in all, Christian had so many land grants that it is doubtful if we can name them all."[8] A survey of land records turns up noncommercial transactions, too. Along with his farm purchases, Amish man Christian Rupp was one of five Lancaster Countians receiving a deed for land to build a community school.[9]

Land transactions also point up other tendencies among Amish families, some of which differentiated them even from other Pennsylvania Dutch immigrants, such as the Mennonites. For example, in contrast to many Mennonite immigrants who purchased unimproved properties, Amish immigrants often bought partially cleared land from

Amish buggies outside a Somerset County, Pennsylvania, meetinghouse (white building) and horse barn (unpainted building.) Amish have lived in the area since 1767. They are one of the only groups of Old Order Amish who worship in church buildings.

non-Amish owners. Despite the benefit of taking over somewhat-improved farms, these Amish were generally buying cheaper, thinner soil in Berks, Lebanon, and Chester counties, rather than the more productive acres in central Lancaster County that Mennonites held. Even in Lancaster's Old Conestoga settlement, where for a time Amish and Mennonites lived side-by-side, tax records show Mennonites to have been generally wealthier than the Amish.[10]

For the most part, though, eighteenth-century Amish did not settle especially close to Mennonites, many of whom had preceded them to North America. While Mennonites had strong communities in Philadelphia, and in Montgomery and Lancaster counties, Amish initially settled elsewhere and only later moved to Lancaster in sizable numbers. For their part, the large Mennonite communities in Philadelphia and Montgomery County had little contact with the Amish. In a 1773 letter to fellow church members in the Netherlands, Philadelphia Mennonites wrote, "As to the Amisch, they are many in number; but they are not here near us, and we can give no further information concerning them except only this, that they hold very fast to the outward and ancient institutions."[11]

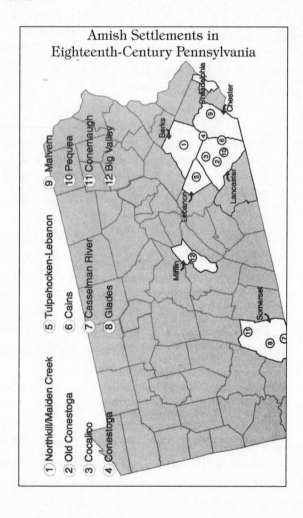

Amish Settlements in Eighteenth-Century Pennsylvania

① Northkill/Maiden Creek
② Old Conestoga
③ Cocalico
④ Conestoga
⑤ Tulpehocken-Lebanon
⑥ Cains
⑦ Casselman River
⑧ Glades
⑨ Malvern
⑩ Pequea
⑪ Conemaugh
⑫ Big Valley

Church in a new land

Holding fast to those "ancient institutions" was hardly accidental. While many Amish immigrated to better their financial standing—and Amish migration within Pennsylvania during the eighteenth century often continued this pattern of economic self-help—the ability to practice their faith unmolested was an important motivation for crossing the Atlantic. The formal side of that practice, though, was less organized than it would be later. Frequent migration, dispersed settlements, and challenging transportation marked colonial life and meant that Amish worship services—like those of many denominations at the time—were infrequent.

Nor were resident church leaders immediately available in all places. While the ranks of early Amish immigrants may have included ministers or deacons, no clear record exists of an Amish bishop (elder) in North America until Jacob Hertzler arrived in 1749 and settled in Northkill.[12] Seeking to provide stability for fledgling congregations in a new environment filled with competing political and religious opinion, Hertzler apparently assumed his role in a winsome way. Family lore holds that the bishop was "very sociable and talkative." Even in his old age he preferred walking rather than riding horseback, trekking many miles on foot to visit and encourage others.[13]

The coming of European-born leaders, and the ordination on American soil of resident ministers and deacons, eventually provided each settlement with church oversight. Bishops performed baptisms and marriages, served the Lord's Supper, and meted out church discipline when needed. Ministers assisted with preaching, and the deacons administered aid to the needy and kept almsbook records.

The religious life of Pennsylvania's Amish was embodied in daily activity as much as in formal Sunday worship services.

It seems that most families were farming, although several household heads, like Lebanon Valley's Hans Gnage and the Old Conestoga community's Michael Garber, were millers. Jacob Beiler of the Northkill settlement was a tanner—an occupation that he might have coupled with farming. And Hans Blank of Lebanon Valley (and later eastern Lancaster County) was said to have been a folk-physician who had converted to the Amish church in Switzerland.[14]

For those who farmed in Lancaster County, wheat was the chief crop of the eighteenth century. Amish estate inventories and wills drawn up in several settlements also point to flax (linen) and apples as typical farm crops, with the apples often converted to cider and distilled. These wills also made specific provisions for Amish widows and directed children who took over farm management to supply their mother with ample produce from garden and field.[15]

Fitting in and standing apart

How much were colonial Amish people like their non-Amish neighbors, and how much did they stand apart? Wills and estate inventories do not suggest a notable presence or absence of particular household goods or equipment. With little visual evidence from the time it is hard to know exactly how distinctive dress may have marked the church's members. English colonists often remarked on what they perceived to be the peculiar dress of Pennsylvania Germans of all religious persuasions. Undoubtedly the Amish demonstrated a commitment to simplicity in appearance, but the form that such plainness took may have been somewhat less striking in their ethnic context.

When it came to westward migration, the Amish appear not to have been much different from their colonial neighbors, German or British. Amish immigrants were sometimes among the first Europeans to settle in the areas in which they chose to live, whether in Berks County or what became Lebanon County. In Somerset County, Amish communities probably put down roots by 1767—two years before the region officially opened for white settlement.[16] Moving into frontier areas, in some cases to locations where Native American populations had only recently been driven away, the Amish participated in the larger story of European land occupation that marked the era.

In large part, the Amish could acquire land as readily as they did because they were *not* like many of their colonial neighbors in an important respect. During the eighteenth century, only about a quarter of all those who came to British North America did so as free labor.[17] The Amish had immigrated as free people with the ability to control the terms and conditions of their work. They may not have realized how unusual their status was, but that status was crucial to their communities' growth and economic success.

If the Amish position as free laborers was notable, so too was their refusal to own slaves. Slavery was a legal part of Pennsylvania life until 1780, and even after that year only a gradual program of emancipation freed human property. No record exists of any Amish family owning slaves.

Probably the refusal to own African-American workers stemmed as much from the Amish insistence on simplicity as it did from Christian humanitarianism. Studies of colonial Pennsylvania slave-owning practices show that slaves were often not so much an economic necessity in Penn's Woods as a status symbol that announced their owner's financial success. Among a people who shied away from ostentatious clothing and home furnishings, the ownership of human ornaments of wealth was naturally taboo.[18]

Some Amish families did purchase redemptioners, however.[19] Redemptioners typically possessed marketable skills but did not have cash to finance their immigration.

Instead, they crossed the Atlantic on credit, and then paid their passage by selling their labor for a negotiated number of years. Amish farmers probably bought redemptioners because their labor, unlike that of slaves, was not a mark of conspicuous consumption. Occasionally a redemptioner even joined the Amish church as a result of contact with Amish employers or neighbors. A testimony to the practice of mutual aid, Amish church almsbook records also show that successful Pennsylvania Amish sometimes paid the immigration costs of European Amish families, thus sparing the newcomers the prospect of becoming redemptioners.[20]

Frontier fires

As frontier settlers the Amish soon found themselves in the midst of the politics of provincial warfare. Pennsylvania became an important battleground for competing claims of British and French imperial designs. The English, taking land from the Atlantic coast westward, and the French, claiming territory from the Great Lakes southeastward, clashed over rights to western Pennsylvania and the Ohio River Valley. Beginning in 1754, a military conflict that became known as the French and Indian War (or Seven Years War) spread death and destruction even into eastern Pennsylvania. Many Native American nations sided with the French and attacked settlements within the English colony's domain. Thus, Pennsylvania's Berks County, and what became Lebanon and Dauphin counties to the west, felt the pressures of international conflict.[21]

Frontier Amish were not immune from the resulting violence, and at least one household, that of Jacob Hochstetler, suffered the death and captivity the war brought. Other families may also have been affected. One Hans Lantz of the

Northkill Amish settlement wrote that his family had "been obligated to flee" their home "on account of the war." The Lantzes had returned only after the English "gained the upper hand . . . [and] fought back the French and the Indians."[22]

Fear of French-inspired attacks balanced other fears of losing religious liberty to the English. After the Pennsylvania government declared war on the Delaware and Shawnee nations in the spring of 1756, the once-pacifist province moved to initiate a militia and fund military defense. The "peace churches"—Religious Society of Friends (Quakers), German Baptist Brethren (Dunkers), Mennonites, and Amish—appealed for exemption. In lieu of direct participation, most proposed to supply material aid to frontier war refugees or provide commissary services to the militia. The measure was short-lived, though, as political feuding in Philadelphia sank all attempts to extend the life of the militia act, and the legal pressures on conscience eased.

After 1763, hostilities in Pennsylvania died down, but the mid-century conflict had tested Amish identity and resolve. The Northkill settlement, hit hard by the fighting, remained the largest Amish congregation into the 1780s. It was the availability of better soil elsewhere—not Native American hostility—that led to Northkill's extinction as families abandoned Berks County. In fact, even after the war, Amish settlers continued to move into areas known to be subject to violent attack. The militia law could have tested the Amish resolve to be a nonresistant people, but both sides seemed open to compromise, and the matter passed without incident. By 1776, however, a new war would test Amish churches more severely.

The Hochstetler Incident

The attack on the family of Jacob Hochstetler in 1757, their refusal to defend themselves, and the account of their captivity are among the most widely known stories in Amish family lore. Folk tradition carried the Hochstetler story through the generations in a somewhat embellished form, but the general outline of that oral narrative matches what official documents and newspapers from the time report.

The Hochstetlers lived in the Northkill Amish settlement in Berks County, Pennsylvania, near the base of the Blue Mountain, an area that, after 1755, was a site of conflict in the so-called French and Indian War. During the night of September 19, 1757, Jacob Junior opened the family's cabin door to see why their dog was barking so intently. Thereupon he was shot in the leg by Shawnee and Delaware Indians who had surrounded the house. The wounded boy and his two brothers, Christian and Joseph, all reached for their hunting guns in order to defend the family, but father Jacob forbade them to shoot and made his sons put the weapons away. Oral tradition says that Jacob reminded his sons that Jesus' teaching to "turn the other cheek" meant they could not resort to violence.

The Hochstetlers instead hid in the cellar under the house, but the attackers set fire to the cabin. Trying to escape through a cellar window opening, the family was caught. Jacob Junior, his mother, and sister (whose names are unknown) were killed, and the Native American party marched father Jacob and sons Joseph and Christian all the way to the French fort at Presque Isle on Lake Erie. There, the three captives were split up. Before parting, Jacob told his sons that they must never forget the Lord's Prayer.

The Native Americans who captured the Hochstetlers were not from eastern Pennsylvania and were acting on orders from French commanders pursuing a wider campaign of imperial strategy. The attack was almost certainly not sparked by any particular action on the part of the Hochstetlers, despite family lore that Jacob's wife had some time earlier turned away a number of local Native hunters looking for food.

The following spring, Jacob Hochstetler's captors allowed him to hunt in the woods alone, and he fled. Over the course of fifteen days he made his way by foot and raft to a British post near Shamokin, Pennsylvania. He was interrogated about his experience by British commander Henry Bouquet, at Carlisle, and then allowed to return to Berks County. Four years later, Hochstetler's two sons were still captives. He issued an appeal to Pennsylvania's lieutenant governor, asking for help in obtaining their release. Eventually, both sons were freed through prisoner exchanges that followed the peace terms of 1763.

The traditional version of this story is told in Rev. Harvey Hostetler, ed., *The Descendants of Jacob Hochstetler, the Immigrant of 1736* (Elgin, Ill.: Brethren Publishing House, 1912), 26-45. Primary sources documenting the incident at the time are found in Beth L. Hostetler Mark, comp. and ed., *Our Flesh and Blood: A Documentary History of the Jacob Hochstetler Family during the French and Indian War Period, 1757-1765* (Elkhart, Ind.: Jacob Hochstetler Family Association, 2003).

Challenge of revivalism

A different sort of challenge to the Amish church came not from military campaigns, but from preachers associated with a wide-ranging evangelical revival movement then spreading across the north Atlantic world.[23] During the mid-eighteenth century, the Amish church lost members to competing Christian groups who charged the Amish with dead formalism and tried to infuse their communities with a more experiential religion.

An atmosphere of religious toleration and relative equality among churches in Pennsylvania created a kind of spiritual open market in which pastors and evangelists spread their wares and sold their products as freely and easily as any merchants. Not only were the Amish reticent about broadcasting their faith, but their particular understandings of salvation and church made them prime targets for proselytizers.

The Amish believed that Christians experienced salvation in everyday living. This was not salvation earned by individuals; it was a gracious gift from God—a gift realized as one's life was transformed day-by-day into the image of Christ. *Nachfolge Christi*—following Jesus daily—was one way in which Amish forebears, the Anabaptists, had described the Christian life. To the Amish mind, being faithful to Christ's commands was a visible indication of faith. The Amish did not downplay Christian conversion, as such—in fact Amish writings stressed the need for regeneration, or the new birth, which would result in a new way of life. They believed they could see quite clearly a marked difference between the Christian and non-Christian life. That difference—when lived out—was sharp enough to authenticate itself without needing to be confirmed by an extraordinary conversion experience.

The revivalism of many evangelical churches stood in some contrast with Amish understandings. For many revivalists, salvation was presented as an instantaneous experience that followed a deep and inner personal struggle, culminating in an emotional release interpreted as forgiveness. It was not that revivalist-oriented church put no emphasis on ethics or the Christian's daily life. But for many evangelicals, these things were secondary, or at least could be presented as such.

They believed that the singular, emotional experience of conversion was the only sure sign of one's being right with God.

The Amish view of the church was also different from that of many evangelicals. The Amish thought of church in community terms. Church members were mutually accountable to each other, even in mundane matters of lifestyle. Baptism symbolized commitment both to God and to fellow believers, while the Lord's Supper was a sign of the local church's unity in matters large and small.

Typically, the revivalists' emphasis on individual salvation weakened the importance and authority of the church. Communion and baptism became rites between the individual and God; that a larger congregation was somehow involved could seem almost incidental. Revivalists viewed accountability differently from the Amish. If a singular conversion experience had validated one's faith, what business did a church have in critiquing pride, wealth, or a worldly lifestyle that might surface later in one's life?

To some revivalist-oriented Methodists, Baptists, and (later in the century) United Brethren, the Amish were stuck in a formal traditionalism. Their church service seemed "cold" to circuit-riding preachers and itinerant evangelists who sought to bring a "warm" spirituality to the Amish. How many Amish abandoned their way for revivalist religion is unclear, but observers thought the numbers were significant. In one well-known case, Abraham Drachsel (Troxel) Jr., an Amish bishop in what became Lebanon County, Pennsylvania, made "too much of the doctrine of regeneration." His congregation silenced him from preaching, and he left the Amish. Apparently a sizable portion of his congregation followed him, and one Amish historian speculated that defection to other churches led to the demise of the Lebanon Valley settlement.[24]

The German Baptist Brethren (also called "Dunkers," today the Church of the Brethren) posed an even greater challenge to the Amish. While sharing many of the revivalists' spiritual emphases, the Brethren stood much closer to traditional Amish understandings of church than did other evangelicals, and such Brethren similarities made their appeals especially inviting. Like the Amish, the Brethren preached in German, emphasized plain dress (including untrimmed beards for men), practiced the footwashing rite, and were nonresistant. In some areas, vigorous Brethren preaching drew many Amish members or members' children into the Brethren camp.[25]

Perhaps one of the reasons some Amish families moved west to Somerset County was to escape the influence of eastern revivalists, but popular evangelists won converts there, too. Evangelists were eager to win Amish followers, but the Amish themselves were slow to put divine faith into human words. They preferred to let their lives speak and allow their responses to life to stand as their own witnesses. Events in Pennsylvania soon tested that response and witness.

Tories, rebels, and pacifists

The storm of the French and Indian War had cleared for only a dozen years when new clouds of imperial warfare gathered. The outbreak of what came to be the American Revolution had a profound impact on the young Amish communities as they became caught up in political and military turmoil.

To many Americans living in seaport towns and cities, the trade policies and taxes of the British Empire seemed both unfair and intolerable. To many southern planters and a few frontier farmers, the government of King George III was burdensome. But for perhaps as many as one-fifth of the thirteen colonies' residents, the British crown was the object of loyal devotion. For these folks, the patriots in Boston and Philadelphia were unlawful insurrectionists who deserved death as traitors. Those loyal to the government of London received the name *Tories*, and they fought for king and empire.

For the Amish and other Christian peace churches, the political choice offered by the patriots, on the one hand, and the Tories, on the other, was insufficient. The peace churches believed they represented a third option: peaceful neutrality. They insisted that Jesus had commanded Christians to live in love with everyone, a standard that put even politically sanctioned military violence off-limits. Thus the Amish (and other pacifists) would not actively support either side in the bloody battle for control of the colonies.[26]

Yet the Amish also taught that Christians were to be subject to government in all matters that did not conflict with conscience. To their non-Amish neighbors, such teaching probably made the Amish peace stance seem sympathetic toward George III.[27] As the war dragged on, other issues complicated the political picture. After 1727, in order to settle in the English colonies, German immigrants had to sign a declaration of loyalty to the British crown. Although some newcomers may have signed the document without much thought, for the Amish the declaration was a matter of ethical concern. If they had promised loyalty to London, then Christian integrity required them to keep that pledge, even if their neighbors now insisted that the monarch lacked all legitimacy.

And what of taxes? The Amish always had paid taxes to proper authority, but during the Revolution two groups—patriots and Tories—both claimed to be the sole authority to which tribute was due.

Wartime events did not wait for theological reflection. Already by mid-1775, energetic Pennsylvania revolutionaries organized Committees of Observation and Safety and Committees of Correspondence, which served as local patriot watchdog groups. The Committees tried to coerce men into militia groups and tried to force households to stop buying British goods. Using social intimidation and physical force, the Committees attempted to make Pennsylvanians fall in line and support the revolutionary cause. Neither side accepted the peace churches' position of neutrality. As one diary entry lamented, "If one objects with the merest word, one is told 'You are a *Tory*!' . . . And those on the other side say, 'You are rebels.'"[28]

On July 1, 1775, as the war's first weeks evaporated any middle ground between patriots and Tories, a small group of Mennonites, Amish, and Brethren met with the Lancaster County Committee of Correspondence. Minutes of that meeting show that Christian Rupp and Michael Garber, "Representatives of the Society of people called Amisch Menonists," were among those present. Rather "than by taking up of Arms, which we hereby declare to be against our Consciences," the Amish and other petitioners asked if they could instead contribute money "to assist the Common Cause." They were aware that the war had brought "Calamities & Misfortunes" to many Americans, and they wished to offer some sort of humanitarian aid.[29]

The Committee agreed, and the churches collected funds in lieu of military service. Surviving records show that Amish and Mennonites did contribute to the fund, even though the Committee kept the purpose of the collection unclear. As historian Richard MacMaster has pointed out, many peace church people "thought they were giving for nearby poor families or to help refugees from British-occupied Boston; in fact, most of the money went for military expenses."[30]

Not all Amish were so accommodating to patriot Committees. In the fall of 1779 in Berks County, Amish man Isaac Kauffman was tried, convicted, and jailed as a Tory. Earlier that year, a militia officer had demanded to use Kauffman's horse. Kauffman refused and retorted, "You are Rebels and

I will not give a horse to such blood-spilling persons." Both Kauffman's opinion and his refusal to hand over his animal clearly revealed to the court that he was "a person of evil and seditious mind and disposition." Despite having "eight young Children" and later apologizing for his "improper Expressions," Kauffman's sentence was the forfeiture of half of his land and goods, as well as imprisonment for the duration of the war.[31]

War weariness

Already in 1777, the Amish were among those Pennsylvanians who refused to deny past pledges to George III or to take new oaths of allegiance to the revolutionary government. They lost the privilege of voting as a result. Beginning the next year, those who were not sworn supporters of the patriot state were assessed double taxes. On one Berks County tax list from 1779 a patriot wrote the word "Tory" after the names of nine Amish heads of households. On that list, Amish families represented more than a quarter of all Tories identified in the county. Amish oral tradition has kept alive a story that several of these Amish tax-list-Tories spent time in jail and were freed only when a sympathetic German Reformed Church pastor interceded on their behalf.[32]

Members of the Chester County Amish community witnessed the war most directly. The September 1777 Battle of Brandywine likely involved British and American troop movement across Amish farms. Several Amish families lost livestock to foraging Crown soldiers returning to Philadelphia. George Washington's men from nearby Valley Forge took all of Amishman Christian Zook's fences for lumber and, legend holds, his wife's freshly baked bread.[33]

If patriot neighbors thought that pacifist Amish were Tories in disguise, perhaps a few almost were. Amishman Hans

Lantz praised George III in a private letter, and then confided: "I also hate and despise with all my heart treachery, rebellion and assassinations. . . . I am also heartily disposed . . . to prevent such as much as possible." Either way, Lantz hoped that the king's "throne might be well fortified with fairness and be handed down so that he may have eternity for his faithful service and have his reward from God."[34]

For some young people, the patriot's "glorious cause," or the social pressure to conform to the revolutionary party, proved so strong that they cast their futures with the revolutionary Committees. A number left—or simply never joined—the Amish church, and family traditions include stories of sons who went off to battle and never returned.[35] The separation in some homes must have been poignant as an older generation who had fled the militarism of Europe watched younger family members follow the sound of the muster drum.

The war carried political implications for peace church people beyond the death and destruction they may have experienced. The patriot takeover of Pennsylvania left them disenfranchised until 1790 and socially marginalized in new ways. Some Quakers who once had been politically active withdrew from government for good, and a few Mennonites later moved to Canada where they believed there was greater civic stability under royal rule. Amish churches apparently lost members to the appeal of revolutionary rhetoric that promised a "New Order of the Ages" in republican, rather than religious, form.[36]

The war drained members and potential members from the church, but on a deeper level the conflict challenged Amish identity: How American was this church going to be? Would freedom in America turn out to be the freedom to surrender the faith for which their forebears had been persecuted?

An Amish Folktale:
"Strong" Jacob Yoder (c.1726-1790)

"Once upon a time," so the story runs, "a certain strong man in Virginia who had heard of this 'Strong' Yoder had a desire to meet him and test his strength. He left his home on horseback and journeyed to Pennsylvania. When he came into the community, he met a neighbor of 'Strong' Jacob's and inquired about him. He said that he was the strongest man in his own community, and he had come to whip this man, who was his rival. The neighbor told the stranger that Yoder was a peaceable man and that he had better let him alone. But the Virginian went on, arriving at 'Strong' Jacob's home after dark.

"The man made all the noise he could on the porch. When 'Strong' Jacob opened the door, the stranger, to get the advantage of 'Strong' Jacob, took hold of him, but Yoder was more than his equal and at once thrust him onto the floor, holding him and calling for a rope. He tied him securely, dragged him beside the fireplace, and let him lie there until morning, then released him and sent him home. The stranger was convinced that he had found a man who was superior to him in physical strength, and went home a wiser, though disappointed man."

From C. Z. Mast and Robert E. Simpson, *Annals of the Conestoga Valley in Lancaster, Berks, and Chester Counties, Pennsylvania . . .* (Elverson, Pa. and Churchtown, Pa.: C. A. Mast and Robert E. Simpson, 1942), 267.

Precarious position

As the Amish concluded their first century as a distinct people, their future was no more certain than it had been in 1693. In North America, after some sixty years of settlement, the church was barely maintaining its numbers. The difficulties of establishing homes, the overtures of revivalists, and the new wealth and mobility that had resulted from immigration had taken their toll. Patriotic war, too, arrested the church's development. Genealogical studies reveal that no Amish immigrant family retained all of its children in the church. In fact, probably less than forty percent of the early generations continued in the Amish tradition. By the close of the eighteenth century, surnames such as Reichenbach, Schenck, and Schowalter, among others, had disappeared entirely from Amish ranks. Although some 500 Amish adults and children had arrived in Pennsylvania before the Revolution, and most had large families, by 1800 there were probably fewer than 1,000 Amish in the new United States.[37]

Several decades earlier, an Amish immigrant had written to friends in Europe, advising them to come to America because "in this country is a very good living."[38] Many Amish had, in fact, survived and prospered in colonial Pennsylvania, although that prosperity had carried its own temptations. At times, living in America had meant becoming American, with all its revivalistic and patriotic trappings. Still, at least some Amish had persisted, and after 1800 they would welcome a new wave of European immigrants eager to join that "good living" in America.

—5—

A Time of Testing: The Amish in Europe, 1790-1860

> *"Our dogmas and principles are simple . . . 'Love God and your neighbor.'"*
>
> —Amish leaders to the
> French Interior Minister, 1809

Toleration and civic responsibility

In the early years of the nineteenth century, the Amish community near the Palatinate town of Kircheimbolanden met for Sunday worship in a second-floor room of an abandoned Roman Catholic monastery known as the Münsterhof. A few hundred yards south of this place of worship ran the so-called Emperor's Road, linking Paris and Berlin. In 1813, French Emperor Napoleon I and his beleaguered army used this thoroughfare as they retreated from their disastrous attack on Russia. Those French forces included several Amish soldiers by the name of Virkler— at least family tradition preserves the memory of Virkler sons marching into Russia with Napoleon and surviving the return.[1] As they struggled back to France, these Amish boys may have passed the old Münsterhof cloister and its surrounding Amish tenant farms.

That possibility is more than an odd historical coincidence. It points to important developments in European Amish life during these years, and it raises provocative questions. Why were Amish men participating in the French military? What did the nearly incessant European warfare in those years mean for rural western Europeans, especially socially marginal religious dissenters?

Military conflict, the demands of the state, and the currents of popular culture all left their mark on men like the Virklers and churches like the one gathered at the Münsterhof. At least one member of the Virkler family, Rudolph, eventually left for America and its promise of freedom of conscience, and within about fifty years, the Münsterhof congregation itself would dwindle and disband.[2] Social and political pressures fueled a wave of emigration that, in turn, further sapped congregations' strength. These were not easy years for the European Amish.

Until the early 1800s, Amish, Mennonites, and other religious and ethnic minority groups experienced frequent legal and social discrimination. Here and there, to be sure, a tolerant noble or an aristocrat in need of reliable tenant farmers would offer a safe haven for unwanted people, but Mennonites and Amish always received such limited freedom as an exceptional gift, never as a civil right. Tolerance and liberty of conscience were privileges dispensed at the good will of local lords and could be revoked at any time.

After 1789, the unfolding French Revolution profoundly changed western European politics. That upheaval not only overthrew the French king and powerful noble elite, but also introduced influential new ways of thinking about how people and governments relate to one another. A major tenet of the Revolution was its new view of *citizenship*—a view that spread after 1800, especially to other French-occupied and -allied countries.

In this new understanding, people were not *subjects* who had peculiar obligations and received uneven privileges based on their ancestry or religious affiliation. Instead, citizenship was universal. Everyone living within a state's borders could claim equal rights and had to bear equal responsibilities.

Ideally, government would not deny rights to the Amish simply because they were members of a minority religious group. In this way the French Revolutionary idea of citizenship opened the door for social acceptance that went beyond toleration. But while the Amish potentially were freed from future discrimination and persecution, they also were expected to engage in a process of acculturation and assimilation that accompanied such civic acceptance.[3]

The French revolutionary government did make one distinction for its Amish and Mennonite population, briefly granting them exemption from military involvement. In 1792, when the French Republic began compelling men to enroll in the National Guard, Amish from Salm and Montbéliard—two areas recently incorporated into France—appealed for some exemption. Local officials objected, grumbling that, "When the Fatherland is in danger, all citizens who are not public functionaries ought to render service in person." But an official inspector from Paris, Philippe Goupilleau de Montaigu, described the Anabaptists he met in Salm, southwest of Strasbourg in the Vosges Mountains, in glowing terms and declared there were "no better people on the face of the earth."[4]

Encouraged by Goupilleau, the Republic's Committee of Public Safety issued a document in the summer of 1793, signed by the Revolution's infamous and powerful leader, Maximilien Robespierre. It directed local French officials "to exercise the same kindness and gentleness towards them [the Amish and Mennonites] as is their character, and to

An Amish farm near Salm, in the French Vosges Mountains. In the nineteenth century, Amish from this area immigrated to Illinois and Ontario.

prevent their being persecuted."[5] Hearing this news, the Salm congregation's elder, Jakob Kupferschmidt, planted an oak tree to commemorate his church's answered prayer. (Two hundred years later, the "Salm peace oak" was still standing.) Under the policy, Paris did expect some type of extra tax or noncombatant work from the Amish in lieu of military service. Before such details were worked out, however, the revolutionary government was itself overthrown by one of its own military heroes.

Napoleon Bonaparte's rise to power in 1799 and his crowning as emperor in 1804 changed the lives of nearly all western Europeans. Not only was the next decade filled with the destruction of Napoleon's many military campaigns, but the new emperor pushed the Revolution's idea of citizenship to its logical conclusion. All citizens would receive the same civic rights and the same civic responsibilities, regardless of religious affiliation.

For the Amish, that decision meant that they no longer were exempt from military service or other civil duties.[6] Napoleon's military and political tactics required more than small, professional armies could accomplish.   He needed a large fighting force that he could raise only through what became known as *levée-en-masse*, or universal conscription. Eventually Napoleon came directly or indirectly to control every area of Europe in which the Amish lived, so virtually all the Amish had to face this newly assigned citizenship duty.

The Amish response to this new situation was mixed. Undoubtedly some were glad to say good-bye to their second-class status. According to one observer, some Alsatian Amish even reluctantly agreed to wear the tricolor cockade—symbol of the French republic—after wearing such "was made a duty."[7] Many liable for military service hoped to avoid direct participation in violence by hiring a draft substitute or joining a noncombatant regiment (though such regiments ceased to exist in 1807 as combat troops assumed those duties, as well).

If little systematic evidence exists to document the Amish response to universal conscription, the reaction of fellow Mennonites along the Rhine may give some clues. In 1803 and 1805, Mennonites met in general conference to discuss the challenges of living in Napoleon's Europe. The Mennonites rejected military participation and civil-office holding. Soldiers were not to receive communion, the gathering declared. While upholding traditional teaching, the conference's tone was so defensive that one may surmise members were, in fact, rejecting customary practice and participating in armed force.[8] The situation could have been the same among the Amish, considering Amish family lore that preserves the memory of sons who were involved in the military.

Negotiating with Napoleon

For their part, Amish leaders made a concerted effort to win freedom from French military demands, presenting several petitions to the highest levels of government.[9] In the summer of 1806, church leaders gathered at the home of Hans Steiner to discuss how to proceed. Two years later they commissioned elders Christian Engel and Christian Güngerich to

An Alsatian Amish couple, early nineteenth century.

carry a petition to Paris, and the two men arrived there early in 1809. Congregations in Lorraine declared January 29 a day of prayer and fasting for the success of the mission. The two elders were able to offer to the interior minister a document contending that "their religious principles expressly forbid them to bear a lethal weapon against their brothers and enjoins them to abandon their goods rather than to preserve them at that price." The Amish were productive citizens, the petition went on to state, who meant no harm to the orderly functioning of society. But that commitment only added to the "perplexity they encounter when they try to reconcile their duty with their religion."

In May, still waiting in Paris for some response to their appeal, Engel and Güngerich wrote again to the interior minister "that our dogmas and principles are simple and received of all Christians. 'Love God and your neighbor' . . . are the basis of our worship and doctrine." The elders tried to press the seriousness of their case by asserting that "an invisible but invincible power keeps us attached to our religious precepts and most importantly the rule of not staining our hands with the blood of our neighbors." While authorities ignored this initial overture, the Amish did not give up, especially since their young men continued to be drafted.

Then in June 1811, fifteen leaders gathering in Bildhäuserhof drew up a second petition, which four ministers carried to Paris and this time presented to the minister of religion. The petition did, in fact, make its way to the State Council and the Emperor himself, but in April 1812 both rejected the appeal as a dangerous loophole in the notion of universal citizenship. They announced "that the tolerance the government shows to opinions that are not harmful to society cannot go so far as proclaiming, with a decree, exemptions that one can too easily predict may be abused." The judgment was clear: eligible men would continue to be drafted. Amish leaders sent yet a third petition in 1814, but before it worked its way through bureaucratic channels, Napoleon was overthrown and the restored French monarchy ended conscription.

Men of conscriptable age had not been the only ones to suffer through the upheaval of the French Revolution and the subsequent decade of Napoleonic campaigns. Joseph and Barbara (Rupp) Roth and their family lived in Alsace where Joseph was a successful miller. In 1802, the Roths had to leave their home and hide in nearby woods for more than a week as the battle lines neared their home and soldiers dealt heavy damage to their mill. Twelve years later, Napoleon's forces returned and stopped at the mill to demand money. Finding nothing, the troops beat Joseph, ruined the milling machinery, and broke all of the building's precious glass windows. Soon thereafter, Joseph and Barbara died, leaving five orphaned sons to live with relatives.[10]

The violence and social disorder of the Revolution did not endear the cause to many Amish, even if they understood the dynamics of power it had unleashed. "One may say that the mighty have to be afraid of the common people," Essingen elder Hans Nafziger wrote in 1790 to a fellow minister in Pennsylvania, "otherwise their life is not safe from the common rabble. There is such an uprising and unrest between the mighty and the common folk, the like of which I have never seen in my lifetime."

Johannes Oesch was more blunt. A leaseholder in the southern Palatinate—a hotbed of radical sentiment—Oesch found his farm surrounded by revolution-minded peasants and confided that "One should not wish to live a life ruled by people of this sort."[11]

Farming fame

Perhaps in many cases the resentment toward Amish leaseholders that local peasants expressed during the French

Revolution was rooted in the fact that these Anabaptist outsiders seemed to have too close and too successful a working relationship with large landowners. Resentment boiled over near Landau where neighbors attacked the Mühlhofen estate farmed by Amish leaseholder Daniel Holly. Local lore credited Holly with amazing strength, able to carry a donkey across a stream, grab an enraged bull by its horns, or single-handedly free a loaded hay wagon that was jammed in a barn door. Yet neighboring peasants ran Holly off the estate in December 1792 and burned his house. Holly fled north to a farm rented by an uncle.[12]

Close relations with the landowning elite could also provide a means of escape. In 1802, widow Katharina (Imhof) Stalter of Zweibrücken, hoping to leave the war-torn Rhine Valley, wrote to the former Zweibrücken duke who was now Elector of Bavaria. Katharina reminded the elector that after revolutionaries had ousted him from Zweibrücken, her late husband, Heinrich, had visited him, and the duke had promised to remember that kindness. Prompted by Katharina's letter, the elector paved the way for the Stalters and other Amish households to obtain leases in Bavaria, leading to the establishment of the first Amish communities in that kingdom.[13]

In Bavaria and elsewhere, the continuing appeal of Amish tenants stemmed from their growing reputation as skilled farmers. Travelers, government agents, and early scientific observers all remarked on Amish husbandry and the way it stood at the forefront of western European farming practices in the 1700s and 1800s. As one French scholar has explained, in an ironic way the very outsider status of the Amish fitted them for their role as agricultural innovators. Because they rarely were able to own land, Anabaptist farmers invested their earnings in livestock and other productive assets rather than real estate. They also experimented with breeding cattle—the Graber family of Montbéliard enjoying notable

Amish living near Millbank, Ontario, descend from nineteenth-century immigrant families.

success in this regard—and emerging veterinary medicine techniques.

As leaseholders with only a limited number of acres under contract, the Amish also needed to find creative ways to expand productivity. They turned to improved methods of clearing land, draining swamps, and fertilizing tilled ground with animal manure and gypsum. The Amish also maximized their resources by pioneering new methods of crop rotation. Traditional rotation patterns sought to renew soil by systematically allowing fields to lay fallow (unplanted) for a year, a process that left up to a third of one's acre-

Early nineteenth-century drawing of a French Amish farmer.

age out of production at any given time. In contrast, the Amish planted every field each year, but devised an order of rotating crops so that the succession of plants themselves replenished the soil. Finally, Amish farmers were successful in part because they used family labor extensively. By the early nineteenth century, in fact, the term Anabaptist became nearly synonymous with good farming.[14]

So common was this popular association that in 1812, a French farming almanac appeared under the title *L'Anabaptiste ou Le Cultivateur Par Experience* (*The Anabaptist, or The Experienced Farmer*), dedicated to promoting innovative agriculture. The almanac's publisher produced the booklet with the cooperation of French Amish man Jacques Klopfenstein, a successful farmer who had received national recognition

"Expert in All Lines of Agricultural Industry"

A French journalist offered this description of Alsatian Amish in 1819: "The entire number of souls may be twelve or fifteen hundred . . . . I do not think that there is a single family living in any of the towns. They are small farmers being found especially as tenants on the estates of noblemen. Through their industry, intelligence, and experience as farmers they have become expert in all lines of agricultural industry. This circumstance as well as their reliability and punctuality in meeting all their financial obligations have made them much sought after by noblemen as farmers on their estates . . . ."

"To their credit be it said that, unlike many others, they pay their debts, not in worthless assignats [government-issued land bonds], but in good coin. They do not use tobacco, nor play cards. To [popular] music they are strangers. They do not go to law. They take care of their poor and come to the rescue of their members who have financial reverses for which they were not responsible personally. On the whole they are rather illiterate, but honest, temperate, industrious, and of good moral character."

Excerpted from C. Henry Smith and Cornelius Krahn, *Smith's Story of the Mennonites,* 5th ed. (Newton, Kans.: Faith and Life Press, 1981), 213.

from Napoleon's Imperial Society of Agriculture for his progressive farming methods. By connecting the almanac with the name of this influential farmer, the publisher hoped to increase the booklet's circulation and popular appeal.[15]

Aux Gouttes, the Graber farm in Pays de Montbéliard, France. The former sheep shed, on the left, also served as the meeting place for the Amish church.

But Klopfenstein also symbolized Amish assimilation in the powerful currents of Napoleonic political culture. Each year for more than a decade, local politicians appointed the successful farmer and almanac-sponsor to his town's governing council. Perhaps not surprisingly, the Klopfenstein farming almanac also included articles supporting the French emperor and his military program. The cover of one of the early issues even included a rural landscape in which the sun in the sky had been replaced with the imperial coat of arms!

Leaving the church or leaving the continent

During the first half of the 1800s, some of Jacques' extended Klopfenstein family immigrated to America, but most remained in French territory where they underwent a process of gentrification and joined the socially respectable state church. These two forces that pulled at the Klopfensteins—immigration or acculturation—tugged at many European Amish. The final fall of Napoleon in 1815 did not end the influence of French Revolutionary thought or slow the tendency of the state to usurp the moral authority of the church. Additionally, the years of upheaval and war had ruined some of the tolerant nobles who earlier had granted the Amish privileges and freedoms in exchange for tenancy. Moreover, the small political states which rose from the ashes of the French Empire had all been brought up on the revolutionary ideals of universal citizenship and the need for standing armies maintained through universal conscription.

The cover of one of the Klopfenstein almanacs showing an Amish farmer.

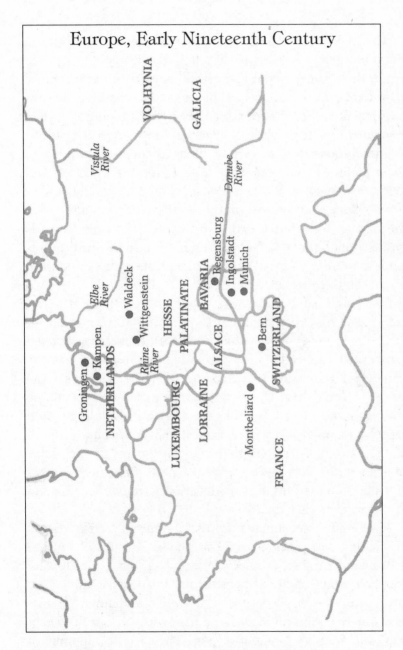

Amish Settlements in Europe early nineteenth century.

Although the Amish had never lived amid static surroundings, these early nineteenth-century years were especially trying, given the tempting new social mobility afforded by universal citizenship and the experience of military conscription. And while state-backed churches had lost much of their political power and influence, the official denominations still offered a measure of social status to their members. Genealogical records for the Waldeck and Wittgenstein communities in Hesse show that people of non-Amish backgrounds joined the Amish congregation there during the early nineteenth century. But the same records indicate that the reverse was equally as true—prosperous Amish families married into and requested membership in official state churches.[16]

Some signs of change were subtle, and shifts in attitudes and social adaptation pointed to potential acculturation. In 1844, the Ixheim congregation near Zweibrücken constructed a meetinghouse.[17] The move was not without controversy, and in fact it divided the local church. But the presence of the issue itself may have signaled a change in self-understanding among some Amish. A physical church building could represent a move away from a traditional Amish understanding of church as the people of God—pilgrims as mobile as their meeting places—and toward a more Protestant idea of church as an institution and a location where preaching and the sacraments are found.

Meanwhile, sometime after 1830, Amish in Hesse began purchasing and playing pianos at home. The use of musical instruments marked another way in which those Amish were adopting popular cultural practices into their own communities.[18]

In some ways, of course, the Amish remained distinctive. Singing from the *Ausbund* during worship services kept fresh the memory of a martyr past. The social component of

"My Children and I Like it Very Much"

In 1840, Johannes and Barbara (Gerber) Güngerich and their children immigrated from Kutzenhausen in Lower Alsace, to Tazewell County, Illinois. In December of that year, Johannes penned a lengthy account of their trip to relatives in Europe, detailing both the difficulties and rewards of the experience. In portions of the letter not reproduced here, Johannes favorably compared life in America with what he had known as a leaseholder in Europe, reported that he had no intention of returning to Germany, and encouraged others to follow.

"To report to you further about where we live, what we are doing, and how our journey went. First, we departed from LeHavre [France] on the eighth of May . . . . We sailed for four days and had good weather, after that we had a little storm . . . [lasting] four days; our ship was running three feet higher on one side than on the other and rising and falling nine or ten feet front and back. We had to tie everything down that was breakable and when we ate, we had to hold up the bowls. . . . During this storm, on the 16th, my wife gave birth to a little daughter, her name is Barbara, her place of birth is the sea. She is a healthy, strong child, everything went well, and the mother and child stayed healthy for the whole trip. . . .

"We spent 48 days on the ocean to New Orleans. . . . [On board] we had a large room—there were 70 people in our group—and all had plenty of room. We did well and brought over the same number of people we started out with: two died and two were born . . . .

"We arrived Friday evening in [New] Orleans and on the next morning we made our declaration to the government, to say what goods we had with us; a man came to search through to see if it was really as we had declared. . . . [The next leg of the journey by river boat] "left at four in the afternoon for a small city called Badarusch [Baton Rouge], about forty hours away from [New] Orleans. Sunday at one o'clock the axle of the paddle wheel broke, and the paddle wheel . . . broke into pieces, and a piece tore a hole down under the ship and it began to sink. . . . [The ship made it to the river bank where] they tied it up quickly with the ropes and anchor chains, otherwise it would have fallen right back. The people were all rescued . . . . [T]here were many property owners, French and English people, who came with horses to ride and with wagons or carriages to console the people. . . . We got back our large trunk with the money and our best clothes and linens, the other things lay in the water for eight weeks. When we had been there for two weeks, many people got sick, and several died. Cousin Nicki Gerber and his wife also died in this place, five days apart. My two sons and the oldest girl were also sick, and when they were well again, I had my wife and children travel ahead to the area where we now live, and I stayed until I got my things back again.

"I have bought land now—250 acres, 150 is tilled land, in all four corners good flat land, with not a stone to be found, neither small stones nor large, and you can plant what you want . . . . My children and I like it very much in America."

Source: Hermann Guth, *Amish Mennonites in Germany: Their Congregations, The Estates Where They Lived, Their Families.* (Morgantown, Pa.: Masthof Press, 1995), 314-18.

church discipline—shunning—underscored the Amish sense that Christian discipleship was practical and demanded integrity in even the routine interactions of life. Holding a literal footwashing service as a part of communion (after the pattern of Jesus and the disciples in John 13) reminded members of their role as servants. Into the 1800s, footwashing still marked the Amish church's communion practice as different from that of neighboring Mennonites, who continued to criticize the rite.[19]

But cooperation marked other aspects of Mennonite and Amish relations, especially in devotional literature. In 1780, an Amish elder and a Mennonite minister cooperated in publishing the Anabaptist history book *Martyrs Mirror,* while the prayer book *Die Ernsthafte Christenpflicht (Devoted Christian's Prayer Book)* was popular in both groups. So, too, was *Christliches Glaubens-Bekentnus* (an edition of the Dordrecht Confession with a collection of prayers and songs) that had been published in 1664 by a Dutch Mennonite elder.[20]

Many Amish congregations also began using a Mennonite catechism commonly known among the Amish as the "Waldeck Catechism."[21] Another Mennonite-written book that was well loved in Amish circles was *Die Wandlende Seel (The Wandering Soul),* which recounted biblical history as its narrator traveled through time and conversed with biblical characters.[22] And common in both Amish and Mennonite homes was a collection of Psalms, put in German verse by Reformed pastor Ambrosias Lobwasser.

In some places, in fact, cooperation between smaller Amish congregations and nearby larger Mennonite ones was so thorough that the Amish were actually absorbed into the Mennonite community. Of the Amish churches in the Netherlands, for example, the group at Kampen merged with the neighboring Mennonites in 1822, and the Groningen Amish did the same in 1824.[23] By 1838 in Eastern Europe, the Volhynian Amish—though still notably conservative in dress and traditional in custom—had joined with neighboring Swiss-descended Mennonites.[24] Meanwhile, the Amish in Bavaria were using their *Ausbunds* less often, and in 1843 produced a new songbook to replace the old Anabaptist hymnal.[25]

The next year, the household of Daniel and Elise (Beller) Oesch moved to Luxembourg, marking the beginning of a church in that place, and one that would go on to nurture a distinctive Amish identity for several generations. But the Luxembourg experience was becoming the exception rather than the rule.[26] For many more Amish, the future of the church seemed to lay across the ocean.

A new wave of Amish emigration

Emigration from Europe had slowed during the years of Napoleon's many campaigns and the War of 1812 between Great Britain and the United States. After about 1815, however, as sea travel became more regular and safe, immigration to North America increased. Between 1820 and 1860, more than five million Europeans left for Canada or the United States, and some twenty-seven percent were German-speakers.[27] Typically, these immigrants were seeking to improve their economic lot, fleeing debt, or seeking adventure.

These motives surely influenced some Amish to venture across the Atlantic. For example, some Swiss Amish and Mennonites left their Jura Mountain farms following crop failures in 1816 and 1819. In the Rhine Valley, meanwhile, opportunities for estate-leasing narrowed as the population of maturing Amish children outstripped such tenant possibilities and forced some young adults, especially after 1830, to look for land abroad.

In a few cases, Amish leaseholders left for North America after accumulating too much debt. Such was the situation of Jakob Nafziger near Darmstadt and Josef Stalter Jr. of Zweibrücken, both of whom emigrated in 1849.[28] For those facing financial difficulties, kin already in America might lure relatives with images of America's golden opportuni-

Amish Immigration from Europe to North America

c.1736–1770: About 500 people. Settled in eastern Pennsylvania. In the years that followed, a few of these immigrants and many of their descendents moved westward.

1804–1816: About a dozen households. Most eventually settled in the Midwest.

1817–1867: About 3,500 people. Nearly all settled in Ohio, Illinois, Indiana, Ontario, New York, Iowa, or Louisiana. A few stayed in Pennsylvania temporarily or permanently. Perhaps 450 were young men of draft-age, immigrating singly.

1870–1914: Fifty or more households and many single individuals. Some settled with relatives in established Midwestern communities; others went to the far West and often without retaining Amish or Mennonite identity.

ties. As one letter from a settler in Bureau County, Illinois, reported to those in Europe, "Cattle you can have as many as you want [in Illinois]. . . . On one small piece of land you make a great deal of hay. You can live a great del more comfortable herr than in Germany [sic]. The land is much more productive."[29]

For other Amish emigrants, faith commitments and convictions also figured into the mix of motives. The pressures and promises of universal citizenship prompted some parents to consider leaving, especially those in France after King Charles X reinstituted military conscription in 1829. Again, Amish ministers sent a petition of protest, asserting that they desired to be good citizens and asking if they could make some civic contribution other than organized violence. They hinted that if the state offered no alternative they might well "go into exile" and emigrate. Since "they all consider themselves happy to be French . . . . there is not one who would not leave the realm with despair in his heart, but you know, my lord [interior minister]," the petition continued, "how powerful religious conviction is."[30]

In the end, this appeal got nowhere since a popular revolt soon ousted King Charles. Conscription, however, remained a tool of successive French and Rhine Valley German states. If some Amish and Mennonites were willing to make peace with war, others considered anew the possibility of emigration for conscience sake.

Families such as Andreas and Elizabeth (Eiman) Ropp left when their sons began to reach draft age.[31] Others, like Daniel and Elizabeth (Bauman) Bender sent only their sons. At age fifteen, Wilhelm Bender sailed alone from Europe to avoid conscription.[32] Nor did all emigrants completely avoid the military. Joseph Wuerkler was actually drafted in the renewed French conscription act of 1829, but escaped the army and fled to America.[33]

The wave of Amish emigration crested in the 1820s–1850s. While a few families and individuals had left during the opening decades of the nineteenth century, most emigrants sailed after 1817.[34] Probably some 3,500 people packed their bags between then and 1860. The rapid loss of members and leaders during these years weakened the church that remained in Europe. At times, nearly an entire congregation from Bavaria or Hesse left together as a large group.[35] Several

Amish communities in those regions were so diminished that they eventually disbanded.

Those leaving Europe took church letters with them, signs of their intent to join or begin a congregation in North America—and perhaps as a way to vouch for their integrity when they asked established U.S. and Canadian Amish for financial aid in the process of settlement. In 1827, Peter Oswald carried a document signed by two ministers and indicating that Oswald "has been received as a brother through the covenant of baptism, and since that time has also conducted himself as a brother to the best of our knowledge." Oswald ended up in Holmes County, Ohio.[36]

But what sort of North American society beckoned these immigrants? Change had affected both sides of the Atlantic since the first Amish had sailed for Pennsylvania a century earlier. While Napoleon had been raising armies in Europe, he was also selling more than 830,000 square miles (2.15 million square kilometers) of Louisiana Territory to the young United States. Opportunities for white settlers to obtain land in America now stretched far beyond eastern Pennsylvania. The former Thirteen Colonies had become an assertive and expansive nation whose restless population pushed relentlessly westward.

Canada was changing, too, as its expanding population began demanding limited self-rule from Britain. A mild nationalism swept through the provinces when they held their own against the Americans in the War of 1812. The challenge of discerning what it meant to "love God and your neighbor"—as Amish elders had summed their practical theology in 1809—would remain as lively a concern in Canada and the United States as it had in Europe.

—6—

Prosperity and Promise in North America, 1800-1865

"We had everything in abundance."
—Amish bishop David Beiler

Fresh frontiers

In 1800, the Amish faced an uncertain future. In the preceding decades, the American Revolution had challenged the church's place in American society, while the influence of revivalism had drawn youth away from their parents' faith. Scattered geographically, the church existed in a new nation that was itself undergoing rapid transformation.

By 1800, the oldest Amish communities in Berks County, Pennsylvania, had mostly disappeared as their members moved to better soils in Lancaster County or farther west. The Lebanon Valley settlement, meanwhile, lost so many members to other denominations that it, too, was practically extinct before the nineteenth century began. Even the Chester County church that seemed healthy in 1800 had dissolved by 1830, as most of its members moved away. And in central and northeastern Lancaster County where two Amish congregations persisted, membership remained small until about 1840.[1]

Households moving west, hoping to establish stronger communities, were not always successful. Of three church settlements in southwestern Pennsylvania's Somerset

Elizabeth Zug (1786–1855) lived in Lancaster County, Pennsylvania, near the village of Eden.

County, only one survived. The freedom of the frontier and the influence of revivalists took their tolls there as well.

Moving to new areas could be a strategy to preserve church and family life, but it could also open new opportunities and possibilities. Amish man Joseph Schantz relocated to the border of Somerset and Cambria counties where, in the fall of 1800, he took the novel step of chartering a town on part of his farm. Schantz (anglicized as *Johns*) laid out lots—including space for a public school and church buildings—and then proceeded to sell them to non-Amish buyers. Even when he later moved to another farm some miles away, the civic-minded Amish man remained a noted local public figure. Although he had chosen the Native American designation "Conemaugh" for his town, the new residents changed its name to *Johnstown* twenty-one years after his death.[2] Such was the worldly civic activity of one Amish man who left the east.

But by that time, Somerset County was itself becoming "the east," as white settlers—Amish among them—pushed relentlessly westward into the Ohio River Valley. In 1809, the family of preacher Jacob Miller moved from Somerset County, Pennsylvania, to Tuscarawas County, Ohio. The Millers' nephew Jonas Stutzmann accompanied them but settled nearby in Holmes County. Four years later, other Amish from Pennsylvania located just to the north of them in Wayne County, Ohio.[3] In time, families that descended from immigrants of the 1700s would establish settlements in the Midwest, such as the community in Logan and Champaign counties, Ohio, that was populated by households from Mifflin County, Pennsylvania's "Big Valley."[4]

New arrivals

These American-born Amish hardly had begun putting down roots in new western locations when hundreds of European Amish immigrants began arriving on North

David Mast, Farming Entrepreneur

James L. Morris was a storekeeper and civic leader in Morgantown, Pennsylvania, whose colorful diaries reported the activities of his neighbors, including members of the Conestoga Amish community. A series of Morris' diary entries point to the agricultural experimentation of Amish deacon David Mast. As a means of replenishing soils poor in phosphorus and potassium, Mast's use of ground animal bone later became common in southeastern Pennsylvania.

September 12, 1845: "This David Mast is one of the most enterprising men of our neighborhood and as an agriculturalist he has scarcely his equal. To a knowledge of the various theories he adds an extensive practice and is not too timid to indulge in experiments."

October 15, 1845: "David Mast purposes manuring the Watts farm (which is very poor) with bone dust. He has offered $5.00 per ton for all the bones that can be collected and wants 30 or more tons. This is the first attempt in this neighborhood to use bone manure."

June 10, 1846: "David Mast whom I mentioned last winter as having erected a bone mill, strewed or sowed a quantity of bone dust upon poor forest land on which he sowed oats. A small patch of land was left unstrewn and the difference is remarkable. On the land on which the bone dust was applied, the oats is [sic] equal to any in the good valley land, while on the other it is merely 'forest oats.'"

Source: James L. Morris "Diary, or Daily Notes of the Weather together with the Events of the Neighborhood, etc., etc.," in 3 vols., Historical Society of Berks County, Reading, Pennsylvania.

American shores. Eventually totaling more than 3,000 people, the nineteenth-century Amish newcomers were, in some cases, fleeing the political and military consequences unleashed by the wars of the French Emperor Napoleon, and in other cases, simply looking to improve their economic lot in life. In the first ripple of what would become a wave of nineteenth-century Amish immigration was Christian Augspurger, of Hesse, who scouted land in Ohio in 1817. Returning to Europe, the Augspurgers rallied more families to join them and in 1819 returned to Ohio's Butler County where they founded a community composed of European immigrants.[5]

Groups of nineteenth-century arrivals settled not only in Butler County, but also in places like Stark County, Ohio (1823); Waterloo County, Ontario (1824); Lewis County, New York (1831); Fulton County, Ohio (1834); and Allen and Adams counties, Indiana (1840s). A few immigrants moved to older, established communities such as those in Lancaster and Somerset counties, Pennsylvania, or joined American-born Amish to form new settlements in places as far west as Johnson County, Iowa (after 1840), and Hickory County, Missouri (about 1855). In Wayne County, Ohio, the new immigrants remained on the edges of the older Amish settlement.[6]

Many of the Amish who came to North America after 1817 arrived not in Philadelphia, as had their eighteenth-century predecessors, but through the port of New York. After sixty-eight days at sea, Catherine (Schertz) Dettweiler and her children landed in New York and took a boat to Albany, where they caught a canal barge to Buffalo. From there they sailed across Lake Erie to Cleveland, took another canal to Cincinnati, and then traveled by riverboat down the Ohio River and up the Mississippi and Illinois rivers to Peoria.[7]

"White" Jonas Stutzmann (1788-1871)

In 1809, Jonas Stutzmann became the first Amish settler in Holmes County, Ohio. More than two centuries later he remains one of the most unusual of that community's residents, best known because he wore white for much of his life.

Stutzmann moved with relatives from Somerset County, Pennsylvania, to Ohio. Three years later he married Magdalena Gerber, and after her death, a woman named Catherine. Jonas had eight children who lived to adulthood.

In 1850, Stutzmann published a thirty-page booklet of writings entitled *First, Second, and Third Appeals to All Men to Prepare for the Approaching Kingdom of God Upon Earth.* The collection is the first known piece of original writing published by an American Amish author. Of the three "appeals," the first was dated July 19, 1849, and the second and third both November 22, 1849. Highly unusual were the book's contents. Stutzmann announced that he had received revelations from God warning all people to repent since the return of Christ was imminent. Church leaders were to stop serving communion and instead earnestly repent and purify themselves for the coming Kingdom of God.

Using a numerology derived from apocalyptic passages of the biblical book of Daniel, Stutzmann predicted Christ's second coming to be 1853. "God has deemed me worthy, his humble servant, to reveal unto me clearly and distinctly that the time of the fulfillment of his plan with mankind is at hand," Stutzmann wrote. "He revealed this unto me not for my sake only, but that I proclaim it before all men, so that everyone may prepare himself." So sure of Christ's return was Stutzmann that he built a chair for Jesus to sit in when Jesus arrived. It was nine inches larger than a standard-size chair.

"White" Jonas' booklet was in English, perhaps because he hoped to communicate with a wide readership. Stutzmann included his address in the book and urged all who were waiting for the predicted return of the Lord to write to him. In 1852, he published a pamphlet, this time in German, that expanded on several of his visions.

One of "White" Jonas' visions affected his choice of clothing and gave him his nickname. "According to what I have seen in the spirit," he wrote in *Appeals*, "there are but three colors for the children of God, viz.: the fallow [beige], gray, and white—the colors of eagles and sheep." For the rest of his life Stutzmann wore only white clothes. Some said he also was obsessed with cleanliness. Even after his predicted date for Christ's return passed without incident, he continued to wear white until he died.

Although the Amish rejected Stutzmann's apocalyptic teaching, he remained a member of the church all his life, and most of his children joined the Old Order Amish. Some of Stutzmann's convictions were typically Amish, including his rejection of expensive clothes, dancing, and church buildings that replaced private homes as the meeting places for worship. Said one Amish historian, "His peculiar views and dress were not seen as a threat to anyone, for he never had any followers." His unusual life grew out of honest conviction, not a spirit of rebellion.

For more information, see Gregory Hartzler-Miller, "'Der Weiss' Jonas Stutzmann: Amish Pioneer and Mystic," *Mennonite Historical Bulletin* 58 (October 1997): 4-12, and David Luthy, "'White' Jonas Stutzman," *Family Life* (February 1980): 19-21.

Others sailed from Europe to New Orleans, then took steamboats up the Mississippi, Ohio, or Illinois rivers to Midwestern destinations. Through the years, a few newcomers stayed on in New Orleans and established a small Amish congregation near the city. Some of the members, such as the families of Christian Oswald and bishop Joseph Maurer, remained in Louisiana only a short time before continuing on to Illinois. But others never left, including preacher Christopher Maurer who served this church from the time of his 1846 arrival from Alsace until his death in 1872.

One way the Louisiana Amish stayed connected to their northern compatriots was through the visits of the remarkable Ohio bishop Peter Naffziger, who twice walked from Ohio to New Orleans to minister to the small city congregation and bring news from fellow believers in the north. The Louisiana group seems to have dissolved in the later 1800s.[8]

The new wave of European immigration also produced the first permanent Amish presence in Canada.[9] In 1822, Christian Nafziger arrived in New Orleans on the first leg of a journey to locate land for members of his Palatinate congregation. Nafziger traveled by foot from Louisiana to Lancaster, Pennsylvania, where fellow Amish informed him of available acres in Canada.

In Ontario, he negotiated the purchase of a large tract in Waterloo County and returned to Europe to share the news of his good fortune. On this return trip, Nafziger's ship stopped in England where, according to family lore, King George IV personally certified the Canadian land deal. Beginning in 1824, European Amish families settled in Waterloo County, and by 1837 they were taking up lands in neighboring Perth County, as well. Soon the settlement also gained new members from Pennsylvania, with members of both groups coming to the aid of the other when needed.[10]

The process of immigration and adjustment was a challenge for all newcomers, but those with ethnic or religious group connections frequently benefited from the help of family networks or the practice of mutual aid. Amish arrivals were no different. Even as "an old man of nearly eighty years," Illinois Amish man Christian Ropp clearly remembered the welcome that the Chester County, Pennsylvania, Zook family had offered the tired Ropps when in 1826 they had arrived in Philadelphia.[11] Individuals without money enough to pay for passage might also receive aid, as young Wilhelm Bender learned when Amish man Peter Kinsinger paid Bender's fare and arranged for him to work for bishop Benedict Miller in Somerset County, Pennsylvania, where some years later Bender and Miller's daughter Catherine married.[12]

Another recipient of her church's generosity was Jacobina (Schwartzentruber) Nafzinger. Widowed during her 1827 Atlantic crossing, Nafzinger and her six young children and two brothers landed in Baltimore but made their way to Philadelphia. When Christian Zook of Chester County heard of the family and its dire situation, he went to Philadelphia to find them.[13] After three months with the Zooks, the Nafzingers settled in Lancaster County where other Amish families helped to take care of and support Jacobina's children.[14]

According to Louis C. Jüngerich, assistance of the sort Nafzinger received was commonplace. An immigrant himself, Jüngerich arrived in Pennsylvania from Hesse in 1821, and then penned numerous letters to European relatives, giving exacting detail on how to finance trans-Atlantic travel. Writing in 1826 to his uncle Christian Iutzi, Jüngerich confirmed that the Amish church "works actively" to assist those "arriving in this country. Entire families often can find shelter with them, as was the case with Johann Brennemann and a hundred more. Members of the congregation paid their passage and picked them up from the ports of entry. Within a few years, the newcomers reimbursed members of the congregation and earned enough more besides to make a start for themselves." New arrivals are "fortunate" to be "taken in by such people," Jüngerich concluded. Prompted by such descriptions, Christian and Maria (Sommer) Iutzi's family immigrated in 1832 and settled in the Butler County, Ohio, Amish community.[15]

A restless people

Like their neighbors in nineteenth-century North America, rural Amish populations were remarkably mobile. Caught up in an emerging market economy that left land values fluid and increased competition, Amish households were among the thousands that packed up and moved each year, often in a quest for affordable and productive land. Even non-farmers such as blacksmith and locksmith Christian Beck of Fulton County, Ohio, or schoolteacher Christian Erismann of central Illinois, were tied to agricultural economies since they lived in predominantly rural communities.[16]

The travels of bishop Isaac Schmucker illustrate Amish mobility and the factors that prompted movement. Schmucker was born in Lancaster County, Pennsylvania, in 1810. He moved with his parents to Mifflin County, and later lived with his wife, Sarah Troyer, in Wayne and Knox counties, Ohio. In late 1841 the Schmuckers became one of the first Amish families to locate in what became the large church community in northern Indiana's Elkhart and LaGrange counties. A decade later he was living in central Illinois, but in another year ill health in the family caused the Schmuckers to return to Indiana.[17]

The northern Indiana settlements typified the processes of migration that produced so many Midwestern Amish settlements. The churches in LaGrange and eastern Elkhart counties, for example, were composed of households from Pennsylvania and Ohio, drawn to new and potentially more profitable western locations. In fact, a small group of eastern Amish land scouts had explored possibilities in Iowa and Illinois before choosing northcentral Indiana in 1840. Many of those who followed were young families with small children. Among the original Elkhart County Amish settlers, the average age of male family heads was thirty-three, and of females only twenty-eight, at the time of their arrival. With the exception of one family of means, the households averaged about as much wealth per person as their non-Amish neighbors.[18]

At the same time, just a few miles to the southwest, another settlement emerged from different migration paths. Here, near what would later become the town of Nappanee, Indiana, recent European arrivals and American-born Amish from the east intermixed, connected by an intricate web of family ties and neighborly connections from Pennsylvania, Ohio, and Ontario.

The forces of migration that took families north and west sometimes brought them back south and east. For three years after their 1829 arrival from Europe, the family of Christian Ebersol Sr. lived near Lancaster, Pennsylvania, and then moved to Waterloo County, Ontario. After settling in Ontario, one of the Ebersol boys returned to Lancaster where he married Elizabeth Stoltzfus—a descendant of 1766 immigrants—and remained in her community. Nevertheless, the Ontario and Pennsylvania Ebersols kept up family contacts through the years, traveling to visit one another by horseback and railroad.[19]

Young people also moved in search of adventure. For about fifteen years, one Andrew Baechler traveled extensively, working in the gold mines of California, Idaho, British Columbia, Montana, and even across the Pacific in Austra-

Bishop Isaac Schmucker spent most of his adult life in northern Indiana as leader of that area's change-minded Amish churches.

lia. Finally, in 1867, Baechler settled among fellow Amish in central Illinois.[20] Others, like Indiana bishop Schmucker, may have pulled up stakes in part to escape conflict and church difficulties in their home communities.[21]

Some reasons for migrating were more personal and preferential. In 1832, the Andreas and Elizabeth (Eiman) Ropp family left Ontario for Butler County, Ohio, because "it was too cold in Canada." The Ropps had come from Alsace and later ended up in central Illinois.[22]

Widowhood seems to have forced Magdalena Augspurger and her children to leave Butler County, Ohio, for Davis County, Iowa, where they homesteaded in that area's small Amish community. In 1854, Augspurger purchased 160 acres of government land for a fraction of the price it would have cost her to expand her holdings in Ohio.[23] Earlier, in 1846, another Butler County farmer, bishop Joseph Goldsmith, had also moved to Iowa in search of cheaper land after financial difficulties forced him to sell his Ohio property and relocate on more affordable farmland in Iowa's Lee County.[24]

Some families bought and sold land without immediate plans to move. In 1837, for example, ten Amish men from Wayne County, Ohio, each purchased land in Adams County, Indiana, but none settled in the area until at least 1841. A few resold their acres without ever living on them.[25]

Complex transactions, land speculation, and the occasional dishonest land agent sometimes combined to cheat families out of money and property, as happened to the Susanna (Nafsinger) Raber family in Hickory County, Missouri. The Rabers paid for 200 acres of land that turned out not to have been for sale.[26] Regardless, migration continued, at times depleting eastern settlements. Only a small cemetery remained in Knox County, Ohio, after the entire Amish community in that place scattered to Illinois, Iowa, and other places in Ohio.[27]

About 1844, European-born Amish immigrants Henry Stahly (1810-1894) and Magdalena Ehrisman Stahly (c. 1812-1879) settled on land that later became the town of Nappanee, Indiana. Photo taken about 1875.

While most Amish searched for what was considered good farmland, others settled on soil deemed useless. Fulton County, in Ohio's northwestern corner, contained the so-called "Black Swamp," an area avoided by most Europeans. In 1834, a sizable group of Amish immigrants arrived in the swamp—so untamed a place it took them eleven days to travel the last twenty miles. Clearing and draining the land, the Amish developed some of the richest fields in the state.[28]

Stress and struggle in the church

The forces of migration had changed not only the size, but also the geographic center, of the Amish world. By 1851, the area with the largest Amish population was not the old Lancaster settlement in southeastern, Pennsylvania, with its four church districts, but rather central Illinois with eight congregations.[29] Population growth was not without tensions. For example, although Amish families—immigrants and old-line households—were instrumental in forming new settlements and organizing churches as they went, the relationship between church and family was not always clear. In many places, extended family networks were prominent and potentially competed with churchly authority.

One way the church strengthened its authority was by trying to hold parents accountable for the actions of their children. As Anabaptists, the Amish practiced adult baptism. Children and younger teens were not members of the church, and thus they were not under church discipline. Still, parents were to bring up their offspring in ways that were congruent with the expectations of the church and that would prepare children for lives as Amish adults, should children eventually choose baptism. Parental permissiveness, then, could stand in tension with churchly expectations.

During the early 1800s, however, church leaders took steps to discipline members who tolerated their children's deviant behavior. No one was to be forced to become a Christian, but neither were parents to encourage children in sin by winking at it. In 1837, the Somerset County minstry declared it would no longer permit parents to dress their children in fancy clothing, as some parents had been doing. Neither should parents turn a blind eye to youthful courting practices where teens "take the liberty to sleep or lie together without any fear or shame." If such happened "with the knowledge of the parents," the Amish concluded, the "parents shall not

Native Americans, First Nation Canadians, and the Amish

The westward migration of Amish families was part of the larger story of European appropriation of North America, and as such, it was also the story of disinheritance for the continent's Native people. In some cases, the Amish moved onto land from which the Indians had been expelled only recently. In Elkhart and LaGrange counties, Indiana, for example, U.S. troops forced Native people to leave in 1840, and the first Amish arrived in 1841. In one case, central Illinois Amish man John Engel assisted with the army's job of Native removal when he served as a teamster during the Black Hawk War of 1832 in which the Sauk tribe was brutally defeated. Engel's experience was highly unusual among the Amish.

Historian Russell Krabill has noted that no documentation exists to show "how the Amish felt about taking over the land which had been taken from Native peoples." Krabill mused that perhaps the Amish, like other white settlers, "were so busy carving out their homes in the wilderness that they did not give it much thought."

After 1840 in Lee County, Iowa, the small Amish community there disbanded when its residents discovered that they were living on land reserved for Indian peoples. Amish family lore suggests that even while they lived in Lee County, the Amish got along well with Native neighbors. One story preserves the memory of one Amish woman offering visiting Indians some of her pumpkin butter and receiving a gift of bear claws in return.

In Ontario, First Nation Canadians got along so well with one of the Amish Schwartzentruber families that the Indians often took young Michael Schwartzentruber on hunting trips and taught him how to use a bow. And apparently in the early days of the Wayne County, Ohio, Amish settlement, both Native and Amish farmers lived peaceably, side-by-side, along the Sugar Creek. While documentation of such encounters is slim, it may be significant that nearly all the stories involving Native Americans passed down through Amish families are ones of goodwill.

Rich H. Meyer, "Why Don't We Tell the Beginning of the Story? Native Americans Were Here First," *Mennonite Historical Bulletin* 60 (July 1999): 1-8; Steven R. Estes, *Living Stones: A History of the Metamora Mennonite Church* (Metamora, Ill.: Metamora Mennonite Church, 1984), 30-32; Orland Gingerich, *The Amish of Canada* (Waterloo, Ont.: Conrad Press, 2002), 33; Russell Krabill, "The Coming of the Amish Mennonites to Elkhart County, Indiana," *Mennonite Historical Bulletin* 52 (January 1991): 3, 4; David Luthy, *The Amish in America: Settlements That Failed, 1840-1960* (Aylmer, Ont. and LaGrange, Ind.: Pathway Publishers, 1986), 115, 116, 227, 263, 328, 356, 380, 381, 472.

go unpunished." Parental authority would have to yield to church standards. Increasingly, the bishops and ministers, not the fathers and mothers, had the final word.[30]

Those Somerset County decisions were concluded at a regional meeting of Amish leaders held in 1837. Similar meetings had been held in 1809, 1826, and 1830 in Pennsylvania, and in 1827 and 1831 in eastern Ohio.[31] At such gatherings, ministers resolved to stress personal humility and reaffirmed their commitments to the social implications of church membership and its disciplinary corollary, shunning the unrepentant. Assembled ministers also denounced expensive furniture, fancy porcelain, decorative dishes, and other signs of popular refinement.

Apostolic Christian Church

Occasionally associated with the Amish, the Apostolic Christian Church has its own distinct roots. The denomination traces its beginnings to 1832 when a Swiss Reformed theology student, Samuel Froehlich, questioned some of his church's doctrinal teaching and was expelled from his church.

Froehlich then traveled throughout Switzerland and met with disaffected Christians—including some Mennonites—eager for church renewal and revival. Two Mennonite ministers disappointed with the spiritual life of their own people joined Froehlich and other supporters at Langnau. Froehlich's group espoused typical Mennonite teachings on adult baptism (but by immersion) and nonresistance to violence. Additionally, they practiced social shunning as a form of church discipline. Deeply important to the Froehlich group was a strong sense of inner Christian repentance, conversion, and sanctification. They eventually received the name Apostolic Christian Church

Harassed in Switzerland, Apostolic Christians began immigrating to the United States in 1847, settling first in Lewis County, New York, which was also home to a sizable Amish community. Especially in New York, and later in Illinois and Ohio, the Apostolic Christians attracted Amish who saw their own tradition as focused too much on human effort and not enough on divine grace. Yet the two groups also shared much in common, and observers nicknamed the Froehlich group "New Amish," both because many of its members once were

Amish and because many Apostolic Christian doctrines seemed to mirror Amish practice.

In 2010, the Apostolic Christian Church had a membership of about 12,700 in eighty-seven congregations in the United States and in two congregations in Canada.

For more information, see Perry A. Klopfenstein, *Marching to Zion: A History of the Apostolic Christian Church of America, 1847-2007* (Eureka, Ill.: Apostolic Christian Church, 2008); and Donald B. Kraybill, *Concise Encyclopedia of Amish, Brethren, Hutterites, and Mennonites* (Baltimore: Johns Hopkins University Press, 2010); http://www.apostolicchristian.org

The Amish also debated a series of doctrinal matters involving baptism and fraternal relationships with Mennonites.[32] After 1850, the practical question of how to administer baptism caused a stir in Amish circles. Traditionally, the Amish held baptismal services, like worship services, in private homes. But some Amish began to argue that because Jesus was baptized in the Jordan River, their own baptismal candidates also should kneel in a stream or river while the bishop poured water on their heads. Debate ended when churches agreed that different districts could use different methods. No bishop would be compelled to baptize in a way with which he was uncomfortable, and very few adopted the innovative stream-baptism style.[33]

Other debates involved interaction with religious competitors. In 1843, Stark County, Ohio, minister George Jutzi had to contend with the ideas of an itinerant preacher associated with William Miller. Miller was the nationally prominent figure who championed the idea that Christ would return in 1844 and bring an end to human history.

Amish Church Structure and Leadership

The Amish church in North America was congregational in organization; that is, each congregation was self-governing, and there were no synods, conferences, dioceses, or other denominational structures. Prior to 1862, regional gatherings of Amish leaders occurred on an occasional basis and never presumed to include every community. Locally, each church had its own leadership, defined in four recognized offices:

1. *Völliger Diener* (fully-approved minister) or bishop. Bishops provided spiritual leadership for the local congregation and conducted baptisms, marriages, and ordinations. Along with preachers, bishops also took regular turns in delivering Sunday morning sermons. If congregations expelled unrepentant members or received them back into fellowship, it was the bishop who carried out these pronouncements. In Europe this office typically was known as *Ältester* (elder); the term bishop was a later English designation.
2. *Diener zum Buch* (minister of the Book/Bible) or preacher. Preachers assisted the bishop in preaching and teaching. Sometimes preachers were simply called ministers.
3. *VölligerArmendiener* (fully-approved minister to the poor) or full deacon. The full deacon performed all the duties of a deacon (see below), plus a number of additional ones. Full deacons assisted with baptisms and in some places also preached on a regular basis. Common in Europe, the office of full deacon was rarely used in North American churches.

4.   *Armendiener* (minister to the poor) or deacon. The deacon looked after the physical welfare of the congregation. Deacons maintained the "alms fund" and distributed money to the needy in the church. In some places deacons also read aloud the Scripture in Sunday morning worship. In addition, deacons assisted bishops in performing baptisms, administering communion, and dealing with matters of church discipline.

It seems that in Europe, church members elected leaders by a simple plurality of votes. Preachers and deacons were chosen from among the male members of the congregation, bishops from among the preachers, and full deacons from the ranks of deacons. Leaders received no formal training and no salary.

In North America the common means of choosing leaders involved not just the voice of the church (voting), but also drawing lots. After church members had voted for candidates to fill a particular position, all those who had received (usually) two or more votes then drew lots. Each candidate selected a book from a set of specially prepared Bibles or hymnbooks, one of which included a slip of paper. Whoever drew the book containing the paper was considered chosen of God and ordained. (The Lewis County, New York, Amish used the European process of simple election, instead of drawing lots, much longer than most other communities.)

Ordination was a lifetime responsibility. If a man moved, his ordination moved with him. Thus, some Midwestern Amish congregations might end up with three or more bishops, if bishops from several areas migrated to the same place. Typically, though, each congregation had one bishop, two preachers, and one deacon.

Congregations met for worship every other Sunday. On "in-between" Sundays, members spent the day visiting family or attending a neighboring Amish church that was meeting for worship that week. Church services included hymn-singing, reading from the Bible, and prayers read from a German prayer book, as well as two sermons. In addition, each ordained man present offered a response, or "testimony," to the sermons.

Twice a year, before the spring and autumn communion services, each congregation had a counsel meeting. During counsel, members were to be reconciled with anyone in the group with whom they had a disagreement. Communion would take place only if all members were at peace with one another. Congregations also addressed new or lingering questions of appropriate lifestyle. The communion service proceeded only if all members reached consensus, a tradition that strengthened congregational unity.

Typically, churches worshiped in private homes. When a congregation grew too large to meet in members' houses, the church divided into two smaller groups. Such divisions always occurred geographically, and eventually congregations came to be called districts, since members living in a given area made up a given congregation. In much of the literature on Amish church life, the term "district" is used in the way "parish" or "congregation" is used in other Christian denominations.

For a great deal more information, see Paton Yoder, *Tradition and Transition: Amish Mennonites and Old Order Amish, 1800-1900* (Scottdale, Pa.: Herald Press, 1991), chapters 3-6.

Jutzi refuted the notion and also critiqued Methodist revivalist techniques that Jutzi thought played on emotionalism.[34]

Other church groups targeted the Amish in particular as candidates for proselytism. A Swiss evangelical movement, later known as the Apostolic Christian Church, drew converts from several Amish settlements.[35] In some areas, in fact, the new group received the designation "New Amish" after scores of former Amish church members joined them. The Lewis County, New York, Amish settlement was especially shaken by Apostolic Christian inroads. After 1847, the Amish there lost not only a majority of their members, but also four preachers and a bishop to the local "New Amish" fellowship. A few families remained Amish and, with the resolute leadership of bishop Michael Zehr, maintained their church in the face of strong opposition.[36] Apostolic Christian congregations also sprang up in Woodford County, Illinois; Wayne and Fulton counties, Ohio; Davis County, Iowa, and elsewhere. In each case many Amish joined them.

Some inter-religious interaction was positive. After 1850 in Waterloo County, Ontario, bishop Peter Litwiller was "known to frequently engage in religious discussion" with his neighbor, Father Eugene Funcken, spiritual overseer of the area's Roman Catholic population. Litwiller and Funcken became good friends, and the priest tolled his church's bell when the Amish man died, and then wrote an appreciative account of Litwiller's life for the local paper.[37]

Cultures in conflict

While these doctrinal debates and religious encounters were important in themselves, the larger context in which they took place was even more significant for the development of Amish identity. The first decades of the nineteenth century were years of profound cultural change in the

United States, and the Amish were not immune from the accompanying social upheaval.

This transformation revolved around popular notions of refinement and respectability. Typically, Americans of earlier generations had valued plainness in dress, decor, and deportment. Patriotic luminary John Adams, for example, counseled against the unnecessary expense of painting barns and other demonstrations of frivolity and waste. Nor was Adams alone. Although a relative handful of Southern planters imitated the British aristocracy, most white Americans made a public virtue of avoiding ostentation. In such an environment, Amish simplicity—even given its Pennsylvania German peculiarity—was a variation on a broader American theme. Between about 1790 and 1850, however, there was a remarkable cultural shift in the United States which affected not only how people lived, but how they thought about how they lived. Americans began to aspire to living in a style that they called *refined*. In about a generation or two, gentility triumphed, and being respectable came to mean something other than plain and simple.[38]

In an ironic way, the fact that white America was relatively free from social class and rank distinctions meant that suddenly the possibility was open for anyone to be an aristocrat. In a society that prized individual liberty, the race was on to the top of the social ladder. Publishers issued exacting guidebooks (based on the old manuals of Renaissance-era nobility) to instruct Americans on how to talk, walk, eat, laugh, and write a letter like a gentleman or a lady. Genteel activities demanded genteel surroundings, including houses with carpets, mirrors, and display objects such as dishes that one did not use, but had only "for show."

Ordinary people worked long and hard to give the appearance of not working at all. Refined people read novels, had more clothes than they could wear, and found creative

Nineteenth-century immigrants formed the so-called "Swiss Amish" settlements in Allen and Adams counties, Indiana. The Swiss Amish drive only "open buggies" without enclosed tops, such as this one in Allen County.

ways to demonstrate that they possessed excess wealth. This refinement of America, as one historian has called it, combined with a market economy to produce a budding consumer culture and joined with popular revivalism to promote a religious endorsement of progress, betterment, and good taste.

In the wake of this realignment of public virtues and values, Amish commitments to separation from the frivolity of the world took on new significance. The Amish were not interested simply in preserving a European heritage. Instead, they struggled to define themselves in a rapidly changing cultural context. Lancaster County bishop David Beiler was sensitive to the implications of the shifting popular mood. Writing in the wake of refinement's triumph, Beiler bemoaned the emphasis on fancy carriages, stylish clothing, and expensive household furnishings that tempted even Amish families. Beiler longed for the good old days when "Christian simplicity was practiced much more, and much more submission was shown toward the ministers."[39] Now Amish youth clamored for months of education each year. Beiler thought that they should be satisfied with knowing how to read and write—anything more would surely lead to a competitive spirit and to pride.

Beiler feared that the Amish were also being enticed by the lure of gentility, patterning their lifestyle after fashionable society rather than the simple teaching of Scripture and the example of the humble Jesus. The world into which Beiler had been born in 1786 had changed dramatically in the course of several decades and left him on the defensive because of his interest in simple things.[40]

At one point Beiler pinned some of his church's mounting interest in genteel habits on more recent Amish arrivals. These "many foreign immigrants with strange manners and customs" clung to the promise of progress more than the steadying anchor of tradition, in Beiler's opinion.[41] It was true that some nineteenth-century immigrants were decidedly change-minded and open to the prospect of refinement. A group of Hessian Amish arriving in Butler County, Ohio, in 1832—some of whom moved to McLean County, Illinois, five years later—was especially known for its genteel sensibilities. Hessian men wore buttons on their coats, and some families even had pianos in their homes, while their leaders appeared flexible with matters of doctrine and discipline.[42]

Yet the picture was more complicated than Beiler may have imagined. Change-minded bishop Isaac Schmucker, for example, had been born into a Lancaster County family that had arrived before the American Revolution, while bishop

Christian Ropp, a recent immigrant of 1826, remained a leading conservative voice throughout his life in Illinois. Then, too, most of the so-called "Swiss Amish" who immigrated to America as late as the 1850s and settled in Allen and Adams counties, Indiana, remained quite plain and tradition-minded.[43]

But Beiler had identified an important impulse that animated much of the struggle in the Amish church during his lifetime. The church's response to an American culture that suddenly prized and promoted the refinement of people and their surroundings would pull the Amish in at least two directions. For some, the invitation to gentility was a welcome overture from the larger society, a sign that not only toleration, but also acceptance was possible for a people once religiously marginalized. For others, the refinement of America highlighted anew the importance of humility, separation, and the wise authority of tradition—rather than the forces of the popular marketplace—in guiding life. As historian Paton Yoder summed up the situation, by the mid-1800s, most Amish were sorting themselves into change-minded and tradition-minded camps. That divide would prove exceedingly critical.

Innovation and involvement

The practical side of the difference in orientation between change-minded and tradition-minded Amish worked its way out in the symbols and substance of church and community. Signaling a shift in their understanding of *church*, some Amish began constructing church buildings, often called *meetinghouses*. While these structures were quite plain and simple, they marked and invited important changes. No longer would the church simply be a pilgrim group of people gathering in private homes. No longer would the congregation remain at the host family's house after worship for a

The South Union Amish Mennonite meetinghouse, Logan County, Ohio (constructed 1876). In 1863, Amish Mennonites in this area launched the first permanent Sunday school among their people anywhere in North America.

meal and afternoon fellowship. Now church could be a place to go to and to leave at selected times during the week.

In 1853, the Amish around Rock Creek near Danvers, Illinois, erected the first permanent Amish meetinghouse.[44] The neighboring Partridge (Metamora), Illinois, Amish church put up a structure the following year. In 1855, the Amish in Logan and Champaign counties, Ohio, built the first of several meetinghouses in their settlement, and the Haw Patch (later Topeka), Indiana, Amish constructed a church building the next year. In the decade that followed, more change-minded Amish churches erected meetinghouses.

The Logan County Amish also became the first to sponsor an ongoing Sunday school program. During the early 1800s,

Sunday schools had become widespread among American Protestants.[45] Many of these Sunday schools were "union schools," supported jointly by several local denominations. An innovative form of Christian education, Sunday schools would increase biblical knowledge, supporters claimed. But, opponents warned, Sunday schools also segregated and compartmentalized religious education by separating children from parents. Furthermore, they used uniform materials written by unknown, inter-denominational authors whose generic messages were calculated to offend no one. Awarding high marks or even prizes to those who performed well in Sunday school promoted the worldly ideals of competition and earned status.[46] None of these aspects of Sunday school made the idea popular with tradition-minded Amish.

In the 1850s, some Amish children from Logan and Champaign counties had attended union Sunday schools. As an alternative, in June 1863, bishop Jacob C. Kenagy and preacher David E. Plank opened the first permanent Sunday school among the Amish.[47] Earlier, Plank had visited a local union school from which he drew his ideas and inspiration. The new school, held in the Amish church house, was not without opposition. Several church members claimed that Sunday school, in session in the afternoons during those early years, disrupted extended-family visiting that otherwise occupied Sunday afternoons. Others were unsure of the doctrinal content of the school's materials. Still, the Sunday school had the support of most of its progressive-minded members.[48]

The nearby Champaign County Amish congregation, under the leadership of preacher John Warye, soon established a Sunday school, as well. A similarly progressive group, the Champaign church permitted members to drive more expensive enclosed carriages instead of the common open buggies used by most Amish at the time. But even progressives drew a line at some point. When two young Pennsylvania Amish men visited a Sunday service in Champaign County and began to show off their harmonic skills during a congregational hymn, "Warye rose to his feet, struck the pulpit desk with his fist, and commanded the congregation to stop and after his stern rebuke, 'Net Bass singa!' [No bass singing!], he permitted the congregation to proceed."[49] Worshipers were to think about what—not how—they were singing.

For conservative-minded Amish who saw the changes in temperament and tone that accompanied the adoption of meetinghouses and Sunday schools, there seemed cause for concern. How much could the church borrow from secular models of organization and efficiency and still remain faithful? Conservatives correctly sensed that adopting styles and patterns from the surrounding culture—be they fashionable clothing trends or more systematic and bureaucratic Christian education programs—were not without implications for other aspects of community life. Biblical teachings on humility, simplicity, and submission to the wisdom of elders did not fit easily with the assertive American notion that bigger was better and new meant improved.

Conservatives noticed that progressives did not stop with innovations in church life. Openness to change seemed to breed interest in the secular activities of larger society. Growing business contacts among enterprising Amish sometimes blurred the line between the church and the world. Mississippi River steamboat-owner and -operator Henry Detweiler managed to balance his social and business life with his Amish church's lifestyle expectations for a time. Eventually, though, Henry and his wife Magdalena Bachman were excommunicated because of their infrequent church attendance, unable to fulfill their duties in both their church and their work.[50] And in other Amish settlements, such as Wayne County,

Ohio, keeping after the world's fads led some Amish to pose vainly and to pay for photographs of themselves.

Despite the growing rift between tradition-leaning and change-minded church members, the Amish remained at least nominally united in spirit, with those on both sides generally recognizing one another and allowing bishops visiting from other communities to preach or assist with communion. An early exception to this pattern was a small Mifflin County, Pennsylvania, group under the leadership of bishops Samuel B. King and "Long Christian" Zook. After 1849, the King and Zook group broke fellowship with the larger Amish church (except for a small group in Lawrence County, Pennsylvania, with which they maintained contact). The exact disagreement between King's congregation and other Amish is no longer clear; however, the King group (later known as the "Byler Amish") represented notably conservative Amish convictions.[51]

Did the Mifflin County schism foreshadow deeper divisions? Certainly innovations in church life and involvements in worldly business had pulled some Amish towards the social mainstream. Though conservatives like David Beiler might warn and protest against too much accommodation with "the world," there was no doubt that some Amish were identifying more closely with broader American culture—including its system of political power and authority.

Democrats, Whigs, Republicans, and Amish

Popular politics became something of a national pastime during the mid-1800s, as democratization promised finally to fulfill Americans' aspirations for liberty and equality. Political parties, organized on a local level after about 1830, served as a channel for civic-minded Americans to involve themselves in their communities. Tree-stump speeches, torchlight parades, and bonfire rallies became standard campaign fare as neighbors vigorously debated the merits of candidates who promised to secure the republic's future.

Although much of the political enthusiasm appealed to English-speaking citizens, it also beckoned ethnic immigrant communities like the bilingual (German dialect and English) Amish by offering an avenue of acceptance and Americanization. Many Amish discouraged participation in politics. Anabaptist sensibilities concerning the separation of church and state, for example, along with a lingering Amish suspicion that governments were agents of persecution and harassment, made many Amish wary of such involvement. An 1837 Amish ministers meeting held in Somerset County, Pennsylvania, had declared public office-holding, jury service, and voting, as taboo. The boastful and haughty nature of electoral politics smacked of competitive pride, if not outright untruth.[52]

Yet undeniably, some Amish had always been involved in civic life. It seems that Chester County, Pennsylvania, bishop Christian Zook likely issued a printed handbill during the War of 1812, urging Amish and other nonresistant church members to elect officials committed to peace and ending the war.[53] More common was direct participation in local government.

Although it seems impossible to know exactly how many Amish served in local offices, enough did to alarm conservative church leaders in several states.[54] One civic-minded Amish man was Christian Ebersol Jr., an immigrant of 1829 who lived most of his adult life in Lancaster County, Pennsylvania, where he remained a rather traditional and conservative member of his church, but was also active in community affairs. He served as his township's first road supervisor and later as one of its public school directors. Since the township had for a time refused to fund common schools, Ebersol's

Bishop Jacob Zehr (1825-1898) and Elizabeth Ehresman Zehr (1830-1902) at their home in Woodford County, Illinois. Jacob immigrated from Bavaria to Illinois in 1848; Elizabeth immigrated to Ohio as a five-year-old girl.

early involvement suggests that he had more confidence in public education than many of his non-Amish neighbors.[55]

Ebersol was a nineteenth-century immigrant, but the descendants of earlier arrivals had also become involved in civic life. In Mifflin County, Pennsylvania, Amish church members held a variety of local posts. Already in 1797 Abraham Yoder served as a township road supervisor. The next year Christian Lantz and Christian Zook were named public overseers of the poor. Historian S. Duane Kauffman has discovered about three dozen Amish men who filled local government offices in Mifflin County through the 1840s.[56]

While the Amish generally avoided law enforcement offices that may have involved the use of violence, they served as township supervisors, overseers of the poor, school directors, assessors, auditors, tax collectors, and, in one case, county commissioner. Most notable was Shem Zook, who not only served multiple terms in at least five different township and county offices, but also took an interest in political party machinery. Zook was one of several Mifflin County Amish active in the Anti-Masonic and Whig political parties, both of which represented conservative business interests. Local lore preserves the legend that the Pennsylvania Railroad, so impressed with Zook's political savvy, asked him to run for governor after Zook successfully negotiated an important track right-of-way.[57]

In the 1840s and 1850s, the McLean County, Illinois, Amish were heavily involved in local civic life. Members held posts as township, road, and school supervisors, and one Joseph W. Zook even served as justice of the peace.

Most of the Amish active in Illinois politics supported the conservative Whig party, but the Hessian Amish lined up behind the Democrats. After the Republican Party formed in 1854, it drew heavy McLean Amish support.

Maverick Illinois Amish schoolteacher Joseph Joder was an ardent Republican and an outspoken abolitionist. Come election day, every "freedom-loving citizen," Joder wrote, was to "come forward to the ballot box and silently decide in favor of freedom."[58] Among Joder's many non-Amish associates was a young lawyer named Abraham Lincoln. A number of Illinois Amish interacted with Lincoln, including McLean County preacher Christian Farni and his brother bishop Peter Farni. In the 1850s, the Farnis became entangled in a St. Louis-based investment scheme that collapsed in the financial panic of 1857. During the ensuing legal wrangling and bankruptcy proceedings, Lincoln offered legal advice to the brothers and on one occasion appeared in court on their behalf. For his part, Christian wrote to Lincoln promising support in the approaching electoral contest.[59]

Yet it was Lincoln's election to the presidency in 1860 that marked, in many ways, the limits of Amish civic participation. With a Republican heading to the White House, Southern states began to secede, and within weeks of Lincoln's inauguration the country was at war with itself. If civic-minded Amish had not sensed acutely enough the moral problems posed by the government's sanction of human slavery, the state's assertion to decide life and death on the battlefield was a claim that could not so easily be ignored.

Uncivil war

The April 1861 bombardment of Fort Sumter outside Charleston, South Carolina, marked the beginning of the violent and bitter struggle between the North and the South, a struggle that would take 600 lives a day for the next four years. Nearly all the Amish lived in northern Union states, and many had sympathies for the ruling Republican Party. Moreover, the Amish had never been friends of slavery, although virtually none had taken an active part in the abolitionist movement, either. How would they respond to a divided nation that had exhausted compromise and demanded its citizens choose sides?

A few families ended up as fractured as the country. In Woodford County, Illinois, for example, two sons of Amish bishop Johannes and Barbara (Gerber) Gingerich chose different paths. While Peter Gingerich refused military induction, in 1862 his older brother Christian enlisted in the Union army. For men such as Christian, the Union cause was clearly just, and moral duty seemed to require joining

Allen County, Indiana, ministers Peter Graber and Jacob Graber, along with laymen Daniel Grabill, Daniel Stoll, Victor Delagrange, Peter Stoll, and John Stoll, signed this notarized January 1865 request for Peter Graber Jr.'s exemption from the Civil War draft.

in the fray. But for Peter and many others, killing was not justified even as a means to a greater good.[60]

Christian was not alone among his people in marching with the Yankees. In 1862, twenty-eight-year-old Emmanuel Hochstetler joined the 22nd Iowa Volunteer Infantry and later died of wounds received at the battle of Vicksburg.[61] Four Yoder brothers—Samuel, Noah, Moses, and Jacob—raised by their widowed mother in Holmes County, Ohio, all went to war. Only Samuel returned unscathed.[62] Some recent immigrants may have grown accustomed to military service in Europe and not seen the American war as a matter of conscience. Valentine Nafziger, of Hessian Amish background, served in the military and then joined a national veterans' organization.[63]

Although some young men did join the Union army, government records reveal that the vast majority refused to do so, even when drafted. State and federal draft laws generally allowed conscripted men the option of paying a commutation fee (eventually set at $300) or hiring substitutes to muster in their place. Paying the commutation fee was the most widespread Amish response, among both traditionalist-leaning and change-minded segments of the church.[64] In some cases, drafted Amish men did hire substitutes, though painful stories kept alive after the war testify to the unease with which those in the church regarded the practice. It was said, for example, that years after the war's conclusion, John S. Stoltzfus of Lancaster County, Pennsylvania, still retained, as a tragic reminder, the uniform that his draft substitute had worn before dying in battle.[65]

Ethical questions also surrounded the practice of contributing money to local civic funds that offered sign-up bounties to volunteers so that a given county could fill its military quota without needing to resort to a draft. It seems some Amish households contributed to such funds, but others were more than a little uncomfortable with an arrangement that suggested

Bishop Jacob Schwarzendruber Speaks Out During the Civil War

During the Civil War, state and federal conscription law allowed draftees to hire substitutes to serve in the draftee's place. Some Amish young men used this provision to avoid induction, but not all Amish were comfortable with such an arrangement. Bishop Jacob Schwarzendruber of Johnson County, Iowa, expressed his opposition in a letter composed in late spring 1865, after the war's conclusion:

"Concerning the draft, or buying volunteer substitutes or paying volunteers to send them out to fight, I hold that it is wrong according to God's Word and the teaching of Jesus and the apostles . . . .

"Are we then still nonresistant according to the teachings of Jesus and the apostles who have proclaimed to us the perfect will of the Father? . . . 'Whoso sheddeth man's blood, by man shall his blood be shed,' for God made man in his image [Genesis 9:6]. So we do not want to go ourselves or to pay others that they would go. How is this right before the eyes of God? . . . The Saviour's teaching is not as we have done, that we should be permitted to buy substitutes or help pay for people and let them go to kill others.

"Are we then still nonresistant? Jesus says* in Luke chapter 3 verse 14 to the soldier, 'Do violence or injustice to no man.' Dare I then pay someone to do injustice? Matthew 5:7, 'Blessed are the merciful for they shall obtain mercy,' and this is before the righteous judge, and how unmerciful things go in war with those who have never harmed us, and are also created after the image of God. Do we do right then voluntarily to support the war with money and to vote for those who want to make war? All vengeance is forbidden to the follower of Jesus . . . . Jesus says 'Love your enemies, bless them that persecute you, do good to them that hate you, pray for those who despitefully use you and persecute you, then we shall be the children of the heavenly Father.' . . . [In Acts 7:60] Stephen prayed for those who stoned him, and what do we do? We send people to fight. Are we then still nonresistant? . . ."

*The quotation is from John the Baptist. Schwarzendruber viewed the entire New Testament in harmony with and reflecting the teachings of Jesus.

Excerpted from Harold S. Bender, ed. and trans., "An Amish Bishop's Conference Epistle of 1865" *Mennonite Quarterly Review* 20 (July 1946): 222-29.

they were encouraging others to fight. "In my meager understanding," wrote Christian Graber, of Stryker, Ohio, in 1863, when such a scheme was being floated in his neighborhood, "I considered it wrong."[66] In Wayne County, Ohio, public pressure to contribute to the county's so-called "Volunteer Fund" was intense. But while Wayne County's nonresistant Mennonites contributed heavily, the Amish there were less willing to give and better resisted the wider community's pressure.[67]

For some Amish, the war's deepest impressions came not so much from the conscription of men and money as from the stark realities of the war itself, realities that left deep memories which became often-repeated family tales. After stealing a wagon load of wheat from a Hickory County, Missouri, farmer, Southern troops forced teenage Christian Raber of the area's local Amish community to haul the grain some thirty or forty miles in Raber's father's wagon. A frightening experience, it was not Raber's last run-in with troops. During the war's later years, an intoxicated Union soldier stopped the wagon which young Raber and a friend were driving. Not satisfied with the answers that the Amish boys gave his questions, the soldier shot and killed Raber's traveling companion. Deeply shaken, Raber drove the twelve miles home with his friend's body.[68]

Soldiers commandeered Amish man Christian Petersheim of Aurora, West Virginia, and forced him to haul supplies for weeks, while his family wondered whether he was dead or alive. And the Amish of Davis County, Iowa, never forgot the fall 1864 morning when Southern sympathizers from nearby Missouri rode through their community, stealing and looting from barns and homes. Such was war, even among neighbors.[69]

"Who is there that has not deserved it?"

The Civil War was the bloodiest conflict in United States history, devastating in its enormity. Beyond the physical and financial toll, some contemporaries saw in the war great moral meaning. On March 4, 1865, at his second inauguration, Abraham Lincoln reflected on the war and concluded that perhaps God was teaching America a lesson through all the death and destruction. In the form of war, the sin of tolerating slavery had visited its curse upon the Union, the president suggested.

Three months later, Amish bishop Jacob Schwarzendruber in Johnson County, Iowa, expressed somewhat similar thoughts in a letter to fellow Amish church leaders. Schwarzen-druber saw God using the war to test the faithfulness of the church. "The war in this country is a permission or a sending of God to punish the people because of their sins," the bishop wrote. "And who is there that has not deserved it?"[70]

The lesson for the Amish was clear to Schwarzendruber. His church had become more worldly and progressive, too much involved in an American culture that included injustice and war. As a result, the Amish were now in part responsible for the nation's tragic calamity. "Our people should all keep themselves apart from all party matters in political things," he warned, "where brother votes against brother and father against son." Entangled in the war machinery, the Amish church had "departed from the example of Jesus and the martyrs," he feared.[71] Conservatives such as Schwarzendruber believed that the tragedy of the Civil War demanded repentance and reform.

Half a continent to the east, in Lancaster County, Pennsylvania, seventy-six-year-old bishop David Beiler had already seen God's judgment in the war's events. "Perhaps with war and strife and bloodshed," Beiler thought, Providence was teaching the Amish church to live more simply and obediently. The first half of the nineteenth century had been a time of material and social prosperity, Beiler was sure. But, he wondered, in having "everything in abundance according to natural things," had some Amish "become forgetful of the great goodness of God?" Looking back over some six decades, he saw a struggle in his church that reminded him of the schism between the American North and South. Just as two sections of the nation had years earlier embarked on divergent social, economic, and political paths, so too had change-minded and tradition-minded Amish set out on apparently incompatible means of relating to the world.[72] Now the nation had divided. Could the church hope for more?

The Amish in North America, both the descendants of the eighteenth century immigrants and the new arrivals of the 1800s, had prospered abundantly. Their prosperity stemmed in a large part from their own beliefs and practices: simplicity, community, mutual aid. But prosperity had also led them to a fork in the road, with one path pointing toward greater integration into North American society and the other pointing toward some type of critical distance. For many Amish, the choice became especially acute in the 1860s, the very decade in which the United States painfully struggled to remain united. The Amish church also struggled during those years—and ultimately divided.

—7—

Years of Division, 1850-1878

"In many places patience has grown cold."
—open letter from a group of Amish ministers, 1861

The context for conflict

As the Amish approached mid-century, some leaders wondered if their church was on a collision course with central values of North American culture. Although Amish families had left Europe in large part to avoid the pressures of political conformity, they now faced the question of how much they would adapt to their new North American environment. In this respect, the Amish were hardly different from many other European-rooted minority groups that sought to balance old values and embody traditional practices in new settings. For the Amish, however, the stakes were particularly high since their understanding of faith was one that placed a premium on embodying Christian values in everyday expressions of discipleship. Since those expressions took specific and public form, they were always more than simply ethnic folkways—regardless of how they appeared to outsiders—and so questions of cultural change were bound up with questions of spiritual faithfulness.

For those living in the United States, tensions existed on multiple fronts. Commitments to self-determination and individual freedom of choice, for example, had become articles of faith for most Americans, and much of popular culture rested on the assumption that defending such freedom was at the heart of national identity. The unchecked celebration of progress and individual achievement had propelled Americans to conquer a continent, produce secular self-government, and place profound hope in the abilities of technology to unleash individuals for lives of autonomous fulfillment. For the Amish, on the other hand, accountability to church and family limited individual choice, separation from the world entailed less-than-full participation in politics, and simplicity and modesty cautioned against always striving for bigger, better, and newer.

But if this posture placed one at odds with larger society, not all Amish agreed on what that meant for their church. Indeed, for some the promise and prospect of American culture was attractive, and they welcomed greater adaptation. They viewed change not as an exercise in wholesale assimilation, but as a necessary means of remaining relevant. After 1850 especially, tension between the push for change and the pull of tradition became acute.

The third quarter of the nineteenth century was a time of remarkable disagreement, dissension, and schism. While Amish churches across the continent were nominally united in 1850, twenty-five years later, controversy had produced permanent divisions. The events of those years remain visible today. Those who resisted the claims of American progressivism and modernization maintain a distinctive integration of faith and life that is still identifiable. Those who chose the path of adaptation eventually blended, for the most part, into larger American society.

While these years are critical for understanding Amish history, the debate and discussion that marked them can be difficult to describe. Part of that difficulty lies in the fact that no single Amish division took place during these years. Though there were key moments of conflict, the formation of competing parties worked its way out at different times in different places. A process of "sorting out," one historian has suggested, would be a better way to describe the alignment of churches into change-minded and tradition-minded camps. For example, the Amish in northern Indiana had broken into progressive-leaning and more tradition-guided factions by 1860, but the Ontario Amish did not split until the 1880s, and the church in Iowa divided only in the 1890s.[1]

Also important for understanding the debate within the Amish church after mid-century was the Amish idea of church order, or *Ordnung*.[2] *Ordnung* embodied the teachings and practices of the church, defined members' lifestyle and conduct, and served to unify the highly congregational Amish. Without a hierarchy or systematic, scholarly theology, it was the practical order of life—the ordinary application of faith in daily life—that held Amish churches together. The Amish *Ordnung* included general principles such as modesty and simplicity, and specific directives such as wearing certain patterns of plain clothes and avoiding costly, showy household furniture. *Ordnung* was not a written code or rulebook, but rather a traditional way of going about life, one that continued slowly to evolve over time and often allowed for gradual, considered change.[3]

During the mid-nineteenth century, though, the purpose and function of church order became unclear. For some Amish, church order was something with which to tamper only very carefully and cautiously. For others, *Ordnung* was a more dynamic principle that guided change and certainly did not prohibit innovation. For conservative-minded Amish, the *Ordnung* gave physical expression to biblical teachings and virtues. For the progressives, those teachings and virtues could be expressed in various ways in an ever-changing world; *Ordnung* simply embodied biblical ideals that guided change.

Different views of order and change ultimately led to a division in the Amish church. With a common *Ordnung* as the church's only organizational glue, disagreement on the purpose and use of *Ordnung* naturally led to fracture.[4]

Clouds of controversy gather

Around 1850, several issues surfaced in Amish communities in northern Indiana, eastern Ohio, and central Pennsylvania. Ripples of dissension in these places soon disturbed the shores of more placid communities, foreshadowing tensions that eventually would split the Amish world. Already in the late 1840s, trouble surfaced in northern Indiana, where Amish households had been living since 1841 after arriving from Ohio and Pennsylvania. Those who settled in eastern Elkhart County—many of whom had Ohio roots—seem to have been less conservative than most of those in neighboring LaGrange County—many of whom hailed from Pennsylvania. When the Elkhart-LaGrange church grew too large to meet comfortably in its members' homes, it separated into two county-defined church districts, and the factions became more distinct.[5]

Under the progressive leadership of bishops Isaac Schmucker and Jonas D. Troyer, the Elkhart County Amish took to wearing somewhat more stylish clothing, obtaining more schooling, and holding local public offices. Such practices were prime examples of a desire to adapt to their social surroundings. How better to be accepted as fellow citizens than to dress and work like one's neighbors and become involved in civic life?

To the more tradition-minded LaGrange Amish, such innovations smacked of compromise and an undermining of the Christian values of simplicity, humility, and

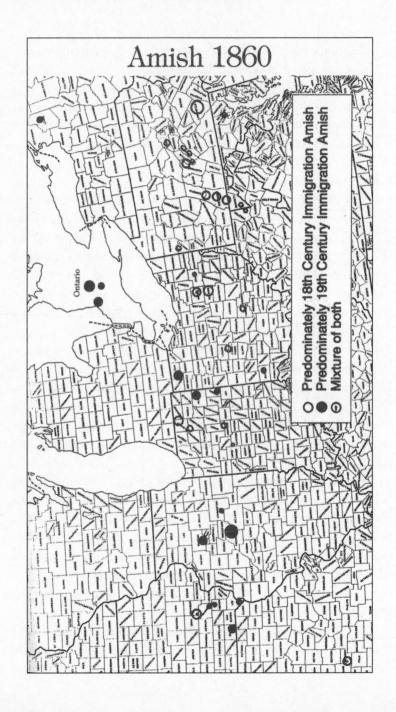

Amish 1860

Predominately 18th Century Immigration Amish
Predominately 19th Century Immigration Amish
Mixture of both

community decision-making. As conservative LaGrange County Amishman John E. "Hansi" Borntreger interpreted the events of the late 1840s, "Most of the church members were in harmony with their [conservative] ministers, but several preachers . . . and part of the church . . . had much to say in opposition, causing the faithful ones much concern and grief."[6] Borntreger believed that the liberals had drifted from their biblical foundation and "started a new church according to their own opinions."[7]

The differences in northern Indiana did not immediately produce schism. Both groups still recognized one another as Amish and hoped that the other would see its way to reconcile with the other. Even Borntreger occasionally attended the worship services of his more progressive Amish neighbors. Yet, in retrospect, the seeds of division had been planted. The differing perspectives obvious in each group could hardly be expected to disappear. To the change-minded Amish, selective innovation was a means of making the church relevant and appealing in a new and constantly changing world. For the Amish opposed to such adaptation, easy and individual change represented a lack of commitment and faith. Was not the church to be different from "the world" in its public life?

Controversies in Pennsylvania and Ohio mirrored the Indiana conflict. In the two eastern states the disagreement began over the proper mode of baptism. Some argued for baptism in a stream, while others held to a traditional baptismal rite performed as part of an indoor church service. Although those on both sides of the baptism issue eventually agreed to recognize either mode of baptism as legitimate, the division in those communities persisted, largely because the baptism dispute had been a surrogate for other issues and attitudes.

Those who championed stream baptism also tended toward a more progressive, innovative church life, while those who favored baptism among fellow church members in a home were more cautious about the church's attempts to catch up with and adapt to its surrounding culture. For example, Mifflin County stream-baptism advocate Shem Zook was also involved in politics, writing and publishing, and big business contacts with major railroad companies. Similarly, the Wayne County proponent of stream-baptism was bishop Jacob D. Yoder, who engaged in sometimes questionable business deals, raced mules, traded in horses, and held a unusual interpretation of the biblical story of Adam and Eve.[8]

Clearly, conservatives thought that they had something to worry about when change-minded Amish introduced new things. Even a new form of baptism—which the conservatives never rejected categorically—appeared to be merely the first step toward wholesale involvement in society and, in the case of bishop Yoder, even questionable doctrine. Tampering with *Ordnung* that regulated baptism had an unsettling effect on other practices. Stiff resistance to change on the part of some Amish grew out of a realization that people cannot easily make selective changes. Choosing to adapt in one area of life often leads to unforeseen and undesirable changes in other areas.

Even though the Indiana, Ohio, and Pennsylvania controversies of the 1850s did not result in outright breaks in fellowship between conservatives and progressives, the tension between the camps grew. While the change-minded and tradition-minded Amish recognized one another as Amish, they also recognized that it was becoming difficult to overlook the growing gap that stood between them. As Lancaster County's David Beiler observed in 1862, "The split appears to be becoming almost irreparable."[9] It was during this time of uncertainty and confusion that conservatives proposed an innovative idea.

Diener-Versammlungen

Two conservative-leaning bishops proposed that the church address knotty questions by assembling a continent-wide gathering of Amish leaders—a *Diener-Versammlung*, or ministers meeting—that would address conflicts roiling particular communities, as well as encourage a renewed sense of unity by reasserting the importance of practical *Ordnung*. Ideally, its tradition-minded proponents hoped, such a North American gathering would bring churches together around practical expressions of humility, simplicity, and peace.

Already in 1851, David Beiler had written to a fellow Holmes County, Ohio, bishop that Beiler had "often thought that a church-wide ministers' meeting" could be a blessing. Such a gathering would serve not only as a forum for discussion, but more importantly as a setting in which the whole church could "take the Word of God as the plumbline" and find unity.[10]

In the past, infrequent regional ministers' meetings in Europe and America had resolved disputes, and at times even issued written guidelines listing agreed-upon principles and practices.[11] Beiler believed a continental meeting held the same potential. Dissension and division might dry up if Amish from across the United States and Canada met to reaffirm common convictions. In the same vein, Holmes County bishop Frederick Hege also suggested that a general ministers' conference could settle local problems, such as those that had sprung up in his part of Ohio. Like Beiler, Hege was a tradition-minded man.[12]

A North American gathering was a novel solution to the problems facing mid-century Amish. No previous ministers gathering had ever been so comprehensive in scope. Nor had an assembly ever set out to address the broad question of the church's general direction and future. Yet while Amish conservatives initially floated the idea, it fell to a somewhat

The 1863 and 1868 Diener-Versammlungen were held in this Mifflin County, Pennsylvania barn owned by Christian B. and Rebecca (Zook) Peachey.

progressive Amish deacon—eastern Lancaster County's John Stoltzfus—to call the first conference. (Although Stoltzfus never broke with the tradition-minded camp while he lived in Pennsylvania, John and his wife, Catherine Holly, later moved to Tennessee where he allied himself with change-minded Amish.) On March 8, 1861, Stoltzfus issued an "Open Letter to Amish Church Leaders," in which he suggested that a continental conference of Amish leaders meet and "put together and achieve [an agreement] suitable to the peace and forbearance of the Gospel."[13]

Responding to Stoltzfus, a group of ministers proposed an initial meeting later that same year in Holmes County, Ohio, noting ruefully that, "It is now the case that in many places patience has grown cold, so much so that neglect and division have crept in."[14] For reasons that are no longer clear,

Rachel Zook (1837-1916), Israel Zook (1833-1919), and Phoebe Zook (1842-1917), children of well-known Amish layman Shem Zook. Rachel and Phoebe watched the proceedings of the 1863 Ministers' Meeting from the hayloft of the Christian Peachey barn.

the gathering did not take place until the following year and in a different location. In any case, these early letters implied that a continent-wide ministers meeting should become an annual event, and for almost seventeen years it was.

In June 1862, more than seventy Amish bishops, ministers, and deacons from settlements across six states convened in Wayne County, Ohio.[15] Scores of lay members—more than 400, according to deacon Stoltzfus—also attended the sessions but did not vote or directly participate in discussions. The number of attendees and observers was so large that the conference was held in the barn of Samuel and Lydia (Schmucker) Schrock. Many attendees arrived by train, taking advantage of the good network of rails in the northern United States.

From the start, it seems, the ministers conferences tended to favor a change-minded Amish agenda. Both the first year's moderator, bishop Jonathan Yoder from McLean County, Illinois, and assistant moderator, bishop John Esh of Juniata County, Pennsylvania, were well-known Amish progressives. The remarkable layman Shem Zook of Mifflin County, Pennsylvania, served as the first recording secretary. Not only did leaders affiliated with the progressive camp attend in greater numbers (about fifty of the seventy-two registrants could be considered change-minded), but conservative Holmes County bishop Levi Miller complained that not all the tradition-minded church districts had been properly informed of the meeting.[16] Miller's charge was not entirely true. Conservative David Beiler and other Lancaster County bishops and ministers, for instance, chose to stay away from the meeting. Although Beiler had originally suggested the ministers conference, he soon sensed that it might simply become a vehicle for bringing more change into the church, rather than creating a unified front against it.

The proceedings of the *Diener-Versammlungen* were fairly informal. Sessions opened with sermons, these being the highlight for many participants who normally had little opportunity to hear preachers from other states. Issues or problems brought to the conference received floor discussion and debate. Special committees took up important questions and formulated written responses that they then presented back to the larger group. The first two annual meetings used an informal consensus method to approve or reject committee findings, but by 1864, the ministers meeting was employing a system of majority voting.[17] Despite this formal mechanism for rendering decisions, Amish polity limited the conference's ability to enforce any decisions. Since Amish churches upheld congregational authority, local churches could ignore conference decisions with which they disagreed.[18]

The Amish ministers meetings of 1862, 1863, and 1864 were reasonably successful in restoring peace to tension-filled Amish communities in northern Indiana, Ohio, and central Pennsylvania. Several local conflicts seemed to move toward resolution—or so attendees thought at the time. Although the change-minded and traditional Amish within those settlements eventually went separate ways, immediately after 1862 there was optimism that the annual conferences might bring harmony to strained relations. The minutes from 1863, for example, reported "there is hope for healing."[19]

On the practical question of defining the roles of deacons and full deacons—an issue hotly debated in Logan and Champaign counties, Ohio, and in Mifflin County, Pennsylvania—the first ministers meetings laid out helpful guidelines.[20] Moreover, *Diener-Versammlungen* attendees were united in their appraisal of the liberal Hessian Amish of Butler County, Ohio. So long as the Hessians insisted on using worldly

The Diener-Versammlungen

The Amish *Diener-Versammlungen* (ministers meetings) met annually from 1862 until 1878 (except 1877). In addition to the registered bishops, ministers, and deacons, the gatherings annually drew up to 1,500 Amish laymen and women who came to hear visiting preachers or simply observe the proceedings. Full deacon (later bishop) Samuel Yoder of Mifflin County, Pennsylvania, was the only leader who attended every gathering.

The *Diener-Versammlung* was held in May or June, and, except for the 1864 meeting, all were held around Pentecost. Bishop Abner Yoder of Somerset County, Pennsylvania (later of Johnson County, Iowa) was the only moderator who eventually sided with the Old Order Amish. All other moderators chose the Amish Mennonite path.

	location	*moderator*	*registered attendance*
1862	Wayne Co., Ohio	Jonathan Yoder	72
1863	Mifflin Co., Pennsylvania	Abner Yoder	42
1864	Elkhart Co., Indiana	John K. Yoder	71
1865	Wayne Co., Ohio	unknown	89
1866	McLean Co., Illinois	Samuel Yoder	75
1867	Logan Co., Ohio	Elias Riehl	42
1868	Mifflin Co., Pennsylvania	John K. Yoder	34
1869	Holmes Co., Ohio	Samuel Yoder	27
1870	Fulton Co., Ohio	John P. King	40
1871	Livingston Co., Illinois	Samuel Yoder	56
1872	LaGrange Co., Indiana	John P. King	56
1873	Wayne Co., Ohio	Samuel Yoder	41
1874	Washington Co., Iowa	John K. Yoder	28
1875	Tazewell Co., Illinois	John P. King	38
1876	Fulton Co., Ohio	Samuel Yoder	30
1877	*not held*		
1878	Woodford Co., Illinois	John K. Yoder	43

musical instruments, other Amish—traditionalists and progressives alike—could not hold them in close fellowship
or participate in ordaining new leaders for their church.[21]
Neither would ministers conference participants approve of
joining state militias, holding membership in secret societies
such as the Masonic Lodge, or posing for photographs, since
picture-taking was a sure sign of vanity and pride that some
ministers suggested might even be a form of graven images
prohibited by the Ten Commandments.[22]

Despite the firm line that the annual meetings drew with
the Hessians and with regard to some other expressions of
popular culture, many conservatives were disappointed in
the tone and outcome of conference discussions and committee reports. On the question of social shunning, long a New
Testament practice in Amish churches, some ministers meeting resolutions and committee reports seemed to waffle.[23]
The conferences also refused to forbid political participation.[24] Moreover, the suggested way to bring peace in most
disagreements was to ask conservatives to be more tolerant.

"It seems to me that each was allowed to have his own
opinion," David Beiler concluded after hearing reports of the
early conferences. Beiler believed that the peace achieved
by the ministers conferences was really "a conciliatory spirit
without coming to the point which was and is the real reason for the differing views." The annual meetings addressed
surface symptoms but not deeper disagreements about the
Ordnung. "If we wish to destroy a weed," Beiler said, drawing on agricultural imagery, "we must pull it up by the roots;
otherwise it will just keep growing." Certainly "if the causes
of offense are not put away, then, according to my opinion,
no real unity can be restored."[25]

A breach in 1865

Although the ministers meetings had been convened to restore harmony between conservatives and progressives, tension between these wings of the Amish church seemed to build, not lessen, in the wake of the early gatherings. With the change-minded group in control of the national forum, conservatives felt ignored by the *Diener-Versammlungen* which they had begun attending in good faith. In 1864, a group of tradition-minded Amish leaders met in Lancaster County to try its hand at resolving the tensions in nearby Mifflin County churches. That gathering fared no better than the national conference, but it did demonstrate that conservatives were keen to work together in addressing church conflicts and were not ignoring the problems at hand.[26]

Tradition-minded Amish were especially disturbed by circumstances surrounding the 1864 national meeting. The gathering rendered a decision on disagreement between northern Indiana conservatives and progressives before all the tradition-minded leaders from Ohio had arrived.[27] Conservatives felt snubbed.

In response, tradition-minded Amish leaders made a final and rather bold attempt the next year to put their views before the Amish church at large. The 1865 ministers meeting was to gather in Wayne County, Ohio, home to a sizable progressive Amish community. Just to the south, in Holmes County, most of the Amish were of a more tradition-minded stripe. Several days before the start of the official *Diener-Versammlung*, thirty-four conservative-leaning leaders from Ohio, Indiana, Ontario, and western Pennsylvania assembled in Holmes County. They drew up a document affirming a traditional *Ordnung* and including specific examples and practices that they believed marked a faithfully humble church. The Holmes County statement served as a manifesto of the tradition-minded Amish position, and conservatives took a firm stand against all that they believed to be "destructive to our salvation and contrary to God's Word."[28]

The church's call in a self-indulgent culture was clear, the conservatives insisted. Among other things, members needed to separate themselves from worldly carnivals, the pride and wasted expense of "speckled, striped, flowered, clothing," and from "unnecessary, grand, household furnishings" and "pompous carriages." Such things "serve to express pomp and pride" and "lead away from God." Activities that unraveled the fabric of community, introduced inequality, or stymied the practice of mutual aid, such as commercial property insurance or operating large-scale businesses "according to the ways of the world," were taboo. Conservatives also addressed church practices, warning against lax discipline and the singing of catchy, popular hymns with spiritually shallow lyrics.[29]

There was no doubting the purpose of the statement. It defined the terms under which the tradition-minded Amish were willing to work. "[A]ll those who affirm such with us and demonstrate with works and deeds," the authors announced, "we are willing to recognize as brothers and sisters and resume fellowship with them." Though blunt and specific, the document ended on a note of grace and invitation. Spiritual renewal—not a list of prescribed practices—was what conservatives intended their call for separation from sin to inspire. Thus, the writers concluded, "the gate is portrayed for us as straight and the way as narrow, but it is not therefore ever closed, but stands open for all repentant souls, and as the Savior says in Luke 14:33, 'Whoever does not forsake all that he has cannot be my disciple.'"[30]

With their position in hand, nearly all of the thirty-four signatories headed north to the 1865 annual meeting in Wayne County. The conference registered the highest atten-

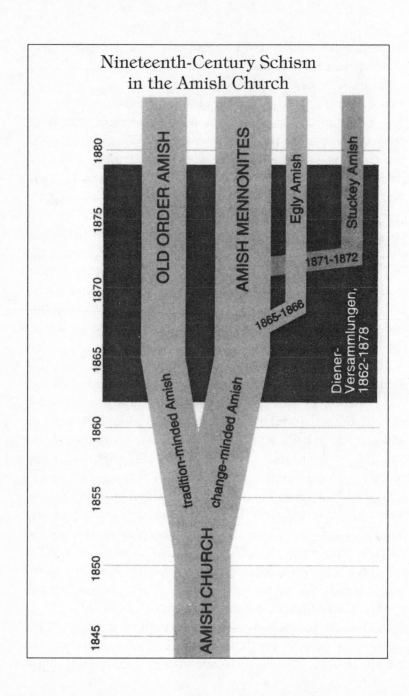

Nineteenth-Century Schism in the Amish Church

dance of any with eighty-nine leaders present. About forty percent of those assembled were tradition-minded Amish, the most significant representation they would ever achieve. Curiously, the printed minutes of the 1865 meeting are the sketchiest of any of the proceedings, so it is difficult to reconstruct the exact order of events. Apparently the ministers meeting acknowledged the conservatives' paper near the end of its business session but did little with it. Although no formal response survives from those who presented the Holmes County manifesto, it appears they were bitterly disappointed with the reception they received at the national meeting.[31] After 1865, only a handful of conservative Amish leaders ever attended another annual conference. Ignored out of their church, the traditionalists withdrew from the activities of an Amish majority increasingly comfortable with change.

Symbolically, the year 1865 stood as a point of public separation between change-minded and tradition-minded Amish. No single schism split the church all at once on that date. Indeed, in some places the informal process by which churches sorted their affiliation stretched over many years and was not especially rancorous. For example, conservative-leaning and progressive-minded Amish in Ontario and some parts of Iowa remained largely united until the 1880s and 1890s. Only then did the differences between the two camps become gulfs large enough to divide the churches. In 1877, division came to the Lancaster County, Pennsylvania, Amish settlement, but most of the members sided with the conservatives.[32] In central Illinois, nearly the opposite situation transpired: all the Amish congregations there chose the course of change.

The conservatives called themselves "Old Amish" but because they had defined their concerns in terms of a traditional understanding of *Ordnung* ("order"), outsiders eventually labeled them "Old Order Amish."[33] Meanwhile,

many in the change-minded group had been constructing closer relations with neighboring Mennonites, many of
whom had an affinity for the Amish progressives. As a result,
the Amish majority coming out of the *Diener-Versammlungen*
embraced the designation "Amish Mennonite." While these
labels were not immediately or universally recognized, after
the 1865 ministers meeting, the terms "Old Order Amish"
and "Amish Mennonite" accurately pointed to two paths that
Amish churches were choosing in their interaction with the
wider world.

Later ministers meetings

Twelve more national gatherings followed the 1865 meeting, and, except for 1877, they were annual affairs. During
these later years, attendance of registered bishops, ministers,
and deacons varied from seventy-five to twenty-seven, though
the assemblies also continued to draw large crowds of lay
members eager to hear the preaching by visiting ministers.
After 1865, however, the nature of the conferences changed
in a significant way.

The ministers meetings had begun as mass consultations
aimed at bringing unity and a sense of common purpose to
the Amish. With the exit of the conservative wing of the
church after 1865, the gatherings took on a more formal,
deliberative—perhaps even legislative—flavor. Rules of order
came into play, and references to precedents established
in past proceedings became more common.[34] In 1867, for
example, the conference "decided that all proceedings of former meetings which were brought to a conclusion remain
in force." Moreover, "no minister who is a member of the
meeting shall have the right to make any changes afterward."[35]
The Amish Mennonites still addressed issues on a case-
by-case basis, but they did so in a more formal way.

Excerpts from the Proceedings of the Amish

Diener-Versammlungen

1863: "Should likeness [photographs] be permitted?" [Answer:] "It was decided almost unanimously that they [the delegates] want to reject this thing [photography]."

1866: "May a person who, for the sake of worldly income, produces intoxicating beverages . . . be considered a useful member of the congregation?" [Answer:] "It was looked upon as improper, and would not throw a good light on the church. We would do much better to stay far away from it and stay away from such drinking places and rather to avoid such and avert the bad consequences which follow. For at such places chains, nets, and snares are set up in order to catch innocent souls."

1867: May church members contribute to the building of Civil War monuments "which cost thousands of dollars, and benefit neither the dead nor the living, and lead only to idolatry"? [Answer:] "There are always poor and needy among us to whom we can be helpful and in that way make better use of that which we have."

1868: "We declare service in the army to be contrary to the Gospel . . . [It] must be forsaken with true penitence and sorrow, and also by leaving off and renouncing everything connected with it . . . [including] pensions. . . . [I]f there is need, it is the duty of the church to support the poor ...."

1870: On frequenting "shows" and "fairs": "It was shown clearly, and with power that, according to God's Word, to frequent such places . . . would give an evil appearance and that, according to the words of Jesus, one cannot let his light shine to good works if he takes part in and supports them. . . . In fact, these [amusements] might be compared to the fair or vanity fair in the City of Vanity, described by John Bunyan [in his book *Pilgrim's Progress*]. . . . All were therefore admonished to avoid all such evil appearance."

1875: "According to God's Word is it right for a brother to . . . borrow money on low interest and then loan it out again with high interest?" [Answer:] "We consider it to be unjust."

Excerpted from Paton Yoder and Steven R. Estes, trans. and eds., *Proceedings of the Amish Ministers' Meetings, 1862-1878* (Goshen, Ind.: Mennonite Historical Society, 1999).

The Old Orders, in contrast, had outlined a clear set of explicit prohibitions and expectations in 1865, but they handled the application of their *Ordnung* in the more informal and personal setting of local congregations. For its part, the Amish Mennonite pattern was taking its cues from the values and methods of larger society that championed bureaucracy and prized formal, large-scale systems of authority. Amish Mennonites were combining a more tolerant attitude toward individual conduct with a more rigid vision of structure and organization. While they neither surrendered church discipline entirely nor established elaborate denominational hierarchies, the progressive Amish Mennonites had clearly moved farther in that direction than had the Old Order Amish, who maintained a tradition-guided, but informally managed, church life.

Change-minded Amish Mennonites did not embrace every aspect of American national life. In the wake of the Civil War, should nonresistant Christians contribute toward

---

Too Much Money in the Offering?

In order to cover conference expenses, the later Amish Mennonite ministers meetings collected donations from attendees. In 1873, the person charged with counting the contributions was surprised by the size of one donation. Several months later, Amish Mennonite leaders ran the following advertisement in the Mennonite periodical *Herald of Truth,* which many Amish Mennonites read:

"Notice.—At the collection taken at the Amish Conference held this year, near Orrville, [Wayne County] Ohio, a twenty dollar bill was thrown in. Bro. Jacob King, who received it thinks the giver probably made a mistake. If so it will be returned to the claimant giving satisfactory evidence that he was the giver."

From *Herald of Truth* 10 (September 1873): 152.

---

the building of war monuments and memorials? The 1867 *Diener-Versammlung* said no.[36] The next year, the Amish Mennonite gathering responded to inquiries for church membership from a veteran who was receiving a government pension. The ministers meeting decided that the applicant could become a church member only if he broke all ties with the military, including his pension, and the church was to provide for him if he was disabled.[37] And what of Grange membership? The Grange was a popular Midwestern-based farmers' union that fought for rural rights and promoted social recreation in farm communities. Given its potential to replace the church as one's primary community and source of identity, Amish Mennonites rejected Grange membership.[38]

The ministers conferences continued to address issues specific to the Amish church, as well, such as modesty in dress and the extent to which members could grow wealthy by patenting inventions.[39] Moderation and gentle tolerance generally guided answers to such queries. Yet things did not always run smoothly for the change-minded Amish Mennonites. After 1865, even without Old Order voices present to offer dissenting opinions and alternative answers, unity remained elusive for progressives.

Division among the Amish Mennonites

It soon became clear that the problems and conflicts in the Amish church had not resulted simply from the presence of protesting conservative-minded folks. Indeed, nearly as soon as the Old Orders opted out of the national forum, change-minded Amish Mennonites who remained engaged in the annual gatherings began to disagree among themselves over what type of changes they should embrace. In the absence of conservative sentiments, change-minded leaders were free to press each other on just how much change each had in mind.

One division among Amish Mennonites occurred already in 1865 and involved the teaching of a European-born, renewal-minded bishop named Henry Egly who lived in Adams County, Indiana.[40] Sometime in the 1840s, while suffering a lengthy illness, Egly experienced a powerful spiritual awakening. The force of Egly's personal conversion convinced him that his was an experience God desired everyone to have.

After his 1854 ordination as a preacher (he had been a deacon since 1850), Egly's sermons highlighted the importance of each individual having a highly personal, experiential encounter with God as a prerequisite to forgiveness and salvation. Only those who could testify to such an experience could be baptized, Egly said. Egly was also critical of the spiritual tone of some Amish congregations. It seemed to Egly that some people were placing too much spiritual stock in their parentage or church attendance. But, he asked, was not baptism without true conversion the same as infant baptism that the Anabaptists had rejected long ago?[41]

To some Amish, Egly's teaching was another version of Protestant revivalism that stressed emotionalism and ignored biblical injunctions for obedience. And if overstated, some feared, Egly's emphasis on experiential conversion weakened similarly important teachings on discipleship. Salvation by grace through faith was a fundamental Amish teaching, but would an inordinate preoccupation with the process of becoming a Christian detract from an emphasis on what being a

Bishop Joseph Stuckey (1826-1902) of Danvers, Illinois.

Christian meant? Although the larger Amish church did not dismiss Egly's personal testimony, nor deny that he may have had a close encounter with God while ill, they did resist his teaching that everyone should come to faith in the same way that he did.

About half of Egly's congregation heartily endorsed his leadership, to the chagrin of the rest. In January 1858, the congregation called on three Amish leaders from Holmes County, Ohio, to mediate the tension between Egly and his local church district. Instead of chiding Egly, as some in the congregation had hoped would happen, the Ohio delegation ordained Egly a bishop![42] Thereafter tension increased, since Egly, as a bishop, now oversaw baptisms and refused to baptize those whom he felt had not experienced a proper conversion. Some of those he rejected protested that he was not taking their claims of Christian faith seriously. In response, Egly argued that baptism without proper conversion was no baptism at all, and he even offered to re-baptize those who subsequently experienced dramatic encounters with God's grace.[43]

By the spring of 1865, conflict in the congregation peaked. Egly refused to discipline a certain church member because, Egly said, she was not really a church member in the first place because she had not been baptized in "the knowledge of godly repentance" as he understood it.[44] Egly's ideas were receiving a hearing outside of Adams County, too, especially in communities in Ohio, Illinois, and Indiana where immigrant family networks tied Amish to supporters in Egly's church.[45] To these sympathizers, Egly was a true reformer. While the ministers meeting of 1865 tried to address some of Egly's concerns, the gathered ministers seemed to be tired of his criticism of them.[46]

That fall, Egly's own congregation was so divided they could not hold their semiannual communion service, and the situation degenerated into a stubborn stalemate.[47] The next year, Egly met with supportive Amish throughout the

Midwest, forming a loose network of like-minded church districts, popularly labeled "Egly Amish." While Egly continued to stay abreast of events in the Amish Mennonite world, he never attended another annual ministers conference. Nor did other Amish Mennonites show much interest in interacting with the Egly Amish. Both sides seem quietly to have agreed to go their separate ways.[48]

The dynamics behind the so-called "Egly division" were complex. Much of what Egly stressed was quite traditional. He defended decidedly conservative dress standards, apparently refused to join the Union army when drafted during the Civil War, and for many years the churches under his leadership worshiped only in the German language.[49] Yet Egly also mixed popular American evangelical sentiments with his Amish tradition. As a church leader, he exercised considerable personal authority over his congregation, downplayed congregational decision-making, and demanded individual experiential conversion of a particular type—all common traits among evangelicals of the day. Additionally, Egly was open to popular social reform movements such as alcohol temperance. Egly's mixture of Amish traditions, American evangelicalism, and popular reformism blended to form a distinct spirituality that appealed to some Amish Mennonites searching for a personal faith in a strange land.

That some Amish found Egly's brand of Christianity attractive illustrates the diversity among the change-minded Amish population. Even if they were relatively open to the winds of popular culture blowing across the North American landscape, different breezes caught the attention of different churches and individuals. For some, change had meant meetinghouses, Sunday schools, and wider latitude in expressing individual wealth and status. For others, change meant reorienting one's religious world to include emphases from American evangelicalism and social reform. Fresh winds bearing the American

Farmer Peter Short (1826-1904) hosted the 1876 Ministers' Meeting in his Fulton County, Ohio, barn.

virtues of tolerance and broad-mindedness could split the Amish Mennonite ministers meetings, too.

Joseph Stuckey

In 1872, a second division transpired within Amish Mennonite ranks. Again, specific doctrinal differences were involved, but the debate centered on the nature of the church, the role of community, and the autonomy of individuals. The person around whom controversy swirled was McLean County, Illinois, bishop Joseph Stuckey.[50] The popular and respected Stuckey had been ordained a minister in 1860 and a bishop four years later. Stuckey was typical of the progressive Amish church leaders in central Illinois. While Old Order appraisals of Stuckey would have characterized him as liberal, he was in certain ways cautious about change. He was cool to portrait photography and at least initially expressed caution about Sunday schools, wondering if they were unnecessary innovations.[51]

Yet clearly Stuckey stood with the change-minded Amish Mennonites. Dress standards in Stuckey's Rock Creek (later named North Danvers) congregation were matters of individual discernment, and members took their grooming cues from store windows more than from traditional understandings of adornment and cautions against pride. Some of the Rock Creek Amish men wore buttons on their coats, styled their hair, and sported neckties. Change was not limited to attire. The Rock Creek Amish used their old Reformation-era *Ausbund* hymnal less and less often, and one family loaned an organ to accompany the singing in a community Sunday school (held in a local schoolhouse) to which many of the families sent their children.[52]

Specific tensions, though, surfaced around Stuckey's practice of allowing Amish who had been disciplined in other churches to join the more tolerant congregations under his oversight without first asking those individuals to make amends with their home churches. In so doing, fellow change-minded ministers charged, Stucky was undercutting neighboring Amish Mennonite churches. Traditionally, Amish leaders had acknowledged the discipline of other congregations, even if those groups' standards differed from their own. This pattern of reciprocal respect was central to the Amish balance of local congregationalism with a broader sense of unity. Stuckey's action might open the door to a consumer approach to church membership, whereby those not liking what they found in one church would simply shop for a group that matched their tastes.[53]

The specific event that sparked a break between Stuckey and other Amish Mennonites centered on schoolteacher and poet Joseph Joder. A member of Stuckey's church, Joder had studied Latin, Greek, and Hebrew, and otherwise cut a rather unusual profile as a nineteenth-century Amishman.[54] One of the peculiar features of Joder's theology was his belief in universalism, the conviction that all people, no matter how they live their lives, will share equally in eternal salvation. There is no place for hell or future consequences for evil in the universalist scheme of thought, and heaven is the destination of all humankind.

Forms of universalist thought have been present throughout church history, though the Christian tradition generally regarded universalism as unorthodox. In the mid-nineteenth century, however, universalism was a relatively popular religious teaching in America, where it seemed to comport well with national affirmations of liberty, equality, and democracy.

Universalist circuit riders spread the teaching throughout the Midwestern United States and founded Universalist churches. By 1850, there were large Universalist congregations in the Illinois cities of Peoria and Champaign. Perhaps Joder learned of the doctrine through these churches, through universalist publications, or through his own private Bible study. Even before Joder's case captured Amish Mennonite attention, universalism had raised Amish eyebrows as Illinois preacher Daniel Holly left his ministry among the Putnam County Amish and joined the Universalists. Nearby, in the late 1850s, Amish lay member Moses Ropp was excommunicated for his universalist views.[55]

Amish schoolteacher Joseph Joder (1797-1887), McLean County, Illinois. Joder's universalism caused a stir among the Amish Mennonites.

Joseph Joder's Controversial Poem

Amish schoolteacher Joseph Joder caused a sensation with his poem *"Die Frohe Botschaft"* (Glad Tidings). Written in German in 1869, the lines of verse drew criticism from many quarters of the Amish Mennonite church. Joder's opponents claimed that the poem advocated *universalism* (a rejection of belief in hell or punishment for the wicked).

The poem was on the whole an affirmation of the Christian doctrine of salvation by grace through faith alone. Interspersed with traditional orthodoxy were several stanzas that supported a universalist perspective. Controversial portions included these lines:

Stanza 2: "Such teachings/As we frequently hear/Of eternal torment in hell/Cannot possibly be the truth:/ They deny God's goodness/And make His spirit harsh."

Stanza 15: "It is not at all reasonable [to believe]/That in the future the torment of hell/Should last forever./ Only insanity can so delude us/As to believe or hear/ What God's word does not teach."

Stanza 16: "It [the idea of eternal punishment for the wicked] is pure fable,/A heathen suggestion;/Lack of understanding honors only/The darkness in the corner;/ Sectarian presumption/Builds up hatred and quarreling."

Stanza 26: "Love flows forth from God/And works its way into the whole of creation,/Makes everything like unto itself,/Until the whole earth/Shall become one universe,/A Heavenly Kingdom of Peace."

When Joder's bishop, Joseph Stuckey, did not discipline Joder quickly enough for promoting these universalist beliefs, other Amish Mennonites censured Stuckey.

Translated by Jennie A. Whitten and published in Steven R. Estes, *A Goodly Heritage: A History of the North Danvers Mennonite Church* (Danvers, Ill.: North Danvers Mennonite Church, 1982), 296-300.

Joder's writing, however, became the celebrated confrontation between the Amish church and universalism. Joder had written several poems that could be interpreted as defenses of universalism, but he had penned them in English, and they attracted little Amish attention. In 1869, though, Joder authored twenty-six stanzas of verse under the title "Die Frohe Botschaft" *(Glad Tidings)*. This new poem was both in German and more explicitly universalist. It did not escape the notice of Amish leaders.[56]

Copies of the poem showed up at the 1872 ministers meeting. Since some fellow ministers long had been suspicious of what they considered Stuckey's lax discipline, the assembly that year decided that the public presence of universalism in Stuckey's congregation demanded direct attention.[57] Several months later, a delegation of three Amish Mennonite leaders visited Stuckey and asked him why he considered Joseph Joder a member of the church when Joder's heretical views were so widely known. Stuckey admitted that his church had not excommunicated Joder, nor was he yet ready to do so. Stuckey's statements could have been interpreted to mean that he agreed with Joder—although Stuckey later denied this. At that point, the delegation withdrew fellowship from Joseph Stuckey and the Illinois congregations that supported him.[58]

Stuckey might have argued that in the congregationally-structured Amish church, he could not single-handedly excommunicate anyone without the support of the congregation, and the congregation wanted to exercise more patience with Joder. Eventually, in 1873, Stuckey and his church did refuse to allow Joder to join them in communion, but only after they found Joder incorrigible.[59] Joseph Stuckey represented a fairly tolerant approach to church administration. Patience was important for Stuckey and the Amish who looked to him for leadership.

At several previous ministers meetings, Stuckey had posed questions that seemed to imply he was unsure whether strict discipline really brought people to repentance. Only God could turn unbelief and disobedience around, he seemed to have said in 1867. The church's role must be patient and loving, waiting for God to work instead of jumping to excommunication and shunning. Rather than bringing erring members back to the church, strict discipline might drive some people further away.[60]

Stuckey was not alone in his approach to church discipline. Several other Illinois congregations allied themselves with Stuckey and collectively became known as the Stuckey Amish. Stuckey also maintained some informal contact with several relatively liberal Amish congregations that remained independent of the larger Amish Mennonite movement represented by the *Diener-Versammlungen*. These more liberal churches included two in Iowa under the leadership of immigrant bishop Benjamin Eicher and preacher Philip Roulet, and two churches in Butler County, Ohio.

In one sense the "Stuckey Amish" represented the limits of change-minded Amish Mennonite tolerance. While rejecting the Old Order option, most Amish Mennonites were not willing to accept the sort of individual latitude that Joseph Stuckey allowed. By the late 1870s, the Amish Mennonite majority saw itself somewhere between the Old Orders on one hand, and the Egly evangelicals and the Stuckey progressives on the other.

An Amish Mennonite future

In 1878, Woodford County, Illinois, hosted what would prove to be the last Amish Mennonite ministers meeting. Since about 1870, the meetings had given more time to sermons and less to church business and controversy. If fewer heated debates remained after the exit of the Old Orders, Egly's followers, and the Stuckey faction, the issue that became more important was the future implications of the annual meetings themselves. What was the purpose of the *Diener-Versammlungen* now that permanent division, instead of unity, had been their result? Should the ministers meetings be discontinued? Should they become a deliberative body to govern Amish Mennonite churches? At the final 1878 gathering, a committee charged with strengthening the work of the assemblies proposed a plan to organize Amish Mennonites into a denomination.[61]

Under the committee's provisions, congregations would operate autonomously, but if ensnared in situations that eluded peaceful resolution, they would be required to bring the matter to a regional meeting of Amish Mennonite leaders. Should that group prove unable to address the local problem successfully, the matter would then come before the annual meeting for North America, and decisions rendered by that body would be final. Such a rational, bureaucratic approach to church government was too much even for change-minded Amish Mennonites open to innovative ideas popular in mainstream society. The three-tiered system of appeal and review seemed more like the polity practiced by mainline Protestants.

Instead of implementing a new national church structure, the annual *Diener-Versammlungen* simply came to an end. Documentation surrounding the gatherings' demise has not survived, but historian Paton Yoder suggested that a personal falling-out between two conference leaders, bishop John K. Yoder of Wayne County, Ohio, and full deacon John P. King of Ohio's Logan County, may have contributed to the fact that no one took the initiative to convene another gathering after 1878.[62] With the leadership of Yoder and King divided, an important piece of the vision that had sustained the yearly schedule was lacking.[63]

But perhaps, too, the meetings ended because they no longer served a purpose. After all, the conferences were originally supposed to settle local disturbances and unify the church. The church had found unity—or rather unities—by dividing into several factions, each of which sought renewal through different means. As the ministers meetings ended, the Amish church was more divided than either conservatives or progressives had contemplated seventeen years earlier when all sides had gathered to find common ground.[64]

In the midst of nineteenth-century social and cultural change, Amish churches across North America had sought renewal. Renewal came, but in multiple and not always compatible ways. The Old Order Amish looked for spiritual renewal through a restored commitment to discipleship guided by a common *Ordnung*. The Egly churches found renewal through a highly personal spirituality, while the Stuckey people embraced Christian broad-mindedness. The turbulent years of the *Diener-Versammlungen* produced several Amish churches—each fairly united, but not with one another. In the decades that followed, the gap between the groups widened as the Old Order Amish continued to maintain a life and faith whose implications made them easily recognizable, while their progressive Amish Mennonite cousins moved toward the American mainstream.

—8—

Merging Traditions: Amish Mennonites and Mennonites in North America and Europe, 1870-1937

> *"We are willing to join hand in hand."*
> —Mennonites and Amish Mennonites in Antrim
> County, Michigan, 1886

Committed to cooperation

"On Sunday Sept. 17th, we met at the house of Joel Detweiler and organized a German Sabbath-school under the auspices of the Omish [sic] Mennonite Church . . . . By the grace of God we hope to derive such spiritual blessings therefrom as will enable us to grow in grace."[1] The news came from an Amish Mennonite community in Knox County, Tennessee, organized just a few months earlier by deacon "Tennessee John" Stoltzfus. The group had lost no time in starting a Sunday school and announced its launch in a Mennonite-published, English-language periodical, *Herald of Truth*.

It was hardly coincidental that Amish Sunday school news appeared in a Mennonite magazine. The article, and others like it in the pages of the *Herald*, pointed to continued promotion among change-minded Amish Mennonites of progressive initiatives such as Sunday schools and to closer ties with Mennonites.[2] Indeed, in the following years such connections would increase substantially. During the early part of the twentieth century, most North American Amish Mennonites would give up their public Amish identity and formally merge with the Mennonites who published the *Herald*. The Sunday school article from Tennessee portended changes to come.

Amish Mennonites were a growing, dynamic group in the later 1800s. As the annual *Diener-Versammlungen* came to an end in 1878, the number of Amish identifying with the Amish Mennonite wing of the movement was still ticking upward. Into the 1880s and 1890s, especially in Ontario, parts of Pennsylvania, and Iowa, the process of sorting affiliations continued, and more congregations chose the Amish Mennonite path.[3] In addition, some change-minded members of conservative churches quietly left for neighboring Amish Mennonite ones. Excommunication and shunning did not always follow such moves.

In the late nineteenth century, there seems to have been a measure of mutual recognition on the part of both the Old Orders and their progressive cousins. Until about 1896, for example, in southeastern Pennsylvania's Conestoga Amish community, shunning was not practiced in cases where individuals left the Old Order group for the more liberal church. Joining the Amish Mennonites may have been frowned upon. But it was tolerated as something of an ecclesial "release valve" for Amish who found Old Order discipline too confining, yet wanted to remain a part of broader Amish community affairs.[4]

Three generations of Amish Mennonite women, Wayne County, Ohio: Mary Conrad Smiley (1825-1912), Elizabeth Smiley Ramseyer (1853-1928), and Clara Ramseyer Miller (1885-1918), holding her son Lloyd (1907-1995). Note the progressive change in dress styles.

Some people ended up in the Amish Mennonite camp for familial reasons. John Lais was a German immigrant and a Roman Catholic who worked as a hired hand on an Indiana Amish farm. Attracted to his employers' faith, Lais wanted to join the Old Order church, but his wife, Susannah (Plank) Lais, did not. Susannah was of Amish background herself and was disenchanted by what she perceived to be Old Order legalism. The Laises joined the Amish Mennonites and moved with fellow church members to Oregon's Willamette Valley.[5]

By century's end, Amish Mennonite churches were spread across the continent. Not only did older settlements in Pennsylvania, Ohio, Ontario, and Indiana include progressive Amish Mennonites, but almost all of the Illinois and many of the Iowa Amish were of the change-minded variety.

So too were many younger Amish settlements in Arkansas, Colorado, Kansas, Missouri, Nebraska, Oklahoma, Oregon, and Tennessee.

Untethered from their Old Order cousins, Amish Mennonites often hastened their pace of change. Naturally there was some variation from place to place, but several notable trends emerged across the late nineteenth-century Amish Mennonite landscape. Members were acculturating, attracted to mainstream American ideals and habits. Less traditional clothing styles, the use of English instead of German in family conversations, and the adoption of popular pastimes were several measures of Amish Mennonite movement toward fuller participation in the privileges of surrounding culture.

Mahala Yoder, a McLean County, Illinois Amish Mennonite woman in her twenties, kept a diary during the 1870s that was filled with observations of life around her home community.[6] While her family affiliated with the decidedly progressive Joseph Stuckey congregation, some of Yoder's comments reflected attitudes common to Amish Mennonites elsewhere, especially of her generation. Mahala confided her disappointment in what she saw as her parents' old-fashioned attitudes. Her father bought "the very plainest wooden" chairs for their home, when Mahala had hoped for fancy new cane-bottoms. And her stepmother gave "the girls so little liberty to visit their friends," that Mahala felt sad for her sisters. Despite the somewhat traditional inclinations of the Yoder parents, the household was rearing a rather different second generation.

The luxuries of an industrial society were becoming common for the Yoder young folks. For her twenty-first birthday Mahala received carpeting for her bedroom. Her room looked so much better, she thought. It needed "only a table and pictures" to be complete. Her sister Mary went to town some weeks later and—with the knowledge of their stepmother—chose new spring hats. "She got white straw hats," Mahala observed, "trimmed with blue ribbons and a pretty red rose."

Recreation, too, was changing. The Yoder family now played what Mahala called "a new game"—the card "game of Authors." And they read *Scribner's* magazine. Although Mahala was kept from traveling much because of a physical disability, her siblings and friends went to town to see "Barnum's [Circus] Show" and an orchestra in Bloomington. Stepsister Magdalena even found a social outlet in political party politics. Around election day 1876 she spent "all afternoon . . . doing up her white dress and making a cap and sash." The next day she was going to a Republican "mass meeting at Bloomington" as part of a delegation of "twenty-nine girls in uniform to represent the states of the Union."

Mahala was usually able to make it to church, and her comments on its services also reveal evolving Amish Mennonite attitudes. Not much longer would congregations be satisfied with preachers who stumbled through traditional sermons or spoke extemporaneously. Mahala strongly approved when a visiting preacher addressed the Stuckey congregation using "pure, rich German . . . which did one's soul good to hear." Proper German or standard English were fine by Mahala, but not the "horrid 'Pennsylvania Dutch'" dialect that she detested as uncouth. Ethnic dialects only detracted from worship. She believed that her "church-going" did her "more good because the sermon was delivered in simple, correct language."

To Mahala's way of thinking, "The beautiful goes with the good and true, always, in God's method." Beyond proper sermons, Yoder found theological insight from reading contemporary novels—one of which she found "as helpful and encouraging and suggestive as so many chapters of the Bible." She wondered why some Amish Mennonites were "ashamed

Amish Mennonites Daniel Graber (1858-1930) and Fanny Conrad Graber (1871-1943) of Wayland, Iowa, about 1890. Daniel served as minister in the Sugar Creek Amish Mennonite Church for 37 years and preferred preaching in German.

to read a good novel." But her wonderment revealed how removed Mahala's generation was from traditional Amish understandings that viewed secular entertainment as frivolous, wasteful, and perhaps even dangerous.

Ripples of reservation

Central Illinois was not the only place where Amish Mennonites were becoming more acclimated to the goings-on of larger society. Near Johnstown, Pennsylvania, Amish Mennonite Isaac Kaufman involved himself in financing toll roads, Johnstown's First National Bank, and various federal bond programs. As an important local financier, Kaufman's portrait hung in the lobby of the Johnstown bank. His heirs received $246,000 from their money-wise forebear.[7] And in eastern Pennsylvania, the Conestoga Amish Mennonite congregation had a bishop, John P. Mast, who served as a local bank director and successful miller.[8]

While such commercially successful financial activity was remarkable even for Amish Mennonites, it illustrates the general acceptability of upward mobility among church members. In the early nineteenth century, a number of Amish had engaged in business and politics or had purchased the latest in household furnishings. But then there had been some resistance to doing so and even an Old Order reaction against it. Since 1865, Amish Mennonite circles included fewer voices willing to speak a word of caution. In 1889, the Oak Grove Amish Mennonite congregation in Ohio's Wayne County granted seven lay members the privilege of drawing up a new, more relaxed church discipline.[9]

In their later years, some of the older, first generation Amish Mennonite leaders became alarmed that change had come so quickly to their congregations. The rapid pace of innovation among the next generations of Amish Mennonites unnerved old *Diener-Versammlungen* promoters "Tennessee

John" Stoltzfus and John P. King.[10] Leaders like Stoltzfus and King had envisioned a church guided by moderate progressive philosophy, not widespread loss of Amish Mennonite values. Nevertheless, as the nineteenth century's last decades closed, Amish Mennonites were taking more hints from the larger society as they organized and operated their churches.

One reaction against the liberal "drift" of the Amish Mennonites came from a number of highly unusual Amish Mennonite lay members known as "sleeping preachers," who addressed audiences while in a deep, sleep-like trance. Convinced that their unconscious sermons were messages from the Lord, these preachers and their adherents preferred to describe the phenomenon as "Spirit preaching." Typically, the Spirit preacher would go to sleep in the early evening, only to rise several hours later and begin to preach (in German or English) on the themes of repentance, spiritual renewal, or the return to simpler lifestyles.[11]

The best-known Spirit preachers were Noah Troyer of Johnson County, Iowa, and John D. Kauffman of Elkhart County, Indiana.[12] Troyer began preaching in 1878 and Kauffman in 1880. Both men claimed to have no knowledge of what happened during their ecstatic states, who listened to them, or what they said. Other Amish Mennonites affirmed the Spirit preachers' messages with revelations of their own. Barbara (Hochstetler) Stutzman, for example, claimed to have received a deathbed revelation which confirmed the Spirit-preaching truth of Kauffman.[13] A member of Elkhart County's Clinton Frame Amish Mennonite Church, Stutzman was disturbed by rapid change in her congregation.[14]

To be sure, the Spirit preachers were not Old Orders, and they did not ask their listeners to forsake the general change-minded agenda. Nor were their messages identical. Troyer, for example, focused more on the need for personal conviction and commitment on the part of Amish Mennonite faithful, while Kauffman's sermons centered on avoiding the temptations of worldly luxury and individual pride. In either case, Spirit preaching emerged and found an audience among people experiencing unsettling change and transition from traditional ways.[15]

For the true believers, Spirit preaching was divine revelation. For the doubters, men like Troyer and Kauffman were either victims of self-induced hypnosis or charlatans. But Spirit preaching was a phenomenon in other groups during the period, too. In nineteenth-century Europe and North America, Spirit preaching occurred among various Protestant denominations and even to a degree among Native Americans' so-called Ghost Dancers.[16]

Most Amish Mennonites eventually discounted the Spirit preachers. In fact, local opposition to Kauffman forced him to move to Shelby County, Illinois, in 1907. There Kauffman and his followers formed their own congregation, nicknamed the "Sleeping Preacher Amish" or the "Kauffman Amish." The group later spread to other states—especially Arkansas and Missouri—and remains active today, although the practice of Spirit preaching itself has long since ceased in the group. Though they now drive cars, members of the loose network of Kauffman churches maintain fairly plain dress and lifestyle traditions reminiscent of nineteenth-century Amish Mennonite custom.[17]

Building an Amish Mennonite institutional world

Remarkable as the sleeping preachers were, they represented few Amish Mennonite interests or intentions. Instead, most change-minded Amish were caught up in creating, supporting, or endowing church institutions. Institution-building occupied the time and energy of a great many Americans during the late nineteenth century.

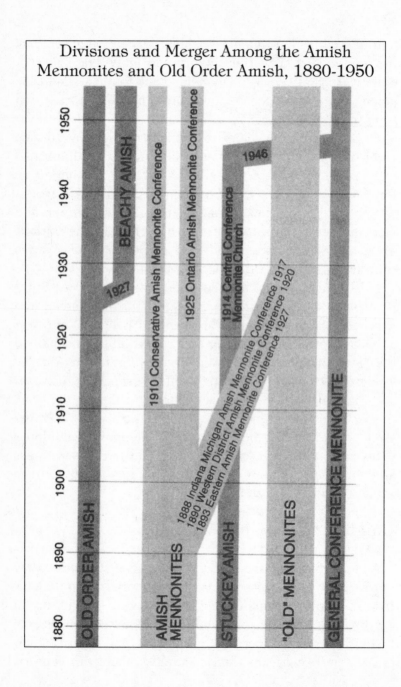

Divisions and Merger Among the Amish
Mennonites and Old Order Amish, 1880-1950

States organized university systems. Banks and businesses formed dozens of new corporations, trusts, and holding companies. Charitable organizations created inner-city settlement houses. Special interest groups—from the National Geographic Society to the American Federation of Labor—formed during this period. Churches were not immune from the spirit of the age, forming national denominational offices, publications, schools, and programs at a rate until then unparalleled in American history.

The Amish Mennonites were institution-builders, as well, and often cooperated with Mennonites who were also hard at work creating their own institutional worlds. News of these organizations and their often cooperative underpinnings traveled through new church magazines, subscribed to by both groups. In fact, so many Amish Mennonites read the Mennonite periodical *Herald of Truth* (and its German language companion *Herold der Wahrheit*) that, for a time, its editor listed the paper as the "Organ of 14 Mennonite and Amish Conferences," even though it never held such official status.[18]

The Amish Mennonite conferences to which the *Herald*'s masthead referred were real Amish Mennonite creations, however. Consolidating congregations into denominational structures was one of the major Amish Mennonite tasks of the 1880s and 1890s. Absorbing the pulse of larger society, the Amish Mennonites adopted apparatus and programs that clearly marked their divergence from the style and tenor of the Old Order. The demise of the *Diener-Versammlungen* had not brought Amish Mennonite connections to an end, and not long after 1878, new structures were taking the place of the old ministers meetings.

Taking their cues from regionally organized Mennonites who reported their church conference activities in the

Herald, Amish Mennonites organized three conferences. In 1888, the Indiana-Michigan Amish Mennonite Conference formed. Two years later, the Western District Amish Mennonite Conference followed, with members in Illinois, Iowa, Missouri, Arkansas, Kansas, Oklahoma, Nebraska, Colorado, and Oregon.[19] In 1893, Amish Mennonites in Ohio and Pennsylvania created the Eastern Amish Mennonite Conference. Ohio bishop John K. Yoder, so active in the workings of the earlier *Diener-Versammlungen*, played a role in the new Eastern Amish Mennonite organization and provided some continuity between the old ministers meetings and the new Conference.

Each of the new groups met regularly, had elected moderators and secretaries, and acted as autonomous, self-governing bodies. Conference gatherings often welcomed fraternal visitors from one of the other Amish Mennonite conferences—or from a Mennonite conference—highlighting the mutual regard the conferences felt for one another. Earlier, Amish Mennonites had emphasized the congregational autonomy that was a part of their Amish heritage. Now, by adopting the Mennonite model of regional conference authority, progressive Amish built another bridge to the Mennonite world and further distanced themselves from their past.

Another field in which the Amish Mennonites demonstrated an American penchant for institution-building was higher education. While Amish families had long supported local public elementary schools, and some Amish served as teachers or township school directors, higher education that cultivated critical thinking and upward social mobility was a different matter. Not all Amish Mennonites immediately supported efforts toward advanced education, but a growing number did. Of course, schooling beyond the elementary level was uncommon for all Americans before 1900 (in 1900 only 6.3 percent of all seventeen-year-old

Americans graduated from high school), but even more so for the Amish who often downplayed the value of worldly knowledge.[20]

By the turn of the twentieth century, however, a noticeable number of Amish Mennonite youth were enrolling in high schools, teachers' colleges (known as "normal schools"), and universities. Wayne County's sizable Oak Grove Amish Mennonite Church had a significant number of young people attend Ada Normal School (now Ohio Northern University) and the College of Wooster.[21] Amish Mennonite leaders were also at the forefront of one of the first Mennonite colleges in the United States. Elkhart Institute, a private institution which opened in 1894 in Elkhart, Indiana (later reorganized as Goshen College), had a board of directors composed of Mennonites and Amish Mennonites. By 1899, the Indiana-Michigan Amish Mennonite Conference was recommending attendance at Elkhart for its youth who aspired to study.[22] One of the school's instructors, C. Henry Smith, was an Amish Mennonite from Metamora, Illinois, who would earn a Ph.D. degree from the University of Chicago in 1907.[23]

Common cause

As the twentieth century approached, Amish Mennonites increased their formal cooperation with Mennonites. Men and women from both groups participated in joint Sunday school teachers' gatherings where they shared ideas and materials. At other times, neighboring Mennonite and Amish Mennonite ministers exchanged pulpits during Sunday services. In still other cases, churches from both groups invited preaching teams composed of one Mennonite and one Amish Mennonite minister to hold "protracted meetings," that is, revival services held several nights in a row. Mennonite bishop John F. Funk and Amish Mennonite bishop Daniel J. Johns were one of the first such teams. Amish Mennonite

The family of Amish Mennonites Samuel J. Miller (1842-1924) and Barbara Yoder Miller (1842-1923), front row, McPherson County, Kansas. Of the couple's 10 children, five joined Mennonite churches, four chose the Church of the Brethren, and one did not affiliate with any group. Two sons-in-law are also pictured.

bishops Jonathan P. Smucker and Jonathan Kurtz also frequently participated in such arrangements.[24]

Such teamwork was not without its hitches. Visiting preachers were supposed to encourage teens and young adults to join their parents' congregations. In 1890, in the Logan County, Ohio, Amish Mennonite community, several youth responded to Johns' and Funk's invitation to follow Christ and join the church. However, the young men and women reported that they wished to join a Mennonite congregation, not their families' Amish Mennonite church. After some embarrassed deliberation, the visiting preachers suggested that local Amish Mennonite leaders allow the young people to form a separate and officially Mennonite fellowship, which they did under the name Bethel Mennonite Church.[25]

The confusion in Logan County pointed up the fact that "Amish Mennonite" and "Mennonite" were still not entirely interchangeable designations. In many places, the Amish Mennonites still dressed a bit more conservatively, their men grew beards, and many were still committed in principle to shunning—although the actual practice of shunning by Amish Mennonites quietly fell into disuse.[26] In some places, the Mennonites were perceived to be the more progressive group. Especially for those young people interested in institution-building, the Mennonites' greater resources—human and capital—were appealing. Mission interests among the Mennonites also ran strong (by 1899 they would have medical missionaries in India), and so those Amish Mennonites interested in international outreach felt a close kinship with the Mennonites.

For several decades, a few Amish Mennonites and Mennonites had been suggesting the merger of their respective groups. Perhaps the first published appeal for such union had come in 1864 from the pen of Elkhart, Indiana, Amish Mennonite minister John Ringenberg. Then, at the 1866 *Diener-Versammlung* there had been talk of bringing the Amish Mennonites and Mennonites "into a closer union."[27] In 1874, the Indiana Mennonite Conference invited any "Amish brethren who are of one mind with us" to participate in Mennonite communion services.[28] Three years earlier, a Mennonite leader had written of his "Omish [sic] brethren," adding, "Now there may be some who think that we are out of place by calling the Omish, brethren." However, his readers "should not be too ready to censure [the

Amish Mennonites]." In fact, "if there was more visiting done [between the two groups], there would be more union of thought," he suggested.[29] Indeed, since the 1860s, the traveling Illinois Amish Mennonite schoolteacher Christian Erismann had referred to his people simply as "Mennonites."

Some "union of thought" did develop on the local level as a few Mennonite and Amish Mennonite congregations quietly merged on their own terms. In 1886, the *Herald of Truth* reported on a church in northern Michigan's Antrim County in which both Mennonites and Amish Mennonites had formed a combined congregation. They were "willing to join hand in hand, and be united as one body in the Lord," the paper reported.[30]

Sometimes unity was the result of the decline of one or another of the groups. "Tennessee John" Stoltzfus' Knox County, Tennessee, community fell on hard times after the old leader's passing. The appearance of a Mennonite minister and several Virginia Mennonite families revived the church, and it became Mennonite. And after 1900, when a few Ontario Amish families moved west to Saskatchewan and Alberta, they joined existing Mennonite congregations rather than establishing new Amish Mennonite ones.[31]

Amish Mennonite and "old" Mennonite unity

The joint ventures and local cooperation between Amish Mennonites and Mennonites in the late 1800s paved the way for formal unification during the first quarter of the twentieth century. For a large majority of Amish Mennonites, the obvious partner in any churchly integration was the so-called "old" Mennonites.[32] Not to be confused with "Old Order," the designation "old" described the largest and oldest existing Mennonite body in North America. Most of its members

Lunch at a Conservative Amish Mennonite Conference Sunday school meeting, Grantsville, Maryland, in 1912.

were of Swiss and south German descent—the very people with whom the Amish had originally divided in Europe.

Over the years, for various reasons, both conservative and progressive minorities had split from the "old" Mennonites, so that by 1900, the "old" Mennonites represented a rather middle-of-the-road Mennonite church. Organized into a dozen fairly autonomous geographic conferences, the "old" Mennonites possessed a structure that allowed them to move toward merger with Amish Mennonites in ways that respected regional wishes and local timing.[33]

In 1917, the Indiana-Michigan Amish Mennonite Conference merged with its "old" Mennonite counterpart in these two states. The new group's name—Indiana-Michigan Mennonite Conference—did not acknowledge the Amish heritage of half its members. But the designation was not necessarily the result of Mennonites trying to squash Amish identity. Apparently, the new conference's former Amish members were eager to forget their past. For example, Noah Long, trustee of the Clinton Frame Amish Mennonite Church in Elkhart County, Indiana, removed the word "Amish" from the meetinghouse sign only a day or two after his conference voted to join the Mennonites, wasting no time in letting passersby know that Clinton Frame was no longer Amish.[34]

The Western District Amish Mennonite Conference was the next to dissolve itself into a new Mennonite family. In 1920, the Western District Amish Mennonites and "old" Mennonites west of Indiana reorganized themselves into five new Mennonite conferences. The Amish Mennonites outnumbered the "old" Mennonites 4,400 to 2,800 in these new groupings, and several congregations continued to use their historic "Amish" name for a time after the merger.[35] In 1927, the Eastern Amish Mennonite Conference brought Mennonite-Amish merger to Ohio and Pennsylvania. The new body judiciously acknowledged both halves of its constituency, using the name "Ohio Mennonite and Eastern Amish Mennonite Joint Conference." By mid-century, however, Amish Mennonite identity seemed so distant that the conference simplified its title to Ohio and Eastern Mennonite Conference.[36]

In Ontario, the Amish Mennonite conference did not merge with the "old" Mennonite conference in that province, choosing instead to retain its independence while working more closely with neighboring Mennonites. Its Amish identity faded, however, and in 1963 the group dropped "Amish" from its name, becoming the Western Ontario Mennonite Conference.[37]

Thus, in a few short years during the early 1900s, several thousand people wittingly or unwittingly lost any public connections to their Amish faith tradition. This was one of

Amish Mennonites Merge with the Mennonites

1865   Egly Amish division.

1872   Joseph Stuckey Amish division.

1888   Indiana-Michigan Amish Mennonite Conference forms.

1890   Western Amish Mennonite Conference forms, covering Illinois, Iowa, Missouri, Arkansas, Nebraska, Kansas, Oklahoma, Colorado, and Oregon.

1893   Eastern Amish Mennonite Conference forms, covering Ohio and Pennsylvania.

1908   Egly Amish become Defenseless Mennonite Church.

1908   Stuckey Amish become Central Illinois Conference of Mennonites.

1910   Conservative Amish Mennonite Conference forms.

1914   Central Illinois Mennonite Conference becomes Central Conference Mennonite Church.

1917   Indiana-Michigan Amish Mennonite Conference merges with the Indiana Mennonite Conference to form the Indiana-Michigan Mennonite Conference.

1920   Western Amish Mennonite Conference merges with several Mennonite conferences in Illinois, Iowa-Missouri, Kansas-Nebraska, and Oregon.

1925   Ontario Amish Mennonite Conference forms.

1927   Eastern Amish Mennonite Conference merges with the Ohio Mennonite Conference to form the Ohio Mennonite and Eastern Amish Mennonite Joint Conference.

1946   Central Conference Mennonite Church joins the General Conference Mennonite Church.

1948	Defenseless Mennonite Church becomes Evangelical Mennonite Church.
1954	Conservative Amish Mennonite Conference becomes Conservative Mennonite Conference.
1955	Ohio Mennonite and Eastern Amish Mennonite Joint Conference becomes Ohio and Eastern Mennonite Conference.
1963	Ontario Amish Mennonite Conference becomes Western Ontario Mennonite Conference.

the profound legacies of the merging of the two streams. As historian Paton Yoder, himself a child of an Amish Mennonite home, lamented, Amish Mennonites paid the price of a lost heritage and "covered their tracks" in the process of so quickly becoming Mennonites. Now Yoder "and all other Mennonites with Amish Mennonite roots, find it necessary to uncover these tracks" in order "to discover—or rediscover— [their] Amish and Amish Mennonite origins."[38]

But the union of the two groups also had far-reaching implications for Mennonites. The addition of 7,500 to 8,000 Amish Mennonites increased the size of the "old" Mennonites significantly. While the "old" Mennonites had been the largest Mennonite group in 1900, they had not been much bigger than the next largest body. With the absorption of the Amish Mennonites, however, the "old" Mennonites clearly became the largest North American Mennonite denomination. Without the addition of the Amish Mennonites in the early 1900s, it is doubtful the "old" Mennonites would have had the resources to engage in the various twentieth-century activities they later did. Then, too, an Amish penchant for local congregational authority continued in many Amish-turned-Mennonite churches. The injection of this congregationalist impulse into "old" Mennonite life would influence Mennonite polity for years to come.

Alternative Amish Mennonite paths

While the majority of change-minded Amish Mennonites who had participated actively in the mid-century *Diener-Versammlungen* merged with the "old" Mennonites, notable minorities followed other paths. These Amish Mennonites had found themselves on the edges of ministers meeting activity, and their subsequent histories as Conservative Amish Mennonites, liberal Central Conference Mennonites, and fundamentalist-inclined Fellowship of Evangelical Churches illustrate the diverse theological paths that some Amish Mennonites traversed.

From independent Amish Mennonites to Conservative Mennonite Conference

Not all Amish Mennonites had warmed to the *Diener-Versammlungen* of the 1860s and 1870s. They chose to chart a moderate path between the Old Orders, on the one hand, and the change-minded ministers meetings, on the other. Although these Amish Mennonites had built meetinghouses and generally embraced Sunday schools and organized mission work, they retained German-language worship, conservative dress, and other marks of traditional Amish life. They were less certain that the benefits of higher education outweighed its unsettling influence on community, and in church matters they had not wanted to adopt, so quickly, the bureaucracy of "old"Mennonite conference structures.

In 1910, representatives of three such independent Amish Mennonite congregations met in Pigeon, Michigan, and formed the nucleus of what came to be known as the Conservative Amish Mennonite Conference.[39] With key leadership from Pigeon's bishop Solomon J. Swartzendruber, the Conservative Conference quickly grew to include churches throughout the Midwest and Mid-Atlantic regions, as well as Lewis County, New York. The sizable Lewis County Amish community had never associated closely with the *Diener-Versammlungen* and was drawn to the Conservative Amish Mennonites' moderate approach that skirted old order and progressive.[40]

For a time, Amish Mennonites in Ontario considered membership in the Conservative Conference, but then decided against it. Interestingly, it seems that the Canadians were unsure they wanted to take the name "Conservative Conference," because they feared the label would link them with their nation's Conservative Party and its politics.

In some ways, the Conservative Amish Mennonite Conference followed the broader pattern of Mennonite and progressive Amish Mennonite institution-building, but at a slower pace. In 1914, Conservative Amish Mennonite churches started a home for orphans, and a mission board charged with sponsoring domestic and foreign mission activities followed four years later. German worship gradually gave way to English services. In 1952, the Conference opened a Bible school near Berlin, Ohio (later moved to Irwin, Ohio, and now known as Rosedale Bible College).

By 1954, most members decided that the word "Amish" in the Conference title held little meaning and shortened their name to Conservative Mennonite Conference. By the 1990s, most Conservative Mennonites had discarded plain dress and other overtly Amish traditions.[41] Instead, they grounded their identity in a mix of Anabaptist theology, American evangelicalism, and strong support for mission work at home and around the world. In the twenty-first century, some members of the Conservative Conference are aware of their group's Amish heritage, but their appraisal of it is mixed. Some are happy to be associated with the conservative family values the tradition represents, while others find it acutely embarrassing that the Amish did not (and do not) engage in verbal evangelism. For today's Conservative Mennonite Conference, an Amish past is both a gift to hold and a stumbling block to overcome.

From Stuckey Amish to Central Conference Mennonites

The Stuckey Amish—those central Illinois churches that looked for leadership to Joseph Stuckey, the beloved McLean County bishop affectionately known as "Father Stuckey"— had also existed on the edges of the Amish Mennonite world of the mid-nineteenth century.[42] Despite his falling-out with Amish Mennonite leaders in 1872 over his leniency with Joseph Joder, Stuckey did occasionally preach in some of the very congregations whose leaders had expelled him, and some of them returned the favor. In 1889, for example, Wayne County, Ohio, bishop John K. Yoder preached at Stuckey's church to an audience that included Stuckey and Illinois Amish Mennonite leader Christian Ropp.[43] Seventeen years earlier, Ropp had asked Yoder to investigate Stuckey's discipline of Joder, an investigation that had led Ropp and Yoder to break with Stuckey.

Despite such signs of repaired relationships, Stuckey's circle of congregations never joined the larger Amish Mennonite conference movement represented by Yoder and Ropp. Instead, Stuckey was drawn to the activities of the progressive General Conference Mennonites, a body formed in 1860 and comprised of more recent and broad-minded European Mennonite immigrants who generally believed that Christianity was compatible with refinement and good taste.

General Conference Mennonites strongly endorsed higher education and organized mission work, while allowing a great deal of congregational autonomy in matters of discipline and everyday life.[44] The lenient stance of the General Conference on matters of dress and church organization appealed to Stuckey and his more tolerant supporters. While the bishop himself retained his beard and somewhat traditional garb, members of his congregation quickly adapted styles from larger society. Within Stuckey's lifetime, women in his churches stopped wearing devotional prayer coverings, and the dress of men became indistinguishable from their neighbors.[45] Stuckey Amish were often at the forefront of the shift from rural to town life.

Father Stuckey's death in 1902 did not stunt the group's growth. Six years later, the Stuckey fellowship had grown to a dozen congregations—including several outside of Illinois—and adopted a formal constitution and new name: Central Illinois Conference of Mennonites (later shortened to Central Conference Mennonite Church).[46] The Central Conference embarked on an ambitious program of witness. It opened city missions in Chicago and Peoria and by 1912 was sending missionaries to the Belgian Congo (now Democratic Republic of Congo). In 1913, the group became a sponsor of Bluffton (Ohio) College, and a similar partnership arrangement saw the Stuckey churches help launch a hospital in Bloomington, Illinois, in 1919.

Although Central Conference Mennonites were eager to cooperate with General Conference partners, the Stuckey people's shared history and geographic clustering in Illinois had given them a distinctive identity and group confidence that resisted formal merger with another body. In 1946, however, the Central Conference became a part of the General Conference Mennonites Church.[47] By then, many Central Conference churches had taken on the trappings of mainline Protestant congregations. Worship often featured robed choirs, organ music, and seminary-trained clergy. Members prized individual freedom of conscience on religious matters, which they saw as an expression of historic Amish conviction. Of course, among the Old Order Amish, conscience was checked by deference to *Ordnung*. Central Conference liberalism, in contrast, promised more freedom and individualism. In any case, their story was another variation on the theme of an Amish heritage.

From Egly Amish to Fellowship of Evangelical Churches

The nineteenth-century Amish Mennonites associated with bishop Henry Egly represented yet a third example of Amish Mennonite adaptation. In this case, the stream defined by Egly's blend of revivalism, evangelical fervor, and Amish background eventually flowed in the direction of American fundamentalism and rarely looked back to its Amish origins.[48]

Under Egly's leadership, the loose association of congregations known colloquially as "Egly Amish" remained rather close to their Amish roots. For example, when the Egly Amish began to construct church buildings, they included a kitchen for preparing and serving dinner, thus continuing in a modified way the old Amish practice of sharing a noon meal together after worship. Egly congregations also remained traditionally Amish in their attitude toward worldly fashion. In 1883, an early conference of Egly-affiliated churches insisted that male church members were not allowed to shave their beards and women could not discard prayer coverings. As one historian observed, during "Egly's lifetime his people appear to have learned from revivalism without departing radically from Amish faith and practice."[49]

But after Henry Egly died in 1890, the churches he had shepherded changed rapidly. A series of annual business

Barbara Naffziger Springer (c.1840-1921) of Hopedale, Illinois, was an Egly Amish church member who continued to wear plain clothes. Photo taken 1917.

meetings convened after 1895, and the group took on an official name—Defenseless Mennonite Church—that did not include the word "Amish." In 1896, the group began sponsoring missionaries in the Belgian Congo (now Democratic Republic of Congo), and two years later established an orphanage near Flanagan, Illinois.[50] The Defenseless Mennonites incorporated in 1908, capping a rapid period of institution building. The quick construction of such structures was one indication of their leaving behind Henry Egly's Amish informality and taking on American ways of organization.

Soon, American-inflected debates over church doctrine were also shaping Defenseless Mennonite church life. Some developments were contentious. Henry Egly's son Joseph, for example, sparked dissent with his novel teaching on the baptism of the Holy Spirit and his interpretation of the end of time. He soon left the church to form the Missionary Church Association (since 1969, a part of the Missionary Church).[51] For the most part, however, Defenseless Mennonites' theological evolution generated little controversy and Egly's group aligned itself more and more with American fundamentalism.

In 1948, the denomination changed its name to Evangelical Mennonite Church (EMC). The loss of the designation "Defenseless" was more than incidental. Few Evangelical Mennonite Church members saw peace and nonresistance as central to Christian practice.[52] By 2003, most EMC congregations had dropped "Mennonite" from their name, and the denomination designated itself the Fellowship of Evangelical Churches, explaining that it was a more accurate label.[53] By then, links to the group's Amish past had long disappeared.

The twilight of the European Amish

While North American Amish Mennonites were joining neighboring Mennonite groups, a somewhat similar pattern was emerging in Europe. In the Old World, no Old Order Amish group ever developed. All the European Amish took the progressive path. European Mennonites, like most of their North American cousins, had often been more a part of the social mainstream than had the Amish. Thus, as the European Amish became more acculturated and gave up distinctive dress and worship practices, they rather naturally identified with the Mennonites. Amish practices of simple apparel, full beards for men, and hook-and-eye coats gradually fell into disuse among the spiritual heirs of Jakob

C. Michel Richard (1829-1871) and Francoise Conrad Richard (1828-1906), members of the Montbéliard, France, Amish community.

Ammann. One practice that continued to distinguish Amish from Mennonites was the observance of footwashing as a part of their communion service. European Mennonites did not practice literal footwashing, but European Amish continued to do so into the twentieth century.

Amish membership in Europe peaked around 1850, with some 5,000 members in Alsace and Lorraine alone.[54] Thereafter, numbers declined, and immigration to North America, especially of young adults, played a key role in draining membership and potential leadership.[55] Although the number of emigrants declined after 1860, scattered Amish individuals and families continued to leave throughout the late nineteenth century, where virtually all joined progressive Amish Mennonite congregations in the American Midwest.[56]

George Guth (1836-1871) and Magdalena Oesch Guth (1844-1870) lived near Bitsche in the French Lorraine region and were members of the Ixheim Amish congregation. Both died of typhoid fever as a result of the Franco-Prussian War.

Over time, interest in emigrating faded as European Amish felt more at home as citizens and participants in society. Young Amish man Christian M. Nafziger fled German conscription in 1883 and ended up in New York's Lewis County Amish Mennonite settlement, but many other members of his European church came to terms with military service.[57] Accepting military service became more common for young Amish (and Mennonite) men. Nor was the world of politics completely foreign. In the 1880s, voters elected Amish elder Peter Schlabbach to the Prussian legislature. Within a decade, Schlabbach's Hessian congregation had merged with the Mennonites.[58]

Indeed, few Amish were left in Hesse, once a territory with a high concentration of the church's members. The few hundred Amish remaining there during the second half of the nineteenth century, like Peter Schlabbach, gradually came to identify themselves with neighboring Mennonites, or else joined socially respectable Lutheran state churches. Many Hessian Amish congregations were quite conscious of their move toward Mennonitism. At a May 1867 Amish ministers conference held in the Hessian town of Offenthal, seventeen leaders from six Amish churches discussed ways to adapt church practices and unite with the Mennonites.[59]

Of the Offenthal Conference's ten-point agreement, four items were especially telling. Regarding footwashing, the conferees decided that "It shall be left to each congregation whether it is to be literally carried out" or not. As a symbol of servanthood, footwashing might be a fine idea, "But it shall not be the basis of a future division," the leaders decided.

On the subject of military participation, the conference offered no clear word. "We leave to the careful consideration of each one," the delegates wrote, how "to do justice first to his own conscience and then also to the government." In a world of conflicting moral claims and intense patriotic pressure, the church would leave such ponderous choices to individuals.

In two other decisions, the Offenthal gathering approved religiously mixed marriages and rejected social shunning in favor of merely excluding the excommunicated from communion. Most of the congregations represented at Offenthal died out in a decade or two. The few that survived became Mennonite. By 1900, no Amish congregations existed in Hesse.

Likewise, the Bavarian Amish declined during the nineteenth century. By the mid-1800s, two of the kingdom's three congregations had nearly dissolved, due simply to heavy emigration to Illinois and Ontario. A third church, near Regensburg, was still 200 members strong in 1888, but was quickly losing its Amish identity. Regensburg member Josef Gingerich long remembered his turn-of-the-century boyhood when "a considerable number left the [Amish] church."[60] In 1908, Gingerich's congregation both ceased the observance of footwashing and formally joined the German Mennonite Conference.

A number of fairly small Amish congregations remained in the French Lorraine, Alsace, and Montbéliard regions, but they, too, found themselves working more closely with German Mennonites. Especially after 1871, when Alsace came under German rule and Lorraine remained French, church connections were divided politically. A new 1872 military conscription law drew little reaction from the Alsatian Amish. In the closing decades of the nineteenth century, these churches often exercised discipline only in cases of religiously mixed marriages.[61]

In 1896, the originally Amish congregations in Alsace, Lorraine, and Basel, Switzerland, created a regional conference. Formally constituted in 1907, the Alsatian-based conference considered itself Mennonite, despite its historic Amish background. Two other small Amish congregations remaining in Switzerland joined the Swiss Mennonite Conference. The two fellowships—Mennonite and Amish—were quietly reuniting after two centuries of separation, but the reunion was always on Mennonite terms.[62]

Not every vestige of Amish heritage disappeared immediately. Often Mennonite churches of Amish background continued the Amish practice of footwashing as a part of the Lord's Supper. The Luxembourg Amish-turned-Mennonites, for example, observed footwashing as late as 1941.[63] Still, the connection to any Amish heritage was faint or foggy for most.

The last European Amish

The few Amish congregations that survived into the twentieth century soon dissolved or merged with surrounding Mennonite groups. The old Bitscherland Amish congregation in Bitsche, Alsace, dissolved after its elder, Christian Schantz, died in 1902.[64] Seven years later, another Amish fellowship, Hornbach-Zweibrücken, also ceased meeting after the death of its elder, Christian Stalter. The deaths of preachers Christian Jordy and Johannes Guth also signaled the demise of the Frönsburg congregation in the Vosges Mountains on the French-German border. Worship services ended there in 1929.[65]

In many of these places, members who wanted to maintain some ties with an Amish fellowship traveled occasionally to worship with the Ixheim or Saar Amish. Then, in 1936, the Saar and Ixheim congregations themselves merged, having a combined membership of 134.[66] Ixheim now represented the lone Amish congregation in Europe since all others had affiliated with the Mennonite conferences in Alsace, Lorraine, or south Germany.

Meetinghouse, built about 1844, used by the Ixheim Amish until 1937 when the group united with local Mennonites.

Long one of the most traditional Amish congregations, the Ixheim church continued to ordain unsalaried, untrained leaders and, at least in theory, held to the social shunning of excommunicated members. Until 1932, they still included a footwashing service as part of their communion observance, and some men wore beards. But Ixheim, too, was considering its future among Mennonites. Serious consideration began after 1929 when Ixheim member Ernst Guth married Mennonite Susanna Weiss. Weiss' Mennonite pastor, Hugo Scheffler, met with Amish elder Christian Guth to discuss the wedding, since the Ixheim Amish had not approved of mixed marriages. Rather surprisingly to Scheffler, the conversation revealed Amish openness to cooperating with the Mennonites.

Otelia Augspurger Compton, American Mother of the Year

In 1939, the J. C. Penney Golden Rule Foundation named Otelia Augspurger Compton its fifth annual American Mother of the Year. The Foundation was seeking to promote a new holiday—Mother's Day—and chose Compton as an exemplary mother because she encouraged education for men and women and because of her achievement in raising four children who collectively held thirty-one college and university degrees.

Born in 1859 in Butler County, Ohio, Otelia Augspurger was a grandchild of Christian and Katharina (Hauter) Augspurger, pioneer Amish Mennonite immigrants of 1817 and 1819. Her parents, Samuel and Eliza (Holly) Augspurger, were members of Butler County's progressive Hessian Amish church, where Otelia was later baptized. As a young woman she wore "plain and modest clothing" but also appreciated instrumental music and learned to play the piano and mandolin.

Otelia completed eight grades of rural public schooling and became a schoolteacher herself—an unremarkable choice for a young woman of her day— but at age seventeen, with the encouragement of her parents, she embarked on a more unusual path by enrolling at Western College in Oxford, Ohio (now part of Miami University of Ohio). When she graduated, she was almost certainly the first Mennonite or Amish Mennonite woman in North America to have earned a bachelor's degree.

In 1886, Otelia married another Butler County schoolteacher, Elias Compton. Thereafter, "although she continued to prize" her Amish Mennonite faith, she increasingly became involved in promoting the programs of her husband's Presbyterian church. Otelia and Elias settled in Wooster, Ohio, where Elias taught philosophy at the College of Wooster.

Otelia's four children all pursued careers in education. Mary Elias was a missionary teacher in India and what is now Pakistan; Karl became president of Massachusetts Institute of Technology; Wilson was president of Washington State University; and Arthur, who won the 1927 Nobel Prize in physics, served as chancellor of Washington University in St. Louis. (Although "struggling with the values of his pacifist Mennonite heritage," Arthur contributed to the University of Chicago's Manhattan Project that developed the atomic bomb.)

In 1932, Western College awarded Otelia an honorary doctorate and named her an outstanding alumna. Seven years later, upon being named Mother of the Year, Otelia responded with "humility," saying "to me the wonder is that I, a daughter of unassuming Mennonite parents, who for fourscore years has merely tried to do her duty as a child of God . . . should now so unexpectedly be honored." Asked by a reporter "if she reared her children in accordance with books and theories, she replied that there wasn't any book to guide her, unless it was the Bible."

Otelia Augspurger Compton was not a typical Amish Mennonite woman, but the trajectory of her life and the lives of her children illustrate one path of change-minded Amish Mennonites who embraced progress and broad accommodation to American culture.

Sources: "Mrs. Compton, 85, 3 Sons Educators: 'American Mother of the Year' in 1939 Dies," *New York Times* (December 16, 1944): 15; Donna Birkey, "Chisholm and the Augspurgers," *Illinois Mennonite Heritage Quarterly* 33 (Winter 2006): 68-69.

Otelia C. Augspurger, age 21

Jakob Schönbeck (1902-1981) of Ingweilerhof, Germany, was one of the last people baptized into the Ixheim Amish congregation before the group merged with neighboring Mennonites.

On January 17, 1937, after several years of discussion, the Ixheim Amish church and the nearby Ernstweiler Mennonite congregation united, taking the name Zweibrücken Mennonite Church. A week later, during a special unity service, the two groups sang together, shared a common meal, listened to Mennonite brass instrumentalists, and watched a slide show about the previous year's Mennonite World Conference gathering. Amish elder Guth read a statement of unity, and Mennonite pastor Scheffler officially took over leadership of the new group. In a formal sense, the Amish church in Europe had come to an end.[67]

Sociologist John A. Hostetler once suggested that such a loss of European Amish identity was perhaps to be expected. Being primarily leaseholders and estate mangers, Amish in

Europe were not always able to live close to one another, existing instead on scattered farms, often some distance apart. Most of their neighbors were members of established churches. The lack of close contact may have worked against the development of strong group solidarity and left them more vulnerable to the influences of the surrounding culture. European Amish, like their North American Amish Mennonite cousins, embraced Western assumptions about the goodness of civic progress, educational advancement, and social mobility.[68]

Within the first few decades of the twentieth century, Amish Mennonites on both sides of the Atlantic had dropped their public Amish identity, signaling their distance from an Amish past. Certainly in giving up the practices of social shunning, the Amish Mennonites surrendered one of the convictions that had set them apart for two centuries. In some quarters, they also discontinued the practice of footwashing in conjunction with communion and surrendered most of their distinctive dress and symbolic separation from the world.

Amish-turned-Mennonites did continue to stress simple, ethical living as a response to God's grace. A commitment to congregational authority, the church as the body of Christ in the world, and Jesus' teaching of peace and forgiveness also marked most erstwhile Amish churches in the twentieth century. However, the Amish Mennonite emphases that such tenets received often expressed themselves through institutions and language that sounded more broadly North American or European than distinctively Amish. The continuation of historic Amish principles in a way that did not easily adopt society's values and idioms fell to the Old Order Amish and related churches.

—9—

Preservation and Perseverance: Old Order Amish, 1865-1900

> *"We are minded, and promise to strive for simplicity and uniformity in all things."*
> —an Iowa Old Order Amish congregation, 1891

Choosing the Old Order

The tradition-minded churches that came to be known as the Old Order Amish were a small group during the last decades of the nineteenth century. In the wake of the annual ministers' meetings, roughly two-thirds of Amish churches had chosen the progressive Amish Mennonite path. By the close of the 1800s, the Old Orders who continued to worship in private homes, maintain traditionally simple clothing patterns, and rigorous church discipline numbered only about 6,300.[1] Yet the Old Order church proved remarkably steady for a body that had undergone a series of wrenching schisms and turbulent unrest.

Even while the debates of the *Diener-Versammlungen* were closing the door to compromise and sealing the reality of a fractured Amish world, conservatives who would make up the Old Order were forming new settlements. In 1866, as progressive Amish Mennonites met for that year's ministers meeting in McLean County, Illinois, tradition-minded families were also heading to the state. The Amish moving to Moultrie County, Illinois, though, were not attending the change-minded church gathering, but rather creating a new Old Order community. Families from Somerset County, Pennsylvania, had settled in Moultrie near the small town of Arthur. Before long, Indiana, Ohio, and Iowa households relocated there as well, and Arthur, Illinois, grew into a sizable Old Order settlement.

A poster advertising land for sale in Michigan noted the presence of "Colonies of Amish and Mennonites" in the state.

The Arthur community symbolized conservatives' ability to grow and thrive, even as the majority of Amish Mennonites moved toward greater social acculturation.[2] Indeed, Old Order life and faith apparently appealed to some Americans, even as it drove other Amish Mennonites away. Around 1863, for example, Jacob Lambright, raised as a Lutheran, joined the Old Order church in northern Indiana. Within a decade, the Bawell, Barkman, Flaud, and Whetstone surnames (among others) became part of Old Order Amish communities in various states, as people bearing those names joined the tradition-minded Amish church.[3]

As the Old Order church slowly grew, important new settlements started in Daviess County, Indiana (1868); Reno County, Kansas (1883); and Geauga (1886) and Madison counties (1896), Ohio. In the late 1800s, new districts formed in a dozen other states, but troubled church affairs or the economic difficulties of homesteading caused these settlements to dissolve.[4]

A congregationally organized church spread across North America and without a national bureaucracy might easily have fragmented. Nevertheless, Old Orders remained remarkably close-knit and connected, considering their dispersed settlements and relatively small numbers. One way in which Amish people kept in contact with one another was through correspondence newspapers such as *The Belleville* (Pennsylvania) *Times* and *The Sugarcreek* (Ohio) *Budget*. Originally published as local papers, periodicals such as *The Budget* regularly printed news items from Amish communities far and wide. Thus, an Indiana *Budget* subscriber could read news not only of the publisher's Tuscarawas County, Ohio, area but also reports from settlements in Iowa, North Dakota, Nebraska, Maryland, and beyond.[5]

Others Who Rejected Modernity or Chose the Way of Tradition

The Old Order Amish were not the only religious group to spurn the progressive spirit of nineteenth-century life. Primitive Baptists, for example, rejected Sunday schools, church bureaucracy, salaried clergy, and innovations to traditional Calvinist doctrine. Some members of the Churches of Christ also rejected progressive institution-building and a professionalized pastorate. During the last quarter of the nineteenth century, an influential Protestant movement known as dispensationalism also dissented from the optimistic tenor of the times. Dispensationalists did not assume that North American society was improving, but rather that the world was becoming more corrupt as the second coming of Christ neared.

Among the Religious Society of Friends (Quakers), a conservative wing emerged between 1845 and 1904. Known as Wilburites, these traditional Friends preserved early Quaker worship practices and theology. Members also stressed the importance of wearing plain attire and maintained traditional Quaker speech patterns.

The Old Order groups that emerged among Amish, Mennonite, and German Baptist Brethren perhaps rejected most strikingly the spirit of nineteenth-century progressivism. Old Order Mennonite groups formed between 1845 and 1901 in Pennsylvania, Indiana, Ohio, Ontario, and Virginia. These tradition-minded Mennonites were concerned that the larger body of Mennonites was moving too quickly down the path of cultural compromise. Old Order Mennonites rejected Sunday school and church bureaucracy, and in most cases, also retained German-language worship. In contrast to the Older Order Amish, Older Order Mennonites met for worship in simple church meetinghouses (rather than members' homes) and did not practice shunning. Old Order Mennonite men were clean-shaven, and, while their dress was plain, it was somewhat different from the Amish. In the twentieth and twenty-first centuries, Old Order Mennonites (like the Old Order Amish) have avoided higher education and continued the use of horse-drawn transportation.

During the 1800s, Old Order groups formed in other Anabaptist-related churches. During the first half of the nineteenth century, the River Brethren divided into Old Order River Brethren and progressive Brethren in Christ camps. Among the German Baptist Brethren ("Dunkers"), an Old Order wing formed after 1881, taking the name Old German Baptist Brethren. The progressive wings of this group became the Church of the Brethren and the Brethren Church. In each case, the Old Order churches among the Brethren have retained plain dress, simple lifestyles, and traditional worship patterns and church structures. Only a very small fraction drive buggies, however, and all use English as their first language.

Members of various Old Order Mennonite, Amish, and Brethren churches often feel a fraternal bond, despite the important differences that exist between them. Old Order Mennonites, for example, often subscribe to and contribute articles to the Old Order Amish magazine *Family Life* and to the Amish-published correspondence newspaper *Die Botschaft*.

For more on other Old Order groups, see Donald B. Kraybill and Carl F. Bowman, *On the Backroad to Heaven: Old Order Hutterites, Mennonites, Amish, and Brethren* (Baltimore: Johns Hopkins University Press, 2001); Stephen Scott, *An Introduction to Old Order and Conservative Mennonite Groups* (Intercourse, Pa.: Good Books, 1996), 11-104; and Beulah Stauffer Hostetler, "The Formation of the Old Orders," *Mennonite Quarterly Review* 66 (January 1992): 5-25. For discussion of a wider cultural context, see T. J. Jackson Lears, *No Place for Grace: Antimodernism and the Transformation of American Culture, 1880-1920* (New York: Pantheon Books, 1981).

Old Order Amish communities also remained connected through personal contacts and visiting. Young people frequently traveled by rail to other settlements. Autograph books of these teens and young adults record the names of friends and acquaintances from across the country.[6] At times, young people—most often young men—took jobs in other Amish communities for a season or a few years. Youth learned to know other areas and families, and their correspondence with relatives at home offered insights even to those who never traveled. The brothers Isaac and Andrew Ebersol, for example, left their parents' eastern Pennsylvania farm and took jobs with their uncle in Arthur, Illinois. During their sojourn in Arthur each wrote to their cousin Sarah E. Lapp, who had remained in Lancaster, Pennsylvania.[7] The boys described life in Illinois, Midwestern commodity prices, Moultrie County weather, church affairs, and the social life of young people in Arthur.

In January 1897, Sarah Lapp received another letter from a traveling Amish youth, one Isaac Zook, a Lancaster boy who had gone to work in Mifflin County, Pennsylvania. Zook described Mifflin's "Big Valley," and then told about a minor accident in which he had been involved. He also listed the names of young Amish couples whose wedding engagements the local bishop had recently "published" (announced to the rest of the church). Zook continued: "If that is the go, I guess I must tell them to have me published while I am here too—" then added, "O excuse me, it takes two Don't it? Well then I'll waite [sic] a while yet I guess."[8] He did wait and returned to Lancaster. Later that year, Isaac and Sarah married.

Weddings and other special occasions were times of celebration in Old Order circles. Although Amish families avoided extravagance, some exchanged holiday greeting cards and, in a few cases, even decorated a tree for the holidays. Two days before Christmas 1888, a young Sallie J. Fisher wrote to her cousin, wishing that the other girl could "see our ever green," because the Old Order Amish Fisher family intended "to make it white with popcorn and candy."[9]

Of course, everyday life also included hard work. One evening when quite tired, Lancaster County teen Bettsy Speicher reported that her family was finally finished with cornhusking and making 100 crocks of apple butter, but still had "the whole house left to clean." Speicher also said that her family kept three cows and "a hundred chickens more or less." The animals provided some income, as selling cream earned the family a few dollars.[10] Several years later, Bettsy's friend Rebecca S. Smucker described her full day of washing and ironing, noting that her mother had been patching

Late nineteenth-century observers considered the Old Order Amish superior farmers. The Amish in Lancaster, Pennsylvania, and else-where, continue to be known for their agricultural skill, even though today a declining percentage makes its living tilling the soil.

clothes, her father caring for the livestock, and her brothers working in the "smith shop" and repairing shoes.[11] Old Order life was like that of other rural Americans—family, fun, and strenuous labor combined to challenge the elements of weather and economic unpredictability.

In general, Amish farmers adopted new agricultural technologies—mechanical hay loaders, grain binders, and grain threshing machines—as they became available, but used these tools toward certain ends. In Johnson County, Iowa, at least, Steven Reschly found that Old Order farmers in the late 1800s maintained a distinctive balance of "livestock, meadows, innovative technology, family labor, and production for the marketplace" in a way that supported mixed agriculture and resisted the sort of intensive cash grain or specialized

S. D. Guengerich, late in life, at his Iowa home.

livestock farming that was becoming common among their non-Amish neighbors. While some observers noted that the Amish often took somewhat seriously almanac folklore that most Americans increasingly considered outdated and unscientific, popular opinion and the national press were already celebrating the Amish as accomplished farmers.[12]

Tradition and change

Although similar in many ways to their rural neighbors, the Amish also stood apart in some easily identifiable ways. Old Order church districts worked diligently to preserve family and community life and stood against pride and wastefulness. Old Orders in the Midwest, for example, continued to drive open carriages throughout the nineteenth century, considering closed-top buggies an unnecessary luxury.[13] They also maintained traditional grooming styles. The plain clothing of Old Order Amish men and women demonstrated humility and pointed to separateness. Men continued the use of hook-and-eye fasteners instead of buttons on their coats (and in some communities, shirts), as well as wearing untrimmed beards. Amish women wore devotional head coverings as a sign of biblical obedience and submission to God.[14]

During the late 1800s, a number of North American denominations—especially churches in the Holiness and Adventist traditions—encouraged or required members to dress simply and conservatively, but Old Order Amish appearance was noticeably plain, even by those standards. In the opinion of one observer in eastern Pennsylvania, Amish men wore "remarkably wide brimmed hats" and coats "plainer than those of the plainest Quakers."[15] Church custom, grounded in biblical principle and supported by the community, shaped everyday life as faith informed even how one got dressed in the morning.

Important as tradition and community were, they were rarely inflexible, and a fair amount of local variation seasoned Old Order life. The Old Order notion of *Ordnung,* after all, was one that prized local custom, so exact uniformity across the continent was never an ideal. Even within a local church district, the peculiar circumstances of a particular person might justify a degree of latitude in tampering with tradition. Old Order prescriptions were flexible in handling special needs.[16]

Nor were tradition and community stifling forces that smothered creative thinking. Those who chose the Old Order path were not uninformed people who retained conservative values because they knew no better. One important Amish lay leader who remained with the Old Order wing of the church for most of his life was the educated and articulate Samuel D. Guengerich.[17] Born in Somerset County, Pennsylvania, Guengerich moved with his family to Ohio and then to Iowa. As a young man, he taught in public schools and decided to return to Pennsylvania to receive formal training in education. In 1864, he received a teaching certificate from Millersville State Normal School (now Millersville University), and then taught several terms in Somerset County before going back to Iowa.

"A good education and well-cultivated mind may be regarded as almost indispensable in many respects," Guengerich wrote at one point in his studies.[18] He cultivated his own mind with visits to such places as Washington, D.C., where in 1889 he saw the Botanical Garden, the Smithsonian Institution the headquarters of the Federal Fish Commission, and the Capitol. At age twenty-eight he had purchased a "telescope and a mikeroscope [sic] and a box of drawing instruments" with which to explore his world.[19] Guengerich also established a private publishing business and issued a German periodical entitled *Herold der Wahrheit* (Herald of Truth).

Near the end of Guengerich's life, his congregation affiliated with the change-minded Amish Mennonites, but Guengerich himself seems to have been satisfied with his life as an Old Order church member and did not view his studies as incompatible with his faith. Although Guengerich's foray into the classroom was unusual, other Old Orders accepted him both as a student and teacher. His diaries record his regular interaction and church fellowship with the Old

The so-called "Nebraska" Amish are among the most conservative of all Old Orders. Clothing styles, for example, reflect early traditions: men and boys wear white shirts with no suspenders and notably wide-brimmed hats. Nebraska Amish drive simple buggies with white cloth enclosures, a practice that has given them the nickname the "white top people" (Weiss-Wegli Leit). Today there are some 20 Nebraska Amish church districts in Pennsylvania (mostly in Mifflin County) and one in Ohio.

Modern Assumptions and the Old Order Worldview

Many members of modern society find Old Order life perplexing and even mistaken. Much of this puzzlement stems from a disconnect between the fundamental assumptions of modern people—assumptions about self and society—and the assumptions of Old Order people. More than simply a collection of distinctive clothes and technological prohibitions, Old Order life is an expression of a distinct worldview and cluster of values.

Historian Theron Schlabach has suggested that North Americans wanting to understand Old Order life need temporarily to set aside modern assumptions and mental habits. This does not mean, Schlabach notes, that "one must romanticize Old Order groups or finally accept the Old Order outlook and critique of modern life. It is only to step outside the prison of mental habits long enough to understand a different view." Modern people seeking to understand Old Orders must *not* assume:

"That ideas expressed and tested in words are brighter and truer than ideas which take their form in personal community life.

"That people who accept the ideas of the eighteenth century's so-called Age of Reason are the 'enlightened' ones of the world.

"That change is usually good, and usually brings 'progress.' (The Old Order-minded accepted this change or that—a new tool, perhaps, or rail travel. But they were not progressiv*ists*.)

"That the individual is the supreme unit, individual rights are the most sacred rights, and human life richest when individuals are most autonomous.

"That the really important human events are those controlled in Washington, New York, Boston, London, Paris, and other centers of power—rather than events around hearths or at barn raisings or in meetings at Weaverland [Pennsylvania] or Plain City [Ohio] or Yellow Creek [Indiana] or Kalona [Iowa].

"That vigor of programs, institutions, activity (including Protestant-style missions) are a test of a Christian group's validity and faithfulness.

"That large organizations, organizational unity, and denominational and interdenominational tolerance are better measures of Christian success than is close-knit congregational life.

"That people who imbibe some alcohol or use tobacco have deeply compromised their Christianity.

"Similarly, that people are poor Christians if their sons and daughters wait until adulthood to put off youthful rowdiness and become sober-minded Christians.

"That a structure of rules and explicit expectations (some moral, others mainly just practical for group cohesion) is always legalistic and at odds with the Christian idea of grace.

"That *salvation* refers almost entirely to the individual's original transaction and covenant with God at the time of personal conversion.

"That in church history, words such as *reform* or *renewal* apply only to movements which share the progressivist faith and apply new methods and new activities; and that leaders who look to the past, or who think faithfulness may come by strict discipline, are simply reactionary and formalistic."

Quotations from Theron F. Schlabach, *Peace, Faith, Nation: Mennonites and Amish in Nineteenth-Century America* (Scottdale, Pa: Herald Press, 1988), 201-203.

Order Amish of Lancaster County, Pennsylvania, while he was a student at Millersville.

Nor was Guengerich the only trained school teacher among the Old Orders. Isaac Huyard, a Millersville student of a generation after Guengerich, joined the Amish. Huyard came from a Lutheran family and from 1886 to 1888 attended the Normal School at Millersville. In 1892 he converted to the Old Order Amish faith and remained a committed member the rest of his life. His wife, Mary Zook, had been raised in an Amish home, and Isaac himself had boarded with an Amish family during some of his growing-up years.[20]

Even in areas of church life and religious ritual, Old Orders were not an entirely uniform lot. The Old Order settlements in Somerset County, Pennsylvania; Kalona, Iowa; and Arthur, Illinois, for example, replaced the old Anabaptist hymnal, the *Ausbund*, with a newer hymn collection. Published in 1860, *Eine Unparteiische Lieder-Sammlung* (called the "Baer book" because it was printed by Johan Baer of Lancaster, Pa.) included *Ausbund* lyrics alongside other songs. Likewise, the Daviess County, Indiana, Amish adopted the 1892 *Unparteiische Liedersammlung* (called the "Guengerich book"), a hymn compilation that also included much *Ausbund* material.[21]

Some Old Orders initiated innovative ways to practice traditional mutual aid. In the mid-1870s, for example, Lancaster County Amish created a special fund to assist families in the event of fire or storm loss. Although the purpose was as old as the church itself, the methods were somewhat novel. Instead of church deacons receiving anonymous donations of alms for those hurt by the elements of nature, Amish Aid Society directors now assessed member families and charged them fixed rates. The whole program was far from bureaucratic and never replaced the work of the deacons who continued to collect money for the needy, but Amish Aid did represent a modest move in the direction of increased formality for a growing church.[22]

Perhaps most unusual were the Somerset County, Pennsylvania, Old Orders who built four church meeting-houses. In 1881, they erected two structures in Pennsylvania and two across the border in Garrett County, Maryland. The appearance of a meetinghouse in an Amish community had always signaled its decided move toward progressive Amish Mennonitism, but the Somerset group built physical church structures and remained Old Order.[23]

Not all communities were so successful in balancing tra-dition and selective change. In 1891, Old Order Amish in Johnson County, Iowa, also built meetinghouses with the intent of remaining conservative. Members even signed a statement which promised, "This church house shall and dare not be a means of granting us more freedom toward worldliness . . . ." In fact, the statement continued, "we are minded, and promise to strive for simplicity and uniformity in all things, and to remain true to the fundamentals of our faith."[24] Such statements summed up Old Order purposes nicely. Yet the two congregations involved proved less than successful; within three decades they had moved into the progressive Amish Mennonite camp, notwithstanding their earlier intentions.

The ability to make selected changes but not be swept away by acculturation and accommodation became something of an Old Order art. Sensing the implicit dangers of certain cultural trends, the Amish reacted in ways that seem today to have had deep sociological insight. But even Old Orders disagreed on how much change was threatening to Christian community and healthy family life. By 1881, some Mifflin County, Penn-sylvania, Amish believed that their own tradition-minded people were becoming caught up in material pursuits. Newer clothing styles, grooming habits, and technological innovation were being slowly accepted even in some conservative families. Because the group of concerned conservatives was comprised only of lay members and a deacon, they wrote to bishop Yost H. Yoder of Gosper County, Nebraska, and asked him to help organize their fellowship. Just a year earlier he had helped found the Gosper settlement.[25]

Yoder traveled to Pennsylvania to help the new ultra-conservative fellowship get started, and his role in the group's beginnings earned them the nickname "Nebraska Amish," despite their Appalachian home. The Nebraska (also called "Old School") Amish maintained especially traditional church and family life. The group retained some clothing standards typical of colonial American dress, and adopted remarkably few technological innovations in farming practices and technology, earning a reputation as being among the most conservative of all Old Orders. After 1904, their numbers increased somewhat as Yoder's Gosper County settlement dissolved and several of its families moved to Pennsylvania and joined the group bearing their old state's name.[26] Within the Old Order circle, then, there was some diversity. From the ultra-traditional "Nebraskans" to Somerset County Old Orders who met in meetinghouses and used new hymnals, the spectrum—though not terribly wide—was broader than many observers realized.

What Old Orders held in common, though, was a commitment to connecting spiritual experience and the very ordinary activity of daily life—and to do so in a church community of mutual accountability. More than anyone in the later nineteenth century, Holmes County, Ohio, bishop David A. Troyer articulated these understandings in his essays and poems, most of which he penned for his children.

In 1870, at age forty-three, Troyer became ill and feared he would not live to see his offspring to maturity. During the next fifteen years or so, he put his convictions on paper as a legacy to his family. Troyer stressed the power of prayer and the goodness of God in offering salvation to stubborn and ungrateful humanity. He also warned against the popular religious sentiment of the day which argued that "the outward has no significance, if only the heart is right." "Oh my beloved," the Old Order father cried, "do not be led astray by this destructive spirit of liberty." If personal freedom was the crown jewel of American political and popular culture, it pointed for Troyer only to self-destruction.

In "a short admonition and instruction relating to the so-called traditional lifestyle," the bishop explored the logic of Old Order living. He began by asserting that every church or social group has some markers of acceptable or expected behavior—some set of boundaries—whether explicit or implicit. The only question is whether or not those habits and practices support Christian faithfulness. Here Troyer could be both critical of and sympathetic toward his Old Order community. Tradition by itself was not the key. Do "not build on an *alte Ordnung* [just] because it is an old lifestyle, but rather because it is based on God's Word," he cautioned. If the orientation of other churches betrayed more of an interest in self-fulfillment than discipleship, "neither is ours praiseworthy in every respect," he admitted. Troyer especially bemoaned the presence of sexual immorality in some Amish families and feared the influence of popular politics and nationalistic patriotism on Christians whose primary loyalty was to be the church. "[Y]ou precious children," he concluded one of his pamphlets, "my sincere admonition to you is: Stay with what you have promised and accepted on bended knee before God and many witnesses, and remain steadfast and faithful and always increase in the work of the Lord."[27]

Debating boundaries

It was hardly surprising that David Troyer connected faithfulness and baptismal vows and the church. The sort of faithfulness he advocated required a discerning church community. The other side of community was accountability, accountability that sometimes took the form of church discipline if members asserted an individual right to privately choose their own path. Commitment and accountability were central to Old Order identity, and during the 1890s, Old Orders engaged in debates over the place and meaning of both. The immediate issues often involved the practice of shunning, but the underlying significance was broader. To which community was a Christian accountable, and how easily could the individual abandon one group and pick a more convenient one? Most specifically, did Old Orders break their baptismal promise to give and receive counsel in the church if they turned their backs on that church and affiliated with the Amish Mennonites?

The children of Moses and Magdalena Hartz in 1934: David (1860-1959), Mennonite; Rebecca (1854-1946), Amish Mennonite; Jacob (1857-1936), Amish Mennonite; and Moses, Jr. (1864-1946), one-time Mennonite, but by 1934 a member of the Religious Society of Friends (Quakers). In the 1890s, controversy over church discipline had swirled around Moses, Jr. and his parents.

During and after the *Diener-Versammlungen*, as the Amish sorted themselves into tradition-minded and change-minded camps, the two groups had maintained an uneasy, but cordial relationship. Those who left Old Order ranks as members in good standing and joined the Amish Mennonites were not excommunicated or shunned by the conservative group.[28] For their part, the Amish Mennonites did not meddle in Old Order church discipline. If someone left the Old Order Amish on bad terms, the Amish Mennonites would not accept that person as a member until the errant party had made peace with his or her former church. In short, those quietly leaving the Old Order church found a welcome among the Amish Mennonites, but the progressive church would not accept those who left the Old Orders in anger or in disobedience.

An incident involving Old Order preacher Moses Hartz Sr., and his wife Magdalena (Nafziger) Hartz, challenged the two groups' delicate balance.[29] Hartz had been a German orphan who found work and a home in the Conestoga Amish community of Lancaster and Berks counties, Pennsylvania.[30] Joining the church as a young man, Hartz was later ordained and served faithfully for many years, remaining with the conservative side during the division of the 1870s.[31] After 1894, trouble erupted in the Hartz home when son Moses Jr., took a job as a traveling mechanic for a millwork company and began routinely missing Sunday worship and wearing worldly clothing. When the church counseled Hartz to find another job, he left the church. But he had trouble finding another church home. The progressive Amish Mennonites denied him membership because of the angry terms on which he had severed his former ties, and so Hartz joined a Mennonite congregation that accepted him, despite his irregular participation in their congregational life.

Unlike joining the Amish Mennonites, taking membership with Mennonites was considered breaking of one's baptismal vows. As a result, the younger Hartz was excommunicated from the Old Order church. Shunning was the ritual corollary of excommunication, but preacher Moses Sr., and Magdalena announced that they would not shun their son. Now two generations of Hartzes were disturbing the community's harmony since the parents refused to practice a key church teaching because of family favoritism. The elder Hartz's congregation silenced him from preaching. Wanting to maintain ties with their son and with their Old Order family and friends, the Hartzes devised a way around their situation. They would simply switch their membership to the nearby Amish Mennonite church. By quietly joining the Amish Mennonites, they could leave the Old Order church without being excommunicated themselves, and once they were Amish Mennonites, they would not need to shun Moses Jr., since Amish Mennonites had abandoned the practice of social avoidance.

The Old Orders now faced a dilemma: should they discipline the elder Hartzes? Some argued that so long as the couple were joining another nonresistant, somewhat plain, Amish-related church, the ban and avoidance were unnecessary. Another party stood for what became known as *streng Meidung* (strict shunning). Advocates of "strict shunning" felt that excommunication and avoidance were required in any case where Old Order members broke their baptismal vows and left the tradition-minded group.

A series of Amish Mennonite and Old Order negotiations, including mediators from Ohio, failed to settle the matter. Under the assumption that the Old Orders would not object to the Hartzes becoming Amish Mennonites, the progressive church accepted them as members. A year later, in 1897, at a special gathering of conservative Amish leaders, most Old Order churches decided it was necessary to excommunicate the Hartzes for leaving under the conditions that they had.

Thereafter, no one would slip into the Amish Mennonite meetinghouse from an Old Order church district without also facing excommunication. The embrace of "strict shunning" marked another break between the Old Orders and the Amish Mennonites.

Not all Amish communities chose the path of "strict shunning," especially in the Midwest, and a situation in the Arthur, Illinois, church concluded differently. There, in the mid-1890s, Joni F. and Anna (Yutzy) Helmuth began attending a new Amish Mennonite church after they were excommunicated from the Old Order church.[32] When the Amish Mennonite church received the Helmuths as members, some Old Order Amish suggested that their excommunication be lifted and the shunning ended. But others in the community felt that the ban should remain in place. In the end, both groups got their way as the Arthur community compromised. Those who felt that the ban should be lifted acted as though it was. Those who wished to continue practicing shunning did as they saw fit.

The "strict shunning" question did not go away entirely. Into the twentieth century it lingered in some areas, demonstrating the seriousness with which many Amish regarded baptismal vows, obedience, and submission, some two centuries after Jacob Ammann and Hans Reist had first debated the issues.

Depression politics

Old Order life was never limited to church affairs. Although intent on remaining symbolically—and often substantially—separate from worldly society, the Amish were never unaware of or unaffected by current events that shaped the surrounding culture. In the 1890s, for example, many Amish families faced the same harsh economic realities that their neighbors did. The depression of 1893-1897

The Budget *and* Die Botschaft

For more than a century, Amish community news has circulated on the pages of *The Budget*, a weekly newspaper published in Sugarcreek, Ohio. Devoid of headlines, photographs, comics, and a sports page, *The Budget* serves its roughly 18,000 subscribers by publishing hundreds of letters, arranged in neat columns, from Amish correspondents across the country. Correspondents (known as "scribes") enumerate local events, including births, deaths, weddings, the weather, illnesses and accidents, visitors to the community, and the names of families who recently hosted church services in their homes. Scribes, most of whom are women, mail their handwritten columns to Sugarcreek, where each week the publisher typesets the material with little editing and no commentary.

Begun in 1890, *The Budget* was at first simply a local paper for the Sugarcreek community. During its early years, however, the paper began including news from scattered communities that included Amish households with kin in eastern Ohio. By 1899, each issue of the paper contained as many as thirty such letters from regular correspondents. The paper's owner was John C. Miller, a progressive Amish Mennonite, and in the early years, probably less than a third of the correspondents were Old Order. After about 1920, however, the paper's content and its subscriber list began to change. Miller sold the paper to Samuel A. Smith, a local Lutheran man who had warm friends among the Old Orders. Under the editorship of Smith and, later, his son, George R. Smith, *The Budget* took on more and more Old Order Amish scribes and readers. Since 1946, the paper has appeared in both a Local Edition and a National Edition. The local run is a conventional newspaper for Sugarcreek's non-Amish community, while the National Edition offers page after page of letters from Amish scribes across the continent. Today *The Budget* continues to be published by a non-Amish firm.

Popular as *The Budget* was, by the 1970s, its content had generated some consternation in certain Old Order circles. Since *The Budget* also included letters from members of more liberal Beachy Amish-Mennonite churches, as well as advertisements for books and musical recordings that flaunted the boundaries of Old Order *Ordnung*, a group of Amish readers launched *Die Botschaft* in 1975 as an alternative. Although it has a German name, *Die Botschaft* also published English-language letters from scribes across the country, though with somewhat tighter editorial control and more restricted advertising than *The Budget*.

Despite their somewhat different editorial lines, the two publications have considerable overlap, and some scribes submit the same letter to both papers. Since 2005, *Die Botschaft* has been issued by an Amish publisher in Dauphin County, Pennsylvania. Much like *The Budget*, *Die Botschaft* in a typical issue includes about 750 letters from 680 communities in twenty-five states and Ontario. Most of its scribes are also women.

The traditional format of these Amish publications serves to draw a sharp line between Amish society and contemporary Facebook and YouTube cultures. Yet although these image-less, black-and-white, hardcopy papers seem to have nothing in common with the Internet-based social media of the twenty-first century, they actually bear intriguing similarities. Like their modern counterparts, *The Budget* and *Die Botschaft* create "imagined communities" in which people who might never meet in person share mutual interests and forge an identity grounded in a common conversation of insider knowledge of acceptable topics and taboo subjects. Without leaving home, readers of these weekly publications participate in a virtual Amish community that stretches well beyond their local neighborhoods and has created a durable sense of what it means to be Amish today.

See Steven M. Nolt, "Inscribing Community: *The Budget* and *Die Botschaft* in Amish Life," 181-98, in *The Old Order Amish and the Media*, ed. by Diane Zimmerman Umble and David Weaver-Zercher (Baltimore: Johns Hopkins University Press, 2008).

was the deepest the United States had experienced in sixty years. During 1893 alone, some 500 banks failed and 16,000 businesses closed their doors for good. Nearly twenty percent of the work force was unemployed for some part of those bleak years.[33]

The farm economy was particularly hard hit, especially in the Midwestern and Plains states, where drought conditions added to the difficulties. Commodity prices dropped sharply and land values plummeted, while anti-inflationary monetary policy made loans harder to repay. Despite lower land costs, productive farms could still be out of reach for young families setting up business on their own, and hard-pressed farmers moved in search of cheaper acres. The Amish were a part of these migration patterns. During the depression years, Old Orders formed eleven new settlements scattered across Illinois, Indiana, Kansas, Michigan, Minnesota, Mississippi, North Dakota, and Ohio. Not all of the new settlements survived. Often the depression that gave them birth soon forced them to dissolve.[34]

One new settlement was located in southern Indiana's Brown County. In October 1896, families from Elkhart County, in the northern part of the state, took a train to scout for affordable acres farther south. Stopping in Indianapolis, Daniel M. Hochstetler, Eli J. Miller, S. J. Slabaugh, David Hochstetler, Joseph Schrock, and Jacob Troyer were surprised by the "immence [sic] crowd of people" on the streets and in the yard of the State house. Soon the men realized that presidential candidate and popular orator William Jennings Bryan "was to arrive and talk on the money question." Evidently the Amish travelers witnessed the parade that escorted Bryan to his hotel, but they "did not hear his speech" because their train was scheduled to leave for Brown County before Bryan began.[35]

The attention that Bryan received in Indianapolis was indicative of the political excitement that year. The 1896 election generated more interest than any since before the Civil War, and the Old Order Amish were aware of its significance. That year's bid for the White House pitted Ohio's Republican Governor William McKinley against Bryan, the 36-year-old spellbinding speaker and Democrat from Nebraska. The depression colored the debates since McKinley stood for strict monetary policies, high interest rates, and gold-backed currency, while Bryan countered with demands for lower interest rates, government regulation or purchase of utilities and railroads, and other seemingly radical economic measures. Even the candidates' personalities were a study in contrast. While McKinley calmly campaigned for office from his home in Columbus, Bryan canvassed the country, making hundreds of speeches and meeting thousands, like those in Indianapolis.[36]

Studying the Amish response to the 1896 election, Amish historian David Luthy concluded that many Amish likely sympathized with Bryan.[37] "Amish people, generally not involved in political affairs, were caught up in the debate and suspense of this election," Luthy discovered as he read letters in *The Budget*. Bryan "had great sympathy for the farmers and the working-class people," Luthy noted. "He appealed to the common man and thus to the Amish." Bryan was well-known as a sincere and theologically conservative Christian, which also may have increased his standing in Amish circles. In communities where some Old Orders voted, Bryan was the clear winner. In Holmes County, Ohio, for example, he logged a 2,300-vote majority.

Nevertheless, Bryan lost the election. The new President McKinley took office and promised that public confidence would bring back prosperity. When conditions in rural America only worsened, many farmers felt abandoned and expressed bitter disappointment with McKinley. Old Order Amish writers in *The Budget* shared the sentiments of other rural folks. When one *Budget* writer expressed satisfaction in McKinley's victory, an Indiana Amish farmer replied, "That hurrahing [for McKinley] was rather out of place for this part of the globe, because corn has dropped 3c a bu[shel] since the election." A Nebraskan Amishman agreed, adding sarcastically, "Prosperity is here and corn has advanced from 10c to 9c. If it keeps on it will soon go up to 5c a bu[shel]. Hurrah for McKinley." Most Amish writers joined in critiquing the president's economic policies.

Slowly the economic picture began to brighten, and by 1900, farmers who had made it through the depression years were pulling their operations together and looking toward turning a profit. The election of 1900 brought little reaction from Amish *Budget* scribes. Bryan once again challenged McKinley and once again lost. Interest in the political sphere seemed to have faded from the pages of *The Budget*, but national affairs would never be far from Amish lives. As the twentieth century unfolded, North American political, military, and economic developments would have far-reaching impact on Amish communities.

As 1899 drew to a close, Old Orders found themselves in circumstances far different from those that had begun the century. A new wave of immigration in the early 1800s had dramatically increased the Amish population, as well as settled the church more firmly in the Midwest and in Ontario. By mid-century, deep differences within the church had led some leaders to propose a series of unity meetings— which ended in permanent division. As the majority (Amish Mennonites) slowly moved toward merger with various Mennonite groups, the smaller (Old Order Amish) branch struggled to define and maintain itself in a world defined by urbanization and material progress. The Old Order response had not been to reject anything and everything that was new. But they did aim to be carefully selective in what they adopted into their communities. While the pace of change seemed rapid enough during the last quarter of the 1800s, it only increased in the new century.

—10—

Finding a Place in Modern America, 1900-1945

> *"If the world should stand another century, who can tell what it might bring forth?"*
> —a Missouri Amish man, 1900

Preoccupied with progress

In 1908, Amish characters took center stage in a novel by an Ohio social-reform advocate, Cora Gottschalk Welty. If larger society had long ignored the Amish, the dawning of the twentieth century brought the prospect of new encounters between modernity and a people who stood apart from its promises and goals. Welty's book pointed to some of these possibilities and problems, as the novel was one of the first to use the Amish for popular affect. On the surface, the book's plot was innocent enough. The main character in *The Masquerading of Margaret,* a young woman from New York City, went to live on an Amish farm and dressed in Amish clothes, a turn of events that concealed her true identity and complicated the romantic situation that developed between her and the book's male hero.[1]

But clearly the novel was more than a romantic comedy. Author Cora Welty was a political Progressive committed to redeeming society, restoring lost virtues, and building a brighter national future.[2] *The Masquerading of Margaret* used the example of the Amish to condemn gambling, political corruption, and unscrupulous monopolies. Readers also learned that Welty favored expanding public welfare and investigative news reporting. In Welty's telling, the Amish became upstanding models for Americans compromised by the quest for individual gain—though she was decidedly vague about how or why the Amish maintained the values she praised. As a political Progressive, she endorsed government intervention and cultural management to shape society as a whole, efforts that often afforded little room for dissenting religious minorities like the Amish to be different.

Without intending to, Welty's novel suggested themes that would take on importance for Amish people in the coming century. The book illustrated an emerging fascination with the Amish on the part of Americans at large. Romance writer Helen Reimensnyder Martin had published an Amish-theme novel about the same time as Welty, and by 1915 a Lancaster, Pennsylvania, tobacco shop owner was selling Amish picture postcards.[3] The development of mass tourism was still decades away, but Amish resistance to modernity already attracted Americans wistful for quieter, simpler days they believed were behind them.

The progressive impulse behind *The Masquerading of Margaret* also foreshadowed conflict with the state that would mark much of the Amish experience after 1900. Reforming society along progressive lines would involve pressing citizens into a common mold, socialized through public high school curricula, integrated through the programs of the welfare state, and given a patriotic sense of identity through participation in global war. If Welty thought her vision of the future was compatible with Amish sensibilities, time would prove otherwise.

The Amish, of course, were hardly oblivious to the claims of social progress and turn-of-the-century technological change. "Many wonderful inventions were made during the past century," a Missouri *Budget* scribe wrote in 1900, "and if the world should stand another century who can tell what it might bring forth?"[4] Phonographs, telephones, electric lights, and other household consumer goods were becoming more common in American homes, soon to be joined by automobiles and "aeroplane" travel. Just two years earlier, the United States had defeated Spain in a quick, calculated war to establish itself as an imperial power with colonies in the Caribbean and the Pacific. Whether such developments implied moral advancement, as progressives believed, remained to be seen—especially since improved communication and intriguing inventions failed to banish war or economic depression in the years that followed.

Technology, *Ordnung*, and identity

Welty's progressive optimism was widespread, in part because of the apparent promise of a brighter economic future, even among rural residents hit hard by the 1890s depression. Now farm profits increased almost annually, and the years 1910-1914 were financially the best in American farm history. As a decidedly rural people, the Amish shared in this turnaround. They remained concentrated in the Midwest and Pennsylvania, though the early twentieth century also saw the beginning of new settlements in Kansas, Ohio, Michigan, Iowa, and Oklahoma. Amish families also moved to Kent County, Delaware, in 1915, taking their church to that state for the first time.[5]

Some of the boost in agricultural output and profitability resulted from the general strength of the larger economy in those years, but changes in technology and farm efficiency also contributed. Yet that new technology brought a variety of

A picture postcard produced about 1910 showing an Amish family on the streets of Ephrata, Pennsylvania.

social changes in its wake, changes involving automation and the transformation of some community "work frolics" into single-operator tasks that made neighborly cooperation and the value of family labor less important. Until then, Old Order identity had not been tethered to technological taboos, but, as the new century opened, the response of the Amish to mechanization and the individualism it spawned sparked a reappraisal.

For example, the automobile, another convenience of the twentieth century's first decades, promised what its name suggested: automatic mobility. For a people who valued community, cars threatened to accentuate the worst of worldly individualism. Autonomous mobility weakened interdependent family ties and encroached on time spent at home. Moreover, the expense of vehicles and the way in which car models quickly became recognized status symbols made them incompatible with Christian stewardship and humility, the Amish believed.

The particularly troubling elements of status and individual choice were linked most closely to car *ownership*, which the Amish forbade, even as they acknowledged that in some cases automobile travel might be beneficial or necessary. The Amish would ride in cars or even hire a driver if circumstances demanded, though they might disagree among themselves on just what those necessary circumstances were. In any case, the advent of American automobile culture was gradual enough that most Old Orders were able to respond to it in a constructive way.[6]

In some cases, however, technological change and the accompanying social implications were sudden enough to create church conflict. During the fall and winter of 1909-1910 in Lancaster County, Pennsylvania, for example, about a fifth of the Old Order church withdrew from their larger fellowship and reorganized under the leadership of a sympathetic Mifflin County bishop. Nicknamed the "Peachey Church," the seceders were still upset about the Moses Hartz incident and wanted to do away with "strict shunning."[7] But the disagreement over excommunication was only part of the story. In addition to favoring a more lenient church discipline, the new group sanctioned in-home telephones and alternating current electricity in houses, barns, and shops.

The quick adoption of such things on the part of the breakaway group pushed the larger Old Order church in Pennsylvania to oppose more firmly such an innovation because it could be disruptive to community stability. Before 1910, Old Orders had not arrived at a consensus on the use and abuse of new gadgetry, but the eager embrace of change by the Peachey faction helped incorporate technological cautions and prohibitions more decidedly within the Old Order church's *Ordnung*.[8]

During the early 1900s, telephones had come into limited use among the Lancaster Amish. Only after serious community problems erupted from gossip spread over the lines did the church take a stand. By 1910, Old Orders prohibited convenient in-home telephone ownership as a dangerous temptation—though phone *use* was never forbidden. Modern means of communication might prove necessary in an emergency, but easy access to private conversation would only lead to trouble, the church decided. The breakdown of face-to-face conversation and community, which rode on the coattails of in-home phones, would not be tolerated in a church that placed the quality of human relationships above individual convenience. Amish families who had purchased phones removed them, and the *Ordnung* barred future in-home installation. The simultaneous "Peachey Church" adoption of the phone galvanized Old Order opposition. The withdrawal of a minority group of Lancaster progressives helped to unite the majority along more definitely conservative lines.[9]

Change and reaction did not follow a uniform pattern, however, and change-minded members were not the only ones to secede into identifiable subgroups. In Washington and Johnson counties, Iowa, it was the more conservative-leaning members who separated from the larger church in order to maintain congregational, farm, and family life as they understood it. The Upper and Lower Deer Creek districts there had been undergoing slow but steady change, erecting meetinghouses in 1890 and abandoning the *Ausbund* in favor of a new hymn collection that included fewer Reformation-era songs.[10]

Some households were displeased with what they saw as the church's progressive "drift," and, in 1914, seven traditionalist families left and moved north to Buchanan County, Iowa. Although they had worshiped in a meetinghouse for nearly a quarter century in their old community, after moving to Buchanan, the group reverted to gathering in homes on Sunday mornings. (The withdrawal of the conservative families may have hastened Lower Deer Creek's pace of change. In 1917, its members embraced in-home telephones, severed ties with other Old Orders, and soon affiliated with a Mennonite conference.)

The new Buchanan County settlement gained a reputation as a notably conservative community, even by Old Order standards. Yet rather than hindering growth, this orientation attracted families from Kansas, Wisconsin, Indiana, and elsewhere who were disappointed with the degree of change they saw in their home districts. The distinctive mix of Old Orders eager to maintain a strict *Ordnung* and unusually suspicious of the promises of progress gave the Buchanan County church a special flavor, something of a conservative conscience within the larger Old Order world.[11]

About the same time as the Buchanan group formed, another markedly tradition-minded movement emerged within the Wayne County, Ohio, settlement. The precise issues that sparked the separation are no longer clear, but after 1913, an ultra-conservative group took shape under the leadership of Apple Creek's bishop, Samuel E. Yoder. Nick-named "Swartzentruber Amish" after a subsequent set of leaders, the movement became a distinct sub-group within the eastern Ohio Old Order community. In the decades that followed, as most Amish in the area adapted some of the century's new technologies for farm and home in limited and selective ways, the Swartzentrubers did not. For example, Swartzentrubers rejected pressure naphtha lamps and indoor bathrooms, virtually all changes in clothing patterns and carriage styles, and nonelectrical appliances such as natural gas refrigerators. Nor did belt power from tractor engines find a place on Swartzentruber farms. While many Swartzentrubers remained in the Wayne and Holmes counties area, by the early twenty-first century there were some 119 Swartzentruber districts in fifteen states.[12]

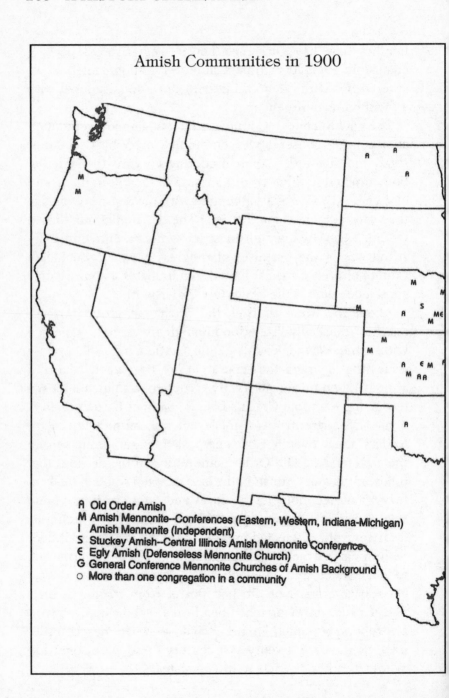

Amish Communities in 1900

A Old Order Amish
M Amish Mennonite--Conferences (Eastern, Western, Indiana-Michigan)
I Amish Mennonite (Independent)
S Stuckey Amish--Central Illinois Amish Mennonite Conference
E Egly Amish (Defenseless Mennonite Church)
G General Conference Mennonite Churches of Amish Background
O More than one congregation in a community

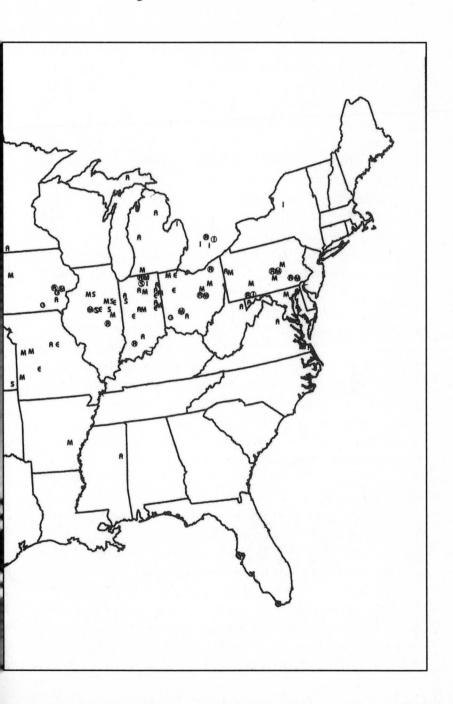

The Buchanan County and Swartzentruber Amish signaled a growing variety within Old Order circles—variety not unrelated to the issues that had divided the Amish in the 1800s, but now stemming more from different visions of how to apply *Ordnung* in an increasingly technologically-driven and -determined world. These ultra-conservatives, along with the older "Nebraska" group in Mifflin County, Pennsylvania, resisted in remarkable ways pressure to accept change as inevitable.

Most church districts, though, combined serious reservations about the claims of progress with a willingness to make selective, practical concessions to modernity. They would impose taboos on things that undermined family and community ties—automobiles, public utility electricity, in-home telephones, for example—but adopt belt power from stationary steam engines to operate threshing machines and other small equipment. In the early 1900s, some began using tractor engines to provide a similar source of belt power, while resisting the use of tractors to do field work. Although all Old Orders remained purposefully out of step with larger society, some were more disciplined than the rest. Soon, the coming of World War I would test the discipline and commitment of Amish throughout North America.

War fever

Church members in Ontario faced the prospect of war in 1914, although Canada did not begin drafting men until late summer 1917. At first, officials freely gave agricultural production deferments to Amish men, but easy releases did not last, and the next spring, Ottawa suddenly canceled all draft exemptions. After April 1918, no one could claim conscientious objector (CO) status in Canada. Instead, Amish men were to join the army and then wait for a government directive asking their commanding officer to issue them

*Patriotic neighbors vandalized the Metamora, Illinois, Amish Menno-
nite Church during World War I.*

indefinite leaves of absence. Most Amish did, in fact, receive
this second-hand military deferment, but the situation was
not satisfactory to the Amish since it meant they remained
officially registered soldiers even when they returned home.
But before anything could be done to change the arrangement, the war ended.[13] The First World War experience of
the Canadian Amish was hardly ideal, but it turned out to be
better than what happened south of the border.

America's spring 1917 entry into World War I came as a
surprise to many Americans. While Europe had been at war,
politicians had preached noninvolvement, insisting that the
United States had no interest in foreign fighting. America would remain "neutral in fact as well as in name . . .
impartial in thought as well as in action," President Woodrow
Wilson had assured the country.[14] So, when the country
suddenly entered the fray, the federal government mounted
a swift and massive public propaganda campaign to rally
national support. Although many Americans were initially
skeptical of the war effort—still sure that the affair was
none of their business—the posters, rallies, war-bond sales,

and organization of patriotic citizen groups soon engendered broad sympathy. The government also systematically used churches and church periodicals to stir up war fever.[15] The Amish, however, would not be stirred.

The first test for many young Amish men came with the military draft.[16] Because of early public opposition to conscription, no draft law immediately followed the declaration of war. By late spring, however, Congress had instituted national conscription with an act that included vague provision for religious conscientious objectors. Still, the possible promise of conscientious objection was enough to prompt some draftees to try and gain exemption. In Mifflin County, Pennsylvania, Amish layman John S. Peachey worked tirelessly as a draft counselor for Amish youth in his area. Peachey kept abreast of changes in conscription regulations, learned how to fill out government forms, and met with Mennonite leaders to discuss questions of draft exemption or deferment. Occasionally Peachey was successful, yet even when young men did receive formal recognition as conscientious objectors from local draft boards they typically had to report to an army camp anyway.[17]

Once COs arrived at their assigned military posts, no specific guidelines detailed what they were supposed to do, nor what the military was to do with them. The Army had planned to send all men to training camps and sort out the CO question there. Once COs were in the camps and part of the military routine, the War Department hoped the men would forget their scruples and join the regular forces. Peer pressure and separation from their parents and church leaders would weaken young conviction, the government hoped.[18]

In some cases, the military strategy worked. Of the dozens of young Amish men drafted and sent to camps, a few did join the fighting corps. Amishman Enos Stutzman, of Buck-

Amish conscientious objectors at Camp Funston, Kansas, during the First World War.

lin, Kansas, gave in to pressure, but took a noncombatant role as a bugler.[19] Some accepted regular infantry positions. Although Secretary of War Newton D. Baker had told a Mennonite leader, "Don't worry. We'll take care of your boys," the Army's policy became one of intimidation and threats to coerce drafted COs into taking up rifles.[20]

But Army tactics did not always produce Amish soldiers. Drafted in October 1918, Holmes County farmer Rudy Yoder reported to Camp Jefferson, Jefferson City, Missouri. Scared and exhausted, he tried to explain that he was a CO, but under intense pressure he agreed to don a uniform, march with the other men, and wait for word on his status from the commander.

After several weeks, it became obvious that no directive would appear, and he was about to begin rifle training. Yoder decided that he would stop wearing his uniform and with-

draw from the routine camp activities in which he slowly had
become involved. The decision was momentous and could
have brought a court martial trial. Officers took him outside
the camp to what looked like three fresh graves. Menacingly
brandishing pistols, the officers told Yoder his would be the
fourth grave if he did not put on his uniform the next morning. After a sleepless night, Yoder reported for breakfast in
civilian clothes. Although other abuse continued, the officers
never carried out their death threat.[21]

Unlike Yoder, most Amish men refused to participate in
the Army from the moment they reported to camp. Despite
threats and pressure, Amish draftees remained unwilling
to fight, wear military uniforms, or perform jobs they felt
aided the Army's war-making ability. At times, the military
kept COs separate from each other in an attempt to wear
down their resolve, while in other camps, COs were herded
together and dealt with as a group.

Either way, many Amish conscientious objectors—along
with other objectors—received verbal abuse, beatings, and
wire-brush scrubbings. In addition, soldiers sometimes forcibly shaved Amish beards. COs might be ordered to stand
for long periods of time in the sun without water, and those
who refused to wear military uniforms were at times left in
cold, damp cells with no clothing at all. In some cases, officers "baptized" Amish objectors in camp latrines in mockery
of their Anabaptist beliefs. Many COs remained in abusive
camp situations until well after the war was over and
demobilization began. For the Amish who endured World
War I military camps, memories remained powerful and
deeply emotional.[22]

Pro-Germanism?

Young men in military camps were not the only ones to
feel the pressures of patriotic war fever. In some communi-

ties, onlookers and officials labeled the Amish as German
sympathizers. After all, they spoke a German dialect, would
not join the Army, and in most cases refused to buy war
bonds. The conclusion seemed inescapable: the Amish (and
members of other ethnically-German peace churches, such
as the Mennonites and Hutterites) wanted Germany to win
the war. Citizens' groups regularly hounded Amish and
Mennonites who would not buy bonds or otherwise financially support the national campaign. Patriotic neighbors
torched two Mennonite meetinghouses, while civic groups
vandalized several Amish Mennonite meetinghouses or
posted American flags in front of them.[23] Not having church
buildings, the Old Order Amish escaped such attacks, but
they were the subjects of official government observation.

"I Make This Humble Plea"

Old Order Amish woman Rosa (Bender) Bontrager
wrote the following letter to Secretary of War Newton
D. Baker a month and a half after her husband, Gideon
J. Bontrager, was drafted and reported as a conscientious
objector to Camp Taylor, Louisville, Kentucky.

Shipshewana, Indiana
August 12, 1918

To the Hon. Secretary of War, Baker
Washington, D.C.

I am informed that the administration does not favor
the practice of taking registrants for military service
whose wives have no means of support other than their
own labor. I therefore take the liberty to present my
case to you and humbly plead that you consider it.

I am a child of an orphan's home. I have no money of any kind and have no inheritance to expect.

I was married on January 25, 1917 at the age of 21 to Gideon J. Bontrager. He was called to camp on July 2, 1918, leaving me alone without any means of support other than my own labor. We have no home of our own and I am compelled to work out[side of the home] for my living. We failed to state all these facts fully when my husband filled out his questionnaire.

I may further state that my husband is a so-called conscientious objector and cannot because of conscientious scruples render any service under the military establishment, and must therefore also refuse to accept any pay from the government, and neither can I as his wife accept any money from the government for my support.

Because of these facts I make this humble plea to you, trusting that you may consider it and give instructions to the effect that my husband be returned to me.

Yours truly,
Mrs. Gideon Bontrager

Tragically, Rosa received her wish. In October 1918 she became ill with influenza and Gideon obtained a leave of absence to visit her from October 16 to 27. On the 25th, Rosa died. Gideon had to report back to Camp Taylor on the day of her funeral. One month later he was given the farm furlough his wife had requested.

The complete story is found in Nicholas Stoltzfus, comp. *Nonresistance Put to Test* (Salem, Ind.: Nicholas Stoltzfus, 1981), 25-27.

Throughout the conflict, the War Department's Military Intelligence Division kept Mennonites and Amish under surveillance. A lengthy Division memorandum detailed the domestic spying. Some of the government's research information came from articles in the 1911 *Encyclopedia Britannica*, but the document also included original espionage material that the Division collected. Names, addresses, and information on church leaders appeared in War Department files, though the decentralized Old Orders were something of a frustration to the Division. Amish congregationalism left no single leader or denominational office to target. About the Old Orders, Military Intelligence could only note: "No organization. Services generally held in German."[24] Nevertheless, Washington officials were watching the Amish.

When Old Order bishop Manasses E. Bontrager of Ford County, Kansas, wrote a lengthy letter for publication in *The Budget*, federal officials caught wind of the content. In the letter, Bontrager urged Amish not to buy government war bonds. He chided those who had voted in the elections that brought the current administration into office, and he praised the young men who remained steadfast in their refusal to join the armed forces, even to the point of spending time in military prisons. "What would become of our nonresistant faith," Bontrager asked rhetorically, "if our young brethren in camp would yield? From the letters I receive from brethren in camp, I believe they would be willing to die for Jesus rather than betray Him." The bishop urged his readers to muster the same resolve: "Let us profit by their example they have set us so far, and pray that God may strengthen them in the future."[25]

Two and a half months later, Bontrager was arrested on grounds that his *Budget* piece was "inciting and attempting to incite insubordination, disloyalty and refusal of duty in the military and naval forces of the United States."[26] Bontrager appeared for trial in Cleveland, Ohio, the jurisdiction of the paper's home state. He and *Budget* editor Samuel H. Miller were convicted and fined $500 each. The freedom to express religious conviction, it seemed, was one of the war's casualties.

Scuffles over schools

Conflicts with state authority did not end with Armistice Day in 1918. The return to post-war "normalcy" brought with it new expectations for higher education and compulsory schooling. Born of Progressive optimism about social engineering and recent war-time anxiety over the place of immigrants in American society, the drive to reform public education was grounded in a belief that schools would produce forward-thinking, assimilated, and patriotic citizens. Exposure to new ideas through a centrally managed curriculum would strip away old values, customs, and traditions and provide a rising generation with a common culture.[27] New state guidelines mandated additional subjects and textbooks, longer school terms, and attendance—often through age sixteen—in an effort to make the social ideal more quickly a reality.

Although the Amish had never opposed education, and had participated in the locally-managed, nineteenth-century system of public primary schools, many Old Orders were wary of the tone and approach of early twentieth-century secondary schools. Parents believed that learning in such settings was of little practical value, and even threatened to undermine their way of life. Troubling, too, was the "worldly wisdom" of competition and individual self-improvement that lay at the heart of the high school curricula championed by public-school reformers.

Formal schooling should remain basic, the Amish believed, in harmony with the church and the home, and be one part of a broader education that included developing work and voca-

The Smoketown, Pennsylvania, consolidated public school, built 1937 and razed 1993. Local Amish opposed the new building.

tional skills on the farm or in family trades. Learning how to live with one's family, church, and community were skills missing from expanded public school studies, yet with longer school years and increased attendance requirements, children had even less time to be with their parents and grandparents.[28]

In 1921, Indiana mandated school attendance through age sixteen and set a new high school curriculum. Amish parents resisted sending their teens beyond eighth grade, objecting to certain high school classes, immodest physical education uniforms, and the general tone of the high school program. Controversy brewed for several years and resulted in the arrest, fining, and in some cases imprisonment of as many as two dozen fathers in the Elkhart and LaGrange counties settlement before the state backed down.[29]

Next door in Ohio, the 1921 Bing Act made school attendance compulsory through age eighteen, though it allowed some children to receive work permits and leave school at age sixteen. Considered a major reform bill in Columbus, the Bing Act was no favorite of the Holmes and Wayne counties Amish who kept their teens at home and objected to content in high school social studies and hygiene texts. In January 1922, officials arrested five fathers on charges of neglecting their children's welfare. Authorities declared most of the men's school-age children wards of the court, sent them to an orphanage, and would not allow them to wear Amish clothes. Distressed parents decided that keeping their families together was more important than opposing the Bing Act and promised to comply with the law. Amish teens would apply for work permits at sixteen and hope the state would be generous.[30]

For some Amish, these school difficulties, coming on the heels of World War I draft difficulties, were enough to start them thinking about leaving the United States. When word arrived in Wayne County of inexpensive, fertile land in northern Mexico, some Amish decided to emigrate.[31] In the fall of 1923, ten household heads signed a contract for 5,000 acres in Paradise Valley, Galeana Municipality, Nuevo León. Eventually, eleven households—most from Ohio, but some from Missouri—moved there. Traveling by rail, they took their household goods and animals with them. The land in Mexico was fertile and with some irrigation proved quite productive. The Amish built adobe homes and traveled the 60 miles to town to buy and sell. Free from restrictive Ohio school laws, they organized their own school without interference.

Although the settlement had the potential for economic growth, it did not last. A promised railroad connecting Paradise Valley with other communities never materialized. Then too, a smoldering guerilla war in northern Mexico caught Amish families in troop-pillaging. Perhaps most importantly, no Amish church ever developed there. No ministers moved to Mexico and no ordinations ever took place there. Without the formation of a more stable spiritual base, the community found life discouraging. By 1929, the Amish had left Mexico, either returning to Ohio or moving to a new settlement in North Carolina.[32]

A legal battle in Pennsylvania

School controversy erupted in eastern Pennsylvania more than a decade after it did in the Midwest. Since 1925, Pennsylvania law had required school attendance until age fourteen, but often school boards—some of which included elected Amish members—gave work permits to Amish youth who left the classroom early. The confrontation that developed in the Keystone State in the mid-1930s had to do with the consolidation of local schools. Lancaster County districts began closing rural one-room schools and busing children out of their immediate communities to larger buildings. By 1937, school centralization came to involve the area in central Lancaster County in which many Amish lived. The resulting public protest on the part of the Amish, while not exactly unprecedented, drew more media attention and cast a higher profile than any previous event involving Old Orders.[33]

That year, East Lampeter Township announced plans to close ten local schools and replace them with a consolidated institution in the village of Smoketown. Breaking with tradition, some Amish and a few non-Amish friends hired Philadelphia lawyers and received a court order halting construction. A higher court overturned the injunction and the building went up, but the Amish had shown their resolve to keep education locally oriented and managed.[34] Amish leaders disapproved of members' resorting to lawsuits, seeing the action as a violation of the church's nonresistant faith, but a solid majority of lay members were set against the new school, and many would not send their children to it.[35]

An Amish parochial school in Elkhart County, Indiana, in 2002.

Added to the mix was new legislation passed in the summer of 1937 that raised to fifteen the age at which students were eligible to leave school on work permits. Now even church leaders thought it was time to petition the legislature. A 130-foot-long letter, almost all of which was given to some 3,000 signatures (including Old Order and conservative Mennonites), went to Harrisburg asking the state to rescind the new requirement.[36] An Amish committee known as the "Delegation for Common Sense Schooling" met with legislators to reach a compromise. The delegation reported that it did "not wish to withdraw from the common public schools," but "at the same time we cannot hand our children over to where they will be led away from us."[37]

As matters grew tense during the 1937-1938 school year, the Amish began to consider withdrawing from the public system. The following November, two private elementary schools opened in Lancaster County, marking the beginning of a new era in Amish parochial education.[38] Meanwhile, new petitions arrived at the capitol asking relief from the age-fifteen requirement. By the end of that school year, the legislature had rolled back the compulsory attendance age to fourteen, though some children might have to attend consolidated public high schools until their fourteenth birthday if they completed eighth grade before that age. Fearful that the agreement would not last, some families made plans to leave Pennsylvania. Beginning in 1940, several households moved to Saint Mary's County, Maryland, where that state seemed more ready to work with the church.[39]

The Beachy Amish-Mennonites

During the 1920s and 1930s, Amish communities faced not only changes in state school law, but also shifting loyalties within their own ranks. After 1927, an important new Amish group emerged—the so-called Beachy Amish-Mennonites. The Beachy movement had roots in the 1890s "strict shunning" controversies. In 1895, the settlement that spanned the border between Somerset County, Pennsylvania, and Garrett County, Maryland, had divided—Old Orders to the north and a Conservative Amish Mennonite congregation in Maryland—but numerous friendly and family connections continued between the two groups. How the Old Order church should respond if someone left for the neighboring progressive group remained something of a question.[40]

For two decades, the traditional leanings of Somerset bishop Moses D. Yoder muted the controversy. Yoder supported "strict shunning" in cases where Old Order individuals switched their allegiance to the Garrett County church. After 1916, however, the dynamics changed when Moses M. Beachy was ordained bishop to assist the aging Yoder, and Beachy let it be known that he would not excommunicate or shun Old Order Amish who became Amish Mennonites. Efforts to mediate the disagreement between Yoder and

George W. Beiler (1884-1959) and Susie Kauffman Beiler (1887-1953) with their four daughters, Hilda, Lillian, Mary, and Katie, going to church in their 1929 Chevrolet. In 1927, George had been ordained minister in the "John A. Stoltzfus Church" in Lancaster County, Pennsylvania, one of the congregations that formed the nucleus of the emerging Beachy Amish fellowship.

Beachy failed, and in June 1927, in the last summer of his life, old Moses Yoder and those who wished to maintain a discipline that included "strict shunning" quietly separated from the rest of the Amish and began holding their own worship and communion services. The majority of the Somerset church followed Beachy's leadership.[41]

But very quickly, the issue of shunning moved into the background. From the Old Order's point of view, the Beachy church's loose application of avoidance symbolized a more significant embrace of change. Indeed, Beachy's congregation soon adopted progressive Sunday schools, and some members wired their homes for electricity. Within a year and a half, the group accepted automobile ownership. Whereas Beachy and his supporters saw their approach to modifying traditional practices as selective and in the service

The Beachy Amish-Mennonites: A Brief Chronology

1909–1910	Thirty-five families, collectively nicknamed the Peachey Church, withdraw from the Lancaster County Old Order church, objecting to "strict shunning." John A. Stoltzfus later becomes bishop.
1927	The Somerset County, Pennsylvania, Amish community divides. Moses Beachy and supporters reject "strict shunning." Moses Yoder leads the Old Orders.
1928	John A. Stoltzfus' church in Lancaster County and Moses Beachy's church in Somerset County both permit automobile ownership.
1929	Leaders from the Beachy and Stoltzfus churches begin fraternal exchanges.
1930s–1940s	Moses Beachy helps organize congregations in other states, forming a loose network of Beachy Amish-Mennonite churches.
1950–1955	Old Order Amish (not Beachy Amish-Mennonites) interested in mission work hold a series of "Amish Mission Conferences," begin publishing *Witnessing* newsletter, and organize a Mission Interests Committee, which sponsors work in Mississippi, Ontario, and Arkansas.
1955	Beachy Amish-Mennonites organize Amish Mennonite Aid, a relief and service organization.

1960s	Amish involved in the 1950s' mission movement leave Old Order circles; many affiliate with Beachy churches. The influx of new members with an interest in evangelism changes the tone and tenor of the Beachy fellowship.
1970	Beachy Amish-Mennonites begin Calvary Bible School, Calico Rock, Arkansas, and begin a monthly periodical, *Calvary Messenger.*
1981	Christian Aid Ministries organizes as an international relief and service ministry and is supported by many Beachy Amish-Mennonites.
1990s	Increasing diversity among Beachy Amish-Mennonites results in calls for greater uniformity in church life and practices among congregations. When uniformity proves elusive, subgroups emerge as distinct constituencies with different emphases, including Maranatha Amish-Mennonites, Berea Amish-Mennonites, and Ambassadors Amish-Mennonites.
2014	There are 153 Beachy Amish-Mennonite and related churches in the United States and Canada with 10,300 members. In addition, there are congregations in Belize, Costa Rica, El Salvador, Ireland, Kenya, Nicaragua, Paraguay, Romania, and Ukraine.

of church renewal, their Old Order neighbors were more apt to find it a rather thoughtless chasing after the world's goods. Regardless of interpretation, the Beachy Amish-Mennonites' use of motor vehicles set them apart from the Old Order Amish, even as they maintained relatively plain dress, German-language worship, and prohibitions against worldly entertainment.[42]

In time, Beachy's change-minded congregation became the center of a network of like-minded Amish in other parts of North America. The first connection was with heirs of the progressive "Peachey Church," who had withdrawn from the Lancaster Old Orders back in 1909. Under the leadership of John A. Stoltzfus, a portion of the Peachey group had adopted automobiles in 1927 and soon began meeting in a church building, thus further distinguishing itself from its Old Order neighbors.[43]

During the 1930s and 1940s, bishops Moses Beachy and John A. Stoltzfus—sometimes together, sometimes separately—helped organize similarly minded congregations in central Pennsylvania, Ohio, Ontario, and Indiana, further expanding the Beachy Amish fellowship. As the Beachy circle grew, it remained loosely structured, in line with traditional Amish congregationalism. This orientation was one way the Beachy churches maintained continuity with their past.[44] Later, in the 1960s and 1970s, the Beachy church would experience an influx of former Old Orders who had a deep interest in mission work and who would change the character and tenor of the Beachy fellowship significantly. At mid-century, however, the Beachy Amish probably still represented equal measures of innovation and tradition.

Depression days

While the Beachy division initially affected only a few Amish settlements, the financial squeeze of the Great Depression troubled virtually all communities. America's farm and small-town families felt the effects of the market collapse of the 1930s as much as did the nation's city-dwellers. One notable effect of the Depression on the Amish was a near halt to the establishment of new settlements. Of the few settlements begun during the Depression years, none survived long. Economic hardship and the lure of cheap land prompted some families to try new ventures in Arkansas, Indiana, North Dakota, Oklahoma, and Pennsylvania, but the same harsh realities that brought the new communities into existence also caused most to fail rather quickly.[45] Some younger men could not afford land anywhere, and in northern Indiana a handful took factory jobs, beginning a shift toward off-farm employment that would later become common among Amish in that region.[46]

Some Amish interpreted the tough times as a challenge to deepen spiritual roots. "The Depression years were such times when we all needed to look to a Higher Power," one Amish minister later thought. He was impressed with "how some people could have patience with each other, the creditor with the debtor."[47] Other members believe fewer controversies surfaced during those years as church districts pulled together in the face of uncertain financial futures. Mutual aid and sharing scarce resources took more frequent and concrete forms.[48]

In 1931, an anonymous Amish man's diagnosis of the country's economic ills found its way onto the front page of the Lancaster, Pennsylvania, *Intelligencer Journal*. Under the title, "Adoption of Too Many Labor Saving Devices Blamed for Depression," the author argued that "Extremity Is Cause of Many Ills Today." Mechanized farming practices, which increased agricultural production faster than population growth, were the root of Depression problems, he insisted. If only farmers and other business leaders had been satisfied with less, they would have avoided the troubles brought on by too much borrowing and debt. The use of so-called labor-saving machinery, he continued, threw hard-working people out of jobs. "They made a profit before they used labor-saving devices," the Amish man charged, but greed had led business down the road of bankruptcy.[49]

When U.S. Department of Agriculture agents visited the Lancaster settlement, however, they found fewer people reflecting philosophically on the Depression's causes and more digging in to the daily task of managing hard times. The USDA was especially taken with the contribution of Amish women to their families' financial well-being, noting that many put in cash-crop potatoes, raised poultry, and sold eggs to make ends meet. Surveys revealed that, on average, farm wives processed the equivalent of $422 worth of food, thanks in large part to their annually canning of 345 quarts of vegetables and fruit per household. Coupled with limited consumer consumption—Amish women also did much of their families' sewing, for example—this productivity led the agents to conclude that "women's labor was central to successful family farming."[50]

Families still struggled, despite a commitment to hard work. By 1933, United States farm income had fallen on average more than sixty percent, and the federal government took drastic steps to stabilize the rural economy.[51] The most famous measure was President Franklin D. Roosevelt's Agricultural Adjustment Administration (AAA). One facet of the AAA that drew response from the Amish was a provision paying farmers to reduce the acres they planted. An attempt to boost prices by reducing supply, the tactic seemed wrongheaded to most Amish, especially when they heard stories of starvation in America's cities. Said one Amish man, "We felt this was a cruel way to get money into circulation again, being so many people were going hungry."[52] While some Amish farmers did reduce their planting in line with AAA guide-

Jonathan Fisher: Traveling Amish man

Jonathan B. Fisher of Bareville, Pennsylvania, was adventurous. As a farmer, cheesemaker, and farmers' market merchant, Fisher led a typical Old Order life. But Jonathan Fisher also harbored a deep desire to explore the world, and as a young man he visited many places in the United States, Canada, and Mexico.

Fisher also took several longer trips and wrote two books about his adventures. In 1908, he sailed for Europe to learn about European methods of cheese production. He visited England, France, Switzerland, Germany, Denmark, and the Netherlands; rode to the top of the Eiffel Tower; and went on an Alpine-mountain climbing expedition. Returning home, he published *A Trip to Europe and Facts Gleaned on the Way*, a 346-page book detailing his excursion. The cover promised that the contents were "interesting reading matter for both young and old; teachers or pupils; country and city folks."

In 1934, Fisher set off again, this time on an around-the-world tour during which he hoped "to take a peep into foreign lands, to note the customs of their natives, the beauty of their sceneries; [and] also, to glean about facts one may learn on the way." By the time he left on this second voyage, Fisher was married, but according to contemporary newspaper accounts his wife Sarah (Farmwald) Fisher "elected to stay at home."

Fisher sailed from New York City to Cuba, then through the Panama Canal and north to Portland, Oregon. From there he headed for Japan, then China, Singapore, and Indonesia. After visiting Sri Lanka and India, he traveled through the Suez Canal and stopped in Egypt. Fisher remained in the Holy Lands for six months of touring biblical sites. Eventually he turned home, but not before visiting Italy, Spain, Portugal, Morocco, and England. In each place his ship docked,

Fisher observed local customs, asked questions, and wrote in his diary.

Fisher kept two thick autograph books while on this world tour and gathered signatures and short sayings from people around the globe, each in their native languages and scripts. Fisher chronicled this second journey in *Around the World by Water and Facts Gleaned on the Way.* He described local history and architecture, as well as his impressions of other places and cultures. For example, the tea produced in Indonesia was superb, he thought, and the traveler in Japan was safer than in many parts of the United States.

Even at age 74, Fisher could not be kept at home. In 1952, he went to Europe again, this time under the auspices of the relief organization Church World Service. Fisher oversaw a shipload of livestock the group was sending to the Continent. While in Europe, Fisher attended the Mennonite World Conference gathering held that year in Basel, Switzerland. He was the only member of the Amish church to attend.

Jonathan and Sarah had three daughters and a foster son. Though interested in learning about other people, he also shared his own convictions and "carried religious pamphlets, which he gave to everyone he met." While on his global trip, he visited the U.S. Navy base in San Diego and engaged officers in a discussion of peace and conscientious objection to war.

A remarkable figure, Jonathan Fisher enjoyed people and learning about other cultures. Sharing his experiences through books, he widened the worlds of many Amish readers, as well.

See Jonathan B. Fisher, *A Trip to Europe and Facts Gleaned on the Way* (New Holland, Pa.: Jonathan B. Fisher, 1911); Jonathan B. Fisher, *Around the World by Water and Facts Gleaned on the Way* (Bareville, Pa.: Jonathan B. Fisher, 1937). Both of these books first appeared as serials in *The Budget.* See also H. Harold Hartzler, *Amishman Travels Around the World: The Life of Jonathan B. Fisher* (Elverson, Pa.: Mennonite Family History, 1991).

lines, virtually all refused government reimbursement.[53] "I don't think it's right to take money that isn't earned," one Amish farmer told a *Philadelphia Inquirer* reporter. "That means, if you come down to it," he continued, "that a farmer is being paid to not work. Then there's farmers that don't tell the truth about their acreage [to get a greater subsidy]. That isn't right. That's just not right."[54]

The Amish also took no part in the 1935 Social Security program, known then as Old Age and Survivors Insurance. The public pension plan was optional for those who were self-employed—a category that included virtually all Amish at the time—and the Amish opted out. Taking care of orphans, the poor, and the elderly was the duty of the church, they believed, and they refused to surrender those responsibilities to the state.[55] The pressure to take part in government farm and social welfare programs would grow after 1935, but the Amish had already begun to resist.

Coincidentally, the Depression era saw the launch of what would become an important Amish publication. In 1930, a Baltic, Ohio, bookstore owner and Amish deacon, John A. Raber, issued the first printing of an annual Amish almanac. *Der Neue Amerikanische Calender* (since 1970 also issued in English as *The New American Almanac*) quickly became a yearly favorite, not least because it included a directory of all Amish church districts and their leaders' addresses. In time, son Ben J. Raber took over publication of his father's almanac and ably continued the Raber tradition of fostering community connections across North America.[56]

A world at war

As the economic depression began to fade, trouble surfaced on another front, as rumbles of war in Europe and the Pacific grew louder. In 1939, Canada was drawn into the Second World War, and two years later the United States entered the global conflict. Already in the 1930s, North American leaders of the Religious Society of Friends, Brethren, and Mennonite churches had been at work on both sides of the border to avoid repeating the difficult experiences of World War I conscientious objectors, should war erupt again.[57] In the United States, twenty-two Old Order Amish bishops from Indiana, Kansas, Michigan, and Pennsylvania signed a letter in 1939 declaring their support of a Mennonite statement entitled "Peace, War, and Military Service." In offering their approval, the bishops wrote that they were expressing not only their personal convictions, but also "that of the entire membership" of their church.[58]

The statement to which the bishops affixed their names explained Christian nonresistance and denounced military involvement. It did, however, offer Washington a willingness "at all times to aid in the relief of those who are in need, distress or suffering, regardless of the danger in which we may be placed in bringing such relief," suggesting an openness to alternative service in lieu of the military.[59]

The draft alternatives that governments offered COs were significantly different from those of World War I, especially in the United States. The programs that emerged in 1940 placed Amish and Mennonite draftees in federally regulated, often geographically isolated work camps instead of sending them to military camps or to jail. Ottawa and Washington both established systems in which COs provided free labor for government projects or agencies. The Canadian Alternative Service Work (ASW) and American Civilian Public Service (CPS) enrolled the labor of thousands of conscientious objectors. ASW men worked in Canadian national parks as ground crews and forest firefighters. Others staffed psychiatric hospitals and cleared land for the Trans-Canada Highway. Additionally, some Canadian Mennonite and many Amish COs received farm furloughs to work at home.[60]

In the United States, the CPS program provided similar jobs for its participants. In addition to receiving forestry and hospital assignments, some COs worked in social work programs or agricultural experimentation stations. Thus, while the Amish had refused farm subsidies and social security payments during the Depression, they later helped to subsidize the government itself by providing virtually free labor for various state and federal projects. While the CPS program was an arm of the government, its participants worked under civilian direction, and the sponsoring peace churches managed and funded the program. And although men in CPS camps often felt local hostility towards their peace stance, they were not subject to the physical abuse that had plagued COs in World War I.[61]

An unknown number of American Old Order Amish men received farm or other deferments from local draft boards during the Second World War, but at least 772 men were drafted. Twenty-three enlisted in regular army service, twenty-seven chose noncombatant military assignments, and 722 declared themselves conscientious objectors and worked in service assignments under CPS auspices.[62]

CPS thrust many participants—Amish and non-Amish, alike—into challenging experiences that stirred new interests and widened parochial horizons. Most Amish COs served in Mennonite-sponsored camps, but the Amish did operate one camp of their own: an experimental farming station near Hagerstown, Maryland. Amish churches purchased the farm in 1942 and managed it under U.S. Soil Conservation Service supervision. The camp had only about thirty-five COs at any one time, but it received strong support from Amish districts. The camp newsletter, *The Sun Beam,* had an extensive circulation to Amish homes.[63]

Life in Mennonite CPS camps was alternately comfortable, eye-opening, and troubling for young Amish men. On the one hand, the Amish were among fellow COs in an environment sympathetic to their historic views and teaching. At the same time, being in a Mennonite-run camp could be challenging, since many Mennonites were unfamiliar with specific Amish customs and convictions, and some looked down on the Amish as "backward" and uneducated.

Rubbing shoulders so closely with Mennonites convinced some Amish that their religious cousins were alarmingly worldly and individualistic, while others found Mennonite-sponsored religious activities and worship services refreshingly innovative and attractive. When a few Amish decided while in camp to leave their church and join the Mennonites, relations were strained on all sides.[64] Nevertheless, most Amish memories of CPS were positive, and COs felt the support of friends and family who wrote regularly or even visited the camps. For his part, the remarkable LaGrange County, Indiana, bishop Eli J. Bontreger made an effort to visit every Amish CPS participant. Crisscrossing the country, mostly by rail, Bontreger once traveled more than 16,000 miles in five months and earned the deep appreciation of Amish draftees.[65]

Some of those relatives and friends experienced problems of their own on the home front. In an especially troublesome situation in Reno County, Kansas, five Amish families lost their farms to the U.S. Navy Department. The Amish-owned acres were part of a four square-mile tract taken over by the government to establish a Navy pilots training base.[66]

The wartime economy produced other problems, as many Amish refused to use the ration stamps distributed by the government for purchasing food and other necessities. The stamps bore the images of tanks, cannons, air corps planes, navy ships, and torpedoes, which some Amish could not use in good conscience.

An Old Order Amish man discusses the World War II military draft with Major General Lewis B. Hershey, Director of Selective Service, as three Mennonites look on.

For others, the idea of state-regulated commerce was troubling. Amish families that decided not to participate in the ration program provided their own food or simply did without other scarce material goods.[67] Wartime thriftiness became their trademark, and in a 1942 *New York Times* article, one reporter called the Amish "models for the nation's consumers."[68] By declaring themselves conscientious objectors and refusing to use war-glorifying ration stamps, the Amish had ironically become models for American patriots. But in a world turned upside down by depressions, dictators, and atomic bombs, irony no longer seemed out of place.

When the war ended, some young Amish men signed on for extended voluntary service as "Sea-Going Cowboys." The Allied relief and reconstruction work in Europe involved sending hundreds of horses, cattle, and donkeys to Germany, Poland, and other parts of the Continent, and the U.S. Merchant Marine needed people with experience in animal handling to care for the livestock during the Atlantic passage. "Not everyone [in the United States] was in favor of rebuilding our enemies," one Illinois Amish man reflected later, "but that is what Christians should do. Not that we approve of war, but the rebuilding surely was the right thing to do." After unloading the animals, these adventuresome Amish youth were able to take in various tourist sites before returning home.[69]

European sightseeing was a new way for Amish teens to spend part of a summer. But after 1945, the Amish were living in a very different world. The turbulent first half of the twentieth century had left Western society reeling. Despite their efforts to remain apart from the turmoil that surrounded them, the Amish were caught up in many of the events of those years. In the decades that followed, most Amish conflicts with the state found amiable resolution, but not before heightened tensions saw scores of Amish sit in prison. Those same years also witnessed the emergence of various renewal movements in Amish circles, impulses that often pointed participants in different directions. In all, the second half the middle years of the twentieth century would prove to be dynamic ones for the Amish.

—11—

Conflict, Compromise, and Renewal, 1945-1975

> *"There can be no assumption that today's majority is 'right' and the Amish and others like them are 'wrong.'"*
> —U.S. Chief Justice Warren E. Burger

With the end of the Second World War, the attention of Americans turned homeward. As states and cities scrambled to capture a share of America's growing leisure time and tourist dollars, the Pennsylvania Department of Commerce issued an advertisement encouraging would-be visitors to take a "post-war vacation." The ad included a picture of an Amish buggy with the caption, "Pennsylvania's Plain People." While the piece did not specifically mention the Amish by name, the image clearly implied that Old Order folks should be a part of every family's excursion fun.[1]

For the Amish, however, life in the mid-twentieth century was no walk in the park. The post-war years were shaped by serious and protracted conflicts with the state over military conscription, public schooling, and the role of the welfare state. In the end, these clashes were often resolved in ways that made space for the Amish to live their lives outside the North American cultural mainstream.

Such outcomes were, in part, a result of the tenor of the times, which by the late 1960s and early 1970s had witnessed a rise in public sympathy and legal support for dissent and minority civil rights. But Amish privileges also resulted from creative flexibility on the part of the church. At times Amish people tenaciously held convictions to the point of prison, while in other cases they negotiated and bargained with the forces of modern bureaucracy to craft alternatives that acknowledged public authority while recognizing Amish values. Midcentury conflicts with the state played out publically against a series of backstage theological debates that disrupted and often divided Amish communities in ways that had not happened in a hundred years.

If post-war tourism advertisements presented the Amish as a changeless people, the Amish who lived through the years following 1945 knew better. Societal change seemed especially sharp in the late 1940s as the country began a long, steady period of economic growth and an accompanying baby boom. Prosperous middle class families entered a golden age of consumerism. In the four years from 1946 to 1950, for example, the number of households owning television sets skyrocketed from a mere 8,000 to nearly four million. Soon the new interstate highway system, sprawling suburbs, and shopping malls encouraged American mobility and changed spending habits. People lived farther from their jobs and spent more time each day on the road. And as household income continued to rise, so did the opportunities to spend it on the latest gadgets promising to revolutionize life.[2]

The Amish remained conspicuously aloof from this hurried buying, selling, suburbanizing, and expanding, and that disturbed some officials. In the spring of 1946, government agriculture agents publicly urged Amish farmers to give up horse-farming and use tractors to help boost American agricultural exports. "By hitching them [tractors]

Amish farmers near Yoder, Kansas, use tractors instead of horses for fieldwork because of the climate and summer heat. The Yoder settlement is one of a handful of Old Order Amish communities that permit tractor farming while continuing to use horse-drawn transportation on the road.

to the plow and harrow they will be serving not only the needs of their owners, but will help to sustain life among the hungry nations in Europe," officials stated in their appeal. The Amish were outdated and unscientific, the Department of Agriculture argued. If they did not mechanize, surely they would not survive.[3]

A few Amish settlements did adopt tractor-farming in the 1940s, but the vast majority continued to use horse-drawn equipment and reserved tractor engines for stationary belt power. Fully automated farming destroyed the need for working together, and the Amish valued cooperation. After the Second World War, non-Amish "neighbors went for bigger tractors and combines and more modern ways of farming," one Amish man remembered, "until no one seemed to have any use for his neighbors anymore."[4] Horse-based farming kept operations small and labor-intensive. As well, tractors were too much like cars, and groups that approved tractor use in fields might soon be driving automobiles on the road.

Sometimes the pressures of life in post-war America proved to be too great. In 1952 the long shadow of the atomic mushroom cloud fell across a newly established Amish settlement in Pike County, Ohio. That year, the federal government announced its intention to build a nuclear power plant in the area. Plans suggested a tripling in the county's population, with associated increases in real estate prices. While the project was a boon to some land-owning locals, it marked the demise of the young Old Order community. The area's winding roads would become too crowded for buggy travel, land quickly became too expensive to buy, and observers guessed the area would become a highly secret military district. Within a year, the Amish began moving away, most immigrating to Ontario. One of the reasons the families chose Canada was because that country had no military draft, and conscription was again becoming an issue in the United States.[5]

Troubling alternative service

Only in 1947 had the United States demobilized the last World War II conscripts, and, nearly as soon as the old Selective Service system completed its business, a new draft took its place. The escalating Cold War between the United States and the Soviet Union persuaded Congress in 1948 to establish a large peacetime standing army for home defense and the ongoing occupation of West Germany and Japan. Amazingly, the new law granted conscientious objectors complete and total exemption. Such deferment lasted only a few years, though, as the outbreak of the Korean War in 1950 turned public opinion against COs, and the government demanded some type of alternative service. Beginning in the summer of 1952, objectors had to complete two-year assignments in a work program commonly known by its Selective Service code, "I-W."[6]

The I-W program placed most COs in city hospitals or nonprofit human services organizations. Most of the hospital assignees worked as orderlies, cooks, and maintenance personnel and public institutions benefited from the inexpensive labor I-W men supplied. The men needed to work outside their home communities, but few other restrictions applied. COs were paid wages, typically lived on their own in private apartments, and had charge of their off-duty hours. At first glance, such conditions seemed much better than those permitted for COs during World War I, or even World War

Conservative Amish Mennonite Conference women chat with a Mennonite delegate from the Netherlands during the 1948 Mennonite World Conference, Goshen, Indiana.

II, but the Amish church was uneasy with the arrangement. The wages, unmonitored free time, and the relative isolation of many I-Ws troubled parents.[7]

Some Amish I-W men had difficulty adjusting to their surroundings. Working in large, impersonal institutions, with no family and few friends nearby, they became lonely and in some cases depressed. Raised in strong extended families and church communities, Old Order youth were often shocked by attitudes and lifestyles of coworkers and superiors. Others reacted by escaping into the surrounding culture. Frequenting popular city nightspots, dating non-Amish hospital employees, and discarding traditional garb, Amish COs could lose themselves in urban society. Some never returned to their home communities. Others came back emotionally distant from their families and disconnected from the church. They had felt out of place in their I-W assignments, but after two years in the city, many no longer were comfortable at home either.

In time, some draftees resisted work in I-W settings. In 1955, for example, three Indiana Amish received five-year prison terms and $2,000 fines for refusing induction.[8] Incarcerated in Mill Point, West Virginia, the men refused to wear prison uniforms after their Amish clothes were confiscated. Officials would not admit the men into the dining hall without their prison garb, but after four weeks of malnutrition, the warden adapted clothing requirements to suit both the state and the men.[9]

The government brought others to trial, as well, including Joni L. Petersheim of Hazelton, Iowa, who in 1957 received a two-month jail term and $5,000 fine.[10] In a Cold War context of popular patriotism, draft resistance by the likes of Holmes County native Aden A. Miller (sentenced to three years in federal work camp prison for rejecting I-W employment) made headlines across the country.[11]

Other media notoriety was much more problematic. At times, local police would arrest rowdy Amish teens for disturbing the peace or underage drinking. In the wake of such news stories, public outcry often demanded that older Amish men liable for the draft not receive conscientious objector status. After police arrested three LaGrange County, Indiana, Amish young people for public intoxication, the county's draft board president declared, "If they can do things like that . . . I don't see how they can refuse to carry a gun in defense of their country."[12]

While such stories ignored the question of how representative the unruly young people were, they represented understandable public sentiment that troubled Amish parents and church leaders alike. Embarrassed Amish adults worked harder to keep teens' behavior in line. Yet the Amish were in some ways limited by their own theology. Parents needed to give children the choice between church membership and a life of worldliness. After all, an Anabaptist understanding of believers baptism included the real possibility that not everyone would take the way of discipleship. Some children would not live as their parents might hope, but that did not invalidate the convictions of those Amish who did.

While draft controversy put the Amish in the national limelight, the church also drew press attention as it applied the principles of peace and nonresistance in a different situation. On a summer 1957 evening, two non-Amish young men recently released from prison rendezvoused in Holmes County, Ohio, to celebrate their freedom. Randomly targeting the Mount Hope home of Old Orders Paul M. and Dora J. (Yoder) Coblentz, the youths robbed the couple and killed Paul. The Amish apparently offered no resistance, and their nineteen-month-old daughter was unharmed.

Using a stolen car, the two assailants fled to Illinois where they shot a sheriff's deputy before surrendering to arrest.

Amish fathers being released from Lancaster County, Pennsylvania, prison in the early 1950s. The men had been jailed for violating compulsory school attendance laws.

Returned to Ohio, they stood trial for the Coblentz murder, and one of them, Cleo Eugene Peters, was eventually convicted and sentenced to death.[13] Shocked and grieving, the Amish community found itself in an uncommon situation.

Since the days of the Anabaptist leader Menno Simons, Mennonites and Amish had taken a decided stand against capital punishment. Human life was too valuable and the possibility of repentance too real for Christians to approve of executions, they believed. But rarely had the issue been so immediate for the Amish. Peters' trial had stirred deep and painful emotions, yet letters offering forgiveness and promising prayer arrived at Peters' cell from Amish settlements in many states. Even the young widow and victim wrote to him. Amish families invited Peters' parents into their homes for meals, and church leaders visited him in prison. In addition, the Amish called for a stay of execution. Wrote one Ontario Amish man, "Will we as Amish be left blameless in the matter if we do not present a written request to the authorities, asking that his life be spared?"[14]

Letters arrived at the office of Governor C. William O'Neill until the November 7, 1958, execution date. Seven hours before the scheduled electrocution, the governor commuted Peters' sentence. The whole event had a marked impact on the Holmes County Amish.[15] Amid conflict over military conscription, the Coblentz tragedy brought into focus the deeper meaning of peace in a violent world.

Crisis of conscience

Meanwhile, as the I-W program moved into its second decade, problems and anxieties remained. Some Amish continued to refuse work in alienating urban environments and received fines or prison terms, even as others considered the program worthwhile. "I have worked in a hospital as an orderly for two years, and I have not lost my Amish faith," one I-W participant wrote to *The Budget.* There certainly were "temptations in these hospitals," he acknowledged, but that did not mean that everyone who went to the city would leave the church.[16] Yet by the mid-1960s some Amish leaders reported that only about half of their drafted men returned home to the church. Old Order Amish and Beachy Amish-Mennonite leaders asked what might be done to change these realities.

The Beachy churches launched a two-part strategy: draftee orientation, coordinated by minister Daniel N. King, and the creation of church-related institutions in which drafted men could fulfill their service obligations in a faith-based context. King divided the country into six districts. Each had a coordinator who worked to keep connections strong between conscripted men and their churches and to help I-W participants see their assignments as a type of church service.

Beachy churches also created their own service positions, which were then designated by Selective Service as approved I-W assignments. These jobs included Beachy-managed homes for the aged and the international relief agency, Amish Mennonite Aid, which employed I-W men in maintenance and clerical tasks.[17]

Old Order Amish were less eager to construct organizational or bureaucratic apparatus, but they, too, considered how to improve the I-W experience. One response was to launch a monthly periodical, *Ambassador of Peace.* Beginning in 1966, each Amish CO received the *Ambassador,* which contained stories by I-W participants, as well as devotional articles and church news.[18] The magazine was the brainchild of Sarah M. Weaver, an Ohio woman living with muscular dystrophy.[19] Weaver spent a good deal of time thinking about and praying for the I-W men, and she suggested a periodical might encourage her church's COs.[20]

But by that time, other Old Order leaders were beginning to discuss the formation of a completely new alternative to military conscription. In November 1966, eighteen Amish men gathered in Washington, D.C. to discuss proposed changes in the country's draft law. The group appointed a three-member National Amish Steering Committee to represent them in negotiations with Selective Service. Three months later, at a Holmes County meeting of more than 100 leaders from nine states, the Steering Committee received broad support from the wider church.[21]

For Old Orders, forming the Steering Committee was a new step, indeed. Decidedly congregational in its organization, the Amish had never had a national hierarchy or single spokesperson. Committee officers were laymen, which helped ensure their authority was limited to Committee work and would not spill over into matters of church practice or doctrine. Such decisions would remain with local church districts.

Almost immediately, Steering Committee chair Andrew S. Kinsinger of Lancaster County met with officials from Selective Service and began negotiating a compromise agreement—finalized in 1969—whereby young men could perform farm labor in lieu of their military service. Under its terms, the church leased privately owned Amish farms for twenty-six-month periods and hired each farm's owner as farm "manager." Drafted Amish men then worked on such farms for two years. During the last few years of conscription, many Amish chose such work, although some still took city hospital jobs. The National Steering Committee had proven to be a helpful liaison, and after the draft ended the Committee continued to function as an intermediary in other church-state conflicts.[22]

More school entanglements

Another source of contention with the state continued to be the proper education of Amish children. The Amish refusal to send their children to large, consolidated elementary schools, or to high schools of any variety, resulted in repeated run-ins with the law.[23] During the late 1950s and 1960s, the pace of public school consolidation ramped up in rural areas and more private Amish schools opened their doors. Amish parents from Kansas to Pennsylvania found themselves before local magistrates, paying fines and serving jail time.

Local officials in some places quietly reached compromise agreements that allowed the Amish to operate private schools without interference, or tailored special rural public schools to match Amish preferences. In a few cases, Amish children took correspondence courses from home in an effort to meet state requirements without attending modern high schools. In 1955, Pennsylvania introduced a "vocational school" plan, later copied by several other states. Under this system, Amish youth who completed eighth grade were free to work at home, but they reported to a special "vocational school" one morning per week until they reached the age of fifteen. Here they continued practicing academic skills and turned in weekly work journals. In 1967, Ontario's government granted the Amish the right to establish and manage their own schools apart from provincial regulations.[24]

In other places, however, working agreements were elusive, and some communities suffered repeated conflicts. One of the most widely publicized cases occurred near the Buchanan County, Iowa, town of Hazelton.[25] After the 1947 school consolidation around Hazelton, local Old Orders withdrew from public school participation. Instead, they retained two abandoned one-room public schools, hired teachers, and maintained the facilities themselves. Fourteen years later, residents of Hazelton and a neighboring town voted to combine their already consolidated school systems. Some Hazelton citizens were upset by the merger and resented their high school moving to the next county. But because the Amish believed that the new combined district would allow them to continue their schools, a number of Amish had voted for the merger. In the end, the Amish votes may have been decisive. Local Hazelton citizens, angry about the combining of the schools, resented the Amish voting for a joint district in which Old Order children did not expect to participate.

To the surprise of the Amish, the new school conglomerate had no intention of allowing the Amish free reign to manage their own schools. Officials visited the one-room schools and declared them too primitive for long-term use. The Amish could use the structures for two more years, and then only through sixth grade. Older students would need to attend the public junior high school.

The Amish balked, and in the fall of 1962, they reopened their buildings with their own uncertified Amish teachers. Locals promised to take action against the schools for failing to meet state instructional standards. Yet the schools were not unusual. Amish private schools like those condemned in Buchanan County routinely received state approval to operate in other parts of Iowa. Nor was the use of uncertified teachers particularly uncommon. At the time, half of all Iowa's public secondary schools employed some uncertified teachers. What was unique in Buchanan County was the civic emotion that forestalled all compromise.

The controversy smoldered until the fall of 1965, when authorities moved to close the Amish schools, citing their uncertified teachers as the basis for action. On the morning of November 19, officials arrived at one of the schoolhouses, intent on loading the students onto a bus and transporting

BERRY'S WORLD

© 1965 by NEA, Inc

"Let's skip the Viet Cong for a moment—what are we gonna do about the Amish school kids in Iowa?"

Amishmen ascending the steps of the U.S. Supreme Court. In 1972, the Court ruled in favor of the Amish request to end formal education with eighth grade.

them to Hazelton Elementary. The children began walking toward the bus in an orderly way when an Amish adult shouted, "Run!" (in German), and the students dashed for the surrounding fields. The resulting mayhem left only a handful of children in police hands and the rest scurrying for home. Press photographers captured images of fleeing children and angry officials, and the day's events appeared in newspapers around the country.

The next week public education administrators and local police arrived at the second Amish school, only to repeat the chaos of the previous Friday. Instead of running, the children here sang "Jesus Loves Me" at the tops of their voices, while

Supreme Court of the United States: State of Wisconsin, Petitioner, v. Jonas Yoder, Adin Yutzy, and Wallace Miller. On Writ of Certiorari to the Supreme Court of Wisconsin. [May 15, 1972], No. 70-110.

Excerpts from the 1972 United States Supreme Court case *Wisconsin v. Yoder, et al.* The court unanimously sided with the Amish defendants. Chief Justice Warren Burger wrote the majority opinion. (Justice William Douglas dissented in part from Warren's opinion, but agreed in the main. Several justices wrote concurring opinions.)

"Amish objection to formal education beyond the eighth grade is firmly grounded in . . . central religious concepts. They object to high school and higher education generally because the values it teaches are in marked variance with Amish values and the Amish way of life. . . . The high school tends to emphasize intellectual and scientific accomplishments, self-determination, competitiveness, worldly success, and social life with other students. Amish society emphasizes learning-through-doing, a life of 'goodness' rather than technical knowledge, community welfare rather than competition, and separation rather than integration with worldly society.

"As the record so strongly shows, the values and programs of the modern secondary school are in sharp conflict with the fundamental mode of life mandated by the Amish religion; modern laws requiring compulsory secondary education have accordingly engendered great concern and conflict. The conclusion is inescapable that secondary schooling, by exposing Amish children to worldly influences in terms of attitudes, goals and values contrary to beliefs, and by substantially interfering with the religious development of the Amish child and his integration into the way of life of the Amish faith community at the crucial adolescent state of development, contravenes the basic religious tenets and practices of the Amish faith, both as to the parent and child . . . . The State's requirement of compulsory formal education after the eighth grade would gravely endanger if not destroy the free exercise of respondents' religious beliefs.

"The State attacks respondents' position as one fostering 'ignorance' from which the child must be protected by the State. No one can question the State's duty to protect children from ignorance but this argument does not square with the facts disclosed in the record. Whatever their idiosyncrasies as seen by the majority, this record strongly shows that the Amish community has been a highly successful social unit within our society even if apart from the conventional 'mainstream.' . . .

"It is neither fair nor correct to suggest that the Amish are opposed to education beyond the eighth grade level. What this record shows is that they are opposed to conventional formal education of the type provided by a certified high school because it comes at the child's crucial adolescent period of religious development . . . .

"We must not forget that in the Middle Ages important values of the civilization of the western world were preserved by members of religious orders who isolated themselves from all worldly influences against great obstacles. There can be no assumption that today's majority is 'right' and the Amish and others like them are 'wrong.' A way of life that is odd or even erratic but interferes with no rights or interests of others is not to be condemned because it is different . . . ."

By the Court: Chief Justice Warren E. Burger, Justices Harry A. Blackmun, William J. Brennan Jr., William O. Douglas, Thurgood Marshall, Potter Stewart, and Byron R. White. (Justices Lewis F. Powell Jr. and William H. Rehnquist took no part in the consideration or decision of the case.)

mothers cried and stern-faced fathers stood in protest by the doorway. Governor Harold E. Hughes declared a three-week suspension on interfering with the schools, and national sympathy began to coalesce around the Amish. Private contributions poured in to pay for fines and penalties, and Governor Hughes asked the state legislature to address the situation. By 1967, the General Assembly agreed to exempt from certain public school requirements any Amish community that had existed in the state for a decade or more. The Buchanan County Amish could now manage their own schools with their own teachers, just as Amish did in other parts of Iowa.

Supreme Court resolution

The Buchanan County incident had attracted wide attention. One person who took special interest was the Rev. William C. Lindholm, an Iowa native who in 1965 was pastor of Grace Lutheran Church in East Tawas, Michigan.[26] Lindholm saw the situation as one of religious liberty and, with the encouragement of the National Council of Churches, decided to get involved. He attended a University of Chicago conference on the regulation of non-public schools and called on those interested in Amish First Amendment rights to organize. The resulting National Committee for Amish Religious Freedom (NCARF) included lawyers, academics, and Christian and Jewish religious leaders. It bore all the moral urgency of civil rights advocacy that flowered during the late 1960s.

By the time NCARF formed, the Iowa conflict had calmed considerably, but new problems were surfacing in Kansas. There, Hutchinson Amish resident LeRoy Garber had been convicted of not sending his daughter to the local high school, and Kansas rejected the Pennsylvania-style "vocational school" compromise. NCARF discussed the situation but

The rise of Amish schools, 1925-2006

Old Order Amish Schools founded by decade

1920s	1
1930s	2
1940s	12
1950s	50
1960s	147
1970s	165
1980s	205
1990s	362
2000-2006	332

Data from a detailed listing of Amish schools for the 2005-2006 school year as compiled by the editors of *Blackboard Bulletin*, an Amish-published monthly periodical for schoolteachers. That year the editors heard from 1,390 schools with 2,077 teachers and 36,896 students. Not all schools responded to the editors' inquiry in time to be included in the report, so the actual numbers of schools, teachers, and students are undoubtedly somewhat higher; 114 schools did not include a founding date in their report and so are not included in this table.

For more information, see Karen M. Johnson-Weiner, *Train Up a Child: Old Order Amish and Mennonite Schools* (Baltimore: Johns Hopkins University Press, 2007); and *Blackboard Bulletin* (Pathway Publishers, 52445 Glencolin Ln, RR 4, Aylmer, ON, Canada, N5H 2R3).

could do nothing without the chance to argue an appeal, and the U.S. Supreme Court had refused to review the case.[27]

For their part, the Garbers and some other Old Orders decided to leave Kansas. Migration always had been an option for Amish facing inflexible state laws. The Adin Yutzy family, for example, had left Buchanan County, Iowa, during the height of that controversy and moved to a settlement in Green County, Wisconsin, which since 1964 had attracted Amish from around the Midwest.[28] Then, in the fall of 1968, Wisconsin authorities arrested three Green County fathers for not sending their children to high school. Ironically, one of the men was Adin Yutzy, who had faced the same situation back in Iowa. Hearing of the arrests, Lindholm contacted Harrisburg, Pennsylvania, attorney William Bentley Ball, who began to prepare a legal defense.

In the spring of 1969, NCARF lost its case in Green County Court.[29] The court acknowledged that the government had violated Amish religious liberty, but the decision held that a "compelling state interest" overshadowed religious rights. On appeal, the Wisconsin Supreme Court decided in favor of the church and parents. No such "compelling right" existed in this incident, the justices said, and the church posed no significant threat to society by choosing an eighth-grade education.[30]

The case was not exhausted, however, as Wisconsin appealed its state's high court verdict to the U.S. Supreme Court. In December 1971, attorney Ball persuasively presented the Amish argument in Washington, D.C. The following spring the Supreme Court handed down its decision in *Wisconsin v. Yoder, et al.*, ruling that the government did not have reason to deny the Amish their right to practice their faith and teach their children, even if such teaching included no certified high school work.[31] Lack of formal secondary education has not made the Amish a social or economic "burden" to American society, Chief Justice Warren E. Burger reasoned in his majority opinion.

Although legal conservatives, such as Robert Bork, criticized the decision as an example of special privilege for undeserving minorities, *Wisconsin v. Yoder* become a key religious freedom case, cited in hundreds of later rulings. Ball

Amishmen wait outside the office of the Internal Revenue Service. Social Security taxes have been a point of tension between the Amish and the government.

saw it as more than a victory for the Amish. "The results of the decision not only helped the Amish people everywhere," he later commented, "but the terrific emphasis on religious liberty and parental rights is just golden."[32]

Since *Wisconsin v. Yoder,* the Old Order Amish (and similar or related groups, such as Old Order Mennonites and Beachy Amish-Mennonites) have had the legal right to establish and operate their own schools or withdraw from public institutions after completing eighth grade.[33] In some places—notably in large and long-established Ohio and Indiana settlements—a significant minority of parents has continued to send their children to public elementary schools. But *Yoder* settled most conflicts surrounding exemption from high school. Only in Nebraska did difficulties persist. Not interested in additional

*Old Order Amish and Old Order Mennonites appear in an Ontario
courtroom for a hearing on provincial education laws in July 1968.*

court cases, the Amish finally left that state in 1982 (though
some began moving back in 2005).[34]

Coming to terms with the welfare state

Schooling and the military draft were only two of the
areas in which the Amish found themselves in conflict
with government during the mid-twentieth century. Modern life was pervasively and profoundly shaped by the rise
of the welfare state, one of the most far-reaching social
developments of the twentieth century, and the Amish did
not embrace the values that those developments represented.

In broad terms, welfare-state philosophy called for delib-
erate government involvement in economic and social policy
to create a better life for all citizens. Rooted in early 1900s'
Progressive thought, the welfare state took identifiable
shape during President Franklin D. Roosevelt's response to
the stark economic realities of the Great Depression. Pub-

lic action on behalf of the unemployed, the poor, the aged, and the disabled were becoming standard public fare by the 1950s and 1960s. In the decades which followed, welfare-state activities grew to include such diverse programs as farm-commodity subsidies, tuition loans for college students, federal funding of airport construction, and environmental regulation, all designed to better citizens' lives.[35]

For the Amish, the welfare state raised concern for two reasons. First, the "better life" toward which these systems strove was not an Amish ideal. Based on middle-class professional values, most programs encouraged individual achievement and ignored the importance of other minority group concerns. Second, the welfare state weakened community-based mutual aid. Public intervention undercut church-centered care and extended-family responsibility.

From the mid-1950s to the 1970s, Amish confrontation with the welfare state was frequent as the church sought the right to care for its members on its own terms. In the end, the Amish were usually able to negotiate their values into the system, but not without protracted struggle.

One prominent conflict erupted in 1955 when Congress extended the Social Security program to include self-employed farmers.[36] Self-employed Amish had never taken part in the twenty-year-old program, and, now that participation was mandatory, many refused to pay. Internal Revenue Service (IRS) agents began collecting through Amish bank accounts, but a few Amish closed their accounts, making it difficult to tap their resources. In 1958, the government foreclosed on several farms to recover lost Social Security funds. During the next two years, the IRS forcibly collected from 130 other Amish households.[37] Such action did not stop Amish opposition to involvement in a system they saw as misdirected and wrong.

The spring of 1961 saw the most dramatic encounter between the Amish and the IRS. Two years earlier, the

federal government had placed a lien on the workhorses of
Valentine Y. Byler, a New Wilmington, Pennsylvania, farmer
who had not paid Social Security. The next summer, authorities arrested Byler after he failed to appear in court. The
judge immediately released him, but the following April
agents arrived at Byler's farm while he was involved in
spring plowing. Meeting Byler in the field, they unhitched
three of his horses and led them away as confiscated property. The IRS then sold the animals to recover Byler's unpaid
Social Security taxes. While officials also seized horses from
other Amish, Byler's case became the celebrated incident.[38]

Since the government's method of recovering funds
deprived the Byler family of its livelihood, Byler sued Washington for damages. However, church leaders forced him to
withdraw the case, rejecting as un-Christian the use of the
courts for self-defense. Nevertheless, the notoriety of the
case and public outcry beyond the Amish community led to
an IRS moratorium on collecting Social Security from Old
Order families.[39]

In the summer of 1965, Congress addressed the problem
in the process of crafting the nation's new Medicare health
insurance program. A subsection of that measure exempted
self-employed Amish from both Medicare and Social
Security.[40] But Amish employers and employees were still
liable for all Social Security taxes.

In 1982, the Supreme Court upheld the necessity of such
payment, but six years later Congress sided with the church
and passed another exemption. Since 1988, if Amish employees work for Amish employers, neither party must pay
Social Security payroll taxes.[41] The IRS still requires Amish
employees of non-Amish employers to contribute fully to
Social Security, even though few such employees ever draw
benefits from the system.

After 1970, Amish men employed in construction rejected
the hard-hats stipulations in the new Occupational Safety

and Health Act, preferring their own felt or straw hats or knit caps. In 1972, federal authorities granted Amish workers a headgear exemption.

Workers Compensation, farm-commodity subsidies, Medicaid, Department of Agriculture dairy-herd reduction plans, and other welfare-state activity all have raised special problems for Amish households. Much publicity resulted from the opposition of a few ultra-conservative Amish to the bright orange, slow-moving vehicle signs required on Amish carriages. Often the National Amish Steering Committee has been involved in finding negotiated settlements agreeable to all sides, but sometimes the state resorts to litigation.[42]

In Canada, too, welfare-state policies resulted in conflict with the church. Ironically, in 1953, American Amish had begun migrating to Ontario, in part, because they perceived Canada to have relatively fewer welfare-state entanglements.[43] Whether or not the Amish rightly judged the situation on that score, the rapid rise and spread of Canadian social programs was soon apparent, and Old Orders confronted their new home's National Pension Plan. By 1967, Revenue Canada was invading Amish bank accounts and garnishing wages to collect unpaid Pension Plan taxes. Finally, in 1974, self-employed Amish received exemption from the system, but the situation for Amish employees and employers remains problematic. Some businesses have become multi-member partnerships so that each employee is a self-employed part owner. Canadian Amish also accepted Social Insurance numbers, but those numbers are digitized so that they cannot be used to receive benefits.

Milk-marketing regulations have also proven difficult for the Amish, and so since 1977, the number of Amish-owned dairy operations in Canada has declined. Many Old Orders

The Amish in Latin America

As conflicts with the state and pressure on rural communities increased in the 1950s and 1960s, some Amish floated the idea of leaving North America behind. In 1951, Samuel Hertzler of Saint Mary's County, Maryland, visited Honduras and decided that "it might be an ideal place for Amish to get away from the turmoil of our modern country including [the military] draft, unreasonable school laws, and high land prices." But Hertzler never pursued his Central American dream.

In 1967, a family with a similar idea—Peter and Anna (Wagler) Stoll, of Aylmer, Ontario—scouted land opportunities in Honduras, and along with a number of other households moved to farms near Guaimaca, in the central part of the country, the next year. Soon, sixteen families from Ontario, Indiana, and Pennsylvania were part of the new community. The soil was productive, and the Amish adjusted to the climate and new crops while trying to master Spanish.

They also recognized the presence of poverty in a new way. In North America, they had lived simpler lives than their neighbors, but in Honduras the Amish were considered wealthy. They owned land, horses, and homes. "We have been challenged," wrote one Amish man from Honduras, "to live less luxuriously as we have come face to face with the poor and hungry." Several families adopted Honduran orphans, and in 1974, the Guaimaca Amish built a school for other children in their area.

Tension within the church proved to be the group's major difficulty. From its beginning, the settlement included those with both New Order and Old Order leanings, and that mix proved problematic, especially as lifestyle and technological innovation increased. By 1977, some families had returned to North America. The next year, almost all of the Old Orders resettled in Aylmer, Ontario, while several of the New

Order-oriented members moved to eastern Ohio. Those who remained in Honduras eventually affiliated with the car-driving Beachy Amish-Mennonites.

While the Honduran experiment was taking shape, other North American families were packing their bags for Paraguay. In 1967, seven families from Orange County, Indiana, moved to Paraguay's Chaco region, already home to a sizable group of conservative Mennonites, and settled near these spiritual cousins. When more families arrived, the community seemed to be off to a good start.

Despite his advanced age, bishop Noah J. Coblentz of Lakeside, Ontario, traveled twice by ship to Paraguay and helped organize the church and ordain resident leaders. The Paraguayan farms prospered, but the Amish there never formed a stable congregation. In 1978, nearly all the settlers returned to the United States.

One participant in these Latin American Old Order settlements later reflected on his disappointment with their demise. He always believed that "our way of life" was actually better suited for an agrarian Latin American context "than a rich and mechanized country such as Canada or the United States," and that "our churches should thrive better spiritually" among the poor.

Since the 1960s several dozen Beachy Amish-Mennonite churches have taken root in Central and South America. Members of these congregations, such as *Iglesia Luz y Esperanza* (Light and Hope Church) in Paraguay, are typically distinctive in their appearance—beards for men, head coverings for women. They drive cars and trucks, have shifted to Spanish as their primary language, and engage in evangelistic mission work.

Sources: Joseph Stoll, *Sunshine and Shadow: Our Seven Years in Honduras* (Aylmer, Ont.: J. Stoll, 1996) and "The Amish Settlement at Guaimaca, Honduras," *The Diary* (October 1972): 200, 196-99; Enos Hertzler, *Time Out for Paraguay* (Gordonville, Pa.: Gordonville Print Shop, 1985); J. Winfield Fretz, "The Amish in Paraguay" [n.d.] and "Witnessing a Community's Death" [1978], unpublished papers, Heritage Historical Library; and *The Amish Moving to Maryland* (Gordonville, Pa.: A. S. Kinsinger, 1965).

In recent decades, Amish employment has shifted away from agriculture. In most settlements, a growing number of men hold non-farm jobs in businesses such as this furniture shop in Holmes County, Ohio.

have moved to other types of farming or non-farming work or returned to the United States.[44]

Renewal at midcentury: mission interests, conservative voices, and a "New Order"

Although conflicts with government were the most public parts of midcentury Amish life, they were hardly the only events to mark those years. Less well known to outsiders were the churchly discussions and debates of the 1950s and 1960s that resulted in renewal and division.

Like the controversy of the 1860s that birthed Old Order and Amish Mennonite groups, the mid-twentieth century mix of ideas and activities is not always easy to simplify or categorize. There were more than two sides to most issues, and when division came, it was typically a sorting-out process over several years rather than a single or decisive break.

Nor was the religious dissension of these years uncon-nected to the conflicts with the state that were occurring simultaneously. Many of the churchly arguments involved the role of parents and teens, as well as interaction with the larger society—all issues that seemed more acute when draft boards, public school administrators, and news reporters were scrutinizing Amish young-adult and family life.

Starting in the late 1940s, a small but vigorous concern for mission work emerged among certain Old Orders, especially in the Midwest.[45] The impulse had several roots, but was fanned into flame by Russell Maniaci, a convert to the Men-nonites who took a keen interest in encouraging scattered Amish interest in evangelism.[46] In 1950, Maniaci organized an Amish mission conference in Iowa that drew about 150 peo-ple and signaled the beginning of an identifiable movement.

Although Amish participants soon tried to distance themselves from Maniaci himself, who was often brash, they clearly were intent on cooperative church work that spanned settlements and worked outside traditional Amish church structures. In 1952, they organized a Mission Inter-ests Committee (MIC) and the next year launched a modest newsletter entitled *Witnessing*.

Eventually, the MIC sponsored Amish mission workers in Mississippi, Ontario, and Arkansas. But another aim of these mission-minded folks was moral reform within Old Order circles. Troubled especially by the rowdiness of some Amish teens, mission-movement advocates stressed tighter parental control and closely supervised social activities for unbaptized youth. Such concerns may have had fairly broad sympathy, but when coupled with other mission-movement ideas, they failed to win widespread Old Order endorsement.

By the mid-1950s, when some younger mission advocates began saying that car ownership might be necessary for effective church work, and then enrolled in college courses to equip themselves for ministry, even once supportive Old Orders expressed dismay.

Added to the mix was the remarkable preaching of David A. Miller, a Thomas, Oklahoma, Amish minister who, during the 1950s, became something of a traveling Amish evangelist. Preaching to sizable groups wherever and whenever he could command a hearing, Miller addressed Amish audiences in the Midwest and Pennsylvania, everywhere provoking a sharply mixed response.[47] Although not formally connected to the mission movement, Miller combined sermons on temperance and courtship chastity with a highly innovative and emotional style, so that the medium often cast a shadow on the message.

Few Old Orders were surprised in 1957 when Miller and his church joined the car-driving Beachy Amish-Mennonites.[48] By then, many mission supporters were making similar choices, leaving their Old Order churches and joining nearby Mennonite or Beachy fellowships. In several Amish church districts, mission-movement support had been nearly unanimous, and an entire district simply evolved into a Beachy congregation without schism.

The emergence and dispersal of the midcentury mission movement had a number of important outcomes. For most Old Orders, it confirmed a suspicion that agitating for reform in one aspect of life probably was linked to a wholesale embrace of modernity. Even the innocent interests of mission-movement supporters quickly produced automobile ownership and higher education. As a result, many Old Orders became more wary of outside religious influences that promised to solve Amish problems with new spiritual insights. Longstanding Amish subscriptions to Mennonite periodicals, for example, began to wane. Significantly, the Old Orders' growing sense of churchly separation after 1960 coincided with their increasing economic integration into surrounding agricultural and business economies.

But the demise of the Old Order mission movement may have had an even greater impact on the Beachy Amish-Mennonites, since it injected a sizable group of energetic new members and congregations into Beachy ranks and brought the MIC and its assortment of projects under Beachy auspices. If the Beachy Amish-Mennonites had once been most easily distinguished from Old Orders in technological terms, after about 1960, their outward evangelistic focus would be central to their identity.[49]

But not all reform currents flowed in the same direction. During the 1950s, a few Old Orders who shared some of the mission advocates' moral concerns took those convictions in decidedly different directions. Troubled by teenage antics and opposed to tobacco use, these Amish combined strict moral standards for young people with a principled desire to avoid technological change, maintain a rural way of life, and uphold the practice of "strict shunning." Launching new settlements in places such as Kenton, Ohio, and Paoli, Indiana, they formed a loose network of especially conservative-minded Amish who saw rigorous commitment to a traditional *Ordnung* as the key to spiritual renewal.[50]

A similar dynamic in 1952 sparked the formation in Holmes County, Ohio, of a new Old Order affiliation under the leadership of bishop Andrew J. Weaver. The group sought to stand by the practice of strict shunning and to stave off creeping technological change and worldliness. But the "Andy Weaver Amish" were also concerned about young people's activities and moved to restrict some of the liberty that was traditionally given to unbaptized Amish teens. For example, the Weaver group disciplined church-member parents who allowed their sons to purchase cars and then continue to live at home. Parents could no longer turn a blind eye to the sometimes wild antics associated with teen car ownership.[51]

In the 1960s, yet a third impulse combining a desire for church renewal and the interests of youth emerged in Amish circles. After 1959 in Holmes County, certain ministers expressed a burden for the spiritual state of their young people. When some teenagers requested special "youth meetings" for Bible study, these leaders gladly obliged.[52] Like the earlier mission-movement advocates, these organizers stressed strict courtship practices and nonuse of alcohol and tobacco. But they pressed their case in terms of the local church and did not link these causes with distant mission activism, higher education, or highly emotional preaching appeals that had discredited the earlier mission movement. Proponents stressed their desire to remain Old Order, though they did not share the highly traditional sentiments of the Andy Weaver folks.

For a time, supporters and skeptics agreed to allow the youth meetings to run their course, but soon the gatherings became entangled in a debate over the doctrine of "assurance of salvation," which detractors charged the meetings were promoting. Citing Jesus' words in Mark 13:13 that "he who endures to the end will be saved," the Amish traditionally had taught that eternal life was God's gift to those who persevered in lifelong reliance upon God's grace.[53] To be sure, in this life Christians had a living hope of salvation, but announcing that one was absolutely certain of one's future smacked both of spiritual pride and human arrogance. After all, the apostle Peter had warned the early church that anyone could be "led away with the error of the wicked" and "fall from . . . steadfastness" (2 Peter 3:17).

For their part, youth-meeting leaders insisted they were misunderstood. In stressing the spiritual basis for upright living, they claimed only that Christians entered a knowable relationship with God, and that one could rely on God's sustaining grace. But all too soon the youth meetings themselves became a symbol for a cluster of potentially divisive issues.

Low-grade tension simmered in Ohio until late 1966, when a district split over the youth meetings and related issues. In short order, a number of other such separations took place, ultimately dividing those who stood by the youth meetings from those who saw them as another religiously coated cover for people unwilling to submit to the *Ordnung*. The youth-meeting Amish received the nickname "New Order Amish," and, while they preferred the designation "Amish Brotherhood," they reluctantly accepted the New Order label. They were most uncomfortable with the word *new*, since they saw themselves standing squarely in Anabaptist and Amish traditions.[54]

At almost exactly the same time as the New Order church was emerging in Ohio, a similar movement took shape in the Lancaster, Pennsylvania, settlement. There, however, the calls for spiritual renewal were, from the beginning, tied up with agitation for in-house telephones and tractor farming, which gave the New Order story there a different feel.[55]

Unlike the earlier mission-movement advocates, the New Order Amish self-consciously retained horse-and-buggy culture and biweekly German language worship, almost always in private homes. Indeed—confusing as the terminology is—the New Order Amish are probably best understood as an affiliation under the broader Old Order Amish canopy, and New Orders typically are included in tabulations of Old Order Amish populations nationally.[56]

Nevertheless, the tone of New Order spirituality is different from most Old Orders. In the words of two leaders, "Many New Orders looked at the Old Order system as having many values, but saw a need for more spiritual convictions to make it effective."[57] Similarly, New Orders have produced a number of articulate tracts and booklets outlining their beliefs and practices in a systematic and logical way that most Old Orders would be slow to do.[58] Although the two groups remain distinct, today a more amiable relationship exists between them than was the case in the 1960s and 1970s. New Orders concede that many Old Order parents and leaders care deeply about their young people's welfare.

In 2012, there were some seventy New Order Amish church districts in a dozen states, with the majority of members in Ohio. All New Orders forbid things like tobacco and "disapprove of the idea that young people need to sow some wild oats before marriage." They also have Sunday schools and church supervised activities for youth. But New Order churches differ among themselves on questions of appropriate technology, with some forbidding public utility electricity and tractor farming, and others accepting them. Dress standards also vary somewhat. In addition, since 1983 there has been a small breakaway group known as the New Order Fellowship, which accepts a much wider range of technology and a more subjective religious experience.[59]

The emergence by the 1970s of the New Order Amish, the Andy Weaver Amish, and other identifiable affiliations suggested to some onlookers a disappointing Amish propensity to disagree and divide. Although the Amish themselves lament schism, they might view these midcentury developments a bit differently. The same tenacity that led Amish church members to stand up to the state and spend time in jail rather than compromise their convictions also injected firm resolve into local church life. At times such determination could degenerate into dogmatism, but more often it pointed to a vital faith that took a lively interest in everyday expression of ethics and a resistance to watering down discipleship. As the Amish moved into the last years of the twentieth century and the early decades of the twenty-first, those characteristics continued to shape their dynamic relationship with a globalizing economy and postmodern society.

—12—

Peoplehood in the Midst
of Modernity ·

> *"The Amish people feel that their mission is to lead an humble life that needs no publicity."*
> —an Amish farmer, 1978

Unity and diversity

On October 2, 2006, the quiet Amish community around Nickel Mines, Pennsylvania, was terrifyingly and tragically brought to the center of world attention when a non-Amish intruder entered an Amish schoolhouse and shot ten young girls, five of them fatally, before turning his gun on himself.

Within an hour, these shocking events became news literally around the globe as commentators added Amish schools to a list of unsafe places and wrung their hands over the outbreak of senseless violence. But within forty-eight hours, the media story shifted from one of lost innocence to one of bewilderment as the victimized Amish families responded not with calls for revenge aimed at the memory of the gunman, but with gracious acts of compassion toward his family, even as the Amish themselves were grieving deeply.

Hours after the shooting, Amish people visited the intruder's relatives, extending sympathy and assuring his family that the Amish would not scapegoat them for what he had done. Six days later, when most non-Amish neighbors stayed away from the gunman's burial, local Amish people, including Amish parents who had buried their own daughters the day before, comprised half of the mourners at his graveside service. The funeral director, who had participated in thousands of funerals in his career, had never seen anything like it and believed he "was witnessing a miracle." About the same time, an ad hoc Amish committee, set up to oversee funds that poured in for the schoolgirl victims from generous donors far and wide, announced that it would be giving some of the money to a second fund for the intruder's children.[1]

Reporters and the public at large were unprepared for these developments and struggled to make sense of them. In the aftermath of Nickel Mines, some commentators praised Amish forgiveness and jumped to apply its example to a host of other social and political issues. Others denounced Amish forgiveness as too fast, emotionally unhealthy, and a denial of some innate human need for retributive justice.

As the story of Nickel Mines played out across the airways and in newspaper columns, it was a reminder that fundamental Amish values remain starkly different from those animating mainstream North America in the twenty-first century.[2] Even as Amish society was surely changing—fewer Amish families rose before dawn to milk cows, for example, and more were making a living by managing small businesses— there remained powerful ways in which Amish peoplehood diverged from the modern norm. "It's just standard Christian forgiveness, isn't it?" one Amish man said when he heard that outsiders were stunned by the Amish response to Nickel

Mines. And yet, judged by the reactions, there was little that onlookers found familiar.

In U.S. society, where people are taught to resist giving up anything due them as individuals, the thought of forgiveness, even when promoted by mainstream religious leaders, seemed to be an unnatural act of superhuman heroism. For the Amish, by contrast, whose lives were shaped by daily rituals and routines of giving up individual choices and personal opportunities, forgiveness was certainly hard work, but they did not see it as unnatural or unusual.

If Nickel Mines highlighted values that unify Amish people across time and space, it is also the case that life in modern and postmodern North America has a way of fragmenting even the Amish. True, some of the fragmentation is a result of Amish society itself. A decentralized, congregational church whose members value local traditions and whose numbers are growing by leaps and bounds has spread across thirty states, living out traditional ways in new contexts amid new neighbors.

Some forty affiliations across the Amish landscape, from highly traditional Swartzentruber Amish to New Order Amish, practice their faith in slightly—and sometimes dramatically—different ways. For example, some Amish refuse routine immunization, while most have few qualms about visiting a doctor, and some take advantage of free health clinics.[3]

Responses to technology also reveal a widening array of practice, from Swartzentrubers who generally will not talk on a phone and continue to cut and store ice for basic refrigeration, to mainline Old Orders who increasingly use cell phones to manage their businesses and operate the latest equipment with innovative hydraulic, pneumatic, and solar power.[4] And while some Amish have erected cultural fences that often separate them from their neighbors, others engage their neighbors by participating in volunteer fire companies, acting as blood donors, and traveling to assist non-Amish communities struck by natural disasters—such as Hurricane Katrina in 2005—as they volunteer with groups such as Mennonite Disaster Service and Disaster Response Services.

Interaction with government also provokes diverse response. Swartzentruber conservatives have battled state and local officials over building codes and laws mandating bright orange, slow-moving-vehicle emblems on buggies, emblems the Swartzentrubers consider unholy talismans that undercut their faith in God's protection.

Most other Amish are puzzled by the Swartzentrubers' stance, and are grateful that conflicts with the state over schools and Social Security have generally turned in their favor. They are, however, greatly inconvenienced by anti-terrorism rules that require photo identification for many routine transactions or for crossing the border with Canada, since nearly all Amish churches forbid voluntarily sitting for a photo.

At the other end of the spectrum from sectarian separatism, in 2004 a small number of Amish men in the Lancaster County settlement publicly campaigned for President George W. Bush's reelection, although most Amish, in Lancaster and beyond, were critical of their actions.[5]

Although Amish people have disagreed over where to draw the lines that marked their lives as strangers and pilgrims in this world, they have shared many common experiences. In the last decades of the twentieth century and the opening years of the twenty-first, Amish life has been marked by three more notable developments: an occupational shift from farming to non-farm employment, rising interest in the Amish on the part of outsiders, and the dynamics of continued Amish population growth and migration.

Occupational diversity and social change

In the last decades of the twentieth century, Amish families began moving off the farm. This development carried enormous implications for a people whose way of life had been rooted in the soil for nearly three centuries. Yet the changes that accompanied the shift to non-farm jobs were more complex than some observers realized. Those households that remained in agriculture also saw their livelihoods change as they often needed to shift the focus of their farming to match changing market conditions.

Volunteers prepacking beans at a Christian Aid Ministries (CAM) warehouse in 2003. CAM receives strong support from Beachy Amish churches, as well as from some Old Order Amish and conservative-minded Mennonites. Some 12,000 volunteers per year donate time at this warehouse, preparing about 8,000 food boxes each month for distribution in Eastern Europe, Latin America, Africa, and the Middle East.

Teaching in Mexico

"I believe I have learned as much about faith in the last nine years as I have in all the rest of my life put together," wrote a young Old Order Amish woman from her school teaching post in Mexico. Since 2000, more than one hundred men and women from across the United States have each spent several months to several years teaching in schools associated with culturally conservative Old Colony Mennonites who live in northern Mexico. This Amish teacher-training program represents a new and creative expression of twenty-first century Amish life.

In the 1920s, highly sectarian Old Colony Mennonites left their homes in Manitoba and moved to Mexico, in large part to avoid Canadian public education laws that mandated instruction in English. There, living in geographically bounded colonies, the migrants maintained traditional ways but also experienced poverty and church conflict. Their parochial schools, which were the very reason they had moved to Mexico, fell into disorder.

In 1995 a group of Amish from Pennsylvania, Ohio, and Indiana traveled by bus to Mexico at the invitation of development workers who had been trying to address social needs among the Mexican Mennonites. The Old Colony people welcomed and trusted the Amish, viewing them as less culturally threatening than the foreign aid workers and Mexican government officials whose advice they had often spurned.

For their part, the Amish were surprised by the highly sectarian nature of the Old Colony world. Although Old Order Amish churches maintain meaningful separation from "the world," they have never lived in socially isolated colonies apart from non-Amish neighbors, and their parochial school system has developed a solid academic reputation despite rejecting high school work.

Initially, Amish visitors to Mexico worked to improve Old Colony Mennonites' dairy herds and helped construct a cheese plant to provide an outlet for colony milk. However, reforming Old Colony schooling soon became the heart of the relationship. In 2000, an Amish committee, based in Indiana, began sending Amish teachers to Mexico to train Old Colony teachers and to start new schools modeled on Amish education practices in the United States and Canada. Amish teachers introduced age-graded classes, phonics-based German language reading instruction, and pedagogies other than memorization. They also decorated classroom walls with charts and student art work.

In many ways, the parameters of the program conform to Amish cultural values. Teachers travel to Mexico by train and bus, for example, never by airplane, and teachers return to their home communities in the North for fall and spring communion services so as to remain in fellowship with their home church districts. Even so, the most tradition-minded Amish do not participate in the program, which tends to attract relatively progressive Old Orders. In fact, the Support Committee project is a novel development, and the Amish teachers—almost all young women—often return from Mexico with new perspectives. Wrote one, "My own way of doing things—the way I grew up with—no longer seems like the only way to do it.... Experiencing a different culture showed me how narrow-minded I was." Said another, in Mexico "we learn to understand better about God's unconditional love for us and His will for us to love one another in the same way."

Source: *Called to Mexico: Bringing Hope and Literacy to Old Colony Mennonites* (Nappanee, Ind.: Old Colony Support Committee, 2011); *Old Colony Mennonite Support Newsletter*, 1998-present.

As early as the 1930s and 1940s, a few Amish men in communities such as Nappanee, Indiana, had taken employment in area industry.[6] But during the 1970s the shift to non-farm labor became much more pronounced, and by 2013 it was a reality in every Amish settlement. In 1973, only thirty-one percent of Old Order household heads in the Geauga County, Ohio, settlement were farming. Two decades later, that percentage had dropped to seventeen percent, and in the early twenty-first century, the figure stood at seven percent. By 2012, in the Elkhart-LaGrange, Indiana, settlement, less than fifteen percent of the men under age sixty-five were farming. And in the Lancaster, Pennsylvania, settlement where farmers had still been a majority in 1986, by 2012 the share had slipped to thirty-six percent.[7] Even in newer settlements begun by Amish exiting densely populated areas for cheaper land and more rural elbow room, farming often is a minority occupation.

The drift away from farming is rooted in long-term demographic and economic changes. Large families produced steady Amish population growth that began to outstrip available farmland. In certain communities—such as those near Lancaster, Pennsylvania; Cleveland, Ohio; and Fort Wayne, Indiana—suburbanization and rising land prices compounded the problem.

Also, Old Order Amish families preferred small-scale, low mechanization farming, which became less viable after 1970. Corporate agriculture consolidated business, and government subsidies tilted the playing field in favor of big producers. Meanwhile, new standards for the rapid cooling of raw milk added to production costs. These standards also often conflicted with the *Ordnung* of more conservative church districts that prohibited high-tech refrigeration and consequently forced their members into selling grade B milk for less money.[8]

In the early twenty-first century, there has been a modest renaissance in Amish agriculture. Some families have focused on growing produce for wholesale and restaurant markets. In 1985, Amish farmers near Leola, Pennsylvania, started a produce auction house. Within a quarter century, Amish and Old Order Mennonites were running more than sixty such auctions across the country, bringing profitability back to small-scale growers. In Missouri, the agriculture extension agents estimate that Old Order households now raise ten percent of the state's vegetables. Across the continent, Amish households have started greenhouse businesses, raising seedlings and bedding plants of all kinds.[9]

Other new approaches to farming have included a focus on intensive grazing, grass-fed beef production, and organic farming. Although some outsiders assume that Amish farmers have always been organic, few twentieth-century Amish farms would have met the standards and procedures necessary to meet the organic label.

The move to organic production on the part of some Amish farmers today stems from both a concern to revitalize small-scale agriculture along profitable lines and from religious conviction. In 2003, a group of Amish farmers in Holmes County, Ohio, began Green Field Farms as an organic cooperative and marketing venture. Ohio farmer, writer, and bishop David Kline is an articulate proponent of sustainable farming methods and Christian care for creation.[10]

Farming remains an esteemed and ideal way of life, and the basis on which many Amish cultural traditions originally rested. Still, the shift away from farming in the Amish world has been pronounced. The abandonment of agriculture certainly carries with it the possibility of significant social change, though it has by no means meant the end of Amish society. Indeed, a variety of studies have shown that children of Amish carpenters or factory workers are as likely to join the church as children of Amish farmers.[11]

The implications of occupational change hinge in part on the type of work Amish choose to take up after laying down their plows. Small businesses, industrial employment, and carpentry work crews constitute three broad categories of contemporary Amish employment. Small businesses— from metal fabrication shops to dry-goods stores—are the most common alternative to farming. These small firms are generally located at or near home and are family-centered enterprises. Like farming, they engage several generations and produce busy schedules that leave little time for leisure. But because they are home-based, they also offer the possibility of introducing change into the center of family life itself.

Although the lack of high school and college credentials keeps Old Orders from professional pursuits, Amish business entrepreneurs have proven remarkably successful and, in some cases, quite wealthy. Many such small businesses are owned and operated by Amish women, which adds a new dimension to Amish gender traditions.[12]

Factory employment has been the most common occupation among Amish men in northern Indiana and Geauga County, Ohio, for several decades. In Nappanee, Indiana, for example, in the early 2000s, almost sixty percent of Amish men worked in factories. Most spent their days on assembly lines building recreational vehicles and mobile homes or in related plants supplying component parts for line assembly. Industrial work introduces a somewhat different set of dynamics from that of at-home entrepreneurship. The forty-hour industrial workweek offers steady paychecks with plenty of free time. It also separates home and work environments, leaving children with fewer ways to contribute to the family's welfare.[13]

Carpentry or other mobile work crews related to the construction trades has been a third popular option among Amish men who are unable to farm or are uninterested in farming. Such work is tied to a recognized Amish tradition of craftsmanship. It is also attractive to Amish who adhere to a more traditional *Ordnung* that bans most newer technology from the home or at-home shop. By working for a non-Amish employer or customer, these Amish carpenters are free to use power tools and other devices in the service of others, which they would not use on their own turf.

The drawbacks of such arrangements, from the Amish perspective, include men's traveling (in a rented vehicle) sometimes great distances to work, and the consequent absence of fathers from home for especially long workdays. Nevertheless, mobile-work crews provide employment for sizable majorities of Amish household-heads in some communities.

Attracting attention

Another significant development has been a growing fascination on the part of larger society with Amish life. From the rise of Amish tourism and the popularity of Amish-themed romance novels, to the easy way politicians and comedians can make allusions to the Amish and safely assume their audiences know who they are talking about, it is clear that a remarkable transformation has taken place. Without any public relations campaign, promotional budget, or celebrity spokesperson, a small and self-effacing group has become exceedingly well known, even as North American interest in other denominational differences and distinctions otherwise declines.

Already in the early 1930s, cookbooks and restaurants in eastern Pennsylvania, all non-Amish in origin and ownership, were using the Amish people, and sometimes the name "Amish" itself, to market regional cookery. Then, in 1937-

1938, Old Order communities received extended national media coverage as *Time, Literary Digest,* and *The New York Times* featured stories about the public school controversy in Lancaster County.[14]

The complex roots of Amish-related tourism included the effects of such notoriety, along with the penchant for travel and vacation among post-World War II Americans, who were anxious about the modern society they were creating. In an age that celebrated the interstate highway system and was caught up in a global "space race," the presence of people who traveled by horse and buggy and refused to embrace transistor radios was both intriguing and troubling. Were the Amish relics from the past or the keepers of wisdom who knew something everyone else was fast forgetting?

Given its proximity to East Coast population centers, Lancaster County, Pennsylvania, became a destination of middle class vacationers eager to catch a glimpse of Amish life. For second-generation Eastern European ethnics who populated northeastern cities at the time, Lancaster offered a convenient and nostalgic connection to an imagined peasant past.

By 1950, a New York City based tour company boasted regular excursions to Lancaster's Amish community. An explosion of picture books and knickknacks satisfied the desires of those eager to consume the commercialized simple life.

In 1955, a non-Amish entrepreneur opened The Amish Farm and House for tours, likely the first paid-admission Amish-themed attraction.[15] Two years later, as the number of annual visitors to Lancaster County approached a million, the local Chamber of Commerce launched the Pennsylvania Dutch Visitors Bureau to handle lodging arrangements and promote tourism in the region.[16]

While Amish-related tourism in the Midwest got off to a slower start, by 1960, organized tours were bringing visitors to see the Holmes County, Ohio, and a June 1967 article in *Travel* suggested visiting northern Indiana's Old Order community. Amish themed restaurants and attractions soon opened in both states.[17]

Interest in the Amish accelerated after 1970 as an oil embargo and energy crisis stoked public curiosity about people who lived off the grid. At the same time, art critics Jonathan Holstein and Gail van der Hoof had discovered the bold colors and stark designs of Amish quilts. In 1971, they included Amish quilts in a show they curated at the Whitney Museum of American Art. Soon, serious collectors and tourists seeking a piece of Amish authenticity were among those who helped spike a national interest in all things Amish.[18] By the early twenty-first century, some eleven million tourists annually flocked to the largest Amish communities in Pennsylvania, Ohio, and Indiana, and poured $1.2 billion into local tourism economies.[19]

Meanwhile, Amish characters were popping up in popular culture. Young children learned about the Amish through Marguerite de Angeli's 1944 story, *Yonie Wondernose,* which received a wide audience after winning the American Library Association's Caldecott Honor for its illustrations.[20] Books for teens and adults—including a Nancy Drew mystery, *The Witch Tree Symbol*—further popularized Amish images, settings, and plots.[21] In 1955, Twentieth Century Fox released "Violent Saturday," an Ernest Borgnine film in which criminals hid on an Amish farm. Earlier that year, the Mark Hellinger Theatre in New York City opened "Plain and Fancy," a popular Broadway musical that celebrated Amish life, even as it criticized the practice of Amish church discipline that underlay that life.[22]

Amish romances

Popular interest in the Amish in the twenty-first century is perhaps nowhere so clear as on retail bookshelves loaded with titles from the burgeoning genre of Amish romance fiction. Although there are also Amish-themed mysteries and science fiction books, Christian romances featuring Amish plot lines have rocketed to the top of sales charts. A dozen new Amish romance novels hit the market in 2008. Two years later there were forty-five new releases, and in 2012 there were eighty-five new titles, or more than a book a week. All totaled, more than twenty-four million "bonnet novels" have passed through readers' hands since 1997, when evangelical Christian writer Beverly Lewis published *The Shunning*, which was among the first commercially successful books in the genre.

What accounts for this phenomenon? Literary critic Valerie Weaver-Zercher has argued that the popularity of these novels is linked to readers' weariness of hypermodern and hypersexualized society. Amish romance novels offer readers "chaste texts and chaste protagonists living within a chaste subculture." Many of the books offer some criticism of Amish culture (or popular perceptions of Amish culture), but the sharpest critiques these books wield is of individualistic and hedonistic North American society.

The Amish romance genre has been dominated by non-Amish writers. The exception is Linda Byler, an Old Order Amish writer living in central Pennsylvania who has published nearly a dozen novels. Byler had been a well-known writer for Amish correspondence newspapers when, as a grandmother, she began writing longer, serialized stories with young women as protagonists. In 2010, she released *Running Around*. That title was followed by books such as *The Disappearances* (2012), set in a Montana Amish settlement, and *The Witnesses* (2014), which takes place in Lancaster, Pennsylvania.

For more information, see Valerie Weaver-Zercher, *Thrill of the Chaste: The Allure of Amish Romance Novels* (Baltimore: Johns Hopkins University Press, 2013).

Occasionally Amish leaders have protested their people's portrayal in such secular formats. When the 1984 filming of Paramount Pictures' "Witness" disturbed the Lancaster Amish community, they addressed their concerns to the Pennsylvania government. ("Witness" portrayed the Lancaster Old Orders innocently entangled in a web of big-city drug crime.) A delegation of Amish leaders, including three bishops, traveled to the state capitol to register their complaint.[23] Nevertheless, sensationalized media images have continued, including so-called reality television shows such as "Amish in the City," "Breaking Amish," and "Amish Mafia," in 2004 and 2012. None of these programs reflected anything like Amish reality, of course, and the head of CBS/UPN entertainment joked that his studio chose Amish subjects because "the Amish don't have a good lobbying group" that can mount any meaningful objection to their exploitation.[24]

Although the Amish are dismayed by the blatantly bigoted messages of such reality shows when newspaper stories and non-Amish neighbors describe the programs to them, they are also uneasy about the excessively admiring images associated with much of the tourist trade and with the genuine popularity of the Amish "brand," fearing that it provides a spiritual temptation to pride rather than an authentic witness. In 1998, when several Amish-reared men became involved in a drug ring more bizarre than even "Witness" had portrayed, the publicity was enormous. Some Amish and other onlookers believed that society's earlier adulation only encouraged the resulting charges of Amish hypocrisy.[25]

Historian David Weaver-Zercher has looked at popular interest in the Amish and helpfully explained how it combines highly romanticized and deeply critical elements. Modern observers are intrigued by people who demonstrate the possibility of countercultural choices and show that life can be different. But, Weaver-Zercher found, moderns also desperately want to believe that such dissenters are deeply flawed, thereby reassuring themselves of modernity's superiority. In the end, pop culture encourages North Americans to admire, but then dismiss, the Amish way.[26]

If popular attention to the Amish reveals much about modern Americans' hopes and fears, it also has an impact on how the Amish think about themselves. In an essay "Being a Witness to Tourists," minister Benuel Blank reflected on the ways "we plain people can learn a good bit from the very people who would come to see firsthand our way of life and living." For Blank, the high expectations that tourists have of Amish people have encouraged him to embrace more fully a life of simplicity, while the probing questions that visitors ask have led him to "resolve to live a better example" before his church, his children, and a watching world. On the whole, conversations with tourists made him "thankful for the teaching that we got from our parents."[27]

In a similar vein, sociologist Donald B. Kraybill has suggested that visitation fortifies Amish life as it "galvanizes the cultural gap between the two worlds and helps define Amish identity." In fact, growing public interest in the Amish may bolster public sympathy for them and discourage government infringement on Amish rights that would force them to move away.[28]

The presence of tourism has other, more immediate results. In some communities, the press of popularity produces overcrowded roads and curious throngs of picture-takers.[29] While some families have chosen to move away from such areas, most remain. Some take jobs in businesses that cater to the tourist trade, and a few operate full-scale retail shops that rely on visitor dollars or sell their wares through non-Amish dealers who host websites devoted to Amish-themed online commerce.

If modern Americans are ambivalent about their response to the Amish, the Amish have mixed feelings about tourism. Some find it a nuisance while others profit from it. Most believe that tourists typically are sincere seekers, genuinely interested in learning about others.

Growth in the midst of modernity

Both the shift toward non-farm employment and the increasing public recognition of the Amish are related to a third feature of recent Amish history: persistent population growth. In the midst of modernity and assorted pressures from the welfare and warfare state, the Amish have remained remarkably resilient. Despite mid-twentieth-century predictions that they would not long survive the currents of assimilation or resist the inevitable logic of individual fulfillment in the liberal state, the Amish have not disappeared. Indeed, they have grown in numbers and, in recent years, even increased their rate of growth.

The explanations and implications of such growth vary, but the increases themselves are readily recognizable. For its part, the Beachy Amish-Mennonite fellowship has expanded to include more than 160 congregations in twenty-four states and one province in North America, as well as nine other countries.[30] Some of this domestic and much of the international growth have come from systematic mission work during the later decades of the twentieth century.[31] While Beachy Amish-Mennonites are keen to engage in verbal evangelism, they also support agencies such as Christian Aid Ministries, an international relief and service organization headquartered in Berlin, Ohio, and founded in 1981 by David N. Troyer, a Beachy church member. CAM receives solid backing from Beachy churches and provides tangible links to other parts of the world.[32]

In contrast, most Old Order Amish harbor serious reservations about the value of organized and bureau-

The Old Order Amish remain a growing group in the twenty-first century, not only because of their large families, but also because an increasing percentage of Amish children choose to follow their parents' faith.

cratized mission programs, skeptical of the possibility of communicating faithful living with words or via large institutions disconnected from daily discipleship.[33]

Yet despite their resistance to missionary strategizing, the Old Orders have grown even more rapidly in recent years. While the Amish do not keep systematic membership records on a national basis, the change in the number of church districts reflects their membership trends. Since Old Orders worship in homes, shops, or barns, whenever a given church district's membership grows too large to comfortably continue such meeting, the church divides into two districts. Those patterns of division and multiplication make it clear that the Old Order circle is growing. In the twenty-one-year period from 1992 to 2013, Old Order Amish population grew 120 percent.[34]

While older communities expand, Amish families establish new settlements annually.[35] Church districts now stretch from Fort Fairfield, Maine to Beeville, Texas, and from Sarasota, Florida to Rexford, Montana. Thirty states and the province of Ontario are home to an ever-growing number of Old Order churches. While Amish populations remain concentrated in Ohio, Pennsylvania, and Indiana, those states account for a smaller share of the Amish population than in the past. In 1974, they were home to three-quarters of all Old Orders, but, by 2014, their share had dropped to sixty-four percent, with New York, Wisconsin, and Michigan, attracting many new settlements. Those states, plus Missouri and Kentucky, now account for almost a quarter of the Amish membership and have eclipsed older areas of residence such as Illinois and Iowa.[36]

Those forming new communities seek available, affordable rural acreage, though not necessarily farms, since even in today's new communities, farming is often a minority occupation.

Although it is possible for those raised in non-Amish homes to join the Old Order church, very few do so.[37] Instead, large families are the key source of Old Order increase. Yet the presence of children is no guarantee of growth, since those reared in Amish homes must choose church membership and baptism as adults. Central to the Old Order Amish story of recent decades has been the rising percentage of Amish offspring who join their parents' church. Comprehensive studies in northern Indiana, northeast Ohio, and eastern Pennsylvania point to identical trends. In the Elkhart-LaGrange, Indiana, settlement, for example, of those born in the 1930s, twenty-one percent did not join the Old Order church, but of those born in the 1950s, the dropout rate dipped to ten percent. In many places, retention rates now are eighty-five to ninety percent or more.[38]

Beachy Amish-Mennonite growth and diversity

Old Order Amish communities have undergone tremendous growth and witnessed new diversity in recent years, and so, too, have the Beachy Amish-Mennonites. Since 1927, the Beachy churches that stem from the leadership of bishop Moses Beachy (see chapter 10) have maintained many aspects of plain life, including simple dress, trimmed beards for men and head coverings for women; resistance to worldly entertainment; parochial education; and *a cappella* worship in simple meetinghouses.

At the same time, Beachy churches have been clearly distinguished from Old Order Amish branches because the Beachys drive cars, almost always worship in English, and engage in verbal evangelism and organized international mission work.

For most of their history, the Beachy Amish-Mennonites embraced the localized, congregational structure of their Amish heritage, although since 1970, many congregations have supported institutions such as Calvary Bible School or Hillcrest Home for the Aged, both in Arkansas.

By the mid-1980s, the growth of the decentralized Beachy fellowship had resulted in increasing diversity— diversity that some Beachy Amish-Mennonites saw as troubling assimilation. In 1991, a five-member Beachy Bishop Committee formed following a continent-wide ministers' meeting held in Wellesley, Ontario. The group developed an eighteen-point statement, entitled "A Charge to Keep I Have," that outlined minimal standards for Beachy church members, including items related to divorce, radio ownership, hairstyling, and suitable recreation on Sundays.

By 1997, it became clear that the Bishop Committee would not be able to corral all Beachy Amish-Mennonites behind a single, detailed statement. In the years that followed, the Beachy fellowship fractured as some congregations, disappointed in the failure of the Bishop Committee to dictate greater uniformity, banded together around stricter rules or a common mission. Some of these groups are:

Maranatha Amish-Mennonites adhere to a somewhat more conservative way of life than other Beachy churches. In 2014, they had fifteen congregations and just over 1,000 members in Kansas, Missouri, New Jersey, Ontario, Pennsylvania, Tennessee, Texas, and Virginia.

Ambassadors Amish-Mennonites are known for their commitment to church planting and mission, and for publishing a monthly devotional entitled *Beside Still Waters*, which is read in many Amish homes. In 2014, they had seven congregations and 482 members in Indiana, Kentucky, and Missouri.

Berea Amish-Mennonites are among the most conservative subgroups in terms of lifestyle, dress, and doctrine. In 2014, their ten churches and 526 members were found in Arkansas, Illinois, Indiana, Iowa, Kentucky, Missouri, Ohio, and Virginia.

The main *Beachy Amish-Mennonite* branch remains the largest Amish-Mennonite fellowship and had 165 congregations in 2014. Its 9,764 members are spread across twenty-four states and Ontario, plus Belize, Costa Rica, El Salvador, Ireland, Kenya, Nicaragua, Paraguay, Romania, and Ukraine.

A related group, *Mennonite Christian Fellowship*, emerged from Beachy roots in the 1970s, but adopted its present name later. Members generally dress more conservatively than those in the mainstream Beachy church. With 1,600 members, MCF has thirty-four congregations in California, Kentucky, Maryland, Missouri, Montana, New York, Ohio, Pennsylvania, and Tennessee, as well as Cuba, Honduras, Nicaragua, and Paraguay.

Source: Cory Anderson, "Retracing the Blurred Boundaries of Twentieth-Century 'Amish-Mennonite' Identity," *Mennonite Quarterly Review* 85 (July 2011): 361-411. See also http://www. beachyam.org and annual statistics in *Mennonite Church Directory* (Harrisonburg, Va.: Christian Light Publications).

Scholars and the Amish themselves suggest possible reasons for the church's increasing attraction. The rise of Amish parochial schools as a resource for socializing children and presenting a learning environment in harmony with the church and the home is one important piece. Private schools enroll an increasing percentage of Amish students, even in settlements where public school attendance is still possible.[39]

Other observers point to the growing gap between Old Order culture and wider society, arguing that increased contact with the world through factory employment or tourism confirms for the Amish their sense of separation. Still others suggest that the growing variety of occupational pursuits in Amish circles now makes it economically easier to remain Amish. The choice to stay, in many communities, is no longer reliant on one's ability to find a farm or succeed in agriculture.[40]

Another factor may be the presence of modest and low-profile institutions that bolster and help to define Amish community. These include the books and magazines of Pathway Publishers, headquartered in Aylmer, Ontario. The monthly periodical *Family Life*, along with *Young Companion* for teens and children, support Amish values through stories and editorials. Pathway also issues historical fiction, devotional books, and Amish school texts. Numerous freelance Amish publishers now issue a plethora of audience-specific magazines that connect housewives, woodshop owners, parents of special-needs children, and many other interest groups.

Meanwhile, historically minded Amish folks in several communities have established historical libraries to support the transmission of heritage and faith, while other settlements have organized trust funds, offering low interest loans to church members for mortgages or small business start-ups.[41]

Amish leaders in some communities have also partnered with mental health professionals to establish residential treatment centers sensitive to Amish cultural values, such as Rest Haven, located in Goshen, Indiana, which opened in 2002. At the same time, a loose network of "People's Helpers" coordinates the efforts of Amish who act as lay counselors, assisting those with a variety of personal or family problems.[42]

None of these newer institutions is uniformly accepted in all Old Order circles, especially among more conservative leaning members, skeptical of activity and organization other than that of the local church. Nevertheless, in many places, these formalized connections have helped nurture a broader sense of peoplehood alongside demographic and geographic expansion.[43]

If some Amish speculate on the social causes of their church's health and strength, they typically are also quick to credit the mystery of divine goodness. There simply is no logical explanation, one Old Order sage remarked, "that can explain the basic fundamentals of their faith that was inherited from ancestors of many generations ago, which was granted to them through the grace of our Lord Jesus Christ." Instead, the Amish man thought, his people had "cultivated as their every day mission" the task of Christian discipleship, and "feel that their mission is to lead an humble life that needs no publicity."[44]

And yet attention comes, even if it is sometimes misguided or misinformed. In a world seeking security in more powerful weapons, happiness in the accumulation of things, and faith in the individual's ability to hasten human progress, Amish life continues to compel many moderns to stop and think about choices and decisions—watching, weighing, and wondering—as the Amish story continues.

Largest Old Order Amish settlements, 2014

Location	Church districts	Estimated population (adults & unbaptized children)
Lancaster County area, Pennsylvania	197	32,900
Holmes-Wayne counties area, Ohio	251	32,630
Elkhart-LaGrange counties, Indiana	163	22,820
Geauga-Trumbull counties area, Ohio	108	15,230
Berne area, Indiana	57	8,210
Nappanee, Indiana	42	5,590
Arthur, Illinois	30	4,200
Daviess County, Indiana	29	4,090
Mifflin County area, Pennsylvania	28	3,360
Allen County area, Indiana	21	3,025
Indiana County area, Pennsylvania	21	2,975
New Wilmington area, Pennsylvania	19	2,415

Source: annually updated data from http://www2.etown.edu/ amishstudies

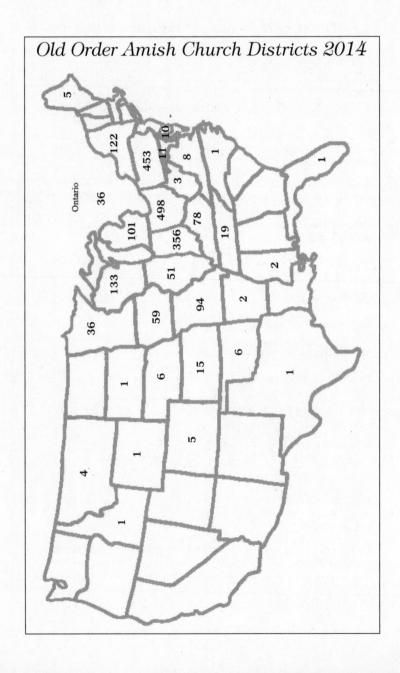

Old Order Amish Church Districts 2014

Old Order Amish Church Districts, 1974 and 2014

	1974 Church districts	*2014 Church districts*	*2014 estimated population (adults & children)*
Canada			
Ontario	16	36	4,860
Honduras	1	—	
Paraguay	1	—	
United States			
Arkansas	—	2	270
Colorado	—	5	675
Delaware	5	10	1,500
Florida	1	1	75
Idaho	—	1	75
Illinois	12	51	7,140
Indiana	91	356	50,195
Iowa	15	59	8,320
Kansas	4	15	2,025
Kentucky	3	78	9,750
Maine	—	5	675
Maryland	3	11	1,485
Michigan	9	101	13,330
Minnesota	3	36	4,535
Mississippi	—	2	150
Missouri	19	94	11,000
Montana	—	4	540

	1974 Church districts	2014 Church districts	2014 estimated population (adults & children)
Nebraska	—	6	810
New York	5	122	16,470
North Carolina	—	1	195
Ohio	136	498	67,230
Oklahoma	1	6	810
Pennsylvania	104	453	67,045
South Dakota	—	1	75
Tennessee	4	19	2,375
Texas	—	1	75
Virginia	1	8	1,080
West Virginia	—	3	225
Wisconsin	11	133	17,025
Wyoming	--	1	75
Total	**444**	**2,119**	**290,090**

Approximately forty percent of the total Amish population are baptized members of the church. The rest are unbaptized children. Statistics in this table are for all horse-driving Amish groups (including New Order Amish and New Order Fellowship).

Sources: David Luthy, "Old Order Amish Settlements in 1974," *Family Life,* (December 1974), 13-16; and for 2014, "Amish Population by State (2014)." Young Center for Anabaptist and Pietist Studies, Elizabethtown College. http://www2.etown.edu/amishstudies/Population_by_State_2014.asp

Endnotes

Abbreviations used in these endnotes:
AMCUSA-G   Archives of the Mennonite Church USA—Goshen, Goshen, Ind.
HHL Heritage   Historical Library, Aylmer, Ont.

Chapter 1 (pages 1-25) Notes

1. Patterson (1996).
2. Miller (1963:11, 23). Miller's book is a mix of typical Amish sentiment and unusual opinion. Her effort to publish her thoughts on life, and especially with their political overtones, are uncommon for an Amish woman of her day. It is doubtful that all of her opinions were widely shared in the Amish community, though some of them probably were.
3. Miller (1963:12, 45). Miller quotes freely, and at times without attribution, from other Amish sources.
4. Miller (1963:11, 15, 40-41, 105-25).
5. Anabaptism was a geographically diverse movement with complex roots and expressions. The summary description in this chapter highlights places, themes, and events most closely tied to the Amish story. For introductions to Anabaptism more broadly, see Snyder (1995) and Snyder (2004). A scholarly and encyclopedic treatment is Roth and Stayer (2007). Selected Anabaptist primary sources appear in English translation as Klaassen (1981) and Dyck (1995).
6. For an overview of Luther's thought, see George (1988). The book also compares Zwingli, Calvin, and Menno Simons, as well as providing an introduction to late medieval Christian theology.
7. The writings of this group, and especially of Konrad Grebel, are available in English as Harder (1985).
8. See Snyder (1995:101-28) on the dynamics of Anabaptism's spread.
9. Stayer (2002: 58-59) and Gregory (1999).
10. Persecution of Anabaptists in the Low Countries lasted about 50 years. In Switzerland and south Germany, executions continued for approximately 90 years after 1525.
11. Yoder (1973:8). The text of the Schleitheim Confession is available at http://www.anabaptistwiki.org/mediawiki/index.php/Schleitheim_Confession.
12. The writings of Menno are available in English as Menno (1956).
13. Snyder (1995:211-24, 317-26, 339-50).
14. Some of the biblical passages that suggest the practice of social shunning are Matthew 18:17; Romans 16:17; 1 Corinthians 5:9-11; 2 Thessalonians 3:6, 14-15; 2 Timothy 2:3-5; Titus 3:10.
15. Shunning was also tied theologically to a particular understanding of Christology among Dutch Anabaptists; see Oyer (1984:222-24).
16. Bender (1927:57-66) and Gross (1991).
17. The most accurate translation is Horst (1988); an older translation by Joseph Sohm is readily available online at http://www.gameo.org/encyclopedia/contents/D674.html. For an Amish perspective, see Stoll (2000). Important though it was, the Confession was not adopted by all Dutch and north German Anabaptist groups.
18. Roth and Springer (1993:95 and n.29).
19. Roth and Springer (1993:145-46). The dissenter was Rudolph Egli; see Roth (1993:106).
20. Hein (1959:110).
21. Background on the Swiss Brethren migration to Alsace is given in Séguy (1984:207-209) and Séguy (1980).
22. Yoder (1973:9).

Chapter 2 (pages 26-49) Notes

1. Oyer (2000).
2. Furner (2001) details these strategies.
3. Quotes from Roth and Springer (1993:8).

4. Beachy (2011:v.1, 35-110).
Beachy presents a wealth of material on early Amish life, although I am not convinced that Ulrich Müller should be regarded as more significant than Jakob Ammann when understanding the events of 1693-1694.

5. Primary source material on the controversy that eventually resulted in schism is contained in a set of contemporary letters written by the participants and translated as Roth and Springer (1993). The letters also appear in German in an issue of the Swiss Mennonite Historical Society periodical as *"Briefsammlung"* (1987:26-61). For an overview of interpretations of the division, see Meyers (1996).

6. Roth and Springer (1993:22).

7. Roth and Springer (1993:31). The "younger ones" here may refer to the relationship between ministers in terms of seniority, rather than to a literal age difference between older and younger men.

8. Roth and Springer (1993:118).

9. Roth and Springer (1993:24, 118).

10. Roth and Springer (1993:24).

11. Roth and Springer (1993:26).

12. Roth and Springer (1993:26).

13. A common Swiss naming practice involved shortening surnames by dropping the last syllable and adding an "i" with a long "e" sound. Thus *Ammann* might have been pronounced as *Ami* (Ah-mee). In this form the transition to *Amisch* or *Amish* is plausible. See Luthy (1978a).

14. Roth and Springer (1993:27-28).

15. As Meier (2008:23-24, 56-61, 97, 115, 143) shows, Ammann was not alone in his conviction. Radical members of the contemporary and widespread Pietist movement also advocated social shunning, and some cited the Mennonites' Dortrecht Confession in support of the practice.

16. On Ammann's followers in the Bernese Oberland, see Gratz (1953:45-48).

17. Furner (2001:467) makes an interesting economic point in this regard.

18. Roth and Springer (1993:94).

19. Roth and Springer (1993:113-14). Apparently Uli Ammann was a tenderhearted pastor, as evidenced in a letter he wrote to the church at Sainte-Marie-aux-Mines, probably around 1720, in Roth and Springer (1993:123-27).

20. Roth and Springer (1993: 69-70).

Chapter 3 (pages 50-71) Notes

1. Baecher (1998) and (2000). The quote from the Catholic priest, Antoine Rice, is from (2000:151).

2. Gerlach (1990:3).

3. Schmölz-Häberlein and Häberlein (2001: 479) note, for example, that after 1722, Anabaptists in the Margravate of Baden-Durlach had to pay an annual protection fee similar to that demanded of resident Jews, but the tax also became a basis for recognized toleration.

4. Séguy (1973) and Guth (1995:5-8).

5. Guth (1995:53-54); Schmölz-Häberlein and Häberlein (2001:475).

6. Springer (2015); Correll (1955:70); Stoll (1974).

7. Guth (1995:59); Schmölz-Häberlein and Häberlein (2001).

8. See examples in Gratz (1952:5-7). A 100-Taler reward went to anyone turning in an Anabaptist minister, 50 Taler for a deacon, 25 for a layman, and 12½ for a female member.

9. MacMaster (1985:53).

10. Guth (1995:57, 264-66). Von Gunten was not the father of Barbara's child (he was related to one of Hans Hochstättler's in-laws and was a man of some means), but his offer of marriage would have allowed her to move away and begin a new life without social stigma, which is perhaps why her father was so eager to have the wedding carried out.

11. For example, Visser (1996:101-102); the Amish disciplines of 1752, 1759, and 1779 discuss marriage and the ban in ways that also suggest this sort of situation. See Springer (2015: 560-71) for texts of these confessions.

12. Wenger (1981); Beiler (1969). For the experience of Lutheran-turned-Amish Martin Bornträger, see Luthy (1991:19).

13. Schmölz-Häberlein and Häberlein (2001: 486-90).

14. Gratz (1952:9).

15. This narrative is found in Gratz (1952:13-18), Smith and Krahn (1981:87-94), and Smith (1929:70-72).

16. See the memory recorded in Bachmann (1934) and Smith (1929:71-72).

17. Visser (1996); Smith and Krahn (1981:92-94, 134); Gratz (1952:5-21).

18. Frost (1990).

19. Luthy (1988:20); Hostetler (1993:55 n.12; 65, n.34).

20. Wokeck (1999: 37-58).

21. MacMaster (1985:69-70).

22. See Fogleman (1996:28-35) on the migration destinations of German-speakers at the time.

23. For the story of the Galician and Volhynian Amish and Mennonites, see Stahly (1994), Schrag (1974), and Stucky (1981).

24. For more on the Hutterites, see Janzen and Stanton (2010).

25. On these meetings and their resulting documents, see Springer (2015: 560-71); quotes that follow are from Springer pp. 560, 562, 567-68.

26. Nafziger's 1788 and 1790 letters appear in Guth (1995:281-90); this quote from p. 286.

27. Correll (1928:66-79, 198-204); Guth (1987:130); Guth (1995:285-86).

28. Correll (1928:200-204); Guth (1995:279).

29. Guth (1995:289).

30. Guth (1995:286).

Chapter 4 (pages 72-96) Notes

1. Fogleman (1996:67-99).

2. See an important series of articles by Joseph F. Beiler, "Our Fatherland in America," which appeared regularly in *The Diary* beginning in May 1972. See also Beiler (1976/1977), (1974a), (1977a), and (1983); Stoltzfus (1954); and Fisher (1984). Reviews of early settlements include MacMaster (1985:86-88, 125-27) and Kauffman (1991:19-24). See also maps and text of *Early Amish* (1991).

3. Beachy (1954); Kauffman (1991).

4. Kauffman (2014: 111-26) corrects earlier sources that stated the Chester County Amish had constructed a meetinghouse as early as 1795. Instead, it seems the group had a schoolhouse as early as 1811 and likely also used it as a church. Sometime between 1817 and 1821, Chester County Amish also participated in the construction of a new school and union meetinghouse, which was shared by several denominations.

5. There is one reference to a meetinghouse in the correspondence surrounding the Ammann-Reist division; see Roth and Springer (1993:81).

6. On the Chester County settlement see Kauffman (2014).

7. Brunk (1982).

8. Beiler (1974b:119-20).

9. Beiler (1978). See also MacMaster (1985:151, n.28).

10. MacMaster (1985:70-72, 86-88, 125-27).

11. Wenger (1937:399).

12. Beiler (1975a) provides biographical data but suggests too strongly that Hertzler was the first Amish leader in America. On suggestions of earlier leaders, see Kauffman (1991:20).

13. Kauffman (1991:32).

14. MacMaster (1985:127), Beiler (1976/1977: 46), Stoltzfus (1954:240), and Murray (1981: 16).

15. Lemon (2002: 154-56, 204-211); Stoltzfus (1954:259-62).

16. Beachy (1954:265).

17. Fogleman (1998:44). Of all arrivals to the British "thirteen colonies" between 1700 and 1775, 47 percent were slaves, 9 percent were sentenced convicts, 18 percent were indentured servants or redemptioners, and 26 percent were free labor.

18. MacMaster (1985:101, and n.47).

19. MacMaster (1985:100). The redemptioner system differed from traditional indentured servitude. Indentured servants arrived in North America with contracts stipulating fixed terms of work; the contract price was negotiable. Redemptioners, in contrast, arrived with a fixed price for passage, and then negotiated the terms and work conditions. In short, shipping transporters bore more of the financial risk of indentured servants, while redemptioners themselves bore more of their own risk; see Fogleman (1998:51-56).

20. MacMaster (1985:74). For nineteenth-century examples, see Hostetler (1989:35) and Gingerich (1961), and the comments of Amish immigrant Louis Jüngerich in Levine, et al. (1997:5).

21. For peace churches in this period, see MacMaster (1979:61-164).

22. Kauffman (1979:15).

23. Butler (1990:164-93).

24. Beiler (1977b) and Hostetler (1989:199-200). It is unclear exactly

when Drachsel was silenced and left the Amish church. He was preaching in a non-Amish congregation by at least 1782 and seven years later attended an organizing conference of the United Brethren in Baltimore. In 1804 he moved from Dauphin (now Lebanon) County to Westmoreland County, where he died.

25. Hostetler (1983); Kaffman (1991:31). For information on the German Baptist Brethren tradition, begin with Durnbaugh (1997).

26. Stievermann (2013).

27. Durnbaugh (1978) provides case study examples.

28. Quoted with context in Ruth (1976:129); the quotation is from the diary of Pennsylvania German Lutheran minister Henry Melchior Muhlenberg.

29. MacMaster (1979:245-46).

30. MacMaster (1985:254).

31. MacMaster (1979:474-77).

32. MacMaster (1979:464-66) and Mast (1952).

33. Kauffman (1991:30-31) and Kauffman (2014: 22-25).

34. Kauffman (1979:16).

35. Beiler (1975b).

36. Beiler (1975b).

37. Gingerich and Kreider (1986:xiii).

38. Kauffman (1979:13).

Chapter 5 (pages 97-119) Notes

1. Gerlach (1990:5-6); Luthy (1986:288). Other Amish members of that invasion force were not so fortunate—see Estes (1993b:50-51 and notes).

2. Gerlach (1990:5-6).

3. On the impact of the French Revolution and the Napoleonic era on French Amish, see Séguy (1984:212-23). Levine (2009:60-62, 65, 68-69) illustrates the impact on those living outside of France; the journal of Christian Iutzi, who lived in Hesse-Kassel, make numerous references to Napoleon and his wars during the years 1813-1815.

4. Brock (2006:74-76).

5. Brock (2006:75); Correll (1955:72).

6. Correll (1956).

7. Smith and Krahn (1981:213).

8. Neff (1957).

9. The quotations in this and two following paragraphs are drawn from translations in Estes (1993b:42-51).

10. Grieser and Beck (1960:34).

11. Guth (1995:290, 15).

12. Guth (1995:17-18).

13. Guth (1995:80).

14. Séguy (1973). Excerpts from letters and reports chronicling the Amish-leased Böhmer estates near Zweibrücken during the years 1838-1853 are reproduced in Guth (1995:291-311). Levine (2009:49-103, 105-117) provides an annotated agricultural journal and log book for the years 1812-1825 of lease-holder Christian Iutzi, who farmed in Hesse-Kassel, was ordained as a minister in 1819, and immigrated to Butler County, Ohio in 1832. On the cattle breeding of the Grabers, see Springer (2015: 555-58).

15. Varry (1984). See also Yoder (1954). The almanac was issued until 1845.

16. Guth (1995:108-48).

17. Sommer and Hostetler (1957); Guth (1995: 74). The two Ixheim groups reunited in 1909.

18. In 1832, some of the Hessian Amish who immigrated to Butler County, Ohio, brought pianos among their belongings, one of which is now on display at Chrisholm Historic Farmstead, Trenton, Ohio, the restored 1874 home of Samuel and Elisa (Holly) Augspurger, son and daughter-in-law of Amish immigrant leader Christian Augspurger.

19. See the comments of Swiss Mennonite Niklaus Wütrich in 1807 who criticized both shunning and footwashing, in Roth and Springer (1993:129-40). For a window into Amish worship during this time, see the sermon by Klopfenstein (1984).

20. Devoted (1984) is the Amish edition; a fresh translation is Gross (1997). See also Luthy (1981b) and Luthy (1984c).

21. Catechism (1905).

22. Schabalie (1975).

23. Zijpp (1956) and (1957).

24. Schrag (1974:62-66) and Stahly (1989). See Stahly (1994:108) for an 1830 observation of a Prussian Mennonite that the Volhynian Amish Mennonites were "very restrictive in external life, on dress, beards, and hooks [instead of buttons on coats]."

25. Gingerich (1982:185).
26. Gerlach (1990:4).
27. Historical (1975:106).
28. Guth (1995:40, 81, 111).
29. Quoted in Smith (1983:78).
30. Estes (1993b:51-56).
31. Smith (1983:57).
32. Hostetler (1989:35).
33. Estes (1984:30).
34. For Amish immigrants during the years 1804-1816, see Beachy (2011:v.2, 6-12) and Luthy (1988:21).
35. See, for example, Gerlach (1990:2-3). Also Luthy (1973:16). An 1821 letter reproduced in Schmidt-Lange (2002) details reasons for migration from Hesse to North America.
36. Levine, et al., (1997:10). Schmidt-Lange (2002:9) provides another example of such a church letter, dated March 18, 1819, for Christian Schwartzentruber and signed by elder Samuel Brennemann. Peter Graber (2012:1-6) reproduces seventeen such church letters, dated 1849 to 1886.

Chapter 6 (pages 120-161) Notes

1. Stoltzfus (1954); Kauffman (2014: 63-82).
2. Luthy (1972a).
3. Beachy (2011: v.1,375-91); Luthy (1986:339-42).
4. Kauffman (1991:100-105).
5. Levine (1997); Page and Johns (1983:9-10); Beachy (2011:v.2, 12-13, 19-20).
6. Beachy 2011: v.2, 213-34) provides a comprehensive list of nineteenth-century Amish immigrants.
7. Estes (1993b:33).
8. Estes (1984:21); Luthy (1986:166).
9. At least one Pennsylvania Amish household, Christian and Barbara (Yoder) Troyer, had lived in Ontario as early as 1789, but had not remained permanently. Christian Troyer had come to Welland County, Ontario, from Bedford County, Pennsylvania; Troyer then returned to Pennsylvania to encourage other family members to join him and then resettled in Norfolk County. By the time they left Canada for Holmes County, Ohio, in 1815, they were living in York County, Ontario. The lack of a larger church community, the defection of family members to other denominations, and

possibly harassment from the Canadian government during the War of 1812 all induced the Amish Troyers to move to Ohio. Christian's son David Troyer and his wife Catherine Hooley remained Amish and also moved to Ohio. Other children joined various denominations and remained in Canada. Roth and Grant (1986:13-17).
10. Guth (1995:312-13); Gingerich (2002:27-41); Roth (1998:9-14).
11. Weber (1931:84).
12. Hostetler (1989:35).
13. There is some debate as to which Christian Zook this was. Steven R. Estes believed it was Christian Zook/Zug (1758-1829) who married Magdalena Mast. Christian Zook who served as an Amish minister in Chester County, Pennsylvania, died 8 October 1826.
14. Mast and Mast (1982:46-47).
15. Levine, et al. (1996:2-3, 6) and (1997:5). Jüngerich became a highly successful and wealthy merchant, eventually leaving the Amish church to join the (Swedenborgian) Church of the New Jerusalem and moving to Philadelphia.
16. Springer (1998).
17. Wenger (1961:328). On the Elkhart-LaGrange settlement beginnings, see Amish and Mennonites (1992:4-18) and Borntreger (1988).
18. Miller (1971).
19. Luthy (1995).
20. Smith (1983:61) and Estes (1990:45-46). Baechler was born in Europe.
21. Yoder (1991:118).
22. Weber (1931:83-87) is a translation of their son's account.
23. Luthy (1986:118-19).
24. Gingerich (1955b:12).
25. Habegger (2002:7-14, 45ff).
26. Luthy (1986:241).
27. Umble (1947:1).
28. Grieser and Beck (1960:26); Stoltzfus (1969:79-80).
29. The eight congregations were Partridge Creek, Busch Gemein, Dillon Creek, Mackinaw River, Rock Creek, Hessian Amish, Bureau Creek, and Ohio Station.
30. Bender (1934:93-95).
31. For more information on the 1809 and 1837 meetings, see Bender (1934). On an 1849 meeting in Ohio, see Gingerich (1965). For a listing of all such known gatherings between

1809 and 1862, see Yoder and Estes (1999:400-403).

32. Yoder (1991:31-32) and (1999); Miller (1959).

33. Yoder (1991:121-34). For the later views of Lancaster County deacon John Stoltzfus, see Yoder (1979:41-42, 44-47, 170-77). A few Amish—mostly in Mifflin County, Pennsylvania—practiced stream baptism until about 1910. Today stream baptism is not practiced in Old Order Amish churches.

34. George Jutzi letter, Hist. Mss. 1-10, Long, AMCUSA-G. Jutzi's critique of the Methodists was of their use of a so-called "anxious bench" where religious seekers figuratively wrestled for their soul's salvation. Jutzi compared the practice with emotionally intense Roman Catholic devotional rituals that involved sitting before particular images. The anti-Catholic Methodist with whom Jutzi discussed the matter was not pleased with the parallel Jutzi drew!

35. The standard history of the Apostolic Christian Church is Klopfenstein (2008).

36. Yousey (1987:46-59).

37. Gingerich (2002:41); Roth (1998) offers helpful context.

38. Bushman (1992).

39. Umble (1948:101-102).

40. Nolt (1999).

41. Umble (1948:103).

42. Estes (1982:11-12). Schmidt-Lange (2002) suggests some of the cultural tensions between nineteenth-century Amish arrivals from Hesse and long-established Somerset County, Pennsylvania Amish churches.

43. Nolt and Meyers (2007:61-62, 101-20); Ringenberg (1976); and Habegger (2002).

44. The Chester County, Pennsylvania, Amish used a meetinghouse during the relatively brief life of their settlement, but that building seems not to have set a precedent for later Amish church buildings. Likewise, the temporary log structure used near Louisville, Stark County, Ohio, in the 1830s and the "log chapels" in some Ontario Amish cemeteries as early as 1859 did not represent the same sort of change-minded approach to church life that the meetinghouses built in 1851 did.

45. Boylan (1988).

46. Umble (1941:20-21).

47. After 1840, a few Ontario Mennonites and Pennsylvania Amish conducted Sunday schools on an occasional basis, but none of these experiments lasted.

48. Umble (1963:1-8) and Umble (1941:16-28).

49. Umble (1933:82).

50. Estes (1984:40-41).

51. Kauffman (1991:118-19).

52. Bender (1934:94).

53. Luthy (1984b).

54. Among those concerned were northern Indiana's John E. "Hansi" Borntreger (1988:12); Lancaster, Pennsylvania's David Beiler, in Umble (1948); Iowa's Jacob Schwarzendruber, in Bender (1946). Political involvement was common in Butler County, Ohio; see Page and Johns (1983); and in the large central Illinois settlement and in Mifflin County, Pennsylvania, discussed below.

55. Ellis and Evans (1883:928, 932-33). In 1849, the Pennsylvania Supreme Court ordered recalcitrant Upper Leacock Township to open a public school after its residents had repeatedly refused. Ebersol was elected a school director in 1858.

56. Kauffman (1991:144-47).

57. Hostetler (1964:280-84). For more on Zook, see Luthy (1989).

58. Estes (1982:47-50). Levine (2009:39) reports that on October 11, 1842 immigrant Christian Iutzi, living in Butler County, Ohio, "cast my vote for the first time, reluctantly for the Democrats."

59. Nolt (1995) and Nolt (1996). Because of its potential interstate nature, the Farnis' case was actually heard by the U.S. Supreme Court as *Farni v. Tesson* (1862).

60. Estes (1984:85-88).

61. Reschly (2000:96-104).

62. Lehman and Nolt (2007:120-22).

63. Estes (1982:50-51). The most prominent Amish-connected member of the military was U.S. Brigadier General Samuel Kurtz Zook, grandson of Chester County, Pennsylvania, Amish church members. Samuel's parents, however, were not Amish and had not raised him in the Amish faith. At some point, the patriotic Zook changed his middle name from *Kurtz* (a common Amish surname) to *Kosciusko*

(after Thaddeus Kosciusko, the Polish and U.S. revolutionary hero).

64. See extensive documentation in Lehman and Nolt (2007:103-11, 166-71).

65. Yoder (1991:95).

66. Peter Graber (2012:37).

67. Lehman (1978:58).

68. Lehman and Nolt (2007: 131-32).

69. Lehman and Nolt (2007:130); Gingerich (1939:62-64).

70. Bender (1946:224).

71. Bender (1946:225).

72. Umble (1948:105).

Chapter 7 (pages 162-196) Notes

1. On the schisms in Ontario and Iowa, see Roth (1993b) and Reschly (2000:158-72).

2. For discussion of *Ordnung* by a twentieth-century Old Order Amish minister, see Beiler (1982).

3. Occasionally local gatherings of ministers had published brief, written *Ordnung*, but these documents were meant to communicate selected important or controversial points and were not meant to be comprehensive statements.

4. Gingerich (1986).

5. This chapter identifies these two northern Indiana church districts by their home counties—Elkhart and LaGrange— even though contemporaries often called the church in LaGrange County the "Elkhart church" because its members lived near the Little Elkhart River (in LaGrange County), and they called the Elkhart County church the "Clinton church" because its members' homes were in Clinton Township (in Elkhart County). See Yoder (1991:117-121).

6. Borntreger (1988:10).

7. Borntreger (1988:11).

8. Yoder (1991:130-34). According to contemporaries, Yoder taught that the sin of the first humans was not disobedience to God's command, but only lying about what they had done. An account of the controversy in Ohio from the perspective of a conservative is Troyer (1998:130-38).

9. Umble (1948:105).

10. Yoder (1987c:37).

11. For a list of these meetings, see Yoder and Estes (1999:401-405).

12. Yoder (1991:142).

13. Yoder (1987c:63-65).

14. Yoder (1987c:65-66). The only surviving copy of this letter is unsigned, making it unclear who was responding to Stoltzfus, although the letter is written in plural, suggesting it was coming from a group.

15. The minutes ("Proceedings") of all 17 *Diener-Versammlungen* are available in German in many Amish and Mennonite historical libraries. Yoder and Estes (1999) provide an English translation of the minutes, as well as related documents.

16. Yoder and Estes (1999:5).

17. Yoder and Estes (1999:47, 49, 53-54, 56).

18. For example, see Yoder and Estes (1999:36, 38).

19. Yoder and Estes (1999:39).

20. Yoder and Estes (1999:49). On these problems, see Yoder (1985:2-9).

21. In a February 12, 1863 letter, Mifflin County, Pennsylvanian Shem Zook informed deacon John Stoltzfus that bishops Jonas D. Troyer and John Schmucker had ordained a bishop for the Hessian Amish church. Zook reported that this had happened because the Hessians' "playthings [i.e., musical instruments] have been put away." See Yoder (1987c:101-102).

22. Yoder and Estes (1999:16-17, 36-38, 53).

23. Yoder and Estes (1999:13-14, 38, 47, 49, 52).

24. Yoder and Estes (1999:51, and possibly 36).

25. Umble (1948:107).

26. Yoder (1991:159-61).

27. Yoder and Estes (1999:47).

28. English translations of the conservatives' statements are Bender (1934:95-98) and Yoder and Estes (1999:258-60).

29. Yoder and Estes (1999:258-59).

30. Yoder and Estes (1999:259).

31. Yoder and Estes (1999:64). David A. Troyer, one of the signatories, later reflected this disappointment in Troyer (1998:136, 138).

32. See Yoder (1996) for a contemporary Lancaster document outlining the issues (meetinghouses, stream baptism, and Sunday school) from the change-minded standpoint.

33. The Old Orders themselves claimed the name *Alt Amisch* (Old Amish). The etymology of "Old Order Amish" is elusive; see discussion in Yoder (1991:261). For a definition of "Old Order" emerging out of a

comparative study of Old Order Amish, Old Order Mennonite, Old German Baptist, and Old Order River Brethren beginnings, see Hostetler (1992).

34. Yoder and Estes (1999:71-72, 74-75).

35. Yoder and Estes (1999:82, 90).

36. Yoder and Estes (1999:84).

37. Yoder and Estes (1999:91-92).

38. Yoder and Estes (1999:202).

39. Yoder and Estes (1999:202).

40. A brief account sympathetic to Egly is Nussbaum (1991:2-11). See also Yoder (1991: 184-87).

41. Helpful discussion of Egly's theology is found in Weaver (1997:126-29, 178-87, 212-15, 302-303). Egly (1965) is a translation of an article he penned, and which has the feel and tone of a sermon, and may suggest the content of his preaching. Egly moved to Indiana in 1850; his initial spiritual awakening in the early 1840s occurred while he was still living in Butler County, Ohio.

42. Claudon and Claudon (1947).

43. Egly's thoughts on baptism were outlined in an 1866 letter available in Yoder and Estes (1999:262-64).

44. Nussbaum (1991:2).

45. Roth (1993a).

46. Jacob Rupp from Fulton County, Ohio, spoke as one sympathetic to Egly's concerns. For Rupp's and others' concerns and the responses of the *Diener-Versammlungen*, see Yoder and Estes (1999:64, 72-73, 119-20).

47. "Henry Egly's autobiography," Hist. Mss. 1-542, Box 1, folder 3 (English translation), AMCUSA-G.

48. An interpretation of the separation is Estes (1982:66-68).

49. Egly's letters to Allen County, Indiana, bishop Peter Graber in Peter Graber (2012:71-75) provide examples of Egly's conventional and even conservative approach to many church matters; on the family tradition around Egly's paying a commutation fee during the Civil war, see Lehman and Nolt (2007:170).

50. Estes (1982:83-86), Yoder (1991:187-94), and Smith (1983:88-91).

51. Estes (1982:52).

52. Estes (1982:53).

53. Weaver (1926:72) offered the sympathetic view that although Stuckey "was sometimes blamed for splitting churches," in fact "he was

only trying to care for those who had left the old church and were without a leader."

54. Estes (1982:48-49, 81) and Clark (1929).

55. Estes (1982:80-81); Yoder and Estes (1999:118-19, and related document 260-62). On universalism and the nineteenth-century American religious scene, see Bressler (2001).

56. Yoder and Estes (1999:155-56). The German poem appears in Estes (1982:291-95); an English translation of the poem is in Estes (1982:296-300) and Yoder and Estes (1999:282-288). A photocopy of what may be Joder's handwritten original is in the Edwin O. Ropp Papers, Illinois Mennonite Archives, Metamora, Ill. Interestingly, *Der Fröhliche Botschafter* was the name of the German-language universalist periodical that was published 1829-1838. It carried articles in German and some poems in the Pennsylvania Dutch dialect. Published in western Lancaster County, Pennsylvania, it circulated in German-speaking communities well beyond that region; see Yoder (1944).

57. Stuckey had been questioned by committees from the *Diener-Versammlungen* of 1871. See Yoder and Estes (1999:136-37).

58. Yoder and Estes (1999:175-76); Estes (1982:70-86).

59. Estes (1982:94-95).

60. Yoder and Estes (1999:136).

61. Yoder and Estes (1999:231).

62. Biographical information on Yoder is found in chapter 4 of Lehman (1978). A brief biography of King is found in Stoltzfus (1969:77).

63. Yoder (1991:196-201).

64. An example of Amish reunion and reconnection facilitated by the ministers meetings deserves mention. In 1874, the Mennonites living in Russian Volhynia immigrated to Kansas and what would become South Dakota. Some of these Mennonites had been of Amish background, for the most part descendants of Alsatian and Montbéliard Amish who had moved to Volhynia and joined Mennonites there. After settling in North America, however, some of the Volhynian immigrant ministers heard about the Amish *Diener-Versammlungen* and attended as Amish ministers. In 1875, 1876, and 1878, preacher Johannes Schrag of Tuner, Dakota Territory,

participated in the gatherings, as did Jacob Stucky of Lakeview, Kansas, in 1875; see Stahly (1994:110-13). Although the *Diener-Versammlungen* temporarily united an extended church family, the Volhynian Amish-turned-Mennonites did not continue their fraternal links with other North American Amish after the ministers' meetings ended. They affiliated instead with the General Conference Mennonites on the Great Plains.

Chapter 8 (pages 197-233) Notes

1. C. B. Neuhauser, et al., "From Tennessee," *Herald of Truth*, October 1871, 152.
2. The *Herald* includes scores of examples of Amish Mennonite and Mennonite cooperation or joint activity. Illustrative examples from Indiana alone include John Ringenberg, "Letter from Locke, Ind." *HT*, July 1864, 43; John M. Christophel, "Letter from Indiana," *HT*, January 1865, 7; Daniel Brenneman, "A Visit," *HT*, January 1867, 11-12; G. Z. Boller, "From Noble Co., Ind.," *HT*, February 1867, 25. Letters and articles also appeared in the German-language companion paper *Herold der Warheit*, such as Ringenberg (above) in *HW*, July 1864, 43.
3. Roth (1993b); and Reschly (2000: 158-72).
4. Yoder (1991:267).
5. Lind (1990:45-46).
6. Quotes here and in the paragraphs that follow from the Mahala Yoder Collection, Hist. Mss. 1-12, 1871-76 Diary, AMCUSA-G.
7. Yoder (1991:228-30).
8. Mast and Mast (1982:63-70).
9. The text of the 1889 sixteen-article Oak Grove discipline is in Lehman (1978:110-11).
10. Yoder (1991:252-60).
11. Hiller (1968/1969); Gingerich (1971); Miller (1970). For an appraisal by C. Henry Smith of Spirit preaching, which he witnessed as a boy, see Smith (1962:132-35).
12. Reschly (2000:132-57); Hostetler (1980).
13. Stutzman's relatives transcribed and printed her revelations as *Revelations* (n.d.).
14. O. A. Graber, "Gleanings from Yesterday," *Die Botschaft*, 8 February 1984, 14.

15. Sermons from the two are found in Troyer (1879) and (1880); and Kauffman (1953).
16. See, for example, Presbyterian Spirit preacher Constantine Blackmon Sanders (1831-1887) and others in Yoder (1968/1969). See also Schlabach (1988:220).
17. Gingerich (1959) and Kraybill (2010:239). The 2012-13 *Anabaptist (Mennonite) Directory*, pp. 34-35, lists 17 Kauffman Amish churches across Arkansas, Colorado, Illinois, Iowa, Missouri, and Wisconsin. More than half the members lived in Missouri.
18. The paper's masthead from April 1, 1893 to December 15, 1895.
19. Amish Mennonite leaders in the West had met as early as 1882 but did not organize a conference until 1890. See Hartzler and Kauffman (1905:306-307) and Weber (1931:187-96).
20. Historical (1975:379).
21. Lehman (1978:134-35) and Yoder (1991:231).
22. On Oak Grove Amish Mennonite (Smithville, Ohio) support for Elkhart Institute, see Lehman (1978:135-42).
23. Bush (2015).
24. For a biography of Smucker, see Yoder and Smucker (1990).
25. Lehman (1990:6-30).
26. See Yoder (1991:220-22) for examples of the last few Amish Mennonite attempts at shunning. Hartzler and Kauffman (1905:306-308) imply that the abandonment of the practice of shunning was a more formal decision on the part of Amish Mennonites.
27. Yoder and Estes (1999:78). The ministers were responding to the hopes for unity expressed by Ohio Mennonite bishop John M. Brenneman, whose proposal "Unity among the Brethren" in the March 1866 *Herald of Truth* is reprinted in Yoder and Estes (1999:264-68).
28. Minutes ([1930]:22).
29. Joseph Holdeman, "A Visit to Clinton and Haw Patch," *Herald of Truth*, February 1871, 25-26.
30. J. D. Troyer, et al., "Correspondence," *Herald of Truth*, 1 March 1886, 73-74.
31. Yoder (1979:124-26); Gingerich (2002:85, 88).
32. A traditional rendering of the history of this group is Wenger (1966). In 2002 the "old" Mennonites

and the General Conference Mennonites merged to form two new denominations: Mennonite Church Canada and Mennonite Church USA.

33. For a chronology, see Bair (1952).

34. Yoder (1991:17).

35. Yoder (1987a:83). The new Iowa-Nebraska Conference used neither the word *Amish* nor *Mennonite* in its name so as not to offend either party; see Erb (1974:468-69).

36. Umble (1964).

37. In 1988 the Western Ontario Mennonite Conference joined two other Mennonite bodies to form the Mennonite Conference of Eastern Canada. For detailed history of Ontario Amish Mennonites and the Western Ontario Conference, see Steiner (2015).

38. Yoder (1991:17).

39. Yoder (2014).

40. Yousey (1987).

41. Scott (1996:122-36). In 2000, eighteen Conservative Conference congregations concerned about the decline in plain dress and other signs of nonconformity in Conservative Conference circles left that group and formed Mennonite Biblical Alliance.

42. For a summary of Stuckey Amish history see Smith (1983:88-110).

43. Yoder (1991:193).

44. Schlabach (1988:127-39); Juhnke (1989:49-51, 136-42).

45. Estes (1982:93-94).

46. Weaver (1926:94-95) and Weber (1931:485-96).

47. The Central Conference became a district conference of the General Conference Mennonite Church in 1946; eleven years later the Central Conference merged with the GC Mennonite Middle District, with which it had overlapped geographically. See Estes (1993a). A few Amish-rooted congregations in Iowa and Ohio that were not part of the Stuckey Amish stream also joined the GC Mennonite Church; see Pannabecker (1968:18-22) and Pannabecker (1975:69).

48. See Nussbaum (1991) and Smith (1983:111-31).

49. Schlabach (1988:116). The first Egly Amish conference was held in 1882 in Illinois; the gatherings became annual affairs starting in 1895.

50. Weber (1931:377-401).

51. For a history of the Missionary Church Association, see Lugibihl (1950).

52. Kauffman and Driedger (1991:174).

53. Estes (2007).

54. Séguy (1982:25).

55. Hostetler (1993:65-66). Gerlach (1990:3) lists Amish church membership statistics for the mid-to-later nineteenth century and estimates only 1,659 to 1,859 total members by 1888.

56. Estes (1990:42-46) and Springer (2015) document this third wave of Amish immigration. Estes cites a European Amish immigrant to America as late as 1924. In many cases, these third wave immigrants joined progressive Amish Mennonite congregations in the Midwest, or if they settled in the Pacific West, they did not maintain any Amish or Mennonite ties. Virtually none became Old Order.

57. Yousey (1987:74-75); Luthy (1986:290).

58. Gerlach (1990:2).

59. Neff (1959) and Yoder and Estes (1999:271-76).

60. Gingerich (1982:182).

61. Séguy (1984:206-17).

62. Correll (1955).

63. Fretz (1957).

64. Yoder (1955).

65. Guth (1995:94).

66. Sommer and Hostetler (1957).

67. Gerlach (1990:8).

68. Hostetler (1955:215, 218-19).

Chapter 9 (pages 234-260) Notes

1. Population (including unbaptized children) estimate calculated by Stephen E. Scott in 2010, based on careful review of local census schedules from 1900 and other available data on the 63 Old Order Amish church districts in existence at the time. See United States (1941:vol. 2, 1005-1006) for official U.S. religious statistics for 1906, 1916, 1926, and 1936, but note that the Old Order Amish numbers are generally too low and sometimes confuse known Old Order churches with decidedly progressive Amish Mennonite ones.

2. Illinois Directory (2012); Smith (1983:132-33).

3. Luthy (1972/1973). The articles cover other time periods, as well.

4. See Luthy (1986) for stories of numerous settlements begun and dissolved in this time. See Stoll (1997) for the Daviess County settlement.

5. Nolt (2008); Yoder (1990).

6. Heritage Historical Library, Aylmer, Ont., has several of these autograph books.

7. Letters from Isaac Ebersol to Sarah Lapp Zook, and from Andrew Ebersol to Sarah Lapp Zook, in the Sarah Lapp Zook Papers, private collection of a relative, Lancaster, Pa. (hereafter SLZ Papers).

8. Isaac Zook to Sarah Lapp, January 8, 1897, SLZ Papers.

9. Sallie J. Fisher to Sarah Lapp, December 23, 1888, SLZ Papers. Christmas trees were a widely shared Pennsylvania German ethnic tradition, see Shoemaker (1999:45-74), and would have been uncommon among Amish in the Midwest.

10. Bettsy Speicher to Sarah Lapp, October 31, 1891; Speicher to Lapp, 2 March 1896, SLZ Papers.

11. Rebecca S. Smucker to Sarah Lapp, March 25, 1896, SLZ Papers.

12. Reschly (2000:43-63, 177-81); Deeben (1992:21-29). Using data somewhat different from Reschly, Cosgel (1993) also argues for a distinct approach to farming among the Kalona, Iowa, Amish.

13. Scott (1981:60, 72). Amish carriages in Pennsylvania were not enclosed until the latter part of the nineteenth century. See Scott (1981:51, 55-56).

14. The biblical text here in Amish teaching is 1 Corinthians 11:1-16. Scott (1986:98-103) gives more explanation.

15. Gibbons (1882:59).

16. See, for example, Luthy (1995) and Stoltzfus (1995).

17. Swartzentruber (1950); Reschly (2000:164-72, 205-209).

18. Samuel D. Guengerich, "Value of Education," Hist. Mss. 1-2, box 8, AMCUSA-G.

19. Samuel D. Guengerich diaries, 10 March 1864, Hist. Mss. 1-2, box 1, AMCUSA-G.

20. Hostetler (1989:180-82); Luthy (1972/1973).

21. Luthy (1981c). Judging from the hymns and hymn numbers recorded in the *Diener-Versammlungen* minutes, the gatherings of 1873, 1875, and 1876 sang from the "Baer book" rather than the *Ausbund*. The Baer book would have been a fairly recent publication at the time, but may have received a warm reception at the ministers' meetings since it had been compiled by *Diener-Versammlung* proponent Shem Zook. See Yoder and Estes (1999:400-401).

22. Amish Aid Society began in 1875 according to Stoltzfus (1984:191-92); Heritage Historical Library, Aylmer, Ont., has a printed statement from the plan dated 1879. Gingerich (1955a) offers a description of similar programs begun by Midwestern Amish in the twentieth century.

23. Luthy (1981a). Later, about half the community (mostly those living south of the Pennsylvania-Maryland border) left the Old Order church to affiliate with the Conservative Amish Mennonite Conference. The Old Order Amish in Somerset County, Pennsylvania, continue to use meetinghouses for their biweekly services.

24. Swartzendruber (1977:12-13).

25. Luthy (1986:271-76).

26. Kauffman (1991:118-19). A study of clothing in this group is Weiser (1998).

27. Troyer (1998:52, 57-64). For a discussion of how two early twentieth-century Amish men thought about theology and ethics, see Biesecker-Mast (1999).

28. Another method of handling such situations followed this procedure: a baptized member of an Old Order church would join an Amish Mennonite congregation. The Old Order group would excommunicate and shun the individual, but, after a period of time, "lift" the ban when the person had demonstrated serious intent to be faithful to the Amish Mennonite church.

29. The story is recounted in Yoder (1991:266-73); Mast and Mast (1982:83-87); and Yoder (1987a:103-106).

30. Mast and Mast (1982:37-39).

31. Mast and Mast (1982:57).

32. See Yoder (1991:273-74); Helmuth (1961); Smith (1983:141, 169); and telephone interview with Joni Helmuth's nephew, Orva Helmuth, Arthur, Illinois, May 14, 1992. The Arthur Amish Mennonite Church existed from 1897 to 1914 as part of the Western District Amish Mennonite

Conference. Orva Helmuth made one correction to Yoder (1991:274, n.38), clarifying that the Joni Helmuth in question was Joni F. (not J.) Helmuth. Joni F. Helmuth later left the Amish Mennonites, as well, and joined the Churches of Christ.

33. Ritter (1997).

34. Luthy (1986:85-91, 134-39, 177-83, 213-18, 221-28, 305-32) for some of these stories.

35. "Notes from the Hoosier State," *The Budget*, October 22, 1896, p. [4]. Thanks to Karl N. Stutzman for this citation.

36. Williams (2010).

37. The material in this paragraph and the one that follows, including quotations from *The Budget*, comes from Luthy (1982:23-26).

Chapter 10 (pages 261-297) Notes

1. Welty (1908). The analysis that follows is dependent upon Weaver-Zercher (2001:14-17).

2. The author's husband, Benjamin Franklin Welty, was an Ohio attorney of Mennonite heritage, who was also a convinced political Progressive and two-term Congressman.

3. Martin (1905) and Weaver-Zercher (2001:34-39). On early tourism and popular images of the Amish in the early twentieth century, see Luthy (1994:113-18) and Weaver-Zercher (2001:47-60).

4. Quoted in Yoder (1990:332).

5. On Delaware, see Clark (1988:21-74). Between 1900 and 1915, new Old Order churches also organized in Alabama, Arizona, California, Colorado, Georgia, Montana, Texas, Virginia, and Wisconsin, but did not survive long; see settlements listed in Luthy (1986).

6. Kline (2000b:55-86). On Lancaster, Pennsylvania, Amish reaction to the automobile, see Kraybill (2001:214-17). For an Old Order Amish discussion of the car, see Wagler (n.d.).

7. Yoder (1987a:106-10).

8. On the role of technology decisions (as opposed to excommunication practice) in the division, see Kraybill (2001: 189-92, 199-200). Amish farm life from 1900 through the 1920s in this community is described in Glick (1994:4-139).

9. Umble (1996:63-133) details the telephone story in this community, including the response of Old Order Mennonites. Kline (2000b:23-54) charts conflicts over rural telephony generally.

10. Gingerich (1939:311-14).

11. History (1999). In the 1920s, two other similarly ultra-conservative settlements formed near Medford, Wisconsin and Atlantic, Pennsylvania.

12. Hurst and McConnel (2010:35-43); Beachy (2011:v.2, 436-51); Luthy (1998); and Kraybill, Johnson-Weiner, and Nolt (2013:139). During 1917-1922 the Swartzentruber Amish divided, leading to the formation of the Daniel Wengerd group. In 1934, the Wengerd group reunited with the majority Holmes County Old Orders; however, they remained somewhat more conservative than that group. Many former Wengerd group members left the mainline Old Order again in 1955-1957 with the conservative Andy Weaver group. Some Swartzentrubers derive belt power from engines mounted on carts in order to power some equipment, but do not use belt power from self-propelled tractors.

13. Janzen (1990:167-97). The larger Canadian story was more complex than the Ontario Amish situation summarized here, since Ottawa dealt with immigrant groups on the basis of historic provisions arranged upon their respective times of immigration. Thus, Mennonites, Doukhobors, and other COs in western Canada who had arrived from Europe in the later 1800s were treated under a set of provisions different from those applied to Ontario Mennonites and Amish who had arrived in the 1700s and early 1800s. Janzen details the entire Canadian picture.

14. Quoted in Keim and Stoltzfus (1988:32).

15. Abrams (1933).

16. See Homan (1994) and Stoltzfus (2013).

17. Letter from Peachey's granddaughter Donella Peachey Clemens, May 26, 1992.

18. Keim and Stoltzfus (1988:46-52).

19. Juhnke (1989:236).

20. Quoted in Keim and Stoltzfus (1988:40).

21. Stoltzfus (1981:7-24).

22. Years later, the stories of men who had lived as COs in army camps were full of emotion. Some men did not want the notoriety of being named but shared anonymous stories; see the collections Stoltzfus (1981) and Beechy and Beechy (1993.

23. Examples include Homan (1994:77-78), Mast and Mast (1982:132-33), and Estes (1984:216-19).

24. Teichroew (1979:107). On local suspicion of Amish loyalty in LaGrange County, Indiana, see Pratt (2004:61-71).

25. Luthy (1972b).

26. Reason cited in File No. 186400-18, Department of Justice, Washington, D.C., as quoted in Luthy (1972b).

27. See, for example, Belfry (1923).

28. For an articulate explanation of Old Order objections to state-sponsored secondary education, see Stoll (1975).

29. Pratt (2004:72-86) details this controversy. While authorities made more than two dozen arrests, the total number of individuals arrested is difficult to determine because some may have been arrested more than once. The controversy lasted from 1921 to 1925. See also Bontreger (1982:20-21).

30. Keim (1975:14-15); Luthy (1986:513-14); Meyers (2003b:93). Already in 1914, Geauga County, Ohio, school officials had fined Amish parents whose children had stopped attending school before age sixteen. For an annotated chronology of Amish school court cases, see Keim (1975:93-98). An expanded and annotated list is Place (2003).

31. Just then conservative Canadian Mennonites were also moving to Mexico to avoid new Manitoba education laws; see Loewen (2013).

32. Luthy (1986:514-21).

33. Weaver-Zercher (2001:60-81) discusses the national notoriety these events generated.

34. The school was originally slated to cost $112,000, but the final cost increased to $125,000. Of that sum, $52,250 was Federal Public Works Administration money. Reporters marveled that people would reject government dollars for constructing a new school when many communities were hoping for increased funding from Washington.

35. "Education: Amish Folk Shun Their New PWA School," *Literary Digest,* December 4, 1937, 32-34. Kraybill (2001:162-68) narrates the story.

36. This petition and the list of signers are reproduced in Lapp (1991:141-67).

37. Text is Hostetler (1989:136-37).

38. Keim (1975:94). A number of East Lampeter Township Amish families had not sent their children to school in 1937 and did not do so in the fall of 1938. The boycott drew national attention, e.g., "Amish Lose Fight for Old Schools," *New York Times,* June 28, 1938, 22; "Amish Threaten School Secession," *New York Times,* July 21, 1938, 23; "New Amish School Strike Looms in Pennsylvania, *New York Times,* September 5, 1938, 15; "Amish Pupils Back in 1-Room School," *New York Times,* November 29, 1938, 25; "Amish Hit High School," *New York Times,* September 21, 1938, 26; "Plain People Win Right to their Own Schools as well as Way of Life," *Newsweek,* December 12, 1938, 32. There was precedent for Amish parochial education, though it was largely unknown, even by most Amish in Pennsylvania. Amish families in Delaware, North Carolina, and Mississippi had opened three small private schools. On the Delaware school, named Apple Grove School, which operated 1925-1926, see Clark (1988:111-28, 195). On the North Carolina school that operated 1925-1926, see Luthy (1986:299-300). On the origins of Lancaster County's Amish school movement, see Esh (1977).

39. Amish Moving (1965).

40. Yoder (1987a:112-16).

41. Yoder (1987a:116-20) and Beachy (1955). For a perspective very sympathetic to Moses Beachy, see Mast (1950).

42. Beachy (1955).

43. Lapp (2003:37-44) is a detailed account.

44. For more chronology, see Yoder (1987a: 126-38) and Anderson (2011:369-81). The website http://www.beachyam.org/ contains a great deal of information about Beachy Amish-Mennonite theology, history, and contemporary life, and includes links to scholarly articles and source materials. The site is maintained by Cory

Anderson, a Beachy Amish-Mennonite church member.

45. See settlements listed in Luthy (1986).

46. The 1940 draft census administered by Mennonite Central Committee and sent to all Amish bishops asked the bishops to report the current employment of conscription-age men in each district. The incomplete returns show a few men listed under factory work. This documentary evidence of industrial employment by 1940 matches local memory. See Peace Section Census, 1940, Questionnaires: Old Order Amish, Indiana, IX-7-1, Box 1, Folder 7, AMCUSA-G.

47. An Amish minister writing anonymously, "Amish Life" (1971:20).

48. "Amish Life" (1971). Depression-era memories are recorded in Yoder and Yoder (1998), Glick (1994:158-77), and Pratt (2004:72-86).

49. "An Amishman Speaks," Lancaster (Pa.) *Intelligencer Journal*, 23 February 1931, 1.

50. Jellison (2002:109-12, 116). The published USDA survey is Kollmorgen (1942). More detailed analysis appears in Reschly and Jellison (1993).

51. Historical (1975:483).

52. "Amish Life" (August 1971:19).

53. "Amish Gratitude," *Time*, 29 November 1937, 37. The article again mentioned the Smoketown school controversy.

54. John M. McCullough, "Amish Curb Crops—But Not for AAA Pay," *Philadelphia Inquirer*, 2 April 1933.

55. It is worth noting, however, that despite the widespread Amish criticism of New Deal-style politics and programs, a tiny number of hard-pressed Amish men did work in federal Works Progress Administration jobs, as documented in the 1940 draft census cited in note 46, above.

56. Luthy (1984a).

57. A detailed history of peace churches in the U.S. between the world wars is Keim and Stoltzfus (1988:56-102); on the Canadian scene, see Janzen (1990:198-208).

58. The Mennonite statement was Peace (1937); the Amish document was "Statement" (1939). See also the statement written by David L. Schwartz (19—), an Adams County, Indiana, Swiss Amish man, and printed as a pamphlet for drafted men

to present to their draft boards when called.

59. Peace (1937).

60. On CO provisions and alternative service in Canada, see Regehr (1996:35-59) and Janzen (1990:198-244).

61. On the CPS program, see Wagler and Raber (1986); Keim (1990); Gingerich (1949); Hershberger (1951); and Keim and Stoltzfus (1988:103-26).

62. Unruh (1952:286). See the Amish CPS directory, which lists some 600 men in Wagler and Raber (1986:97-127). The book also includes first-person accounts of Amish who served as forest firefighters, on dairy farms, in psychiatric hospitals, in public health projects, in Puerto Rico, for the Fish and Wildlife Service, and as human "guinea pigs" for medical research.

63. Hostetter (1999).

64. For an Amish critique of the Mennonite-administered CPS camp to which he was assigned, see Wagler (1991). Wagler found the administrators liberal and out of touch with Old Order values.

65. Bontreger (1982:23-25, 30-33); Wagler and Raber (1986:75).

66. Luthy (1978b).

67. "Rationing" file collection, Heritage Historical Library, Aylmer, Ont.

68. Dick Snyder, "Amish Undisturbed by War Shortages, Have Always Done without Autos and Such," *New York Times*, April 12, 1942, II-10.

69. Unruh (1952:227-29); quote from Fred Schrock in Illinois Directory (2012:13). See also "Sea-Going Cowboys" file collection, Heritage Historical Library, Aylmer, Ont.

Chapter 11 (pages 298-331) Notes

1. Luthy (1994:119).

2. Patterson (1996). On TV ownership, see Historical (1975:796).

3. "Urge Amish Use Tractors to Boost Yield of Wheat," newspaper clipping dated Saturday, April 27, 1946, 5, likely from a Lancaster, Pennsylvania, newspaper; copy pasted inside a copy of Steinfeldt (1937) housed in the Lancaster Mennonite Historical Society. On the dramatic transformation of agriculture during the mid-twentieth century, see Shover (1976). See also Kline (2000b:77-79).

4. "Amish Life" (1971:20). The Kokomo, Indiana, and Kalona, Iowa, settlements were among the few that adopted tractor farming at this time. Oral interviews suggest that in some cases the impetus for mechanization was lack of field hands during World War II when men were drafted out of the community and into alternative service assignments. Kraybill (2001:222-30) discusses the debate over field tractor use in the Lancaster settlement.

5. Luthy (1986:366-69).

6. The story of the 1948 conscription law, the Korean War demand for alternative service for COs, and the development of the I-W program is recounted in Keim and Stoltzfus (1988:127-46) and Bush (1999:171-73).

7. Bush (1999:196-97, 239) discusses some of the negative aspects of the I-W program, though from a Mennonite perspective. Amish reservations and frustrations would have been somewhat different. Some of the negative implications of the program for the Amish are discussed in Keim (2003:56-61).

8. A fourth man received a suspended sentence and probation after he agreed to take an I-W assignment.

9. Huntington (1956:579).

10. Associated Press story carried in the Lancaster, Pa. *Intelligencer Journal*, June 28, 1957.

11. On Aden Miller's experience, see "Amish Farmer Jailed," *New York Times*, March 19, 1960, 9; and Miller (1963:115-25). The latter source also includes stories of several other men. Other examples available in the file "Amish," Clippings Collection, AMCUSA-G; many of the clippings are from the *South Bend* (Ind.) *Tribune*, but other newspapers are represented. Stories of Amish convicted of refusing induction into the I-W program also are found in the pages of *The Reporter for Conscience Sake*, the publication of the National Service Board for Religious Objectors, Washington, D.C. A different type of news story from the national press noted the Amish peace position in 1955: *New York Times* ran a story calling attention to the Amish as "pacifists." ("Amish Visit U.N. as Peace Symbol," *New York Times*, May 25,

1955, 35.) The article described a group of Lancaster, Pa., Amish visiting New York for another reason and arranging for a tour of the United Nations. Led by 76-year old Daniel Bawell, the Amish said they wanted to visit the U.N. because it works for peace.

12. *South Bend* (Ind.) *Tribune*, October 28, 1953, 1. This case drew particular attention because the LaGrange County draft board halted all induction and demanded state and federal officials take action against the Amish. No action was taken against the church, however, and Selective Service persuaded the draft board to resume regular activity.

13. Information from various *Wooster* (Ohio) *Daily Record* articles, including Alma Kaufman, "Murder Violence Leaves Holmes Amish Bewildered but Not Seeking Vengeance," July 20, 1957; and "Arguments on State's Use of Alleged Confession on Monday; Father of Victim is Witness," December 6, 1957. The story was sensationalized in a true crime magazine as White (1957).

14. David Wagler writing in *The Budget*, quoted in Yoder (1990:279).

15. Quoted in Yoder (1961:3).

16. The letter appeared in "The Editor's Corner," *The Budget*, 15 April 1965, 6; however, the editor clearly was not the author.

17. Yoder (1987a:229-30, 293-95) and Keim (2003:59).

18. Stoll (1966:1).

19. Anderson (1966:3).

20. Keim (2003:59).

21. On Steering Committee formation and function, see Olshan (2003) and Olshan (1994). The Committee's first officers were Andrew S. Kinsinger, Lancaster County, Pa., chair; David Schwartz, Allen County, Ind., secretary; and Noah Wengerd, Adams County, Ind., treasurer. Kinsinger served as chair until 1989 when Christian Blank, also of Lancaster, succeeded him. See Kinsinger (1997) for his Amish perspective on the Steering Committee.

22. Primary sources detailing the meeting and agreements are Steering (1973).

23. Meyers (2003b) surveys these conflicts. See also lists of cases in Keim (1975:93-98) and Place (2003). Amish-published histories include

Hershberger (1985), Lapp (1991), and
Farmwald (2004).

24. Primary sources appear in
Lapp (1991:191-518). The vocational
school compromise was in place April
10, 1956. For narrative, see Kraybill
(2001:171-72). Ontario information
from David Luthy, Aylmer, Ontario.

25. The Hazelton story summarized
here is detailed in Erickson (1975b);
see also "The Old Order," *Newsweek*,
December 6, 1965, 38.

26. Lindholm (2003) details his
involvement.

27. Erickson (1975a) and Keim
(1975:97-98).

28. Erickson (1975a:73).

29. Keim (1975:98, 114-23).

30. Keim (1975:98) and Ball
(1975:120).

31. Supreme (1972). The decision's
text also appears in Keim (1975:149-
81). For newspaper accounts of the
Yoder case, see Lapp (1991:547-56).
Discussions of the case include
Hostetler (1975) and Peters (2003).

32. Ed Klimuska, "A Harrisburg
Attorney Won the Supreme Court Case
for the Amish," *Lancaster* (Pa.) *New
Era*, May 26, 1989, A-10. Ball reflected
on the implications in Ball (1988) and
(2003).

33. Nearly all Beachy Amish-
Mennonite children, for example,
attend private Beachy schools, and not
all complete high school; see Yoder
(1987a:209-10, 270-71). On Old Order
Amish school students, teachers, and
education, see Johnson-Weiner (2007)
and Kraybill, Johnson-Weiner, and Nolt
(2013:250-71).

34. "Amish Families Abandon
Nebraska Colony," *Mennonite Weekly
Review*, April 15, 1982, 7.

35. Graham (1976).

36. Conflict with the Internal
Revenue Service is detailed in Ferrara
(2003).

37. "Unto Caesar," *Time*, November
3, 1958, 21; Robert Metz, "The Amish
and Taxes," *New York Times*, May 22,
1961, 45.

38. "U.S. Sells 3 Mares for Amish Tax
Debt," *New York Times*, May 2, 1961,
34; and Robert Metz, "The Amish
and Taxes," *New York Times*, May 22,
1961, 45. Mark Andio of Youngstown,
Ohio, bought Byler's animals. Byler
owed $308.96. The horses sold for
$460. Auction costs were $113.15. The

remaining $37.89 was refunded to
Byler.

39. Clarence W. Hall, "The Revolt
of the Plain People," *Reader's Digest*,
November 1962, 74-78.

40. "Amish are Granted Exclusion,"
New York Times, July 31, 1965, 8. An
earlier attempt was Pennsylvania's Rep.
Richard S. Schweiker, reported as "Bill
Would Exempt the Amish," *New York
Times*, November 7, 1963, 29.

41. Ferrara (2003).

42. For complete treatment of the
issues involved, see Olshan (2003),
Zook (2003), Huntington (2003), and
Bontrager (2003).

43. Regehr (1995) argues that
in 1953, Canada had a more fully
developed welfare state than the U.S.
Nevertheless, it is clear that the Amish
did not perceive this to be the case.

44. Thomson (1993) includes more
detail. See also Janzen (1990:245-71)
for context.

45. The Amish mission movement
summarized here is detailed in Nolt
(2001).

46. On the related Mennonite
context of those years, see Toews
(1996:54-55, 207-208, 226-28, 285-97).

47. Yoder (1987a:79-80); Huntington
(1956: 693-700). In fact, as early as
1952 after Miller preached in the
Lancaster, Pennsylvania, settlement,
bishops there told him he should not
return.

48. The congregation took the name
Zion Amish Mennonite.

49. Nolt (2001:33-36) and Anderson
(2011:373-76).

50. Nolt (2001:35).

51. Hurst and McConnell (2010:43-
48). The "Dan church" is another
nickname for the Andy Weaver
affiliation, because in the group's
early years most of the ordained men
coincidentally had the first name
Daniel.

52. New Order Amish origins are
detailed in Waldrep (2008:396-413),
Kline and Beachy (1998), Beachy
(2011:v.2, 447-51), and Hurst and
McConnell (2010:48-52).

53. Parallels in Matthew 24:13, Mark
13:22, Luke 21:19; see also Revelation
2:5. On the other side, a vocal advocate
of assurance of salvation teaching was
Mifflin County, Pennsylvanian John R.
Renno. He was excommunicated by his
Amish church for insisting too strongly

on the matter of assurance. His sharp defense is Renno ([1976]).

54. Kline and Beachy (1998:8); Waldrep (2008:397n.6).

55. Beiler (n.d.), Scott (1991), Waldrep (2008:398-99), and Lapp (2003:271-79). In February and April 1966 about 100 families withdrew from the Lancaster Old Order church and formed two so-called "New Order" church districts. The Lancaster Old Orders did not excommunicate or shun those who left at that time, because they considered the incident a church schism and not an act of individual disobedience or independence on the part of those who left.

56. Such as those in Raber's *Almanac*; Luthy (1974), (1985), and (2009); and the statistics at http://www2.etown.edu/amishstudies/

57. Kline and Beachy (1998:16); A nice summary of New Order beliefs is available in Waldrep (2008:404-13).

58. See, for example, Beachy (n.d.), Burkholder (n.d.), Kline (n.d.a) and (n.d.b), Miller (n.d.), and Truth (1983). A good discussion of Old Order Amish theology is Oyer (1994).

59. Kline and Beachy (1998:14-17); Kraybill, Johnson-Weiner, and Nolt (2013:139, 148-49).

Chapter 12 (pages 332-358) Notes

1. Kraybill, Nolt, and Weaver-Zercher (2007).

2. On the distinctive nature of Amish spirituality and its countercultural expressions, see Kraybill, Nolt, and Weaver-Zercher (2010).

3. Amish diversity, including the sorts of examples mentioned in this and the following paragraph, is a theme in Kraybill, Johnson-Weiner, and Nolt (2013); see especially the section on diverse affiliations on pp.137-54. In addition to the many Old Order Amish affiliations, Waldrep (2008:413-20) details a number of what he calls "para-Amish" or "near-Amish" groups.

4. Johnson-Weiner (2014).

5. Kraybill and Kopko (2007); Zook (2003); Bontrager (2003).

6. Meyers (1994a:170-71); the 1940 draft census administered by Mennonite Central Committee and sent to all Amish bishops asked the bishops to report the current employment of conscription-age men in each district. The incomplete returns show a few men listed under factory work. This documentary evidence of industrial employment by 1940 matches local anecdotal memory. See Peace Section Census, 1940, Questionnaires: Old Order Amish, Ind., IX-7-1, Box 1, Folder 7, AMCUSA-G.

7. Greksa and Korbin (2002:377); unpublished data from the 2012 Elkhart-LaGrange church directory; and Kraybill, Johnson-Weiner, and Nolt (2013:282).

8. In parts of Ohio and Indiana, Amish farmers selling grade B milk helped establish cheese factories that have supported dairy farms.

9. Kraybill, Johnson-Weiner, and Nolt (2013:283-89).

10. Kline (2000a); Kline (1990). Kline was instrumental in helping launch the periodical *Farming: People, Land, and Community* in 2001. See also a three-part article in *Family Life*, "Poisoning the Earth," April 1990, 16-20; May 1990, 29-33; and June 1990, 29-33.

11. Meyers (1994b); Greksa and Korbin (2002) actually found a reverse relationship between these factors.

12. Kraybill and Nolt (2004) explore many aspects of small-business ownership among the Amish. See also Kraybill, Nolt, and Wesner (2010).

13. Meyers (1994a) and Nolt and Meyers (2007:87-90).

14. Weaver (2013: 67, 126-37) and Weaver-Zercher (2001:60-81).

15. See the historical background provided in Trollinger (2012:25-43) and Luthy (1994:119-22).

16. First known as the Chamber Tourism Committee, it is today known as the Pennsylvania Dutch Convention and Visitor's Bureau; see Stoltzfus (2000).

17. Bill Thomas, "Ohio's Amish Country," *Travel: The Magazine that Roams the Globe,* April 1968, 52-53, 62-63; and Dorothy E. Steinmeier, "Overlooked Indiana," *Travel: The Magazine That Roams the Globe,* June 1967, 28-33. Trollinger (2012) provides a close reading of today's Amish-themed tourism in Holmes County, Ohio, as does Meyers (2003a) for northern Indiana. The first Amish-theme attraction in Indiana was Amishville, near Berne, which opened in 1968; the much larger Amish Acres complex near Nappanee opened to

the public two years later. Both were located on formerly Amish-owned farms.

18. Smucker (2013:65-84).

19. Trollinger (2012:26).

20. de Angeli (1944).

21. Keene (1955).

22. Weaver-Zercher (2001:104-14).

23. Kraybill (2001:280-84) and Weaver-Zercher (2001:152-80).

24. Eitzen (2008:134).

25. For example, Nadya Labi, "Amiss among the Amish," *Time*, July 6, 1998, 81. For analysis, see Umble and Weaver-Zercher (2008:221-41).

26. Weaver-Zercher (2001:181-96). See also Trollinger (2012:41-42) and Umble and Weaver-Zercher (2008).

27. Blank (2009:151-56)

28. Kraybill (2001:287-94).

29. For one Amish perspective, see Fisher (1978:361-70).

30. Data from the 2013 *Mennonite Church Directory* published by Christian Light Publications, Harrisonburg, Va.

31. See, for example, Paul [Pablo] Yoder (1998).

32. See Nolt (2011a) for a brief history of CAM. CAM's "primary purpose is to be a trustworthy and efficient channel for Amish, Mennonite, and other conservative Anabaptist groups and individuals to minister to physical and spiritual needs around the world"; see http://www.christianaidministries.org/. CAM annually distributes fifteen million pounds of clothing, seeds, and other aid; $96 million in medicine and vitamins; and Christian literature, in dozens of countries. Founder David Troyer is of New Order Amish background, but later joined the Beachy Amish. For an example of Beachy Amish mission and service efforts in one congregation, see details in Lapp (2003).

33. Many Amish, especially in Ohio and northern Indiana, support CAM's work by volunteering to pack shipping containers at CAM warehouses. See Nolt (2011a) on Old Order Amish support for CAM and for Mennonite Central Committee (MCC). Old Orders in Lancaster, Pennsylvania, regularly volunteer at the MCC warehouse in Akron, Pennsylvania. Old Orders in various communities volunteer to help with MCC meat-canning or CAM clothing-packing.

34. "Amish Population Trends 1992-2013, 21-Year Highlights." Young Center for Anabaptist and Pietist Studies, Elizabethtown College. http://www2.etown.edu/amishstudies/Population_Trends_1992_2013.asp.

35. Donnermeyer and Cooksey (2010). Not all new settlements thrive or endure; see Luthy (2012).

36. For historical statistics, see Luthy (1974), (1985), (1992), (2003), (2009); and Donnermeyer and Luthy (2013), along with annually updated statistics at http://www2.etown.edu/amishstudies. A study of Amish community growth in Kentucky is Donnermeyer and Anderson (2014).

37. For an exceptional story, see Miller (2015).

38. Meyers (1991) and (1994b), though Meyers shows that retention/defection is not uniform, and certain factors influence the decision to join or leave. Greksa and Korbin (2002) for Geauga and adjacent counties, Ohio, demonstrate the same retention trends and nearly identical percentages, though they found somewhat different variables affecting choice. Greksa and Korbin also review the literature on similar studies in other places, especially Lancaster, Pa. See also Kraybill, Johnson-Weiner, and Nolt (2013:162-65).

39. Johnson-Weiner (2007).

40. Meyers (1991:319) and Meyers (1994b).

41. For *Family Life* excerpts, see Igou (1999). Pathway catalogues are available from Pathway Publishers, 52445 Glencolin Ln, RR 4, Aylmer, ON N5H 2R3. On Amish publishing, see Kraybill, Johnson-Weiner, and Nolt (2013:373-75). Amish Libraries include the Heritage Historical Library, Aylmer, Ontario; Ohio Amish Library, Millersburg, Ohio; Pequea Bruderschaft Library, Gordonville, Pa.; and Northern Indiana Amish Library, LaGrange, Ind. Early revolving mortgage funds were the Family Assistance Fund in the Arthur, Illinois, Amish community, followed in 1990 by the Amish Mutual Mortgage Fund in the Nappanee, Indiana settlement.

42. Nolt (2011b).

43. Kraybill, Johnson-Weiner, and Nolt (2013:186-90).

44. Fisher (1978:320).

Bibliography

Archival sources, newspaper, and news magazine articles appear only in the Endnotes.

Abbreviations used in this bibliography:

FL Family Life, monthly magazine issued by Amish Pathway Publishers, Aylmer, Ont., since 1968.

ME Mennonite Encyclopedia. Scottdale, Pa.: Herald Press, 4 vols., 1955-1959; vol. 5, 1990. Its contents and some updated articles are available online at http://www.gameo.org

MFH Mennonite Family History, a genealogical magazine published at Elverson, Pa., since 1982.

MHB Mennonite Historical Bulletin, published by Mennonite Church USA Historical Committee, 1940-2012.

ML Mennonite Life, journal published by Bethel College, North Newton, Kans., since 1946.

MQR Mennonite Quarterly Review, journal published at Goshen, Ind., by Goshen College and Anabaptist Mennonite Biblical Seminary, since 1927.

PMH Pennsylvania Mennonite Heritage, journal of the Lancaster Mennonite Historical Society, Lancaster, Pa. since 1978.

TD The Diary, monthly magazine by and for Old Order Amish, published at Bart, Pa. (formerly at Gordonville, Pa.) since 1969.

Abrams, Ray H.
1933 *Preachers Present Arms*. Philadelphia: Round Table Press.
Amish and Mennonites in Eastern Elkhart and LaGrange Counties, Indiana, 1841-1991
1992 Goshen, Ind.: The Amish Heritage Committee.
"An Amish Church Discipline of 1781"
1930 *MQR* 4 (April): 140-48.
"Amish Life in the Great Depression, 1930-1940"
1971 *FL* 4 (July): 18-21; (August): 18-21.
The Amish Moving to Maryland
1965 Gordonville, Pa.: A. S. Kinsinger.
Anabaptist (Mennonite) Directory
2003 Harrisonburg, Va.: Sword and Trumpet.
Anderson, Calvin E.
1966 "[Editorial] Introduction," *Ambassador of Peace* 1 (February): 3-4. *Ambassador of Peace* was an Amish-published periodical for conscientious objectors, published from 1966-1970.
Anderson, Cory
2011 "Retracing the Blurred Boundaries of Twentieth-Century 'Amish Mennonite' Identity," *MQR* 85 (July): 361-412.
Ausbund, Das ist: Etliche schöne christliche Lieder
1997 Lancaster, Pa.: Verlag von den Amischen Gemeinden in Lancaster County, Pa. First partial edition was in 1564.
Bachman, Peter
1934 *1784-1934, Mennoniten in Kleinpolen: Gedenkbuch . . . .* Lemberg: Verlag der Lemberger Mennonitengemeinde in Lemberg.
Baecher, Robert
1998 "1712: Investigation of an Important Date," *PMH* (April): 2-12.
2000 "'The Patriarche' of Sainte-Marie-aux-Mines," *MQR* 74 (January): 145-58.
Bair, Ray
1952 "The Merger of the Mennonite and the Amish Mennonite Conference[s] from 1911 to 1928," *MHB* 13 (October): 2-4.

Ball, William Bentley
1975 "Building a Landmark Case: Wisconsin v. Yoder," in *Compulsory Education and the Amish: The Right Not to be Modern*, ed. by Albert N. Keim, 114-23. Boston: Beacon Press.
1988 "An External Perspective: The Constitutional Freedom to be Anabaptist," *Brethren Life and Thought* 33 (Summer): 200-204.
2003 "First Amendment Issues," in *The Amish and the State*, ed. by Donald B. Kraybill, 253-65. Baltimore: Johns Hopkins University Press.
Beachy, Alvin J.
1954 "The Amish Settlement in Somerset County, Pennsylvania," *MQR* 28 (October): 263-92.
1955 "The Rise and Development of the Beachy Amish Mennonite Churches," *MQR* 29 (April): 118-40.
Beachy, Leroy
2011 *Unser Leit: The Story of the Amish*. 2 vols. Millersburg, Ohio: Goodly Heritage Books.
Beachy, Lester
n.d. *The Cross: Bitter or Sweet?* Baltic, Ohio: Amish Brotherhood Publications.
Beechy, William and Malinda Beechy, comps.
[1993] *Experiences of C.O.s in C.P.S. Camps, in I-W Service in Hospitals, and during World War I*. LaGrange, Ind.: W. and M. Beechy.
Beiler, Abner F.
n.d. "A Brief History of the New Order Amish Church, 1966-1976," unpublished paper, Lancaster Mennonite Historical Library, Lancaster, Pennsylvania.
Beiler, Joseph F.
1969 "Two Hundred Years in America: The Stoltzfus Family," *TD* 1 (January): 6, 8.
1974a "The Amish in the Pequea Valley Before 1800," *TD* 6 (July): 162-64.
1974b "Landgrants," *TD* 6 (May): 120, 119.
1975a "Bishop Jacob Hertzler," *TD* 7 (July): 165-68.
1975b "Revolutionary War Records," *TD* 7 (March): 71.
1976/1977 "Eighteenth Century Amish in Lancaster County," *Mennonite Research Journal* 17 (October): 37, 46; 18 (January): 1, 10; (April): 16.
1977a "Amish History in Lancaster County," *Mennonite Research Journal* 17 (April): 16.
1977b "The Drachsel Family," *TD* 9

(March): 70.
1978 [land grant map including Christian Rupp parcel], *TD* 10 (January): 13, 32.
1982 "Ordnung," *MQR* 56 (October): 382-84.
1983 "A Review of the Founding of the Lancaster County Church Settlement," *TD* 15 (December): 17-22.
Belfry, Paul E.
1923 *The Community and Its High School*. New York: D. C. Heath.
Bender, Harold S.
1927 ed., "The Discipline Adopted by the Strasburg [sic] Conference of 1568," *MQR* 1 (January).
1934 ed., "Some Early American Amish Mennonite Disciplines," *MQR* 8 (April): 90-98.
1946 ed., "An Amish Bishop's Conference Epistle of 1865," *MQR* 20 (July): 222-29.
Biesecker-Mast, Gerald J.
1999 "Anxiety and Assurance in the Amish Atonement Rhetorics of Daniel E. Mast and David J. Stutzman," *MQR* 73 (July): 525-38.
Blank, Benuel S.
2001 *The Amazing Story of the Ausbund*. Narvon, Pa.: B. S. Blank.
2009 *The Scriptures Have the Answers: Inspirational Writings by Ben Blank*. Parksburg, Pa.: The Blank Family.
Bontrager, Herman D.
2003 "Encounters with the State, 1990-2002," in *The Amish and the State*, ed. by Donald B. Kraybill, 235-50. Baltimore: The Johns Hopkins University Press.
Bontreger, Eli J.
1982 *My Life Story*. [Goshen, Ind.: Manasseh E. Bontreger].
Borntreger, John E. (Hansi)
1988 Elizabeth Gingerich, trans., *A History of the First Settlers of the Amish Mennonites and the Establishment of Their First Congregation in the State of Indiana . . . .* Topeka, Ind.: Dan Hochstetler. First issued in German by Bontreger in 1907.
Boylan, Anne M.
1988 *Sunday School: The Formation of an American Institution, 1790-1880*. New Haven: Yale University Press.
Braght, Thieleman J. van
1998 *The Bloody Theater; or Martyrs Mirror of the Defenseless Christians*. Joseph F. Sohm, trans. Scottdale, Pa.: Herald Press.
Bressler, Ann Lee
2001 *The Universalist Movement in America, 1770-1880*. New York: Oxford

University Press.
Briefsammlung
1987   *Informations-Blaetter/Feuilles d'Information: Schweizerischer Verein fuer Taeufergeschichte/Societé Suisse d'Histoire Mennonite* 10: 26-61. A German edition of the letters detailing the Amish schism of 1693-97.
Brock, Peter
2006   *Against the Draft: Essays on Conscientious Objection from the Radical Reformation to the Second World War.* Toronto: University of Toronto Press.
Brunk, Ivan W.
1982   "Mennonites in the Carolinas," *PMH* 5 (January): 14-21.
Burkholder, David G.
n.d.   *The Inroads of Pietism.* Baltic, Ohio: Amish Brotherhood Publications.
Bush, Perry
1999   *Two Kingdoms, Two Loyalties: Mennonite Pacifism in Modern America.* Baltimore: Johns Hopkins University Press.
2015   *Peace, Progress, and the Professor: The Mennonite History of C. Henry Smith.* Harrisonburg, Va.: Herald Press.
Bushman, Richard L.
1992   *The Refinement of America: Persons, Houses, Cities.* New York: Alfred A. Knopf.
Butler, Jon
1990   *Awash in a Sea of Faith: Christianizing the American People.* Cambridge, Mass.: Harvard University Press.
Byler, Linda
2010   *Running Around (and Such).* Intercourse, Pa.: Good Books.
Called to Mexico: Bringing Hope and Literacy to the Old Colony Mennonites
2011.   Nappanee, Ind.: Old Colony Mennonite Support.
Catechism, or Plain Instruction From the Sacred Scriptures
1905   Elkhart, Ind.: Mennonite Publishing Company. An English translation of the well-loved 1797 "Waldeck Catechism" of the Waldeck, Hesse, Amish. The Waldeck Catechism was itself originally the 1783 Elbing, Prussia, Mennonite catechism.
Clark, Allen B.
1988   *This Is Good Country: A History of the Amish of Delaware, 1915-1988.* Gordonville, Pa.: Gordonville Book Shop.
Clark, Olynthius
1929   "Joseph Joder, Schoolmaster-Farmer and Poet, 1797-1887," *Transactions of the Illinois State Historical Society* (1929): 135-65.
Clauden, David N. and Kathryn Egly

Claudon
1947   *Life of Bishop Henry Egly, 1824-1890.* n.p.
Correll, Ernst
1928   "The Value of Family History for Mennonite History, Illustrated from Nafziger Family History Material of the Eighteenth Century," *MQR* 2 (January): 66-79; (July): 198-204.
1955   "Alsace," s.v. in *ME*, 1:66-75.
1956   "French Revolution," s.v. in *ME*, 2:392.
Coşgel, Metin M.
1993   "Religious Culture and Economic Performance: Agricultural Productivity of the Amish, 1850-80," *Journal of Economic History* 53 (June): 319-31.
de Angeli, Marguerite
1944   *Yonie Wondernose.* New York: Doubleday.
Deeben, John P.
1992   "Amish Agriculture and Popular Opinion in the Nineteenth and Twentieth Centuries," *PMH* 15 (April): 21-29.
A Devoted Christian's Prayer Book
1984   Aylmer, Ont. and Lagrange, Ind.: Pathway Publishing Corp. An English language translation of *Die Ernsthafte Christenpflicht.*
Donnermeyer, Joseph F. and Cory Anderson
2014   "The Growth of Amish and Plain Anabaptist Communities in Kentucky," *Journal of Amish and Plain Anabaptist Studies* 2 (Autumn): 215-44.
Donnermeyer, Joseph F. and Elizabeth C. Cooksey
2010   "On the Recent Growth of New Amish Settlements," *MQR* 84 (April):181-206.
Donnermeyer, Joseph F. and David Luthy
2013   "Amish Settlements across America: 2013," *Journal of Amish and Plain Anabaptist Studies* 1 (October): 107-29.
Durnbaugh, Donald F.
1978   "Religion and Revolution: Options in 1776," *PMH* 1 (July): 2-9.
1983   ed. *The Brethren Encyclopedia.* Philadelphia, Pa.: The Brethren Encyclopedia, Inc.
1997   *Fruit of the Vine: A History of the Brethren, 1708-1995.* Elgin, Ill.: Brethren Press.
Dyck, Cornelius J.
1995   trans. and ed. *Spiritual Life in Anabaptism.* Scottdale, Pa.: Herald Press.
Early Amish Land Grants in Berks County, Pennsylvania

1991 Gordonville, Pa.: Pequea Bruderschaft Library.

Egly, Henry
1965 "The Kingdom of Peace of Jesus Christ," *The Evangelical Mennonite*, August, 8-10.

Eitzen, Dirk
2008 "Hollywood Rumspringa: Amish in the City," in *The Amish and the Media*, ed. by Diane Zimmerman Umble and David L. Weaver-Zercher, 133-58. Baltimore: Johns Hopkins University Press.

Ellis, Franklin and Samuel Evans
1883 *History of Lancaster County, Pennsylvania, with Biographical Sketches of Many of its Pioneers and Prominent Men*. Philadelphia: Everts and Peck.

Erb, Paul
1974 *South Central Frontiers: A History of the South Central Mennonite Conference*. Scottdale, Pa.: Herald Press.

Erickson, Donald A.
1975a "The Persecution of LeRoy Garber," in *Compulsory Education and the Amish: The Right Not to be Modern*, ed. by Albert N. Keim, 84-92. Boston: Beacon Press.
1975b "Showdown at an Amish Schoolhouse," in *Compulsory Education and the Amish: The Right Not to be Modern*, ed. by Albert N. Keim, 43-83. Boston: Beacon Press.

Esh, Levi A.
1977 "The Amish Parochial School Movement," *MQR* 51 (January): 69-75.

Estes, Steven R.
1982 *A Goodly Heritage: A History of the North Danvers Mennonite Church*. Danvers, Ill.: North Danvers Mennonite Church.
1984 *Living Stones: A History of the Metamora Mennonite Church*. Metamora, Ill.: Metamora Mennonite Church.
1990 *From Mountains to Meadows: A Century of Witness of the Meadows Mennonite Church*. Chenoa, Ill.: Historical Committee of Meadows Mennonite Church.
1993a "The Central Conference and Middle District Merger of 1957," *ML* 48 (March): 11-15.
1993b *Love God and Your Neighbor: The Life and Ministry of Christian Engel*. Metamora, Ill.: Illinois Mennonite Historical and Genealogical Society.
2007 "Fellowship of Evangelical Churches: The Progression of a Name," *Illinois Mennonite Heritage Quarterly* 34 (Spring): 12-21.

Farmwald, Delbert
2004 *History and Directory of Indiana Amish Parochial Schools*. Topeka, Ind.: Study Time Publishers.

Ferrara, Peter J.
2003 "Social Security and Taxes," in *The Amish and the State*, 2nd ed., ed. by Donald B. Kraybill, 125-43. Baltimore: Johns Hopkins University Press.

Fisher, Amos L.
1984 "History of the First Amish Communities in America," *TD* 16 (September): 35-39.

Fisher, Gideon
1978 *Farm Life and Its Changes*. Gordonville, Pa.: Pequea Publishers.

Fisher, Jonathan B.
1911 *A Trip to Europe and Facts Gleaned on the Way*. New Holland, Pa.: Jonathan B. Fisher.
1937 *Around the World by Water and Facts Gleaned on the Way*. [Bareville, Pa.]: Jonathan B. Fisher.

Fogleman, Aaron S.
1996 *Hopeful Journeys: German Immigration, Settlement, and Political Culture in Colonial America, 1717-1775*. Philadelphia: University of Pennsylvania Press.
1998 "From Slaves, Convicts, and Servants to Free Passengers: The Transformation of Immigration in the Era of the American Revolution," *Journal of American History* 85 (June): 43-76.

Fretz, Clarence Y.
1957 "Luxembourg," s.v. in *ME*, 3:422-23.

Fretz, J. Winfield
1978 "Witnessing a Community's Death." Unpublished paper, Heritage Historical Library, Aylmer, Ontario.
n.d. "The Amish in Paraguay." Unpublished paper, Heritage Historical Library, Aylmer, Ontario.

Friedmann, Robert
1949 *Mennonite Piety Through the Centuries: Its Genius and Its Literature*. Goshen, Ind.: The Mennonite Historical Society.

Frost, J. William
1990 *A Perfect Freedom: Religious Liberty in Pennsylvania*. Cambridge: Cambridge University Press.

Furner, Mark
2000 "On the Trail of Jakob Ammann," *MQR* 74 (April): 326-28.
2001 "Lay Casuistry and the Survival of Later Anabaptists in Bern," *MQR* 75 (October): 429-70.

Geiser, Samuel
1959 "Reist, Hans," s.v. in *ME*, 4:281-82.

George, Timothy
1988 *Theology of the Reformers*. Nash-

ville, Tenn.: Broadman Press.

Gerlach, Horst
1990 "Amish Congregations in Germany and Adjacent Territories in the Eighteenth and Nineteenth Centuries," *PMH* 13 (April): 2-8.

Gibbons, Phebe Earle
1882 *"Pennsylvania Dutch," and Other Essays.* Philadelphia: J. P. Lippincott.

Gingerich, Hugh F. and Rachel W. Kreider
1986 *Amish and Amish Mennonite Genealogies.* Gordonville, Pa.: Pequea Publishers.

Gingerich, James Nelson
1986 "Ordinance or Ordering: Ordnung and Amish Ministers Meetings, 1862-1878," *MQR* 60 (April): 180-99.

Gingerich, Josef
1982 Elizabeth Horsch Bender, trans. "The Amish Mennonites in Bavaria," *MQR* 56 (April): 179-88.

Gingerich, Melvin
1939 *The Mennonites in Iowa.* Iowa City: State Historical Society of Iowa.
1949 *Service For Peace: A History of Mennonite Civilian Public Service.* Akron, Pa.: Mennonite Central Committee.
1955a "Amish Aid Plan," s.v. in *ME*, 1: 89.
1955b intro. *Joseph Goldsmith (1796-1876) and His Descendants.* Kalona, Ia.: John W. Gingerich.
1959 "Sleeping Preacher Churches," s.v. in *ME*, 4: 543-44.
1961 "Mennonite Indentured Servants," *ML* 16 (July): 107-109.
1965 "A List of Amish Ministers in 1849," *MHB* 26 (July): 7.
1971 "Sleeping Preachers," *MHB* 32 (January): 4-6.

Gingerich, Orland
2002 *The Amish of Canada.* Kitchener, Ont.: Pandora Press. First ed., 1972.

Glick, Aaron S.
1994 *The Fortunate Years: An Amish Life.* Intercourse, Pa.: Good Books.

Graham, Otis Jr.
1976 *Toward a Planned Society: From Roosevelt to Nixon.* New York: Oxford University Press.

Gratz, Delbert L.
1951 The Home of Jacob Amman [sic] in Switzerland," *MQR* 25 (April): 137-39.
1952 "Bernese Anabaptism in the Eighteenth Century, I," *MQR* 26 (January): 5-21.
1953 *Bernese Anabaptists and Their American Descendants.* Goshen, Ind.: The Mennonite Historical Society.

Gregory, Brad P.
1999 *Salvation at Stake: Christian Martyrdom in Early Modern Europe.* Cambridge, Mass.: Harvard University Press.

Greksa, Lawrence P. and Jill E. Korbin
2002 "Key Decisions in the Lives of the Old Order Amish: Joining the Church and Migrating to Another Settlement," *MQR* 76 (October): 373-98.

Grieser, Orland R. and Ervin Beck Jr.
1960 *Out of the Wilderness: History of the Central Mennonite Church, 1835-1960.* Grand Rapids: The Dean Hicks Co.

Gross, Leonard
1991 "The First Mennonite Merger: The Concept of Cologne," in *Mennonite Yearbook, 1991-1992.* Scottdale, Pa.: Mennonite Publishing House.
1997 trans. and ed. *Prayer Book for Earnest Christians.* Scottdale, Pa.: Herald Press.

Guth, Hermann
1987 "Preacher Johannes Nafzinger of Essingen, Germany," *MFH* 6 (October): 129-31.
1995 *Amish Mennonites in Germany: Their Congregations, The Estates Where They Lived, Their Families.* Morgantown, Pa.: Masthof Press.

Habegger, David L.
2002 *The Swiss of Adams and Wells Counties, Indiana, 1838-1862.* Fort Wayne: D. L. Habegger.

Harder, Leland, ed.
1985 *The Sources of Swiss Anabaptism: The Grebel Letters and Related Documents.* Scottdale, Pa.: Herald Press.

Hartzler, H. Harold
1991 *Amishman Travels Around the World: The Life of Jonathan B. Fisher.* Elverson, Pa.: Mennonite Family History.

Hartzler, Jonas S. and Daniel Kauffman
1905 *Mennonite Church History.* Scottdale, Pa.: Mennonite Book and Tract Society.

Hartzler-Miller, Gregory
1997 "'Der Weiss' Jonas Stutzmann: Amish Pioneer and Mystic," *MHB* 58 (October): 4-12.

Hege, Lydie and Christoph Wiebe
1996 eds., *Les Amish: Origine et Particularismes, 1693-1993.* Ingersheim: Association Française d'Histoire Anabaptiste-Mennonite.

Hein, Gerhard
1959 "Palatinate," s.v. in *ME* 4:106-12.

Helmuth, Orva

1961 "History of the Arthur Amish Mennonite Church," *MHB* 22 (October): 3-4.

Hershberger, Guy F.
1951 *The Mennonite Church in the Second World War*. Scottdale, Pa.: Herald Press.

Hershberger, Noah L.
1985 *A Struggle to Be Separate: A History of the Ohio Amish Parochial School Movement*. n.p.: N. L. Hershberger,

Hertzler, Enos
1985 *Time Out for Paraguay*. Gordonville, Pa.: Gordonville Print Shop.

Hiller, Harry H.
1968-1969 "The Sleeping Preachers: An Historical Study of the Role of Charisma in Amish Society," *Pennsylvania Folklife* 18 (Winter): 19-31.

Historical Statistics of the United States: Colonial Times to 1970
1975 Washington, D.C.: United States Department of Commerce, Bureau of the Census.

History and Happenings of the Buchanan County Amish, 1914-1997
1999 Sugarcreek, Ohio: Carlisle Printing.

Homan, Gerlof D.
1994 *American Mennonites and the Great War, 1914-1918*. Scottdale, Pa.: Herald Press.

Horst, Irvin B.
1988 trans. and ed. *Mennonite Confession of Faith*, ... Lancaster, Pa.: Lancaster Mennonite Historical Society.

Hostetler, Beulah Stauffer
1992 "The Formation of the Old Orders," *MQR* 66 (January): 5-25.

Hostetler, Harvey
1912 ed., *The Descendants of Jacob Hochstetler, the Immigrant of 1736*. Elgin, Ill.: Brethren Publishing House.

Hostetler, John A.
1955 "Old World Extinction and New World Survival of the Amish: A Study of Group Maintenance and Dissolution," *Rural Sociology* 20 (September-December): 212-19.
1964 "Memoirs of Shem Zook," *MQR* 38 (July): 280-99.
1975 "The Cultural Context of the Wisconsin Case," in *Compulsory Education and the Amish: The Right Not to be Modern*, ed. by Albert N. Keim, 99-113. Boston: Beacon Press.
1983 "Amish," s.v. in *The Brethren Encyclopedia*, ed. by Donald F. Durnbaugh. Philadelphia: Brethren Encyclopedia, Inc.
1989 ed., *Amish Roots: A Treasury of History, Wisdom, and Lore*. Baltimore: Johns Hopkins University Press.
1993 *Amish Society*, fourth ed. Baltimore: Johns Hopkins University Press.

Hostetler, Pius
1980 *Life, Preaching and Labors of John D. Kauffman*. Gordonville, Pa.: Gordonville Print Shop.

Hostetter, John M.
1999 *CPS Camp #24, 1942-1946 and Mennonites of Washington County, Maryland*. Hagerstown, Md.: J.M. Hostetter.

Huntington, Gertrude Enders
"Dove at the Window: A Study of an Old Order Amish Community in Ohio." Ph.D. dissertation, Yale University.
2003 "Health Care," in *The Amish and the State*, ed. by Donald B. Kraybill, 163-89. Baltimore: Johns Hopkins University Press.

Hüppi, John
2000 "Identifying Jakob Ammann," *MQR* 74 (April): 329-39.

Hurst, Charles E. and David L. McConnell
2010 *An Amish Paradox: Diversity and Change in the World's Largest Amish Community*. Baltimore: Johns Hopkins University Press.

Igou, Brad
1999 comp. *The Amish in Their Own Words: Amish Writings from 25 years of Family Life Magazine*. Scottdale, Pa.: Herald Press.

Illinois Directory of the Arthur Community and History of the Arthur Community
2012 Tuscola, Ill. : LaVern and Dorothy Schlabach.

Janzen, Rod and Max Stanton
2010 *The Hutterites in North America*. Baltimore: Johns Hopkins University Press.

Janzen, William
1990 *Limits on Liberty: The Experience of Mennonite, Hutterite, and Doukhobor Communities in Canada*. Toronto: University of Toronto Press.

Jellison, Katherine
2002 "The Chosen Women: The Amish and the New Deal," in *Strangers at Home: Amish and Mennonite Women in History*, eds. Kimberly D. Schmidt, Diane Zimmerman Umble, and Steven D. Reschly, 102-18. Baltimore: Johns Hopkins University Press.

Johnson-Weiner, Karen M.
2007 *Train Up a Child: Old Order Amish and Mennonite Schools*. Baltimore: The Johns Hopkins University Press.

2014 "Technological Diversity and Cultural Change among Contemporary Amish Groups," *MQR* 88 (January): 5-22.
Juhnke, James C.
1989 *Vision, Doctrine, War: Mennonite Identity and Organization in America, 1890-1930.* Scottdale, Pa.: Herald Press.
Kauffman, J. Howard and Leo Driedger
1991 *The Mennonite Mosaic: Identity and Modernization.* Scottdale, Pa.: Herald Press.
Kauffman, John D.
1953 *Kauffman's Sermons.* Saint Joe, Ark.: Martin Printers.
Kauffman, S. Duane
1979 "Miscellaneous Amish Mennonite Documents," 2 *PMH* (July): 12-16.
1991 *Mifflin County Amish and Mennonite Story, 1791-1991.* Belleville, Pa.: Mifflin County Mennonite Historical Society.
2014 *The Amish of the Chester Valley (1767-1834): A Challenging and Puzzling Venture.* Perkasie, Pa.: S. D. Kauffman.
Keene, Carolyn
1955 *The Witch Tree Symbol.* New York: Simon and Schuster, Inc.
Keim, Albert N.
1975 ed., *Compulsory Education and the Amish: The Right Not to be Modern.* Boston: Beacon Press.
1990 *The CPS Story: An Illustrated History of Civilian Public Service.* Intercourse, Pa.: Good Books.
2003 "Military Service and Conscription," in *The Amish and the State,* ed. by Donald B. Kraybill, 43-65. Baltimore: Johns Hopkins University Press.
Keim, Albert N. and Grant M. Stoltzfus
1988 *The Politics of Conscience: The Historic Peace Churches and America at War, 1917-1955.* Scottdale, Pa.: Herald Press.
Kinsinger, Andrew S.
1997 *A Little History of Our Parochial Schools and Steering Committee from 1956-1994.* Gordonville, Pa.: Gordonville Print Shop.
Klaassen, Walter
1981 ed., *Anabaptism in Outline: Selected Primary Sources.* Scottdale, Pa.: Herald Press.
Kline, David
1990 *Great Possessions: An Amish Farmer's Journal.* San Francisco: North Point Press.
2000a "God's Spirit and a Theology for Living," in *Creation and the Environment: An Anabaptist Perspective on a Sustainable*

World, ed. by Calvin Redekop, 61-69. Baltimore: Johns Hopkins University Press.
Kline, Edward A.
n.d.[a] *A Sure Path for Mankind.* Baltic, Ohio: Amish Brotherhood Publications.
n.d.[b] *A Theology of the Will of Man and Some Practical Applications for the Christian Life.* Baltic, Ohio: Amish Brotherhood Publications.
Kline, Edward A. and Monroe L. Beachy
1998 "History and Dynamics of the New Order Amish of Holmes County, Ohio," *Old Order Notes* 18 (Fall-Winter): 7-19.
Kline, Ronald R.
2000b *Consumers in the Country: Technology and Social Change in Rural America.* Baltimore: Johns Hopkins University Press.
Klopfenstein, Joseph
1984 Elizabeth Horsch Bender, trans. "An Amish Sermon," *MQR* 58 (July): 296-317.
Klopfenstein, Perry A.
2008 *Marching to Zion: A History of the Apostolic Christian Church of America, 1847-2007.* Eureka, Ill.: Apostolic Christian Church.
Kollmorgen, Walter M.
1942 *Culture of a Contemporary Rural Community: The Old Order Amish of Lancaster County, Pennsylvania.* [Washington, D.C.]: U.S. Dept. of Agriculture.
Krabill, Russell
1991 "The Coming of the Amish Mennonites to Elkhart County, Indiana," *MHB* 52 (January): 1-5.
Kraybill, Donald B.
2001 *The Riddle of Amish Culture,* rev. ed. Baltimore: Johns Hopkins University Press.
2003 ed. *The Amish and the State,* rev. ed. Baltimore: Johns Hopkins University Press.
2010 *Concise Encyclopedia of Amish, Brethren, Hutterites, and Mennonites.* Baltimore: Johns Hopkins University Press.
Kraybill, Donald B. and Carl F. Bowman
2001 *On the Backroad to Heaven: Old Order Hutterites, Mennonites, Amish, and Brethren.* Baltimore: Johns Hopkins University Press.
Kraybill, Donald B., Karen M. Johnson-Weiner, and Steven M. Nolt
2013 *The Amish.* Baltimore: Johns Hopkins University Press.
Kraybill, Donald B., and Kyle C. Kopko

2007 "Bush Fever: Amish and Old Order Mennonites in the 2004 Presidential Election." *Mennonite Quarterly Review* 81 (April): 165-205.

Kraybill, Donald B. and Steven M. Nolt
2004 *Amish Enterprise: From Plows to Profits*, 2nd ed. Baltimore: Johns Hopkins University Press.

Kraybill, Donald B., Steven M. Nolt, and David L. Weaver-Zercher
2007 *Amish Grace: How Forgiveness Transcended Tragedy*. San Francisco: Jossey-Bass.
2010 *The Amish Way: Patient Faith in a Perilous World*. San Francisco: Jossey-Bass.

Kraybill, Donald B., Steven M. Nolt, and Erik J. Wesner
2010 "Amish Enterprise: The Collective Power of Ethnic Entrepreneurship," *Global Business and Economics Review*, 12/1: 3-20.

Lapp, Aaron, Jr.
2003 *Weavertown Church History: Memoirs of an Amish Mennonite Church*. Sugarcreek, Ohio: Carlisle Printing.

Lapp, Christ S.
1991 *Pennsylvania School History, 1690-1990*. Gordonville, Pa.: Christ S. Lapp.

Lears, T. J. Jackson
1981 *No Place for Grace: Antimodernism and the Transformation of American Culture, 1880-1920*. New York: Pantheon Books.

Lehman, James O.
1978 *Creative Congregationalism: A History of the Oak Grove Mennonite Church in Wayne County, Ohio*. Smithville, Ohio: Oak Grove Mennonite Church.
1990 *Uncommon Threads: A Centennial History of Bethel Mennonite Church*. West Liberty, Ohio: Bethel Mennonite Church.

Lehman, James O. and Steven M. Nolt
2007 *Mennonites, Amish, and the American Civil War*. Baltimore: Johns Hopkins University Press.

Lemon, James T.
2002 *The Best Poor Man's Country: Early Southeastern Pennsylvania. With a New Preface*. Baltimore: Johns Hopkins University Press.

Levine, Neil Ann Stuckey
1997 "The Augspurgers of Butler Co., Ohio, in Napoleonic France," *MFH* 16 (January): 4-18; 16 (April): 54-66.
2009 ed., *Transplanted German Farmer: The Life and Times of Christian Iutzi (1788-1857), 1832 Immigrant to Butler County, Ohio, in His Own Words*. Trenton, Ohio:

Friends of Chrisholm Historic Farmstead.

Levine, Neil Ann Stuckey, Ursula Roy, and David J. Rempel Smucker
1996 "Trans-Atlantic Advice: An 1822 Letter by Louis C. Jüngerich (1803-1882)," *PMH* 19 (July): 2-16.
1997 "The View of Louis C. Jüngerich (1803-1882) in 1826: It is Best to Come to This Country Well Prepared," *PMH* 20 (July): 2-15.

Lind, Hope Kauffman
1990 *Apart and Together: Mennonites in Oregon and Neighboring States, 1876-1976*. Scottdale, Pa.: Herald Press.

Lindholm, William C.
2003 "The National Committee for Amish Religious Freedom," in *The Amish and the State*, ed. by Donald B. Kraybill, 109-23. Baltimore: Johns Hopkins University Press.

Loewen, Royden
2013 *Village Among Nations: "Canadian" Mennonites in a Transnational World, 1916-2006*. Toronto: University of Toronto Press.

Lugibihl, Walter H.
1950 *Missionary Church Association*. Berne, Ind.: Economy Printing Concern.

Luthy, David
1972a "An Amishman's City," *FL* 5 (February): 23-25.
1972b "The Arrest of an Amish Bishop—1918," *FL* 5 (March): 23-27.
1972/1973 "New Names Among the Amish," *FL* 5 (August/September): 31-35; (October): 20-23; (November): 21-23; 6 (February): 13-15; (June): 13-15.
1973 "The Amish in Europe," *FL* 6 (March): 10-14; (April): 16-20.
1974 "Old Order Amish Settlements in 1974," *FL* 7 (December): 13-16
1978a "Concerning the Name Amish," *MHB* 39 (April): 5.
1978b "Forced to Sell Their Farms," *FL* 11 (January): 19, 20.
1980 "'White' Jonas Stutzman," *FL* 13 (February): 19-21.
1981a "Amish Meetinghouses," *FL* 14 (August/September): 17-22.
1981b "A History of *Die Ernsthafte Christenpflicht*," *FL* 14 (February): 19-23.
1981c "Replacing the *Ausbund*," *FL* 14 (November): 21-23.
1982 "An Amish View of the Panic of 1893 and the Election of 1896," *FL* 15 (May): 23-26.
1984a "A History of Raber's Bookstore," *MQR* 58 (April): 168-78.
1984b "An Important Pennsylvania

Broadside of 1812," *PMH* 7 (July): 1-4.
1984c "Significant Books for Amish and Mennonites: A Brief Summary," *PMH* 7 (January): 6
1985 *Amish Settlements Across America*. Aylmer, Ont.: Pathway Publishers.
1986 *The Amish in America: Settlements That Failed, 1840-1960*. Aylmer, Ont. and Lagrange, Ind.: Pathway Publishers.
1988 "Two Waves of Amish Migration to America," *FL* 21 (March): 20-24.
1989 "Two Amish Writers: The Zook Brothers, David and Shem," *FL* 22 (November): 19-22; (December): 19-21.
1991 "Martin Bornträger and His Descendants," *FL* 24 (March): 19-21.
1992 "Amish Settlements across America: 1991," *FL* 25 (April): 19-24.
1994 "The Origin and Growth of Amish Tourism," in *The Amish Struggle with Modernity*, ed. by Donald B. Kraybill and Marc A. Olshan, 113-29. Hanover, N.H.: University Press of New England.
1995 *Amish Folk Artist Barbara Ebersol: Her Life, Fraktur, and Death Record Book*. Lancaster, Pa.: Lancaster Mennonite Historical Society.
1998 "The Origins and Growth of the Swartzentruber Amish," *FL* 31 (August/September): 19-22.
2003 "Amish Settlements across America: 2003," *FL* 36 (October): 17-23.
2009 *Amish Settlements Across America: 2008*. Aylmer, Ont.: Pathway Publishers.
2012 *Why Some Amish Communities Fail: Extinct Settlements, 1961-2011*. Aylmer, Ont.: Pathway Publishers.
MacMaster, Richard K.
1979 et al., *Conscience in Crisis: Mennonites and Other Peace Churches in America, 1739-1789, Interpretation and Documents*. Scottdale, Pa.: Herald Press.
1985 *Land, Piety, Peoplehood: The Establishment of Mennonite Communities in America, 1683-1790*. Scottdale, Pa.: Herald Press.
Mark, Beth L. Hostetler
2003 comp. and ed. *Our Flesh and Blood: A Documentary History of the Jacob Hochstetler Family during the French and Indian War Period, 1757-1765*. Elkhart, Ind.: Jacob Hochstetler Family Association.
Martin, Helen Reimensnyder
1905 *Sabina: A Story of the Amish*. New York: The Century Publishing Company.
Mast, C. Z.
1952 "Imprisonment of Amish in Revolutionary War," *MHB* 13 (January): 6-7.
Mast, C. Z. and Robert E. Simpson

1942 *Annals of the Conestoga Valley in Lancaster, Berks, and Chester Counties, Pennsylvania . . . .* Elverson, Pa. and Churchtown, Pa.: C. Z. Mast and Robert E. Simpson.
Mast, J. Lemar and Lois Ann Mast
1982 *As Long as Wood Grows and Water Flows: A History of the Conestoga Mennonite Church*. Morgantown, Pa.: Conestoga Mennonite Historical Committee.
Mast, John B.
1950 ed., *Facts Concerning the Beachy A. M. Division of 1927*. Myersdale, Pa.: Menno J. Yoder.
Meier, Marcus
2008 *The Origin of the Schwarzenau Brethren*, trans. by Dennis L. Slabaugh. Philadelphia, Pa.: Brethren Encyclopedia, Inc.
Menno Simons
1956 John C. Wenger, ed. *The Complete Writings of Menno Simons, c.1496-1561*. Scottdale, Pa.: Herald Press.
Mennonite Church Directory
1999 Harrisonburg, Va.: Christian Light Publications.
Meyer, Rich H.
1999 "Why Don't We Tell the Beginning of the Story? Native Americans Were Here First," *Mennonite Historical Bulletin* 60 (July): 1-8.
Meyers, Thomas J.
1991 "Population Growth and Its Consequences in the Elkhart-Lagrange Old Order Amish Settlement," *MQR* 65 (July): 308-21.
1994a "Lunch Pails and Factories," in *The Amish Struggle with Modernity*, ed. by Donald B. Kraybill and Marc A. Olshan, 165-81. Hanover, N.H.: University Press of New England.
1994b "The Old Order Amish: To Remain in the Faith or to Leave," *MQR* 68 (July): 378-395.
1996 "The Amish Division: A Review of the Literature," in *Les Amish: Origine et Particularismes, 1693-1993*, ed. by Lydie Hege and Christoph Wiebe, 72-93. Ingersheim: Association Française d'Histoire Anabaptiste-Mennonite.
2003a "Amish Tourism: Visiting Shipshewana is better than going to the Mall," *MQR* 77 (January): 109-126.
2003b "Education and Schooling," in *The Amish and the State*, ed. by Donald B. Kraybill, 87-107. Baltimore: Johns Hopkins University Press.
Miller, Elizabeth M.
1963 *From the Fiery Stakes of Europe to*

the Federal Courts of America. New York: Vantage Press.

Miller, Harvey J.
1959   "Proceedings of Amish Ministers Conferences," 1826-1831," MQR 33 (April): 132-42.

Miller, John S.
1971   "A Statistical Survey of the Amish Settlers in Clinton Township, Elkhart County, Indiana, 1841-1850." Unpublished manuscript at the Mennonite Historical Library, Goshen, Indiana.

Miller, Levi D.
1970   "Another Sleeping Preacher," MHB 31 (April): 5-6.

Miller, Levi P.
n.d.   Teaching Emphases That Hinder Discipleship. Baltic, Ohio: Amish Brotherhood Publications.

Miller, Marlene C.
2015   Called to be Amish: My Journey from Head Majorette to the Old Order. Harrisonburg, Va.: Herald Press.

Minutes of the Indiana-Michigan Mennonite Conference, 1864-1929
[1930]   Scottdale, Pa.: Mennonite Publishing House.

Murray, John F.
1981   "Blank/Plank Ancestry of the Amish Mennonite Tradition," PMH 4 (July): 13-19.

Neff, Christian
1957   "Ibersheim Resolutions," s.v. in ME, 3:2.
1959   "Offenthal Conference," s.v. in ME, 4:21-22.

Neff, Christian and Nanne van der Zijpp
1957   "Napoleon I," s.v. in ME, 3:812.

Nolt, Steven M.
1995   "The Rise and Fall of an Amish Distillery: Economic Networks and Entrepreneurial Risk on the Illinois Frontier," Illinois Mennonite Heritage 22 (September): 45, 53-63; and (December): 65, 75-79.
1996   "Christian Farni and Abraham Lincoln: Legal Advice and the Election of 1860," Illinois Mennonite Heritage 23 (March): 1, 13-14.
1999   "Plain People and the Refinement of America," MHB 60 (October): 1-11.
2001   "The Amish 'Mission Movement' and the Reformulation of Amish Identity in the Twentieth Century," MQR 75 (January): 7-36.
2008   "Inscribing Community: The Budget and Die Botschaft in Amish Life," 181-98, in The Amish and the Media, ed. by Diane Zimmerman Umble and David

L. Weaver-Zercher. Baltimore: Johns Hopkins University Press.
2011a   "MCC's Relationship with 'Plain' Anabaptists in Historical Perspective," 135-66, in A Table of Sharing: Mennonite Central Committee and the Expanding Networks of Mennonite Identity, ed. by Alain Epp-Weaver. Telford, Pa.: Cascadia Publishing House.
2011b   "Moving Beyond Stark Options: Old Order Mennonite and Amish Approaches to Mental Health," Journal of Mennonite Studies 29:133-51.

Nolt, Steven M. and Thomas J. Meyers
2007   Plain Diversity: Amish Cultures and Identities. Baltimore: Johns Hopkins University Press.

Nussbaum, Stan
1991   You Must Be Born Again: A History of the Evangelical Mennonite Church. Fort Wayne, Ind.: Evangelical Mennonite Church.

Olshan, Marc A.
1994   "Homespun Bureaucracy: A Case Study in Organizational Evolution," in The Amish Struggle with Modernity, ed. by Donald B. Kraybill and Marc A. Olshan, 199-213. Hanover, N.H.: University Press of New England.
2003   "The National Amish Steering Committee," in The Amish and the State, ed., by Donald B. Kraybill, 67-85. Baltimore: Johns Hopkins University Press.

Oyer, John S.
1984   "The Strasbourg Conferences of the Anabaptists," MQR 58 (July): 218-29.
1994   "Is There an Amish Theology?" in Les Amish: Origine et Particularismes, 1693-1993, ed. by Lydie Hege and Christoph Wiebe, 278-302. Ingersheim: Association Française d'Histoire Anabaptiste-Mennonite.
2000   "Bernese Mennonite Religion at the Time of the Mennonite-Amish Division," 83-108, in "They Harry the Good People Out of the Land": Essays on the Persecution, Survival, and Flourishing of Anabaptists and Mennonites. Goshen, Ind.: Mennonite Historical Society.

Oyer, John S. and Robert S. Kreider
2003   Mirror of the Martyrs, second ed. Intercourse, Pa.: Good Books.

Oyer, V. Gordon
1994   ed. Proceedings of the Conference: Tradition and Transition, An Amish Mennonite Heritage of Obedience. 1693-1993. Metamora, Ill.: Illinois Mennonite Historical and Genealogical Society.

Page, Doris L. and Marie Johns

1983 *The Amish Mennonite Settlement in Butler County, Ohio*. Trenton, Ohio: Trenton Historical Society.

Pannabecker, Samuel Floyd
1968 *Faith in Ferment: A History of the Central District Conference*. Newton, Kans.: Faith and Life Press.
1975 *Open Doors: The History of the General Conference Mennonite Church*. Newton, Kans.: Faith and Life Press.

Patterson, James T.
1996 *Grand Expectations: The United States, 1945-1974*. New York: Oxford University Press.

Peace, War, and Military Service: A Statement of the Position of the Mennonite Church
1937 Resolutions adopted by the Mennonite General Conference at Turner, Oregon. August.

Peter Graber Collection. Letters from 1848 to 1925, from Various Amish Communities
2012 Trans. by Josiah D. Beachy. Hicksville, Ohio: J. D. Beachy.

Peters, Shawn Francis
2003 *The Yoder Case: Religious Freedom, Education, and Parental Rights*. Lawrence, Kans.: University Press of Kansas.

Place, Elizabeth
2003 "Appendix: Significant Legal Cases," in *The Amish and the State*, ed. by Donald B. Kraybill, 277-88. Baltimore: Johns Hopkins University Press.

Pratt, Dorothy A. O.
2004 *Shipshewana: An Indiana Amish Community*. Bloomington, Ind.: Indiana University Press.

Raber, Ben J.
1930 comp., *Der Neue Amerikanische Kalendar*. Baltic, Ohio: Raber's Bookstore. Since 1970 the Almanac has also been issued under the title *The New American Almanac*.

Regehr, T. D.
1995 "Relations Between the Old Order Amish and the State in Canada," *MQR* 69 (April): 151-77.
1996 *Mennonites in Canada, 1939-1970: A People Transformed*. Toronto, Ont.: University of Toronto Press.

Renno, John R.
[1976] *A Brief History of the Amish Church in Belleville*. Danville, Pa.: John R. Renno.

Reschly, Steven D.
2000 *The Amish on the Iowa Prairie, 1840 to 1910*. Baltimore: Johns Hopkins University Press.

Reschly, Steven D. and Katherine Jellison
1993 "Production Patterns, Consumption Strategies, and Gender Relations in Amish and Non-Amish Farm Households in Lancaster County, Pennsylvania, 1935-1936," *Agricultural History* 67 (Spring): 134-62.

The Revelation of Barbara Stutzman, Deceased, to All Mankind
n.d. n.p. copy at the Mennonite Historical Library, Goshen, Indiana.

Ringenberg, William C.
1976 "Development and Division in the Mennonite Community in Allen County, Indiana," *MQR* 50 (April): 114-31.

Ritter, Gretchen
1997 *Goldbugs and Greenbacks: The Antimonopoly Tradition and the Politics of Finance in America, 1865-1896*. New York: Cambridge University Press.

Roth, Donald W.
1993a "Hunches about Family History Relationships in the Origins of the Evangelical Mennonite Church," *Illinois Mennonite Heritage* 20 (June 1993): 25, 40-42.

Roth, John D. and Joe Springer
1993 trans. and eds., *Letters of the Amish Division: A Sourcebook*. Goshen, Ind.: Mennonite Historical Society. Note: pagination differs slightly in a 2003 reprinting; citations in *A History of the Amish* are from the original 1993 printing.

Roth, John D. and James M. Stayer
2007 eds. *A Companion to Anabaptism and Spiritualism, 1521-1700*. Leiden: Brill.

Roth, Lorraine
1993b "The Amish Mennonite Division in Ontario, 1886-1891," *Ontario Mennonite History* 11 (March): 1-7.
1998 *The Amish and Their Neighbours: The German Block, Wilmot Township, 1822-1860*. Waterloo, Ont.: Mennonite Historical Society of Ontario.

Roth, Lorraine and Marlene J. Grant
1986 "Canadian Amish Mennonite Roots in Pennsylvania," *PMH* 9 (April): 13-17.

Ruth, John L.
1976 *'Twas Seeding Time: A Mennonite View of the American Revolution*. Scottdale, Pa.: Herald Press.

Schabalie, John Philip [Schabaelje, Jan Philipsz.]
1975 *The Wandering Soul, or Conversations of the Wandering Soul with Adam, Noah, and Simon Cleophas*. Baltic, Ohio: Raber's Book Store. First edition was 1635 in Dutch.

Schlabach, Theron F.

1988   *Peace, Faith, Nation: Mennonites and Amish in Nineteenth-Century America.* Scottdale, Pa.: Herald Press.

Schmidt, Kimberly D. Schmidt, Diane Zimmerman Umble, and Steven D. Reschly

2002   eds. *Strangers at Home: Amish and Mennonite Women in History.* Baltimore: Johns Hopkins University Press.

Schmidt-Lange, Anne Augspurger

2002   "Roast Bear? No, Thank You!—An 1821 Letter from Kurhessen, Germany, to Daniel and Christian Schwartzentruber in Somerset County, Pennsylvania," *PMH* (October): 9-20.

Schmölz-Häberlein, Michaela and Mark Häberlein

2001   "Eighteenth-Century Anabaptists in the Margravate of Baden and Neighboring Territories," *MQR* 75 (October): 471-92.

Schrag, Martin H.

1974   *The European History (1525-1874) of the Swiss Mennonites from Volhynia.* North Newton, Kans.: Swiss Mennonite Cultural and Historical Association.

[Schwartz, David L.]

19--   "Articles of Faith of the Old Order Amish Mennonite Church, Berne, Indiana." [Berne, Ind.: David L. Schwartz].

Scott, Stephen E.

1981   *Plain Buggies: Amish, Mennonite, and Brethren Horse-Drawn Transportation.* Intercourse, Pa.: Good Books.

1986   *Why Do They Dress That Way?* Intercourse, Pa.: Good Books.

1991   "Information About the Groups Originating from the New Order Division Among the Lancaster County Amish," unpublished paper.

1996   *An Introduction to Old Order and Conservative Mennonite Groups.* Intercourse, Pa.: Good Books.

Séguy, Jean

1973   "Religion and Agricultural Success: The Vocational Life of the French Anabaptists from the Seventeenth to the Nineteenth Centuries," *MQR* 47 (July): 179-224.

1980   "The Bernese Anabaptists in Sainte-Marie-aux-Mines," *PMH* 3 (July): 2-9.

1982   "The French Mennonites: Tradition and Change," *International Journal of Sociology and Social Policy* 2 (1): 25-43.

1984   "The French Anabaptists: Four and One-Half Centuries of History," *MQR* 58 (July): 206-17.

Shoemaker, Alfred L.

1999   *Christmas in Pennsylvania: A Folk-Cultural Study.* Mechanicsburg, Pa.: Stackpole Books.

Shover, John L.

1976   *First Majority, Last Minority: The Transformation of Rural Life in America.* DeKalb, Ill.: Northern Illinois University Press.

Smith, C. Henry

1929   *The Mennonite Immigration to Pennsylvania in the Eighteenth Century.* Norristown, Pa.: Pennsylvania German Society.

1962   *Mennonite Country Boy: The Early Years of C. Henry Smith.* Newton, Kans.: Faith and Life Press.

Smith, C. Henry and Cornelius Krahn

1981   *Smith's Story of the Mennonites,* fifth ed. Newton, Kans.: Faith and Life Press.

Smith, Willard H.

1983   *Mennonites in Illinois.* Scottdale, Pa.: Herald Press.

Smucker, Janneken

2013   *Amish Quilts: Crafting an American Icon.* Baltimore: Johns Hopkins University Press.

Snyder, C. Arnold

1995   *Anabaptist History and Theology: An Introduction.* Kitchener, Ont.: Pandora Press.

2004   *Following in the Footsteps of Christ: The Anabaptist Tradition.* Maryknoll, N.Y.: Orbis.

Sommer, Pierre and John A. Hostetler

1957   "Ixheim," s.v. in *ME,* 3:58.

Songs of the Ausbund: History and Translations of Ausbund Hymns

1998, 2011   2 vols. Millersburg, Ohio: Ohio Amish Library.

Springer, Joe A., trans. and ed.

2015   *Montbéliard Mennonite Church Register, 1750-1958: A Sourcebook for Amish Mennonite History and Genealogy.* Goshen, Ind.: Mennonite Historical Society.

Springer, Nelson P.

1998   "Schoolteacher by Accident, Churchman without Office: Christian Erismann, 1835-1905," *Illinois Mennonite Heritage* 24 (December): 73, 78-93.

Stahly, Jerold A.

1989   "The Montbeliard Amish Move to Poland in 1791," *MFH* 8 (January): 13-17. Stahly followed this article with other MFH pieces that traced the stories of individual families who had been a part of the migration and later immigration.

1994   "The Amish in Eastern Europe," in *Proceedings of the Conference: Tradition and Transition, An Amish Mennonite Heritage of Obedience. 1693-1993*, ed. by V. Gordon Oyer, 101-16. Metamora, Ill.: Illinois Mennonite Historical and Genealogical Society.

"**Statement in 1939 Concerning the Position of Non-resistance signed by Old Order Amish bishops . . . "**

1939 original copy at the Heritage Historical Library, Aylmer, Ont.

Stayer, James M.

2002 "Numbers in Anabaptist Research," in *Commoners and Community: Essays in Honour of Werner O. Packull*, ed. by C. Arnold Snyder, 51-73. Kitchener, Ont.: Pandora Press.

Steering Committee

1973 *Minutes of the Old Order Amish Steering Committee, vol. 1, 1966-1972*. Gordonville, Pa.: Gordonville Print Shop.

Steiner, Samuel J.

2015 *In Search of Promised Lands: A Religious History of Mennonites in Ontario*. Harrisonburg, Va.: Herald Press.

Steinfeldt, Bernice

1937 *The Amish of Lancaster County: A Brief, but Truthful Account of the Actual Life and Customs of the Most Unique Class of People in the United States*. Lancaster, Pa.: Arthur G. Steinfeldt.

Stievermann, Jan

2013 "Defining the Limits of American Liberty: Pennsylvania's German Peace Churches During the Revolution," 207-45, in *A Peculiar Mixture: German-Language Cultures and Identities in Eighteenth-Century North America*, ed. by Jan Stievermann and Oliver Scheiding. University Park, Pa.: Pennsylvania State University Press.

Stoll, Joseph

1966 "Introducing a New Paper," *Ambassador of Peace* 1 (January): 1, 2.

1972 "The Amish Settlement at Guaimaca, Honduras," *TD* 4 (October): 200, 196-99.

1974 "The Amish Church of Montbéliard, France (Founded 1713)," *TD* 6 (January): 19-23.

1975 "Who Shall Educate Our Children?" in *Compulsory Education and the Amish: The Right Not to be Modern*, ed. by Albert N. Keim, 16-42. Boston: Beacon Press.

1996 *Sunshine and Shadow: Our Seven Years in Honduras*. Aylmer, Ont.: J. Stoll.

1997 *The Amish in Daviess County, Indiana*. Aylmer, Ont.: J. Stoll.

2000 *How the Dordrecht Confession Came Down to Us*. Aylmer, Ont: Pathway Publishers.

Stoltzfus, Amos J.

1984 *Golden Memories*. Gordonville, Pa.: Pequea Publishers.

Stoltzfus, Duane C. S.

2013 *Pacifists in Chains: The Persecution of Hutterites during the Great War*. Baltimore: Johns Hopkins University Press.

Stoltzfus, Grant M.

1954 "History of the First Amish Mennonite Communities in America," *MQR* 28 (October): 235-62.

1969 *Mennonites of the Ohio and Eastern Conference from the Colonial Period in Pennsylvania to 1968*. Scottdale, Pa.: Herald Press.

Stoltzfus, Louise

1995 *Two Amish Folk Artists: The Story of Henry Lapp and Barbara Ebersol*. Intercourse, Pa.: Good Books.

2000 *The Story of Tourism in Lancaster County, Pa*. Lancaster, Pa.: Pennsylvania Dutch Convention and Visitors Bureau.

Stoltzfus, Nicholas

1981 comp. *Nonresistance Put to Test*. Aylmer, Ont.: Pathway Publishing Service.

Stucky, Solomon

1981 *The Heritage of the Swiss Volhynian Mennonites*. Waterloo, Ont.: Conrad Press.

Supreme Court of the United States

1972 *State of Wisconsin, Petitioner, v. Jonas Yoder, Adin Yutzy, and Wallace Miller*. On Writ of Certiorari to the Supreme Court of Wisconsin. [May 15], No. 70-110.

Swartzendruber, A. Lloyd

1950 "Samuel D. Guengerich," *MHB* 11 (October): 1, 3.

Swartzendruber, William

1977 et al., *Upper Deer Creek Conservative Mennonite Church Centennial Anniversary*. n.p.: Upper Deer Creek Conservative Mennonite Church.

Teichroew, Allan

1979 ed., "Military Surveillance of Mennonites in World War I," *MQR* 53 (April): 95-127.

Thomson, Dennis L.

1993 "Canadian Government Relations," in *The Amish and the State*, ed. by Donald B. Kraybill, 235-48. Baltimore: The Johns Hopkins University Press. Note: this chapter appears only in the 1993 edition of this book, not in the 2003 revised edition.

Toews, Paul

1996 *Mennonites in American Society, 1930-1970: Modernity and the Persistence of Religious Community*. Scottdale, Pa.: Herald Press.

Trollinger, Susan L.
2012   *Selling the Amish: The Tourism of Nostalgia.* Baltimore: Johns Hopkins University Press.
Troyer, David A.
1998   Paton Yoder, trans. *The Writings of David A. Troyer Published after his Death: An English Translation.* Aylmer, Ont.: Pathway Publishers.
Troyer, Noah
1879   *Sermons Delivered by Noah Troyer, the Celebrated Amishman.* Iowa City, Ia.: Daily Republican Job Printers.
1880   *Sermons Delivered by Noah Troyer, a Member of the Amish Mennonite Church, of Johnson Co., Iowa, while in an Unconscious State. Second book, Containing Six Sermons not before Published . . . .* Elkhart, Ind.: Mennonite Publishing Company.
The Truth in Word and Work: A Statement of Faith by Ministers and Brethren of Amish Churches of Holmes Co., Ohio, and Related Areas
1983   Baltic, Ohio: Amish Brotherhood Publications.
Umble, Diane Zimmerman
1996   *Holding the Line: The Telephone in Old Order Mennonite and Amish Life.* Baltimore: Johns Hopkins University Press.
Umble, Diane Zimmerman and David L. Weaver Zercher
2008   eds., *The Amish and the Media.* Baltimore: Johns Hopkins University Press.
Umble, John S.
1933   "Amish Mennonites of Union County, Pennsylvania," *MQR* 7 (April): 71-96; (July): 162-90.
1939   ed., "Amish Ordination Charges," *MQR* 13 (October): 233-50.
1941   *Ohio Mennonite Sunday Schools.* Goshen, Ind.: Mennonite Historical Society.
1947   "Why Congregations Die," *MHB* 8 (October): 1-3.
1948   ed., "Memoirs of an Amish Bishop," *MQR* 22 (April): 94-115.
1963   *One Hundred Years of Mennonite Sunday Schools in Logan County, Ohio.* West Liberty, Ohio: South Union Mennonite Church.
1964   "The Background and Origin of the Ohio and Eastern Amish Mennonite Conference," *MQR* 38 (January): 50-60.
United States Department of Commerce Bureau of the Census
1941   *Religious Bodies: 1936.* Washington, D.C.: Government Printing Office.
Unruh, John D.
1952   *In the Name of Christ: A History of*

the Mennonite Central Committee and Its Service, 1920-1951.* Scottdale, Pa.: Herald Press.
Varry, Dominique
1984   "Jacques Klopfenstein and the Almanacs of Belfort and Montbeliard in the Nineteenth Century," *MQR* 58 (July): 241-57.
Visser, Piet
1996   "Some Unnoticed Hooks and Eyes: The Swiss Anabaptists in the Netherlands," in *Les Amish: Origine et Particularismes, 1693-1993,* ed. by Lydie Hege and Christoph Wiebe, 95-116. Ingersheim: Association Française d'Histoire Anabaptiste-Mennonite.
Wagler, David
1991   "Our Forefathers Left the Church," *FL* 24 (March): 40, 32-34.
n.d.   *Are All Things Lawful?* Aylmer, Ont.: Pathway Publishers. An Amishman discusses automobile ownership.
Wagler, David and Roman Raber
1986   *The Story of the Amish in Civilian Public Service.* North Newton, Kans.: Bethel Press. A reprint of the 1945 edition with an expanded directory of Amish who served in CPS.
Waldrep, G. C.
2008   "The New Order Amish and Para-Amish Groups: Spiritual Renewal Within a Tradition," *MQR* 82 (July): 395-426.
Weaver, J. Denny
1997   *Keeping Salvation Ethical: Mennonite and Amish Atonement Theology in the Late Nineteenth Century.* Scottdale, Pa.: Herald Press.
Weaver, William B.
1926   *History of the Central Conference Mennonite Church.* Danvers, Ill.: William B. Weaver.
Weaver, William Woys
2013   *As American as Shoofly Pie: The Foodlore and Fakelore of Pennsylvania Dutch Cuisine.* Philadelphia: University of Pennsylvania Press.
Weaver-Zercher, David L.
2001   *The Amish in the American Imagination.* Baltimore: Johns Hopkins University Press.
Weaver-Zercher, Valerie
2013   *Thrill of the Chaste: The Allure of Amish Romance Novels.* Baltimore: Johns Hopkins University Press.
Weber, Harry F.
1931   *Centennial History of the Mennonites of Illinois, 1829-1929.* Goshen, Ind.: Mennonite Historical Society.
Weiser, Frederick S.

1998 "The Clothing of the 'White Top' Amish of Central Pennsylvania," *PMH* 21 (July): 2-10.
Welty, Cora Gottschalk
1908 *The Masquerading of Margaret.* Boston: C. M. Clark.
Wenger, John C.
1937 *History of the Mennonites of the Franconia Conference.* Telford. Pa.: Franconia Mennonite Historical Society.
1961 *The Mennonites in Indiana and Michigan.* Scottdale, Pa.: Herald Press.
1966 *The Mennonite Church in America, Sometimes Called Old Mennonites.* Scottdale, Pa.: Herald Press.
Wenger, Samuel S.
1981 "Nicholas Stoltzfus in Europe and America," *PMH* 4 (April): 15-17.
White, Hal
1957 "Terror at the Amish Farmhouse," *True Detective,* (November), 16-21, 83.
Williams, R. Hal
2010 *Realigning America: McKinley, Bryan, and the Remarkable Election of 1896.* Lawrence, Kans.: University Press of Kansas.
Wokeck, Marianne S.
1999 *Trade in Strangers: The Beginnings of Mass Migration to North America.* University Park, Pa.: Pennsylvania State University Press.
Yoder, Don
1944 "*Der Fröhliche Botschafter*: An Early American Universalist Magazine," *American-German Review* 10 (June): 13-16.
1968/1969 "Trance-Preaching in the United States," *Pennsylvania Folklife* 18 (Winter): 12-18.
Yoder, Elmer S.
1987a *The Beachy Amish Mennonite Fellowship Churches.* Hartville, Ohio: Diakonia Ministries.
1990 *I Saw It in* The Budget. Hartville, Ohio: Diakonia Ministries.
Yoder, Freeman L. and Lizzie Yoder
1998 comps. *Echoes of the Past: Experiences of the Plain People 1920's through 1940's, during the Depression Years and More.* Middlebury, Ind: F. L. and L. Yoder.
Yoder, John Howard
1954 "Mennonites in a French Almanac," *ML* 9 (October): 154-56.
1955 "Bitscherland," s.v. in *ME,* 1:349.
1961 *The Christian and Capital Punishment.* Newton, Kans.: Faith and Life Press.
1973 trans. and ed., *The Schleitheim Confession.* Scottdale, Pa.: Herald Press. Written in 1527.

Yoder, Nathan E.
2014 *Together in the Work of the Lord: A History of the Conservative Mennonite Conference.* Harrisonburg, Va.: Herald Press.
Yoder, Paton
1979 *Eine Würzel: Tennessee John Stoltzfus.* Lititz, Pa.: Sutter House.
1985 "The Preaching Deacon Controversy Among the Nineteenth-Century American Amish," *PMH* 8 (January): 2-9.
1987b "The Structure of the Amish Ministry in the Nineteenth Century," *MQR* 61 (July): 280-97.
1987c *Tennessee John Stoltzfus: Amish Church-Related Documents and Family Letters.* Lancaster, Pa.: Lancaster Mennonite Historical Society.
1991 *Tradition and Transition: Amish Mennonites and Old Order Amish, 1800-1900.* Scottdale, Pa.: Herald Press. The major interpretation of the time period, thoroughly researched and based on primary sources.
1996 trans. and ed. "A Plea by a Change-Minded Pennsylvania Amish Leader to the Traditionalists," *PMH* (April): 25-28.
1999 "A Controversy among the Amish Regarding the Rebaptism of Mennonites, 1820-1845: A Newly-Discovered Document," *MQR* 73 (January): 87-106.
Yoder, Paton and Steven R. Estes
1999 eds. and trans. *Proceedings of the Amish Ministers' Meetings, 1862-1878.* Goshen, Ind.: Mennonite Historical Society.
Yoder, Paton and Silas J. Smucker
1990 *Jonathan P. Smucker, Amish Mennonite Bishop.* Goshen, Ind.: Silas J. Smucker.
Yoder, Pablo [Paul]
1998 *Angels Over Waslala.* Summersville, Mo.: Harbor Lights Publishers.
Yousey, Arlene R.
1987 *Strangers and Pilgrims: A History of Lewis County Mennonites.* Croghan, N.Y.: Arlene R. Yousey.
Zijpp, Nanne van der
1956 "Groningen," s.v. in *ME,* 2:592-95.
1957 "Kampen," s.v. in *ME,* 3:141-42.
Zook, Lee J.
2003 "Slow Moving Vehicles," in *The Amish and the State,* ed. by Donald B. Kraybill, 145-61. Baltimore: Johns Hopkins University Press.
Zürcher, Isaac
1992 "Hans Reist House and the 'Vale of Anabaptists,'" *MQR* 66 (July): 426-427.

Index

About the Author

Steven M. Nolt is a professor of history at Goshen College in Goshen, Indiana, where he teaches courses in American history and Mennonite history. Over the past twenty years he has visited dozens of Amish communities in numerous states and in Ontario. His research has often been collaborative, including projects with sociologists Donald B. Kraybill and Thomas J. Meyers; anthropologist Karen M. Johnson-Weiner; and religion scholar David L. Weaver-Zercher.

Nolt graduated from Goshen College and also earned degrees at Anabaptist Mennonite Biblical Seminary (M.A.) and the University of Notre Dame (M.A., Ph.D.). He is the author or co-author of a dozen books, most recently *The Amish* (Johns Hopkins University Press, 2013) and *Seeking Places of Peace*, the North American volume in the Global Mennonite History Series (Good Books, 2012).

A native of Lancaster, Pennsylvania, Steve is married to Rachel Miller of Engadine, Michigan. They are the parents of two daughters, Lydia and Esther.